T. S. Eliot

Robert Frost

Wallace Stevens

Carl Sandburg

John Crowe Ransom

Hart Crane

W. H. Auden

E. E. Cummings

Edna St. Vincent Millay

Marianne Moore

Oscar Williams

Gene Derwood

The New .... of

AMERICAN VERSE

SPECIAL .... LISTS .... LIBRARIES

BOOKS
by
OSCAR WILLIAMS

〜〜〜〜〜〜〜〜〜〜〜〜〜

BOOKS OF POEMS

The Golden Darkness
The Man Coming Toward You
That's All That Matters
Selected Poems

•

ANTHOLOGIES

The New Poems Series
The War Poets
A Little Treasury of Modern Poetry
A Little Treasury of Great Poetry
A Little Treasury of American Poetry
A Little Treasury of British Poetry
Immortal Poems of the English Language
Palgrave's The Golden Treasury (revised)
The Pocket Book of Modern Verse
The New Pocket Anthology of American Verse

The New Pocket Anthology of

AMERICAN VERSE

FROM COLONIAL DAYS TO THE PRESENT

The New Pocket Anthology of

AMERICAN VERSE

From Colonial Days to the Present

EDITED BY

OSCAR WILLIAMS

THE WORLD PUBLISHING COMPANY

CLEVELAND AND NEW YORK

Library of Congress Catalog Card Number: 55–8250

SECOND PRINTING

PS586
W53

A variant edition of this book, slightly abridged, is published by Pocket Books, Inc.

2WP1160

ACKNOWLEDGMENTS AND COPYRIGHT NOTICES

Most of the poems in this anthology are protected by copyright, and may not be reproduced in any form without the consent of the poets, their publishers or their agents. Since this page cannot legibly accommodate all the copyright notices, the five pages following (pages 5 through 9) constitute an extension of the copyright page. Thanks are due to the following poets, their representatives and publishers for permission to include certain poems in this anthology.

CONRAD AIKEN—for his two poems "The Return" and "A Is for Alpha: Alpha Is for A" from *The Partisan Review* and *The London Times.*

JOSEPH BENNETT—for the poems by Joseph Bennett from *Decembrist*, copyright, 1951, by Joseph Bennett, published by Clarke & Way; from *The Hudson Review*, Vol. IV, No. 3, Autumn 1951, copyright, 1951, by The Hudson Review, Inc., reprinted by permission of The Hudson Review, Inc.

Acknowledgments and Copyright Notices

Acknowledgments and Copyright Notices

Acknowledgments and Copyright Notices

Chronological Contents

*(For a full list of authors and titles, see Index
of Authors and Titles on pages 659-670)*

13

Preface

This collection, although it covers a period of three centuries, has virtually three-quarters of its space devoted to the poetry of the Twentieth. Further, more poets of the Twentieth Century than of the entire preceding time are represented. For, in the last fifty-five years, American poetry has become not only more American but mature, able, abundant and permanently established in world literature. While it expands and continues the tradition of English poetry, it is no longer the provincial simulacrum of what was made in the British Isles as, for the preceding two hundred and fifty years, it tended, with few exceptions, to be.

Most anthologies of American poetry have been compiled more from the historical point of view than from absolute vision of poetic value. In textbooks of American literature many poets have been given inflated importance for the simple reason that, in their periods, not much of value was produced, and the poets, for lack of rivals of immortal stature, dominated their contemporary scenes. Thus Longfellow, Lowell, Bryant, Whittier, etc. rather sparingly represented in this volume, have become entrenched in the schools although their work can stand scarcely any comparison with the immortal poetry of the English tongue, at no matter what level the comparison might be made. This cultural near-tragedy is the more to be regretted since the work of such men is not even American in spirit, weakly imitative as it is of English models, Elizabethan, Victorian, etc. Even when seemingly American because of the use of American place-names, the spirit and technique of such a poet as Longfellow remained that of second-rate English writers. *Hiawatha*, for example, expresses none of the actual Indian personality, outlook or culture in spite of its superficial use of Indian names.

This criticism, severe as it may sound, is by no means a disparagement of American poetry; it is a happy wonder that even in the youth of our nation, in spite of the fact that with the English tongue as our medium and English culture as our cultural nutriment, we should so quickly have produced such definitely American poets as Edgar Allan Poe, Walt Whitman and Emily Dickinson. But although we have had these important figures before 1900 it cannot be said that we had a full and definite volume of American poetry. Only when the many minor poets make substantial contributions to a literature and that literature has an expansive and indigenous audience can we make the claim of a homogeneous and important culture.

15

The Twentieth Century has seen this rapid and spectacular development in the United States. Not only has our poetry become a genuine American expression, it has also, due to its endemic character, begun for the first time to exercise an influence upon English poets. This phenomenon began in the 1920's and has steadily become more marked. American poetry, in its best exemplars, has also, being confident and more at ease with itself, become more balanced. An American characteristic has always been overfulsomeness, a kind of biting off of more than could be chewed. Poe, for instance, in his efforts at technical complication and innovation went to such an extreme of onomatopoeia in *The Bells* that today we find it almost a word-game.° Whitman, stirred by the vastness of America (and his own ego), poured out magnificently but too endlessly. This straining at the impossible must, of necessity, have its failures, but only by such effort could we have been wrenched away from the motherland and produced a literature of our own. This urgent and zealous experimentation is still an American method and to it we owe the best, and what is original, of our poetry.

In spite of the publisher's co-operation and generosity, the space available in a book of this kind is limited. Nevertheless the richness of such major figures as Emily Dickinson, Walt Whitman, Edgar Allan Poe, E. A. Robinson, T. S. Eliot, Wallace Stevens, Robert Frost, Robinson Jeffers, Ezra Pound, Vachel Lindsay, Hart Crane, E. E. Cummings, W. H. Auden, etc. is allowed full scope by the inclusion of substantial selections from their work. At the same time the new and younger contemporary poets, swarming across the poetic horizons of the Forties and Fifties in ever brightening waves, are here represented in greater number than in any previous modern collection chosen by this editor. This makes *The New Pocket Anthology of American Verse* the most comprehensive as well the most representative all-American volume of its kind—more than 500 poems by more than 100 poets—a veritable American Golden Age of Poetry. It is to be hoped that the reader will be stimulated into getting the books of the established poets and into demanding the publication of the younger poets.

The poets have been arranged in alphabetical instead of chronological order chiefly in order to break down prejudices in favor of the older poets which childhood education will have built up in the minds of some readers. The book is so arranged that modern and older poems are likely to be read in juxtaposition, thus enabling the reader to compare his responses without bias or textbook compulsions.

OSCAR WILLIAMS

°*The word-game is included.* ED.

The New Pocket Anthology of

AMERICAN VERSE

FROM COLONIAL DAYS TO THE PRESENT

Léonie Adams

THE RUNNER WITH THE LOTS

We listen, wind from where,
And two have heard
The step across the field
That went from us unseen,
The word that scarcely stirred
Along the corn's stiff green,
Or in their hair who bend among the corn.

And two have understood:
Though the great sails untorn
Of high September bear,
Toward harbour, earth and yield,
The amber-dwindled mood
Is come, the bronze, the blue,
And every hue entering its solitude.

And all about we seize,
Of all that summers knew
Or autumns reconciled,
Sense of some utmost thing,
Some clasp unransoming,
Proffered the destinies,
And on the face recalled to its grave love.

Piercing on each, one air
Has touched them, earth and child;
And fairest here,
Fair now, whom love has sealed;
But fair unseen there move
Before us unbeguiled
The equal feet of love,
And the blind hands bearing the luck of the year.

GRAPES MAKING

Noon sun beats down the leaf; the noon
Of summer burns along the vine
And thins the leaf with burning air,
Till from the underleaf is fanned,
And down the woven vine, the light.
Still the pleached leaves drop layer on layer
To wind the sun on either hand,
And echoes of the light are bound,
And hushed the blazing cheek of light,
The hurry of the breathless noon,
And from the thicket of the vine
The grape has pressed into its round.

The grape has pressed into its round,
And swings, aloof chill green, clean won
Of light, between the sky and ground;
Those hid, soft-flashing lamps yet blind,
Which yield an apprehended sun.
Fresh triumph in a courteous kind,
Having more ways to be, and years,
And easy, countless treasuries,
You whose all-told is still no sum,
Like a rich heart, well-said in sighs,
The careless autumn mornings come,
The grapes drop glimmering to the shears.

Now shady sod at heel piles deep,
An overarching shade, the vine
Across the fall of noon is flung;
And here beneath the leaves is cast
A light to colour noonday sleep,
While cool, bemused, the grape is swung
Beneath the eyelids of the vine.
And deepening like a tender thought

Green moves along the leaf, and bright
The leaf above, and leaf has caught,
And emerald pierces day, and last
The faint leaf vanishes to light.

Conrad Aiken

THIS IS THE SHAPE OF THE LEAF

This is the shape of the leaf, and this of the flower,
And this the pale bole of the tree
Which watches its bough in a pool of unwavering water
In a land we never shall see.

The thrush on the bough is silent, the dew falls softly,
In the evening is hardly a sound.
And the three beautiful pilgrims who come here together
Touch lightly the dust of the ground,

Touch it with feet that trouble the dust but as wings do,
Come shyly together, are still,
Like dancers who wait, in a pause of the music, for music
The exquisite silence to fill.

This is the thought of the first, and this of the second,
And this the grave thought of the third:
'Linger we thus for a moment, palely expectant,
And silence will end, and the bird

'Sing the pure phrase, sweet phrase, clear phrase in the
     twilight
To fill the blue bell of the world;
And we, who on music so leaflike have drifted together,
Leaflike apart shall be whirled

'Into what but the beauty of silence, silence forever?' . . .
. . . This is the shape of the tree,
And the flower, and the leaf, and the three pale beautiful
     pilgrims;
This is what you are to me.

THE ROOM

Through that window—all else being extinct
Except itself and me—I saw the struggle
Of darkness against darkness. Within the room
It turned and turned, dived downward. Then I saw
How order might—if chaos wished—become:
And saw the darkness crush upon itself,
Contracting powerfully; it was as if
It killed itself, slowly: and with much pain.
Pain. The scene was pain, and nothing but pain.
What else, when chaos draws all forces inward
To shape a single leaf? . . .
                    For the leaf came
Alone and shining in the empty room;
After a while the twig shot downward from it;
And from the twig a bough; and then the trunk,
Massive and coarse; and last the one black root.
The black root cracked the walls. Boughs burst the window:
The great tree took possession.
                    Tree of trees!
Remember (when time comes) how chaos died
To shape the shining leaf. Then turn, have courage
Wrap arms and roots together, be convulsed
With grief, and bring back chaos out of shape.
I will be watching then as I watch now.
I will praise darkness now, but then the leaf.

WATCH LONG ENOUGH, AND YOU WILL SEE THE LEAF

Watch long enough, and you will see the leaf
Fall from the bough. Without a sound it falls:
And soundless meets the grass . . . And so you have
A bare bough, and a dead leaf in dead grass.
Something has come and gone. And that is all.

But what were all the tumults in this action?
What wars of atoms in the twig, what ruins,

Fiery and disastrous, in the leaf?
Timeless the tumult was, but gave no sign.
Only, the leaf fell, and the bough is bare.

This is the world: there is no more than this.
The unseen and disastrous prelude, shaking
The trivial act from the terrific action.
Speak: and the ghosts of change, past and to come,
Throng the brief word. The maelstrom has us all.

THE TIME HAS COME, THE CLOCK SAYS TIME HAS COME

The time has come, the clock says time has come.
Here in the mid-waste of my life I pause,
The hour is in my hand, and in my heart
Miscellany of shards and shreds. The clock
Ticks its iambics, and the heart its spondees,
Time has come, time has come and gone,
Winter has taken its toll, summer its harvest,
Spring has brought and taken away its illusion.

What is time, the clock says what is time,
Never the past, never the future, always the now,
What is time, the seed says it is all
Fertility turned deep by the foot of the plow.

The hour has added to the spirit's peace,
Seed has added to minute, and world to flower,
Tears have flowed to the heart till it is rotted,
Hands have worn the hand till it is hard.
Why, I have seen the all, have seen the nothing,
Have heard the monosyllable of the tomb,
Have buried stars and resurrected them,
And watched the shadow moving across a wall.

What is time, the stitch says what is time,
Always the future, never the past, never the now;

Only the seam foresees the future, but even
The longest seam will feel the foot of the plow.

Stand, take off the garments time has lent you,
The watch, the coins, the handkerchief, the shoes,
Your soul, also, and wrap it in a thought;
Display your shards and shreds on the windowsill
Among geraniums and aspidistras,
The week before, and the week before the last,
Ridiculous chronicle, taste, touch, and smell.

What is time, the heart says what is time.
The heart is ticking on the mantelpiece.
The heart says all is past and nothing future.
The heart says heart will never cease.

THEN CAME I TO THE SHORELESS SHORE OF SILENCE

Then came I to the shoreless shore of silence,
Where never summer was nor shade of tree,
Nor sound of water, nor sweet light of sun,
But only nothing and the shore of nothing,
Above, below, around, and in my heart:

Where day was not, not night, nor space, nor time,
Where no bird sang, save him of memory,
Nor footstep marked upon the marl, to guide
My halting footstep; and I turned for terror,
Seeking in vain the Pole Star of my thought;

Where it was blown among the shapeless clouds,
And gone as soon as seen, and scarce recalled,
Its image lost and I directionless;
Alone upon the brown sad edge of chaos,
In the wan evening that was evening always;

Then closed my eyes upon the sea of nothing
While memory brought back a sea more bright,
With long, long waves of light, and the swift sun,
And the good trees that bowed upon the wind;
And stood until grown dizzy with that dream;

Seeking in all that joy of things remembered
One image, one the dearest, one most bright,
One face, one star, one daisy, one delight,
One hour with wings most heavenly and swift,
One hand the tenderest upon my heart;

But still no image came, save of that sea,
No tenderer thing than thought of tenderness,
No heart or daisy brighter than the rest;
And only sadness at the bright sea lost,
And mournfulness that all had not been praised.

O lords of chaos, atoms of desire,
Whirlwind of fruitfulness, destruction's seed,
Hear now upon the void my late delight,
The quick brief cry of memory, that knows
At the dark's edge how great the darkness is.

KEEP IN THE HEART THE JOURNAL NATURE KEEPS

Keep in the heart the journal nature keeps;
Mark down the limp nasturtium leaf with frost;
See that the hawthorn bough is ice-embossed,
And that the snail, in season, has his grief;
Design the winter on the window pane;
Admit pale sun through cobwebs left from autumn;
Remember summer when the flies are stilled;
Remember spring, when the cold spider sleeps.

Such diary, too, set down as this: the heart
Beat twice or thrice this day for no good reason;

For friends and sweethearts dead before their season;
For wisdom come too late, and come to naught
Put down 'the hand that shakes,' 'the eye that glazes';
The 'step that falters betwixt thence and hence';
Observe that hips and haws burn brightest red
When the North Pole and sun are most apart.

Note that the moon is here, as cold as ever,
With ages on her face, and ice and snow;
Such as the freezing mind alone can know,
When loves and hates are only twigs that shiver.
Add in a postscript that the rain is over,
The wind from southwest backing to the south,
Disasters all forgotten, hurts forgiven;
And that the North Star, altered, shines forever.

Then say: I was a part of nature's plan;
Knew her cold heart, for I was consciousness;
Came first to hate her, and at last to bless;
Believed in her; doubted; believed again.
My love the lichen had such roots as I,—
The snowflake was my father; I return,
After this interval of faith and question,
To nature's heart, in pain, as I began.

THE NAMELESS ONES

Pity the nameless, and the unknown, where
bitter in heart they wait on the stonebuilt stair,
bend to a wall, forgotten, the freezing wind
no bitterer than the suburbs of the mind;

who from an iron porch lift sightless eyes,
a moment, hopeless, to inflaming skies;
shrink from the light as quickly as from pain,
twist round a corner, bend to the wall again;

are to be seen leaning against a rail
by ornamental waters where toy yachts sail;
glide down the granite steps, touch foot to float,
hate, and desire, the sunlight on the boat;

explore a sullen alley where ash-cans wait,
symbols of waste and want, at every gate;
emerge in sun to mingle with the crowd,
themselves most silent where the world most loud;

anonymous, furtive, shadows in shadow hidden;
who lurk at the garden's edge like guests unbidden;
stare through the leaves with hate, yet wait to listen
as bandstand music begins to rise and glisten;

the fierce, the solitary, divine of heart,
passionate, present, yet godlike and apart;
who, in the midst of traffic, see a vision;
and, on a park bench, come to a last decision.

RIMBAUD AND VERLAINE, PRECIOUS PAIR OF POETS

Rimbaud and Verlaine, precious pair of poets,
Genius in both (but what is genius?) playing
Chess on a marble table at an inn
With chestnut blossom falling in blond beer
And on their hair and between knight and bishop—
Sunlight squared between them on the chess-board,
Cirrus in heaven, and a squeal of music
Blown from the leathern door of St. Sulpice—

Discussing, between moves, iamb and spondee
Anacoluthon and the open vowel
God the great peacock with his angel peacocks
And his dependent peacocks the bright stars:
Disputing too of fate as Plato loved it,
Or Sophocles, who hated and admired,
Or Socrates, who loved and was amused:

Verlaine puts down his pawn upon a leaf
And closes his long eyes, which are dishonest,
And says 'Rimbaud, there is one thing to do:
We must take rhetoric, and wring its neck! . . .'
Rimbaud considers gravely, moves his Queen;
And then removes himself to Timbuctoo.

And Verlaine dead,—with all his jades and mauves;
And Rimbaud dead in Marseilles with a vision,
His leg cut off, as once before his heart;
And all reported by a later lackey,
Whose virtue is his tardiness in time.

Let us describe the evening as it is:—
The stars disposed in heaven as they are:
Verlaine and Shakspere rotting, where they rot,
Rimbaud remembered, and too soon forgot;

Order in all things, logic in the dark;
Arrangement in the atom and the spark;
Time in the heart and sequence in the brain—

Such as destroyed Rimbaud and fooled Verlaine.
And let us then take godhead by the neck—

And strangle it, and with it, rhetoric.

SEA HOLLY

Begotten by the meeting of rock with rock,
The mating of rock and rock, rocks gnashing together;
Created so, and yet forgetful, walks
The seaward path, puts up her left hand, shades
Blue eyes, the eyes of rock, to see better
In slanting light the ancient sheep (which kneels
Biting the grass) the while her other hand,
Hooking the wicker handle, turns the basket

Of eggs. The sea is high to-day. The eggs
Are cheaper. The sea is blown from the southwest,
Confused, taking up sand and mud in waves,
The waves break, sluggish, in brown foam, the wind
Disperses (on the sheep and hawthorn) spray,—
And on her cheeks, the cheeks engendered of rock,
And eyes, the colour of rock. The left hand
Falls from the eyes, and undecided slides
Over the left breast on which muslin lightly
Rests, touching the nipple, and then down
The hollow side, virgin as rock, and bitterly
Caresses the blue hip.

                              It was for this,
This obtuse taking of the seaward path,
This stupid hearing of larks, this hooking
Of wicker, this absent observation of sheep
Kneeling in harsh sea-grass, the cool hand shading
The spray-stung eyes—it was for this the rock
Smote itself. The sea is higher to-day,
And eggs are cheaper. The eyes of rock take in
The seaward path that winds toward the sea,
The thistle-prodder, old woman under a bonnet,
Forking the thistles, her back against the sea,
Pausing, with hard hands on the handle, peering
With rock eyes from her bonnet.

                              It was for this,
This rock-lipped facing of brown waves, half sand
And half water, this tentative hand that slides
Over the breast of rock, and into the hollow
Soft side of muslin rock, and then fiercely
Almost as rock against the hip of rock—
It was for this in midnight the rocks met,
And dithered together, cracking and smoking.

                              It was for this
Barren beauty, barrenness of rock that aches

On the seaward path, seeing the fruitful sea,
Hearing the lark of rock that sings, smelling
The rock-flower of hawthorn, sweetness of rock—
It was for this, stone pain in the stony heart,
The rock loved and laboured; and all is lost.

IF MAN, THAT ANGEL OF BRIGHT CONSCIOUSNESS

If man, that angel of bright consciousness,
that wingless mind and brief epitome
of god's forgetfulness, will be going forth
into the treacherous envelope of sunlight—
why, the poor fool, does he expect, does he expect
to return at evening? or to return the same?
Those who have put on, in the morning,
that cloak of light, that sheath of air,
wrapped themselves suddenly, on the exit,
in the wild wave of daybreak, which has come
from cruel Alpha,—what has become of them?
They will return as the sons of darkness.

If woman, that demon of unconsciousness,
that wingèd body of delightful chaos,
that quick embodied treason and deceit,
will go forth sinuously from the opening door
and take to herself the garment of daylight—
who will vouch for her, go her surety,
who will her bondsman be, or swear by the cloud
that she, who thus went forth, will thus come back?
If she took darkness with her, will she return
with luminous heart, and a soft light within?
For that which goes forth comes back changed or dead.

If the child, that frail mirror of the sky,
that little room of foolish laughter and grief,
transient toucher and taster of the surface,
assembler and scatterer of light,—if he go forth
into the simple street to count its stones,

its walls, its houses, its weeds and grassblades,
so, in the numbered, to sum the infinite—
infant compendium of the terrible—:
will the changed man, and the changed woman,
await him, with full knowledge, in the evening—
salute him gravely, with a kiss or handshake,
oblique embrace of the young wingless shoulders—
will they, unknowing, unknown, know this Unknown?

All three at evening, when they return once more
from the black ocean of dark Omega,
by those wild waves washed up with stars and hours,
brought home at last from nowhere to nothing—
all three will pause in the simple light,
and speak to each other, slowly, with such queer speech
as dead men use among the asphodels;
nor know each other; nor understand each other;
but tread apart on the wind, like dancers
borne by unearthly music to unearthly peace.

The house of evening, the house of clouds, vast hall
of which the walls are walls of everywhere,
enfolds them, like a wind which blows out lights.
And they are there, lying apart, lying alone,
those three who went forth suddenly in the morning
and now return, estranged and changed;
each is alone, with his extinguished lamp;
each one would weep, if he had time to weep;
but, before tears can fall, they are asleep.

THE RETURN

Dear tiger lily, fanged and striped! you are the bravest,
you as well as another will serve to chant
tongued with flame our vernal madrigal,
sowing among sequins of last year's locust
love's golden rhetoric:

you and the celandine
of immaculate green.
Wraiths of snow run from the stallion sun,
quicksilver lizards of water
flick their tails into cisterns,
and on the tarnished grass
where north wind sheered his drifts
in phantom edifice
melts the last sickle of pale ice:
and there, in a little while, where late was snow,
the Indian Pipes will blow.
O darling, listen—from the orchised bog
chuckles the ancient and omniscient frog
his gross venereal hymn:
and the reed-scented wind, the bulrush-rattling wind,
dreams like memory through the mind.
Now love returns once more, our lost and antique love,
dear tiger lily! above
the sad detritus of death:
fling we then out of doors and into hearts,
where the year freshly starts,
and join the song-sparrow
in Hymen's favorite song:
for treason late and long,
in the sly shibboleth
of treason to death; and love, and another season!

The oak leaves rustle in the thicket,
loosen themselves, detach, and fall,
pale brown, pale purple, harsh still;
the hawk hangs over his beloved hill,
as love hangs over the destined heart;
and once more joyfully we begin
the ancient dance of meet and part,
wherein
each is in turn the hawk and each the heart.
We touch and meet, we touch and greet,
kiss gravely, tread apart,

next glance, and eye askance,
curtsey in courtship's bashful dance,
retreat, and then advance.
O unknown love,
unknown and treacherous as that sky above
and as my own heart is,
what is the meaning of your kiss?
Each lover asks and answers this
in blinded bliss.

Glad, glad, the sound
of two hearts beating, together bound,
O but tumultuous the rest
of your face, love, that rests upon my breast,
tumultuous the rest
of each upon the other resting:
two worlds at war we are,
star dancing against star.

For each must learn in each
all the dark-rooted language under speech:
here, look! new love, the roots we did not know,
strong stems, dark stains, rich glories never guessed:
disparate origins and desperate sins,
acknowledged or unacknowledged, understood
or misunderstood; the labyrinthine windings
through the lewd galleries of the mind, to find
something or nothing; illusory findings
which vanish at the touch, or on exposure to the air,
and of which only in default are we aware;
hatred derived from love, love from terror,
the roots not knowing their own fruits;
the unpracticed, and then the all-too-practiced vices
deliberate dishonesties and rehearsed voices;
purpose becoming mean, meanness purpose,
wants promoted to obsessions, and the obsessions
near to madness. Who am I, who are you,
that one to the other must be true, untrue,

or dissect untrue from true?
Who shall possess, or be possessed? possession
of how much? and what ecstasy, or duration?
Where, too, and in what characters shall we meet,
playing what parts of the multitude we have played,
wearing what masks and scented costumes
on the strewn stage of habit? The attitudes
are predictable, and therefore false, they belong
to another situation, are the inheritance
of other loves and lusts. What beatitudes
can the wingèd god invoke from these? In what divine dance
instruct these stained and stinking puppets?
Out of such mouths, what song, what song?

And yet the tiger lily, under the snow,
heedless alike of year ago or long ago,
and the endless history of her repeated love,
dares yet again to thrust above
the sad detritus of death and grow:
and speaks with the song-sparrow the sly shibboleth
of another season, another treason!
Lost memory, lost love, lost to return,
can we, too, not be brave like these, relearn
O as if all were virginal and new,
the hawk and heart of "I" and "You"?
O daring darling, can we not trust
once more that innocent sky
once more to break our hearts and die?

Comes now, comes she!
comes the unknown, the unpredictable,
she who is half spring, half summer,
between the lilac and the wrinkled apple blossom,
the unknown, all-unimagined newcomer,
birch foot, beech heart, myrtle hand,
and the indecipherable mind
and virgin bosom
and windflower grace

and timeless Etruscan pace
and the tiger's heart, cruel to be kind:
comes like the sunshot southwest wind
bidding the elm bough, soliciting
the fan of the iris under snow
for one more spring, one more spring:
while the hawk's wing
sickles the white-blossoming hill
with shadow of death, the scythe's shadow
shadowing the redwing into the meadow.
O innocence in guilt, and guilt in innocence,
she stoops, she hovers,
fiercest and subtlest, and yes, tenderest of lovers,
the ruthless one
whose eye is in the sun!

A IS FOR ALPHA: ALPHA IS FOR A

I

Now it begins. Now the subaqueous evening
exemplary as the inalterable moon
begins again to begin. With slight starts
of organ-grinder music (if the scene
is of city) or of—"*dee-dee-dee—!*"
chickadee trill if (as it is) it is country.
The shadow, complex, seven-branched, of the ancient lyre-
    tree,
prolongs itself on the sensual lawn and fades away,
predicting a reverse shadow at daybreak. The star
(for look, love, there is a star)
trills through the sunset like a bird
diamond point in crimson word
and melts, and we are heard.
So, now, the casual evening begins, and its slow texture
weaves us into a casuistry. We, who were just now thought-
    less,
or lost in a loss of thought,
come to a breaking and dissolving

sunset of our own. The world ends
and another begins. The love ends—or does it?—
and another begins. But the light
lasts forever, there is no night.

The hands you lift are sunset, and the hands
are the exemplary moon. The eyes you lift
change with the texture of the evening,
Venus it might be one way, Sirius the other;
the lengthening shadow, so intricate, so various, of the lyre-
      tree,
prolongs our listening nerves into the coming light
of to-morrow. My love, observe a moon
unobserved by any till now. Bland and bleak
as any lovestruck human.   Such as we?
Such as we.   We are the silver rind
of moonlight, for now it hardens, now is crystal,
on this tree, this virgin locust tree, and we
are moon and tree.
Fade, fade, all into darkness fade,
but also into light
since one the other closes.
The texture of the evening is of roses,
and we are, for the moment, roses too.
Love is not much: it is a touch: but it is true.

II

Evening, which evens all things.   Hand in hand
brindled by sunset thought we stand
prolonging our nerves, and with them nature, into another day.
We are the sacred players and the play:
we are the music, and what the musicians say:
and always our new title is To-day.
To-day, and yesterday; the divine dance
moves under heart and heaven, the wave of light
gathers its all for a breaking of time
and then falls inward. We are the rhyme
paired like two words in love, and move
in the twinned discord of a chord, our love

hidden in its own secret, like the rose.
Will the rose unclose, disclose?
finding—how naturally!—a reason for season?
It is ourselves that open, even
to the innermost heaven.
It is ourselves magically disguised
as harp-string and harp-song, birdsong and petal,
ice-metal, rain-metal,
ourselves curving the air with a wing
ourselves the air for the wing to find and follow
ourselves the sunlight and the swallow.
Divisibly indivisible we sing
the begin-all-end-all thing:
night becomes a god, and we the night,
for the unfolding and enfolding of our delight.

III

Intervals and interstices of texture
enthrall us, bring us to a standstill, bemuse
fingertip and eyebeam, idea and eye;
while the mind fills with wonders. The voice
is of what? Who said to it, "rejoice"?
You there, I here; you with your mountains of snow,
and your seven golden seas, and the woven Nile,
and the sky piled high with purple clouds;
and I with my rocky Sahara, ribbed with lapis lazuli,
and the last sail melting into sunset:
these are the language of interval, the interstices
subtle and gigantic, unfathomable, inaudible,
hieroglyphic and hieratic, by which we speak.
The exchange is golden. It is thesaurus. The exchange
beggars us only then to endow us again,
exhausts us only to replenish. The simple rain
walking before us down the country lane
shuttling before us down the country lane
says it with silver, syllables it slowly,
repeats its holy, holy,
and into it, and into night,
we weave this love, this light.

W. H. Auden

MUSÉE DES BEAUX ARTS

About suffering they were never wrong,
The Old Masters: how well they understood
Its human position; how it takes place
While someone else is eating or opening a window or just
    walking dully along;
How, when the aged are reverently, passionately waiting
For the miraculous birth, there always must be
Children who did not specially want it to happen, skating
On a pond at the edge of the wood:
They never forgot
That even the dreadful martyrdom must run its course
Anyhow in a corner, some untidy spot
Where the dogs go on with their doggy life and the torturer's
    horse
Scratches its innocent behind on a tree.

In Brueghel's *Icarus*, for instance: how everything turns away
Quite leisurely from the disaster; the ploughman may
Have heard the splash, the forsaken cry,
But for him it was not an important failure; the sun shone
As it had to on the white legs disappearing into the green
Water: and the expensive delicate ship that must have seen
Something amazing, a boy falling out of the sky,
Had somewhere to get to and sailed calmly on.

HERMAN MELVILLE

Towards the end he sailed into an extraordinary mildness,
And anchored in his home and reached his wife
And rode within the harbour of her hand,
And went across each morning to an office
As though his occupation were another island.

Goodness existed: that was the new knowledge
His terror had to blow itself quite out

To let him see it; but it was the gale had blown him
Past the Cape Horn of sensible success
Which cries: "This rock is Eden. Shipwreck here."

But deafened him with thunder and confused with lightning:
—The maniac hero hunting like a jewel
The rare ambiguous monster that had maimed his sex,
Hatred for hatred ending in a scream,
The unexplained survivor breaking off the nightmare—
All that was intricate and false; the truth was simple.

Evil is unspectacular and always human,
And shares our bed and eats at our own table,
And we are introduced to Goodness every day,
Even in drawing-rooms among a crowd of faults;
He has a name like Billy and is almost perfect
But wears a stammer like a decoration:
And every time they meet the same thing has to happen;
It is the Evil that is helpless like a lover
And has to pick a quarrel and succeeds,
And both are openly destroyed before our eyes.

For now he was awake and knew
No one is ever spared except in dreams;
But there was something else the nightmare had distorted—
Even the punishment was human and a form of love:
The howling storm had been his father's presence
And all the time he had been carried on his father's breast.

Who now had set him gently down and left him.
He stood upon the narrow balcony and listened:
And all the stars above him sang as in his childhood
"All, all is vanity," but it was not the same;
For now the words descended like the calm of mountains—
—Nathaniel had been shy because his love was selfish—
But now he cried in exultation and surrender
"The Godhead is broken like bread. We are the pieces."

And sat down at his desk and wrote a story.

VOLTAIRE AT FERNEY

Perfectly happy now, he looked at his estate.
An exile making watches glanced up as he passed
And went on working; where a hospital was rising fast,
A joiner touched his cap; an agent came to tell
Some of the trees he'd planted were progressing well.
The white alps glittered. It was summer. He was very great.

Far off in Paris where his enemies
Whispered that he was wicked, in an upright chair
A blind old woman longed for death and letters. He would
    write,
"Nothing is better than life." But was it? Yes, the fight
Against the false and the unfair
Was always worth it. So was gardening. Civilize.

Cajoling, scolding, scheming, cleverest of them all,
He'd had the other children in a holy war
Against the infamous grown-ups; and, like a child, been sly
And humble, when there was occasion for
The two-faced answer or the plain protective lie,
But, patient like a peasant, waited for their fall.

And never doubted, like D'Alembert, he would win:
Only Pascal was a great enemy, the rest
Were rats already poisoned; there was much, though, to be
    done,
And only himself to count upon.
Dear Diderot was dull but did his best;
Rousseau, he'd always known, would blubber and give in.

Night fell and made him think of women: Lust
Was one of the great teachers; Pascal was a fool.
How Emilie had loved astronomy and bed;
Pimpette had loved him too, like scandal; he was glad.
He'd done his share of weeping for Jerusalem: As a rule,
It was the pleasure-haters who became unjust.

Yet, like a sentinel, he could not sleep. The night was full of
    wrong,
Earthquakes and executions: Soon he would be dead,
And still all over Europe stood the horrible nurses
Itching to boil their children. Only his verses
Perhaps could stop them: He must go on working: Overhead,
The uncomplaining stars composed their lucid song.

FUGAL-CHORUS FROM "FOR THE TIME BEING"

Great is Caesar: He has conquered Seven Kingdoms.
The First was the Kingdom of Abstract Idea:
Last night it was Tom, Dick and Harry; tonight it is S's with
    P's;
Instead of inflexions and accents
There are prepositions and word-order;
Instead of aboriginal objects excluding each other
There are specimens reiterating a type;
Instead of wood-nymphs and river-demons,
There is one unconditioned ground of Being.
Great is Caesar: God must be with Him.

Great is Caesar: He has conquered Seven Kingdoms.
The Second was the Kingdom of Natural Cause:
Last night it was Sixes and Sevens; tonight it is One and Two;
Instead of saying, "Strange are the whims of the Strong,"
We say, "Harsh is the Law but it is certain";
Instead of building temples, we build laboratories;
Instead of offering sacrifices, we perform experiments;
Instead of reciting prayers, we note pointer-readings;
Our lives are no longer erratic but efficient.
Great is Caesar: God must be with Him.

Great is Caesar: He has conquered Seven Kingdoms.
The Third was the Kingdom of Infinite Number:
Last night it was Rule-of-Thumb, tonight it is To-a-T;
Instead of Quite-a-lot, there is Exactly-so-many;
Instead of Only-a-few, there is Just-these;

Instead of saying, "You must wait until I have counted,"
We say, "Here you are. You will find this answer correct";
Instead of a nodding acquaintance with a few integers
The Transcendentals are our personal friends.
Great is Caesar: God must be with Him.

Great is Caesar: He has conquered Seven Kingdoms.
The Fourth was the Kingdom of Credit Exchange:
Last night it was Tit-for-Tat, tonight it is C.O.D.;
When we have a surplus, we need not meet someone with a
    deficit;
When we have a deficit, we need not meet someone with a
    surplus;
Instead of heavy treasures, there are paper symbols of value;
Instead of Pay at Once, there is Pay when you can;
Instead of My Neighbour, there is Our Customers;
Instead of Country Fair, there is World Market.
Great is Caesar: God must be with Him.

Great is Caesar: He has conquered Seven Kingdoms.
The Fifth was the Kingdom of Inorganic Giants:
Last night it was Heave-Ho, tonight it is Whee-Spree;
When we want anything, They make it;
When we dislike anything, They change it;
When we want to go anywhere, They carry us;
When the Barbarian invades us, They raise immovable shields;
When we invade the Barbarian, They brandish irresistible
    swords;
Fate is no longer a fiat of Matter, but a freedom of Mind.
Great is Caesar: God must be with Him.

Great is Caesar: He has conquered Seven Kingdoms.
The Sixth was the Kingdom of Organic Dwarfs:
Last night it was Ouch-Ouch, tonight it is Yum-Yum;
When diseases waylay us, They strike them dead;
When worries intrude on us, They throw them out;
When pain accosts us, They save us from embarrassment;

When we feel like sheep, They make us lions;
When we feel like geldings, They make us stallions;
Spirit is no longer under Flesh, but on top.
Great is Caesar: God must be with Him.

Great is Caesar: He has conquered Seven Kingdoms.
The Seventh was the Kingdom of Popular Soul:
Last night it was Order-Order, tonight it is Hear-Hear;
When he says, You are happy, we laugh;
When he says, You are wretched, we cry;
When he says, It is true, everyone believes it;
When he says, It is false, no one believes it;
When he says, This is good, this is loved;
When he says, That is bad, that is hated.
Great is Caesar: God must be with Him.

THE LABYRINTH

Anthropos apteros for days
Walked whistling round and round the Maze,
Relying happily upon
His temperament for getting on.

The hundredth time he sighted, though,
A bush he left an hour ago,
He halted where four alleys crossed,
And recognised that he was lost.

"Where am I? Metaphysics says
No question can be asked unless
It has an answer, so I can
Assume this maze has got a plan.

If theologians are correct,
A Plan implies an Architect:
A God-built maze would be, I'm sure,
The Universe in miniature.

Are data from the world of Sense,
In that case, valid evidence?
What in the universe I know
Can give directions how to go?

All Mathematics would suggest
A steady straight line as the best,
But left and right alternately
Is consonant with History.

Aesthetics, though, believes all Art
Intends to gratify the Heart:
Rejecting disciplines like these,
Must I, then, go which way I please?

Such reasoning is only true
If we accept the classic view,
Which we have no right to assert,
According to the Introvert.

His absolute pre-supposition
Is—Man creates his own condition:
This maze was not divinely built,
But is secreted by my guilt.

The centre that I cannot find
Is known to my Unconscious Mind;
I have no reason to despair
Because I am already there.

My problem is how *not* to will;
They move most quickly who stand still;
I'm only lost until I see
I'm lost because I want to be.

If this should fail, perhaps I should,
As certain educators would,
Content myself with the conclusion;
In theory there is no solution.

All statements about what I feel,
Like I-am-lost, are quite unreal:
My knowledge ends where it began;
A hedge is taller than a man."

Anthropos apteros, perplexed
To know which turning to take next,
Looked up and wished he were the bird
To whom such doubts must seem absurd.

SEPTEMBER 1, 1939

I sit in one of the dives
On Fifty-Second Street
Uncertain and afraid
As the clever hopes expire
Of a low dishonest decade:
Waves of anger and fear
Circulate over the bright
And darkened lands of the
    earth,
Obsessing our private lives;
The unmentionable odour of
    death
Offends the September night.

Accurate scholarship can
Unearth the whole offence
From Luther until now
That has driven a culture mad,
Find what occurred at Linz,
What huge imago made
A psychopathic god:
I and the public know
What all schoolchildren
    learn,
Those to whom evil is done
Do evil in return.

Exiled Thucydides knew
All that a speech can say
About Democracy,
And what dictators do,
The elderly rubbish they talk
To an apathetic grave;
Analysed all in his book,
The enlightenment driven
    away,
The habit-forming pain,
Mismanagement and grief:
We must suffer them all
    again.

Into this neutral air
Where blind skyscrapers use
Their full height to proclaim
The strength of Collective
    Man,
Each language pours its vain
Competitive excuse:
But who can live for long
In an euphoric dream;
Out of the mirror they stare,
Imperialism's face
And the international wrong.

Faces along the bar
Cling to their average day:
The lights must never go out,
The music must always play,
All the conventions conspire
To make this fort assume
The furniture of home;
Lest we should see where we
    are,
Lost in a haunted wood,
Children afraid of the night
Who have never been happy
    or good.

The windiest militant trash
Important Persons shout
Is not so crude as our wish:
What mad Nijinsky wrote
About Diaghilev
Is true of the normal heart;
For the error bred in the
    bone
Of each woman and each
    man
Craves what it cannot have,
Not universal love
But to be loved alone.

From the conservative dark
Into the ethical life
The dense commuters come,
Repeating their morning
    vow;
"I *will* be true to the wife,
I'll concentrate more on my
    work,"

And helpless governors wake
To resume their compulsory
    game:
Who can release them now,
Who can reach the deaf,
Who can speak for the
    dumb?

All I have is a voice
To undo the folded lie,
The romantic lie in the brain
Of the sensual man-in-the-
    street
And the lie of Authority
Whose buildings grope the
    sky:
There is no such thing as the
    State
And no one exists alone;
Hunger allows no choice
To the citizen or the police;
We must love one another
    and die.

Defenceless under the night
Our world in stupour lies;
Yet, dotted everywhere,
Ironic points of light
Flash out wherever the Just
Exchange their messages:
May I, composed like them
Of Eros and of dust,
Beleaguered by the same
Negation and despair,
Show an affirming flame.

IN MEMORY OF W. B. YEATS

(d. Jan. 1939)

I

He disappeared in the dead of winter:
The brooks were frozen, the air-ports almost deserted,
And snow disfigured the public statues;
The mercury sank in the mouth of the dying day.
O all the instruments agree
The day of his death was a dark cold day.

Far from his illness
The wolves ran on through the evergreen forests,
The peasant river was untempted by the fashionable quays;
By mourning tongues
The death of the poet was kept from his poems.

But for him it was his last afternoon as himself,
An afternoon of nurses and rumours;
The provinces of his body revolted,
The squares of his mind were empty,
Silence invaded the suburbs,
The current of his feeling failed: he became his admirers.

Now he is scattered among a hundred cities
And wholly given over to unfamiliar affections;
To find his happiness in another kind of wood
And be punished under a foreign code of conscience.
The words of a dead man
Are modified in the guts of the living.

But in the importance and noise of to-morrow
When the brokers are roaring like beasts on the floor of the
Bourse,
And the poor have the sufferings to which they are fairly ac-
customed,
And each in the cell of himself is almost convinced of his
freedom;

A few thousand will think of this day
As one thinks of a day when one did something slightly unusual.

O all the instruments agree
The day of his death was a dark cold day.

II

You were silly like us: your gift survived it all;
The parish of rich women, physical decay,
Yourself; mad Ireland hurt you into poetry.
Now Ireland has her madness and her weather still,
For poetry makes nothing happen: it survives
In the valley of its saying where executives
Would never want to tamper; it flows south
From ranches of isolation and the busy griefs,
Raw towns that we believe and die in; it survives,
A way of happening, a mouth.

III

Earth, receive an honoured
    guest;
William Yeats is laid to rest:
Let the Irish vessel lie
Emptied of its poetry.

Time that is intolerant
Of the brave and innocent,
And indifferent in a week
To a beautiful physique,

Worships language and
    forgives
Everyone by whom it lives;
Pardons cowardice, conceit,
Lays its honours at their feet.

Time that with this strange
    excuse
Pardoned Kipling and his
    views,
And will pardon Paul
    Claudel,
Pardons him for writing well.

In the nightmare of the dark
All the dogs of Europe bark,
And the living nations wait,
Each sequestered in its hate;

Intellectual disgrace
Stares from every human
    face,

And the seas of pity lie
Locked and frozen in each
    eye.

With the farming of a verse
Make a vineyard of the curse,
Sing of human unsuccess
In a rapture of distress;

Follow, poet, follow right
To the bottom of the night,
With your unconstraining
    voice
Still persuade us to rejoice;

In the deserts of the heart
Let the healing fountain
    start,
In the prison of his days
Teach the free man how to
    praise.

PERHAPS

O Love, the interest itself in thoughtless Heaven,
Make simpler daily the beating of man's heart; within,
There in the ring where name and image meet,

Inspire them with such a longing as will make his thought
Alive like patterns a murmuration of starlings,
Rising in joy over wolds, unwittingly weave.

Here too on our little reef display your power,
This fortress perched on the edge of the Atlantic scarp,
The mote between all Europe and the exile-crowded sea;

And make us as *Newton* was who, in his garden watching
The apple falling towards *England,* became aware
Between himself and her of an eternal tie.

For now that dream which so long had contented our will,
I mean, of uniting the dead into a splendid empire,
Under whose fertilising flood the Lancashire moss

Sprouted up chimneys, and *Glamorgan* hid a life
Grim as a tidal rock-pool's in its glove-shaped valleys,
Is already retreating into her maternal shadow;

Leaving the furnaces gasping in the impossible air,
That flotsam at which *Dumbarton* gapes and hungers;
While upon wind-loved *Rowley* no hammer shakes

The cluster of mounds like a midget golf-course, graves
Of some who created these intelligible dangerous marvels,
Affectionate people, but crude their sense of glory.

Far-sighted as falcons, they looked down another future;
For the seed in their loins were hostile though afraid of their
    pride,
And, tall with a shadow now, inertly wait.

In bar, in netted chicken-farm, in lighthouse,
Standing on these impoverished constricted acres,
The ladies and gentlemen apart, too much alone,

Consider the years of the measured world begun,
The barren virtuous marriage of stone and water.
Yet, O, at this very moment of a hopeless sigh,

When, inland, they are thinking their thoughts but watching
    these islands
As children in *Chester* look to *Moel Fammau* to decide
On picnics by the clearness or withdrawal of her treeless
    crown.

Some possible dream, long coiled in the ammonite's slumber
Is uncurling, prepared to lay on our talk and reflection
Its military silence, its surgeon's idea of pain;

And out of the future into actual history,
As when *Merlin*, tamer of horses, and his lords to whom
Stonehenge was still a thought, the *Pillars* passed

And into the undared ocean swung north their prow,
Drives through the night and star-concealing dawn
For the virgin roadsteads of our hearts an unwavering keel.

LAKES

A lake allows an average father, walking slowly,
    To circumvent it in an afternoon,
And any healthy mother to halloo the children
    Back to her bedtime from their games across:
(Anything bigger than that, like Michigan or Baikal,
    Though potable, is an 'estranging sea').

Lake-folk require no fiend to keep them on their toes;
    They leave aggression to ill-bred romantics
Who duel with their shadows over blasted heaths:
    A month in a lacustrine atmosphere
Would find the fluvial rivals waltzing not exchanging
    The rhyming insults of their great-great-uncles.

No wonder Christendom did not get really started
    Till, scarred by torture, fresh from caves and jails,
Her pensive chiefs converged on the Ascanian Lake
    And by that stork-infested shore invented
The life of Godhead, making catholic the figure
    Of three small fishes in a triangle.

Sly Foreign Ministers should always meet beside one,
    For, whether they walk widdershins or deasil,
The path will yoke their shoulders to one liquid centre
    Like two old donkeys pumping as they plod;
Such physical compassion may not guarantee
    A marriage for their armies, but it helps.

Only a very wicked or conceited man,
    About to sink somewhere in mid-Atlantic,
Could think Poseidon's frown was meant for him in person,
    But it is only human to believe
The little lady of the glacier lake has fallen
    In love with the rare bather whom she drowns.

The drinking water of the city, where one panics
    At nothing noticing how real one is,

May come from reservoirs whose guards are all too conscious
    Of being followed: Webster's cardinal
Saw in a fish-pool something horrid with a hay-rake;
    I know a Sussex hammer-pond like that.

A haunted lake is sick, though; normally, they doctor
    Our tactile fevers with a visual world
Where beaks are dumb like boughs and faces safe like houses;
    The water-scorpion finds it quite unticklish,
And, if it shudder slightly when caressed by boats,
    It never asks for water or a loan.

Liking one's Nature, as lake-lovers do, benign
    Goes with a wish for savage dogs and man-traps:
One Fall, one dispossession, is enough I'm sorry;
    Why should I give Lake Eden to the Nation
Just because every mortal Jack and Jill has been
    The genius of some amniotic mere?

It is unlikely I shall ever keep a swan
    Or build a tower on any small tombolo,
But that's not going to stop me wondering which class
    Of lake I would decide on if I should.
Moraine, pot, oxbow, glint, sink, crater, piedmont, dimple. . . .
    Just reeling off the names is ever so comfy.

WOODS

Sylvan meant savage in those primal woods
Piero di Cosimo so loved to draw,
Where nudes, bears, lions, sows with women's heads
Mounted and murdered and ate each other raw,
Nor thought the lightning-kindled bush to tame
But, flabbergasted, fled the useful flame.

Reduced to patches owned by hunting squires
Of villages with ovens and a stocks,

They whispered still of most unsocial fires,
Though Crown and Mitre warned their silly flocks
The pasture's humdrum rhythms to approve
And to abhor the licence of the grove.

Guilty intention still looks for a hotel
That wants no details and surrenders none;
A wood is that, and throws in charm as well,
And many a semi-innocent, undone,
Has blamed its nightingales who round the deed
Sang with such sweetness of a happy greed.

Those birds, of course, did nothing of the sort,
And, as for sylvan nature, if you take
A snapshot at a picnic, O how short
And lower-ordersy the Gang will look
By those vast lives that never took another
And are not scared of gods, ghosts, or stepmother.

Among these coffins of its by-and-by
The Public can (it cannot on a coast)
Bridle its skirt-and-bargain-chasing eye,
And where should an austere philologist
Relax but in the very world of shade
From which the matter of his field was made.

Old sounds re-educate an ear grown coarse,
As Pan's green father suddenly raps out
A burst of undecipherable Morse,
And cuckoos mock in Welsh, and doves create
In rustic English over all they do
To rear their modern family of two.

Now here, now there, some loosened element,
A fruit in vigor or a dying leaf,
Utters its private idiom for descent,
And late man, listening through his latter grief,
Hears, close or far, the oldest of his joys,
Exactly as it was, the water noise.

A well-kempt forest begs Our Lady's grace;
Someone is not disgusted, or at least
Is laying bets upon the human race
Retaining enough decency to last;
The trees encountered on a country stroll
Reveal a lot about that country's soul.

A small grove massacred to the last ash,
An oak with heart-rot, give away the show:
This great society is going smash;
They cannot fool us with how fast they go,
How much they cost each other and the gods!
A culture is no better than its woods.

THE TRIAL

"When rites and melodies begin
    To alter modes and times,
And timid bar-flies boast aloud
    Of uncommitted crimes,
And leading families are proud
    To dine with their black sheep,
What promises, what discipline,
    If any, will Love keep?"
        So roared Fire on their right:
        But Tamino and Pamina
            Walked past its rage,
            Sighing O, sighing O,
        In timeless fermatas of awe and delight,
        (Innocent? Yes. Ignorant? No.)
            Down the grim passage.

"When stinking Chaos lifts the hatch,
    And Grotte backward spins,
And Helen's nose becomes a beak,
    And cats and dogs grow chins,
And daisies claw and pebbles shriek,

    And Form and Color part,
What swarming hatreds then will hatch
    Out of Love's riven heart?"
      So hissed Water on their left:
        But Pamina and Tamino
        Opposed its spite,
      With his worship, with her sweetness.
        O look, now, see how they emerge from the cleft,
        (Frightened? No. Happy? Yes.)
        Out into sunlight.

PLAINS

I can imagine quite easily ending up
    In a decaying port on a desolate coast,
Cadging drinks from the unwary, a quarrelsome,
    Disreputable old man; I can picture
A second childhood in a valley, scribbling
    Reams of edifying and unreadable verse;
But I cannot see a plain without a shudder;—
    "O God, please, please, don't ever make me live there!"

It's horrible to think what peaks come down to,
    That pecking rain and squelching glacier defeat
Tall pomps of stone where goddesses lay sleeping,
    Dreaming of being woken by some chisel's kiss,
That what those blind brutes leave when they are through is
    nothing
But a mere substance, a clay that meekly takes
The potter's cuff, a gravel that as concrete
    Will unsex any space which it encloses.

And think of growing where all elsewheres are equal!
    So long as there's a hill-ridge somewhere the dreamer
Can place his land of marvels; in poor valleys
    Orphans can head downstream to seek a million:
Here nothing points; to choose between Art and Science
    An embryo genius would have to spin a stick.

What could these farms do if set loose but drift like clouds,
    What goal of unrest is there but the Navy?

Romance? Not in this weather. Ovid's charmer
    Who leads the quadrilles in Arcady, boy-lord
Of hearts who can call their Yes and No their own,
    Would, madcap that he is, soon die of cold or sunstroke:
These lives are in firmer hands; that old grim She
    Who makes the blind dates for the hatless genera
Creates their country matters. (Woe to the child-bed,
    Woe to the strawberries if she's in Her moods!)

And on these attend, greedy as fowl and harsher
    Than any climate, Caesar with all his They.
If a tax-collector disappear in the hills,
    If, now and then, a keeper is shot in the forest,
No thunder follows, but where roads run level,
    How swift to the point of protest strides the Crown.
It hangs, it flogs, it fines, it goes. There is drink.
    There are wives to beat. But Zeus is with the strong.

Born as a rule in some small place (an island,
    Quite often, where a smart lad can spot the bluff
Whence cannon would put the harbor at his mercy),
    Though it is here they chamber with Clio. At this ditch
The Christian cross-bow stopped the Heathen scimitar;
    Here is a windmill whence an emperor saw
His right wing crumple; across these cabbage fields
    A pretender's Light Horse made their final charge.

If I were a plainsman I should hate us all,
    From the mechanic rioting for a cheap loaf
To the fastidious palate, hate the painter
    Who steals my wrinkles for his Twelve Apostles,
Hate the priest who cannot even make it shower.
    What could I smile at as I trudged behind my harrow
But bloodshot images of rivers screaming,
    Marbles in panic, and Don't-Care made to care?

As it is, though, I know them personally
    Only as a landscape common to two nightmares:
Across them, spotted by spiders from afar,
    I have tried to run, knowing there was no hiding and no
        hope;
On them, in brilliant moonlight, I have lost my way
    And stood without a shadow at the dead center
Of an abominable desolation,
    Like Tarquin ravished by his post-coital sadness.

Which goes to show I've reason to be frightened
    Not of plains, of course, but of me. I should like
Who wouldn't?—to shoot beautifully and be obeyed
    (I should also like to own a cave with two exits);
I wish I weren't so silly. Though I can't pretend
    To think these flats poetic, it's as well at times
To be reminded that nothing is lovely,
    Not even in poetry, which is not the case.

UNDER SIRIUS

Yes, these are the dog-days, Fortunatus:
    The heather lies limp and dead
  On the mountain, the baltering torrent
    Shrunk to a soodling thread;
Rusty the spears of the legion, unshaven its captain,
    Vacant the scholar's brain
    Under his great hat,
  Drug as she may the Sibyl utters
    A gush of table-chat.

And you yourself with a head-cold and upset stomach,
    Lying in bed till noon,
  Your bills unpaid, your much advertised
    Epic not yet begun,
Are a sufferer too. All day, you tell us, you wish
    Some earthquake would astonish

Or the wind of the Comforter's wing
Unlock the prisons and translate
The slipshod gathering.

And last night, you say, you dreamed of that bright blue
          morning,
The hawthorn hedges in bloom,
When, serene in their ivory vessels,
The three wise Maries come,
Sossing through seamless waters, piloted in
By sea-horse and fluent dolphin:
Ah! how the cannons roar,
How jocular the bells as They
Indulge the peccant shore.

It is natural to hope and pious, of course, to believe
That all in the end shall be well,
But first of all, remember,
So the Sacred Books foretell,
The rotten fruit shall be shaken. Would your hope make sense
If today were that moment of silence
Before it break and drown
When the insurrected eagre hangs
Over the sleeping town?

How will you look and what will you do when the basalt
Tombs of the sorcerers shatter
And their guardian megalopods
Come after you pitter-patter?
How will you answer when from their qualming spring
The immortal nymphs fly shrieking
And out of the open sky
The pantocratic riddle breaks—
"Who are you and why?"

For when in a carol under the apple-trees
The reborn featly dance,
There will also, Fortunatus,

Be those who refused their chance,
Now pottering shades, querulous beside the salt-pits,
  And mawkish in their wits,
    To whom these dull dog-days
  Between event seem crowned with olive
    And golden with self-praise.

IN PRAISE OF LIMESTONE

If it form the one landscape that we the inconstant ones
  Are consistently homesick for, this is chiefly
Because it dissolves in water. Mark these rounded slopes
  With their surface fragrance of thyme and beneath
A secret system of caves and conduits; hear these springs
  That spurt out everywhere with a chuckle
Each filling a private pool for its fish and carving
  Its own little ravine whose cliffs entertain
The butterfly and the lizard; examine this region
  Of short distances and definite places:
What could be more like Mother or a fitter background
  For her son, for the nude young male who lounges
Against a rock displaying his dildo, never doubting
  That for all his faults he is loved, whose works are but
Extensions of his power to charm? From weathered outcrop
  To hill-top temple, from appearing waters to
Conspicuous fountains, from a wild to a formal vineyard,
  Are ingenious but short steps that a child's wish
To receive more attention than his brothers, whether
  By pleasing or teasing, can easily take.

Watch, then, the band of rivals as they climb up and down
  Their steep stone gennels in twos and threes, sometimes
Arm in arm, but never, thank God, in step; or engaged
  On the shady side of a square at midday in
Voluble discourse, knowing each other too well to think
  There are any important secrets, unable
To conceive a god whose temper-tantrums are moral
  And not to be pacified by a clever line

Or a good lay: for, accustomed to a stone that responds,
  They have never had to veil their faces in awe
Of a crater whose blazing fury could not be fixed;
  Adjusted to the local needs of valleys
Where everything can be touched or reached by walking,
  Their eyes have never looked into infinite space
Through the lattice-work of a nomad's comb; born lucky,
  Their legs have never encountered the fungi
And insects of the jungle, the monstrous forms and lives
  With which we have nothing, we like to hope, in common.
So, when one of them goes to the bad, the way his mind works
  Remains comprehensible: to become a pimp
Or deal in fake jewelry or ruin a fine tenor voice
  For effects that bring down the house could happen to all
But the best and the worst of us . . .

                              That is why, I suppose,
  The best and worst never stayed here long but sought
Immoderate soils where the beauty was not so external,
  The light less public and the meaning of life
Something more than a mad camp. "Come!" cried the granite
    wastes,
  "How evasive is your humor, how accidental
Your kindest kiss, how permanent is death." (Saints-to-be
  Slipped away sighing.) "Come!" purred the clays and
    gravels.
"On our plains there is room for armies to drill; rivers
  Wait to be tamed and slaves to construct you a tomb
In the grand manner: soft as the earth is mankind and both
  Need to be altered." (Intendant Caesars rose and
Left, slamming the door.) But the really reckless were fetched
  By an older colder voice, the oceanic whisper:
"I am the solitude that asks and promises nothing;
  That is how I shall set you free. There is no love;
There are only the various envies, all of them sad."

They were right, my dear, all those voices were right
And still are; this land is not the sweet home that it looks,

Nor its peace the historical calm of a site
Where something was settled once and for all: A backward
   And delapidated province, connected
To the big busy world by a tunnel, with a certain
   Seedy appeal, is that all it is now? Not quite:
It has a worldly duty which in spite of itself
   It does not neglect, but calls into question
All the Great Powers assume; it disturbs our rights. The poet,
   Admired for his earnest habit of calling
The sun the sun, his mind Puzzle, is made uneasy
   By these solid statues which so obviously doubt
His antimythological myth; and these gamins,
   Pursuing the scientist down the tiled colonnade
With such lively offers, rebuke his concern for Nature's
   Remotest aspects: I, too, am reproached, for what
And how much you know. Not to lose time, not to get caught,
   Not to be left behind, not, please! to resemble
The beasts who repeat themselves, or a thing like water
   Or stone whose conduct can be predicted, these
Are our Common Prayer, whose greatest comfort is music
   Which can be made anywhere, is invisible,
And does not smell. In so far as we have to look forward
   To death as a fact, no doubt we are right: But if
Sins can be forgiven, if bodies rise from the dead,
   These modifications of matter into
Innocent athletes and gesticulating fountains,
   Made solely for pleasure, make a further point:
The blessed will not care what angle they are regarded from,
   Having nothing to hide. Dear, I know nothing of
Either, but when I try to imagine a faultless love
   Or the life to come, what I hear is the murmur
Of underground streams, what I see is a limestone landscape.

THE UNKNOWN CITIZEN

(To JS/07/M/378 This Marble Monument Is Erected by the State)

He was found by the Bureau of Statistics to be
One against whom there was no official complaint,
And all the reports on his conduct agree
That, in the modern sense of an old-fashioned word, he was a
　　saint,
For in everything he did he served the Greater Community.
Except for the War till the day he retired
He worked in a factory and never got fired,
But satisfied his employers, Fudge Motors Inc.
Yet he wasn't a scab or odd in his views,
For his Union reports that he paid his dues,
(Our report on his Union shows it was sound)
And our Social Psychology workers found
That he was popular with his mates and liked a drink.
The Press are convinced that he bought a paper every day
And that his reactions to advertisements were normal in every
　　way.
Policies taken out in his name prove that he was fully insured,
And his Health-card shows he was once in hospital but left it
　　cured.
Both Producers Research and High-Grade Living declare
He was fully sensible to the advantages of the Installment Plan
And had everything necessary to the Modern Man,
A phonograph, a radio, a car and a frigidaire.
Our researchers into Public Opinion are content
That he held the proper opinions for the time of year;
When there was peace, he was for peace; when there was
　　war, he went.
He was married and added five children to the population,
Which our Eugenist says was the right number for a parent
　　of his generation,
And our teachers report that he never interfered with their
　　education.

Was he free? Was he happy? The question is absurd:
Had anything been wrong, we should certainly have heard.

THE SHIELD OF ACHILLES

> She looked over his shoulder
>> For vines and olive trees,
> Marble, well-governed cities
>> And ships upon wine-dark seas;
> But there on the shining metal
>> His hands had put instead
> An artificial wilderness
>> And a sky like lead.

A plain without a feature, bare and brown,
   No blade of grass, no sign of neighborhood,
Nothing to eat and nowhere to sit down;
   Yet, congregated on that blankness, stood
   An unintelligible multitude,
A million eyes, a million boots, in line,
Without expression, waiting for a sign.

Out of the air a voice without a face
   Proved by statistics that some cause was just
In tones as dry and level as the place;
   No one was cheered and nothing was discussed,
   Column by column, in a cloud of dust,
They marched away, enduring a belief
Whose logic brought them, somewhere else, to grief.

> She looked over his shoulder
>> For ritual pieties,
> White flower-garlanded heifers,
>> Libation and sacrifice:
> But there on the shining metal
>> Where the altar should have been
> She saw by his flickering forge-light
>> Quite another scene.

Barbed wire enclosed an arbitrary spot
   Where bored officials lounged (one cracked a joke)

And sentries sweated for the day was hot;
   A crowd of ordinary decent folk
   Watched from outside and neither moved nor spoke
As three pale figures were led forth and bound
To three posts driven upright in the ground.

The mass and majesty of this world, all
   That carries weight and always weighs the same,
Lay in the hands of others; they were small
   And could not hope for help, and no help came;
   What their foes liked to do was done; their shame
Was all the worst could wish: they lost their pride
And died as men before their bodies died.

        She looked over his shoulder
           For athletes at their games,
        Men and women in a dance
           Moving their sweet limbs,
        Quick, quick, to music;
           But there on the shining shield
        His hands had set no dancing-floor
           But a weed-choked field.

A ragged urchin, aimless and alone,
   Loitered about that vacancy; a bird
Flew up to safety from his well-aimed stone:
   That girls are raped, that two boys knife a third,
   Were axioms to him, who'd never heard
Of any world where promises were kept
Or one could weep because another wept.

        The thin-lipped armorer
           Hephaestos hobbled away;
        Thetis of the shining breasts
           Cried out in dismay
        At what the God had wrought
           To please her son, the strong
        Iron-hearted man-slaying Achilles
           Who would not live long.

Joel Barlow

ADVICE TO A RAVEN IN RUSSIA DECEMBER, 1812

Black fool, why winter here? These frozen skies,
Worn by your wings and deafen'd by your cries,
Should warn you hence, where milder suns invite,
And day alternates with his mother night.
    You fear perhaps your food will fail you there,
Your human carnage, that delicious fare
That lured you hither, following still your friend,
The great Napoleon, to the world's bleak end.
You fear, because the southern climes pour'd forth
Their clustering nations to infest the north,
Bavarians, Austrians, those who Drink the Po
And those who skirt the Tuscan seas below,
With all Germania, Neustria, Belgia, Gaul,
Doom'd here to wade through slaughter to their fall,
You fear he left behind no wars, to feed
His feather'd cannibals and nurse the breed.
    Fear not, my screamer, call your greedy train,
Sweep over Europe, hurry back to Spain,
You'll find his legions there; the valliant crew
Please best their master when they toil for you.
Abundant there they spread the country o'er
And taint the breeze with every nation's gore,
Iberian, Lusian, British widely strown,
But still more wide and copious flows their own.
    Go where you will; Calabria, Malta, Greece,
Egypt and Syria still his fame increase,
Domingo's fatten'd isle and India's plains
Glow deep with purple drawn from Gallic veins.
No Raven's wing can stretch the flight so far
As the torn bandrols of Napoleon's war.
Choose then your climate, fix your best abode,
He'll make you deserts and he'll bring you blood.
    How could you fear a dearth? have not mankind,
Though slain by millions, millions left behind?

Has not CONSCRIPTION still the power to wield
Her annual falchion o'er the human field?
A faithful harvester; or if a man
Escape that gleaner, shall he scape the BAN?
The triple BAN, that like the hound of hell
Gripes with three jowls, to hold his victim well.

Fear nothing then, hatch fast your ravenous brood,
Teach them to cry to Bonaparte for food;
They'll be like you, of all his suppliant train,
The only class that never cries in vain.
For see what mutual benefits you lend!
(The surest way to fix the mutual friend)
While on his slaughter'd troops your tribes are fed,
You cleanse his camp and carry off his dead.
Imperial Scavenger! But now you know
Your work is vain amid these hills of snow.
His tentless troops are marbled through with frost
And change to crystal when the breath is lost.
Mere trunks of ice, though limb'd like human frames
And lately warm'd with life's endearing flames,
They cannot taint the air, the world impest,
Nor can you tear one fiber from their breast.
No! from their visual sockets, as they lie,
With beak and claws you cannot pluck an eye.
The frozen orb, preserving still its form,
Defies your talons as it braves the storm,
But stands and stares to God, as if to know
In what curst hands he leaves his world below.

Fly then, or starve; though all the dreadful road
From Minsk to Moskow with their bodies strow'd
May count some myriads, yet they can't suffice
To feed you more beneath these dreary skies.
Go back, and winter in the wilds of Spain;
Feast there awhile, and in the next campaign
Rejoin your master; for you'll find him then,
With his new million of the race of men,
Clothed in his thunders, all his flags unfurl'd,
Raging and storming o'er the prostrate world.

War after war his hungry soul requires,
State after State shall sink beneath his fires,
Yet other Spains in victim smoke shall rise
And other Moskows suffocate the skies,
Each land lie reeking with its people's slain
And not a stream run bloodless to the main.
Till men resume their souls, and dare to shed
Earth's total vengeance on the monster's head,
Hurl from his blood-built throne this king of woes,
Dash him to dust, and let the world repose.

Joseph Bennett

AUTUMNALL

You walk the floor of autumn where her corpse,
Four feet of leaves, decays like rotting fur.
Her immense limbs shift with the strewing wind
And in the scattering mounds the furious horse
Plunge and veer, racing through such flesh.

She cups the flame of autumn in her flesh
Where thick and settled carnage stops the wind.
The smoke suffuses from her wasting corpse
From paleness hidden deep within this fur
And urine stains the leaves beneath the horse.

O sense the massive blending of these horse
As one by one they sink beneath the flesh.
It is the slow liquescence of the fur;
It is the thickened burning of the corpse.
O all this plumage loosened by the wind.

Evolving gases in the fluent wind
Abstract the memories of sunken horse;
The trees, the blinding trees, that cast their flesh.

The leaves erode within the fusing corpse;
The fissures blaze along the drifts of fur.

Endure the spurting grapes within this fur;
Endure the fuels, the thickened fuels of flesh.
The gases drench the eyes of strangled horse.
The flames, spouting in the pores of wind,
Have seized the focussed phrasing of the corpse.

The corpse in flames, all naked to the wind,
The smouldering horse, diffused in fur,
The leaves, the quenching leaves that drown upon the flesh.

TO ELIZA, DUCHESS OF DORSET

In the negro gardens negro birds
Plummet in the shadows, falling thirds.
Dorset in sable plumage comes.
A hawk! A raven in his tediums.

Daughter to that good Earl, once President
Of England's Council, and her Parliament,
Duchess, if that falling shadow strikes
And strikes no more, as Dorset softly likes,

And in your heart the spike its purple draws,
And on your coral neck the marble claws—
O Duchess feel the negro soil beneath
Your crushed mouth and your splintered teeth.

Eliza strangling on the lawn at Knole,
The flowers sinking toward the twilit Pole,
And walking, calling, Dorset now distends;
Dorset cock and cockatoo; and raven ends.

ON THE NATIVITY OF CHRIST OUR LORD

Once in winter shone the ground and full sped
The heavenly spheres, high ghosts of all that frost
And funnelled snow which sways its topless cone

Above these cabined hills. And downsled,
Downing, down the night we flew;
Scorching the brilliant snow we fell
Toward that bright Diamond in the east
Sky fire burning in the east
Great glittering drop that pulses in its web
Of coal-blue coldest night. And brightest coal
Of all, in its rich tint of rippling rose,
Moves above the sleeping towns and snowdrift steppe.

A simple mother, shining in the east,
Drew from her bowels the tiny jewel,
Gave up the strenuous ghost that pierced her ear.
About her spreading cloak of purest blue
Posed the dusky kings with cabinets
Of pearl, and swirled the incense round her beams,
Her raftered baldachino. The wine-wealth
Of their ruddy robes, the paleness
Of her icy blue, blaze forever
Motionless, as in a glassy scene,
A window to the darkling, dazen west.

And pines and bells broke out their loud uproar,
Clarions shaking up and down the west,
The tall cathedrals twined with sprays of pine,
The congressed candles fuming in the nave.

HEADSONG

O Lord, the whistling sword is beauty
Both to ear and eye; and trembling,
Held by hair, the wordwise head
Cants and chants, cantata to
The whirling blade, the elegance
That swings. So trembling goes the head,
So swayed, so resonant it falls.

O Lord, the spirit was bestowed so carelessly,
It worked through many forms and many mouths
And burnt them all. Earth is cinders

It deposed. Earth is solid lava,
Pocked with bubbles where the air escaped,
But the spirit works the earth and clings.

This graveyard of persistent bones that will
Not wear away, this graveyard still can bloom
In earthly glory, but the soft
Insistent growth of death gathers all the forms
And fruits and dries them in its treasury.
The growth of death is the persistence of skeletons
And the drainage of the earth, to wash it pure.

O Lord, the growth of death is the cancerous breast,
Is the shriveled petal, is the bleeding bird.

For death is a garment exceeding pain,
And fitted when the flesh is newly cut.
The head sings of severance; the sword whirls.
What falls becomes the deep and rooted
Skeleton which will not fail, but glowing
When the earth has turned to ash
Preserves intact its careful structure.

The phosphorescent spirit hovers:
Exhumation of the well-washed bones
Does not relieve its luminous task.
It is the life of ash and cinders.
It craves no atmosphere, and when
Earth's ponderous axis tips across
The poles and balance stops the sphere,
It glimmers in the absolute
Imaginable cold assigned by space
To heavy planets come to rest:
One side in death; the other burning.

EARTHLY LOVE

Cling together in your dust: the frost
Across the spirit hisses and is lost.

Let us hang our few old bodies in
The sun; we benedict and flapping on
Our several trees would cause the surging flesh
To flower on the oak and strew the yews
With fruit as pale and faultless as a bruise.

Floating in our midst the lovely sun
Is mild and dancing in its cooking pot.
Tossing and swimming in the fluid air,
His cool and circular light is closely spun
About our glistening ears and wrought
Among us are his tremorous particles.
Shake this light deep in your glittering limbs, O lovers,
Fallow and wise on your purest trees. You share
The fragments of that flayed and flowering pear.

Perhaps there were twelve of us and not a word
Of greeting passed, but all this light exchanged
And smiling. And twelve trees stripped of branches bore us
In this watery light. Twelve trees bore
Our long and tranquil limbs of glass, and hung us
In the sun, slender as grasshoppers.
Sculptured and polished, corded at the tendons
And the knee and ankle bones we hung
In glass, and watery glass, pale and streaming,
Glittered on each trunk and bole. Exchanged
And fluttering was the light that held us
In our circle. And at the center, where
The sun drank deep within his cup, there rose
The flowering door of life, the flesh-strewn boughs.

O lovers pale on your frangible stems,
Trembling in sight of the faultless seed,
Exult in the guise of the clarified sun;
Exult where he blinded, flooded in mead,
Rises of crucial tree the crest
While rock-doves tear at his flowering breast.

Vine clings to tree in winter and midsummer,
Green in the blasts of snow, green in the dust of summer.

Blade strikes the sun at the point of high midsummer,
Sharp is the curving edge, swift is the waste of summer;
The scythe flashes gold, the scythe for flesh midsummer,
Cutting, cutting the vine of summer;
Cutting the wine of life with a plunging blade.

Was it the sun the Tree of Life pushed upward
With its head when first it broke the center
Of our gravelled soil? And if so why
Does it now hang green enormous on the crown,
A heavy head for the growing tree?
The sun becomes its single fruit, and flowing.

Green, green it grows, green sucks its sap
From every root of the tunneling tree.
Who had not shared twelve leaves
Within their whimsical and separate forest
Now behold colossal greenery
Aerial roots, and giant flowers crimson
On the tree.   A thousand colored birds
Upon it, and the insects swarming up and down.
The bees in sonorous quick clouds hung
Slowly on each pistillate and throbbing flower.

The sun hangs flush at the crucial height,
Frangible, a honeycomb of pores.

John Berryman

CONVERSATION

Whether the moorings are invisible
Or gone, we said we could not tell.
But argument held one thing sure
That none of us that night could well endure:
The ship is locked with fog, no man aboard
Can see what he is moving toward,
There's little food, less love, no sleep,
The sea is dark and we are told it's deep.

Where is an officer who knows this coast?
If all such men long since have faced
Downward, one summon. Who knows how,
With what fidelity his voice heard now
Could shout directions from the ocean's floor?
Traditional characters no more
Their learnéd simple parts rehearse,
But bed them down at last from the time's curse.

A broken log fell out upon the hearth,
The flaming harbinger come forth
Of holocausts that night and day
Shrivel from the mind its sovereignty.
We watched the embers cool; those embers brought
To one man there the failing thought
Of cities stripped of knowledge, men,
Our continent a wilderness again.

These are conclusions of the night, we said;
And drank, and were not satisfied.
The fire died down, smoke in the air
Took the alarming postures of our fear;
The overhead horror, in the padded room
The man who cannot tell his name,
The guns and enemies that face
Into this delicate and dangerous place.

CANTO AMOR

Dream in a dream the heavy soul somewhere
struck suddenly & dark down to its knees.
A griffin sighs off in the orphic air.

If (Unknown Majesty) I not confess
praise for the rack the rock the live sailor
under the blue sea,—yet I may You bless

always for hér, in fear & joy for hér
whose gesture summons ever when I grieve
me back and is my mage and minister.

—Muses, whose worship I may never leave
but for this pensive woman, now I dare,
teach me her praise! with her my praise receive.—

Three years already of the round world's war
had rolled by stoned & disappointed eyes
when she and I came where we were made for.

Pale as a star lost in returning skies,
more beautiful than midnight stars more frail
she moved towards me like chords, a sacrifice;

entombed in body trembling through the veil
arm upon arm, learning our ancient wound,
we see our one soul heal, recovering pale.

Then priestly sanction, then the drop of sound.
Quickly part to the cavern ever warm
deep from the march, body to body bound,

descend (my soul) out of dismantling storm
into the darkness where the world is made.
Come back to the bright air. Love is multiform.

Heartmating hesitating unafraid
although incredulous, she seemed to fill
the lilac shadow with light wherein she played,

whom sorry childhood had made sit quite still,
an orphan silence, unregarded sheen,
listening for any small soft note, not hopeful:

caricature: as once a maiden Queen,
flowering power comeliness kindness grace,
shattered her mirror, wept, would not be seen.

These pities moved. Also above her face
serious or flushed, swayed her fire-gold
not earthly hair, now moonless to unlace,

resistless flame, now in a sun more cold
great shells to whorl about each secret ear,
mysterious histories, strange shores, unfold.

New musics! One the music that we hear
this is the music which the masters make
out of their minds, profound solemn & clear.

And then the other music, in whose sake
all men perceive a gladness but we are drawn
less for that joy than utterly to take

our trial, naked in the music's vision,
the flowing ceremony of trouble and light,
all Loves becoming, none to rest upon.

Such Mozart made,—an ear so delicate
he fainted at a trumpet-call, a child
so delicate. So merciful that sight,

so stern, we follow rapt who ran awild.
Marriage is the second music, and thereof
we hear what we can bear, faithful & mild.

Therefore the streaming torches in the grove
through dark or bright, swiftly & now more near
cherish a festival of anxious love.

Dance for this music, Mistress to music dear,
more, that full storm through the disordered wood
ravens at midnight of my thirtieth year

and only the trial of our music should
still this irresolute air, only your voice
spelling the tempest may compel our good:

Sing then beyond my song: whirl & rejoice!

Elizabeth Bishop

THE FISH

I caught a tremendous fish
and held him beside the boat
half out of water, with my
  hook
fast in a corner of his mouth.
He didn't fight.
He hadn't fought at all.
He hung a grunting weight,
battered and venerable
and homely. Here and there
his brown skin hung in strips
like ancient wall-paper,
and its pattern of darker
  brown
was like wall-paper:
shapes like full-blown roses
stained and lost through age.
He was speckled with
  barnacles,
fine rosettes of lime,
and infested
with tiny white sea-lice,
and underneath two or three
rags of green weed hung
  down.
While his gills were
  breathing in
the terrible oxygen
—the frightening gills
fresh and crisp with blood,
that can cut so badly—
I thought of the coarse white
  flesh
packed in like feathers,
the big bones and the little
  bones,
the dramatic reds and blacks
of his shiny entrails,
and the pink swim-bladder
like a big peony.
I looked into his eyes
which were far larger than
  mine
but shallower, and yellowed,
the irises backed and packed
with tarnished tinfoil
seen through the lenses
of old scratched isinglass.
They shifted a little, but not
to return my stare.
—It was more like the tipping
of an object toward the light.
I admired his sullen face,
the mechanism of his jaw,
and then I saw
that from his lower lip
—if you could call it a lip—
grim, wet, and weapon-like,
hung five old pieces of fish-
  line,
or four and a wire leader
with the swivel still attached,
with all their five big hooks
grown firmly in his mouth.
A green line, frayed at the
  end

where he broke it, two
heavier lines,
and a fine black thread
still crimped from the strain
and snap
when it broke and he got
away.
Like medals with their ribbons
frayed and wavering,
a five-haired beard of wisdom
trailing from his aching jaw.
I stared and stared

and victory filled up
the little rented boat,
from the pool of bilge
where oil had spread a rainbow
around the rusted engine
to the bailer rusted orange,
the sun-cracked thwarts,
the oarlocks on their strings,
the gunnels—until everything
was rainbow, rainbow, rainbow!
And I let the fish go.

ROOSTERS

At four o'clock
in the gun-metal blue dark
we hear the first crow of the first cock

just below
the gun-metal blue window
and immediately there is an echo

off in the distance,
then one from the back-yard fence,
then one, with horrible insistence,

grates like a wet match
from the broccoli patch,
flares, and all over town begins to catch.

Cries galore
come from the water-closet door,
from the dropping-plastered henhouse floor,

where in the blue blurr
their rustling wives admire,
the roosters brace their cruel feet and glare

with stupid eyes
while from their beaks there rise
the uncontrolled, traditional cries.

Deep from protruding chests
in green-gold medals dressed,
planned to command and terrorize the rest,

the many wives
who lead hens' lives
of being courted and despised;

deep from raw throats
a senseless order floats
all over town. A rooster gloats

over our beds
from rusty iron sheds
and fences made from old bedsteads,

over our churches
where the tin rooster perches,
over our little wooden northern houses,

making sallies
from all the muddy alleys,
marking out maps like Rand McNally's:

glass-headed pins,
oil-golds and copper-greens,
anthracite blues, alizarins,

each one an active
displacement in perspective;
each screaming, "This is where I live!"

Each screaming,
"Get up! Stop dreaming!"
Roosters, what are you projecting?

You, whom the Greeks elected
to shoot at on a post, who struggled
when sacrificed, you whom they labelled

"Very combative . . ."
what right have you to give
commands, and tell us how to live,

cry, "Here!" and "Here!"
and wake us here where are
unwanted love, conceit, and war?

The crown of red
set on your little head
is charged with all your fighting-blood.

Yes, that excrescence
makes a most virile presence,
plus all that vulgar beauty of iridescence.

Now in mid-air
by twos they fight each other.
Down comes a first flame-feather,

and one is flying,
with raging heroism defying
even the sensation of dying.

And one has fallen,
but still above the town
his torn-out, bloodied feathers drift down;

and what he sung
no matter. He is flung
on the gray ash-heap, lies in dung

with his dead wives
with open, bloody eyes,
while those metallic feathers oxidize.

St. Peter's sin
was worse than that of Magdalen
whose sin was of the flesh alone;

of spirit, Peter's,
falling, beneath the flares,
among the "servants and officers."

Old holy sculpture
could set it all together
in one small scene, past and future:

Christ stands amazed,
Peter, two fingers raised
to surprised lips, both as if dazed.

But in between
a little cock is seen
carved on a dim column in the travertine,

explained by *gallus canit;*
flet Petrus underneath it.
There is inescapable hope, the pivot;

yes, and there Peter's tears
run down our chanticleer's
sides and gem his spurs.

Tear-encrusted thick
as a medieval relic
he waits. Poor Peter, heart-sick,

still cannot guess
those cock-a-doodles yet might bless,
his dreadful rooster come to mean forgiveness,

a new weathervane
on basilica and barn,
and that outside the Lateran

there would always be
a bronze cock on a porphyry
pillar so the people and the Pope might see

that even the Prince
of the Apostles long since
had been forgiven, and to convince

all the assembly
that "Deny deny deny,"
is not all the roosters cry.

In the morning
a low light is floating
in the backyard, and gilding

from underneath
the broccoli, leaf by leaf;
how could the night have come to grief?

gilding the tiny
floating swallow's belly
and lines of pink cloud in the sky,

the day's preamble
like wandering lines in marble.
The cocks are now almost inaudible.

The sun climbs in,
following "to see the end,"
faithful as enemy, or friend.

John Peale Bishop

ODE

Why will they never sleep   20
Those great women who sit
Peering at me with parrot eyes?
They sit with grave knees; they keep
Perpetual stare; and their hands move
As though hands could be aware—
Forward and back, to begin again—
As though on tumultuous shuttles of wind they wove
Shrouds out of air.

The three are sisters. There is one
Who sits divine in weeping stone
On a small chair of skeleton
And is most inescapable.
I have walked through many mirrors
But always accompanied.
I have been as many men, as many ghosts,
As there were days. The boy was seen
Always at rainfall, mistily, not lost.
I have tried changing shapes
But always, alone, I have heard
Her shadow coming nearer, and known
The awful grasp of striding hands
Goddess! upon
The screaming metamorphosis.

One has a face burned hard
As the red Cretan clay,
Who wears a white torso scarred
With figures like a calendar.

She sits among broken shafts
Of stone; she is and still will be
Who feeds on cities, gods and men,
Weapons of bronze and curious ornaments,
Reckoning the evens as the odds.
Her least movement recalls the sea.

The last has idiot teeth
And a brow not made
For any thought but suffering.
Tired, she repeats
In idiot singing
A song shaped like a ring:
"Now is now and never Then
Dead Virgins will bear no men
And now that we speak of love, of love,
The woman's beneath
That's burdened with love
And the man's above
While the thing is done and done.
One is one and Three is three
Children may come from a spark in the sun
But One is one and never Three
And never a Virgin shall bear a Son
While the shadow lasts of the gray ashtree!"

Phantasmal marbles!

There was One who might have saved
Me from these grave dissolute stones
And parrot eyes. But He is dead,
Christ is dead. And in a grave
Dark as a sightless skull He lies
And of His bones are charnels made.

PERSPECTIVES ARE PRECIPICES

Sister Anne, Sister Anne,
Do you see anybody coming?

> I see a distance of black yews
> Long as the history of the Jews.

> I see a road sunned with white sand
> Wide plains surrounding silence. And

> Far-off, a broken colonnade
> That overthrows the sun with shade.

Sister Anne, Sister Anne,
Do you see nobody coming?
                                    A man

> Upon that road a man who goes
> Dragging a shadow by its toes.

> Diminishing he goes, head bare
> Of any covering, even hair.

> A pitcher depending from one hand
> Goes mouth down. And dry is sand.

Sister Anne, Sister Anne,
What do you see?

> His dwindling stride. And he seems blind
> Or worse to the prone man behind.

Sister Anne! Sister Anne!

I see a road. Beyond nowhere
Defined by cirrus and blue air.

I saw a man but he is gone
His shadow gone into the sun.

THIS DIM AND PTOLEMAIC MAN

For forty years, for forty-one,
Sparing the profits of the sun,
This farmer piled his meagre hoard
To buy at last a rattly Ford.

Now crouched on a scared smile he feels
Motion spurt beneath his heels,
Rheumatically intent shifts gears,
Unloosing joints of rustic years.

Morning light obscures the stars,
He swerves avoiding other cars,
Wheels with the road, does not discern
He eastward goes at every turn,

Nor how his aged limbs are hurled
Through all the motions of the world,
How wild past farms, past ricks, past trees,
He perishes toward Hercules.

Louise Bogan

MEN LOVED WHOLLY BEYOND WISDOM

Men loved wholly beyond wisdom
Have the staff without the banner.
Like a fire in a dry thicket,
Rising within women's eyes
Is the love men must return.
Heart, so subtle now, and trembling,
What a marvel to be wise,
To love never in this manner!
To be quiet in the fern
Like a thing gone dead and still,
Listening to the prisoned cricket
Shake its terrible, dissembling
Music in the granite hill.

M., SINGING

Now, innocent, within the deep
Night of all things you turn the key
Unloosing what we know in sleep.
In your fresh voice they cry aloud
Those beings without heart or name.

Those creatures both corrupt and proud,
Upon the melancholy words
And in the music's subtlety,
Leave the long harvest which they reap
In the sunk land of dust and flame
And move to space beneath our sky.

HENCEFORTH, FROM THE MIND

Henceforth, from the mind,
For your whole joy, must spring
Such joy as you may find
In any earthly thing,
And every time and place
Will take your thought for grace.

Henceforth, from the tongue,
From shallow speech alone,
Comes joy you thought, when young,
Would wring you to the bone,
Would pierce you to the heart
And spoil its stop and start.

Henceforward, from the shell,
Wherein you heard, and wondered
At oceans like a bell
So far from ocean sundered—
A smothered sound that sleeps
Long lost within lost deeps,

Will chime you change and hours,
The shadow of increase,
Will sound you flowers
Born under troubled peace—
Henceforth, henceforth
Will echo sea and earth.

OLD COUNTRYSIDE

Beyond the hour we counted rain that fell
On the slant shutter, all has come to proof.
The summer thunder, like a wooden bell,
Rang in the storm above the mansard roof,

And mirrors cast the cloudy day along
The attic floor; wind made the clapboards creak.
You braced against the wall to make it strong,
A shell against your cheek.

Long since, we pulled brown oak-leaves to the ground
In a winter of dry trees; we heard the cock
Shout its unplaceable cry, the axe's sound
Delay a moment after the axe's stroke.

Far back, we saw, in the stillest of the year,
The scrawled vine shudder, and the rose-branch show
Red to the thorns, and, sharp as sight can bear,
The thin hound's body arched against the snow.

Anne Bradstreet

THE AUTHOR TO HER BOOK

Thou ill-form'd offspring of my feeble brain,
Who after birth didst by my side remain
Till snatcht from thence by friends less wise than true
Who thee abroad expos'd to publick view,
Made thee in raggs, halting to th'press to trudge
Where errors were not lessened (all may judge)
At thy return my blushing was not small,
My rambling brat (in print) should mother call.
I cast thee by as one unfit for light,
Thy Visage was so irksome in my sight;
Yet being mine own, at length affection would
Thy blemishes amend, if so I could:
I wash'd thy face, but more defects I saw,
And rubbing off a spot, still made a flaw.
I stretcht thy joints to make thee even feet,
Yet still thou run'st more hobling than is meet;
In better dress to trim thee was my mind,

But nought save home-spun Cloth i'th'house I find.
In this array 'mongst Vulgars mayst thou roam,
In criticks hands beware thou dost not come,
And take thy way where yet thou art not known.
If for thy Father askt, say, thou hadst none:
And for thy Mother, she alas is poor,
Which caus'd her thus to send thee out of door.

THE FLESH AND THE SPIRIT

In secret place where once I stood
Close by the Banks of *Lacrim* flood,
I heard two sisters reason on
Things that are past, and things to come.
One Flesh was call'd, who had her eye
On worldly wealth and vanity;
The other Spirit, who did rear
Her thoughts unto a higher sphere:
Sister, quoth Flesh, what liv'st thou on—
Nothing but Meditation?
Doth Contemplation feed thee so
Regardlessly to let earth goe?
Can Speculation satisfy
Notion without Reality?
Dost dream of things beyond the Moon
And dost thou hope to dwell there soon?
Hast treasures there laid up in store
That all in th' world thou count'st but poor?
Art fancy sick, or turn'd a Sot
To catch at shadowes which are not?
Come, come, Ile shew unto thy sence
Industry hath its recompence.
What canst desire, but thou maist see
True substance in variety?
Dost honour like? Acquire the same,
As some to their immortal fame:
And trophyes to thy name erect

Which wearing time shall ne're deject.
For riches dost thou long full sore?
Behold enough of precious store.
Earth hath more silver, pearls and gold,
Than eyes can see, or hands can hold.
Affect'st thou pleasure? Take thy fill,
Earth hath enough of what you will.
Then let not goe what thou maist find
For things unknown, only in mind.
                Spirit:
Be still thou unregenerate part,
Disturb no more my setled heart,
For I have vow'd (and so will doe)
Thee as a foe still to pursue.
And combate with thee will and must
Untill I see thee laid in th' dust.
Sisters we are, yea, twins we be,
Yet deadly feud 'twixt thee and me;
For from one father are we not,
Thou by old Adam wast begot,
But my arise is from above,
Whence my dear Father I do love.
Thou speak'st me fair, but hat'st me sore,
Thy flatt'ring shews Ile trust no more.
How oft thy slave hast thou me made
When I believ'd what thou hast said,
And never had more cause of woe
Than when I did what thou bad'st doe.
Ile stop mine ears at these thy charms,
And count them for my deadly harms.
Thy sinfull pleasures I doe hate,
Thy riches are to me no bait,
Thine honours doe nor will I love,
For my ambition lyes above.
My greatest honour it shall be
When I am victor over thee,
And triumph shall, with laurel head,
When thou my Captive shalt be led.

How I do live thou need'st not scoff,
For I have meat thou know'st not of:
The hidden Manna I doe eat,
The word of life it is my meat.
My thoughts do yield me more content
Than can thy hours in pleasure spent.
Nor are they shadows which I catch,
Nor fancies vain at which I snatch,
But reach at things that are so high,
Beyond thy dull Capacity.
Eternal substance I do see,
With which inriched I would be;
Mine Eye doth pierce the heavens, and see
What is Invisible to thee.
My garments are not silk nor gold,
Nor such like trash which Earth doth hold,
But Royal Robes I shall have on,
More glorious than the glistring Sun;
My Crown not Diamonds, Pearls, and Gold,
But such as Angels heads infold.
The City where I hope to dwell,
There's none on Earth can parallel:
The stately Walls both high and strong,
Are made of pretious Jasper stone;
The Gates of Pearl, both rich and clear,
And Angels are for Porters there;
The Streets thereof transparent gold,
Such as no Eye did e're behold;
A Chrystal River there doth run,
Which doth proceed from the Lamb's Throne.
Of Life there are the waters sure,
Which shall remain for ever pure;
Nor Sun, nor Moon, they have no need,
For glory doth from God proceed;
No Candle there, nor yet Torch light,
For there shall be no darksome night.
From sickness and infirmity
For evermore they shall be free,

Nor withering age shall e're come there,
But beauty shall be bright and clear.
This City pure is not for thee,
For things unclean there shall not be.
If I of Heaven may have my fill,
Take thou the world, and all that will.

TO MY DEAR AND LOVING HUSBAND

If ever two were one, then surely we.
If ever man were lov'd by wife, then thee.
If ever wife was happy in a man,
Compare with me, ye women, if you can.
I prize thy love more than whole Mines of gold,
Or all the riches that the East doth hold.
My love is such that Rivers cannot quench,
Nor ought but love from thee give recompence.
Thy love is such I can no way repay;
The heavens reward thee manifold I pray.
Then while we live, in love lets so persever,
That when we live no more, we may live ever.

William Cullen Bryant

TO A WATERFOWL

Whither, midst falling dew,
While glow the heavens with the last steps of day
Far, through their rosy depths, dost thou pursue
   Thy solitary way?

Vainly the fowler's eye
Might mark thy distant flight to do thee wrong
As, darkly seen against the crimson sky,
   Thy figure floats along.

Seek'st thou the plashy brink
Of weedy lake, or marge of river wide,
Or where the rocking billows rise and sink
    On the chafed ocean-side?

There is a Power whose care
Teaches thy way along that pathless coast—
The desert and illimitable air—
    Lone wandering, but not lost.

All day thy wings have fanned,
At that far height, the cold, thin atmosphere,
Yet stoop not, weary, to the welcome land,
    Though the dark night is near.

And soon that toil shall end;
Soon shalt thou find a summer home, and rest,
And scream among thy fellows; reeds shall bend,
    Soon, o'er thy sheltered nest.

Thou'rt gone, the abyss of heaven
Hath swallowed up thy form; yet, on my heart
Deeply has sunk the lesson thou hast given,
    And shall not soon depart.

He who, from zone to zone,
Guides through the boundless sky thy certain flight,
In the long way that I must tread alone,
    Will lead my steps aright.

TO THE FRINGED GENTIAN

Thou blossom, bright with autumn dew,
And colored with the heaven's own blue,
That openest when the quiet light
Succeeds the keen and frosty night;

Thou comest not when violets lean
O'er wandering brooks and springs unseen,
Or columbines, in purple dressed,
Nod o'er the ground-bird's hidden nest.

Thou waitest late, and com'st alone,
When woods are bare and birds are flown,
And frosts and shortening days portend
The aged Year is near his end.

Then doth thy sweet and quiet eye
Look through its fringes to the sky,
Blue—blue—as if that sky let fall
A flower from its cerulean wall.

I would that thus, when I shall see
The hour of death draw near to me,
Hope, blossoming within my heart,
May look to heaven as I depart.

THANATOPSIS

To him who in the love of Nature holds
Communion with her visible forms, she speaks
A various language; for his gayer hours
She has a voice of gladness, and a smile
And eloquence of beauty, and she glides
Into his darker musings, with a mild
And healing sympathy, that steals away
Their sharpness ere he is aware. When thoughts
Of the last bitter hour come like a blight
Over thy spirit, and sad images
Of the stern agony, and shroud, and pall,
And breathless darkness, and the narrow house,
Make thee to shudder, and grow sick at heart;—
Go forth, under the open sky, and list
To Nature's teachings, while from all around—

Earth and her waters, and the depths of air,—
Comes a still voice—Yet a few days, and thee
The all-beholding sun shall see no more
In all his course; nor yet in the cold ground,
Where thy pale form was laid, with many tears,
Nor in the embrace of ocean, shall exist
Thy image. Earth, that nourished thee, shall claim
Thy growth, to be resolved to earth again,
And, lost each human trace, surrendering up
Thine individual being, shalt thou go
To mix for ever with the elements,
To be a brother to the insensible rock
And to the sluggish clod, which the rude swain
Turns with his share, and treads upon. The oak
Shall send his roots abroad, and pierce thy mould.

Yet not to thine eternal resting-place
Shalt thou retire alone,—nor couldst thou wish
Couch more magnificent. Thou shalt lie down
With patriarchs of the infant world—with kings,
The powerful of the earth—the wise, the good,
Fair forms, and hoary seers of ages past,
All in one mighty sepulchre. The hills
Rock-ribbed and ancient as the sun; the vales
Stretching in pensive quietness between;
The venerable woods; rivers that move
In majesty, and the complaining brooks
That make the meadows green; and, poured round all,
Old ocean's grey and melancholy waste—
Are but the solemn decorations all
Of the great tomb of man. The golden sun,
The planets, all the infinite host of heaven,
Are shining on the sad abodes of death,
Through the still lapse of ages. All that tread
The globe are but a handful to the tribes
That slumber in its bosom.—Take the wings
Of morning, traverse Barca's desert sands,
Or lose thyself in the continuous woods

Where rolls the Oregon, and hears no sound,
Save his own dashings—yet—the dead are there:
And millions in those solitudes, since first
The flight of years began, have laid them down
In their last sleep—the dead reign there alone,
So shalt thou rest, and what if thou withdraw
In silence from the living, and no friend
Take note of thy departure? All that breathe
Will share thy destiny. The gay will laugh
When thou art gone, the solemn brood of care
Plod on, and each one as before will chase
His favourite phantom; yet all these shall leave
Their mirth and their employments, and shall come,
And make their bed with thee. As the long train
Of ages glides away, the sons of men,
The youth in life's green spring, and he who goes
In the full strength of years, matron, and maid,
And the sweet babe, and the grey-headed man—
Shall one by one be gathered to thy side,
By those, who in their turn shall follow them.

    So live, that when thy summons comes to join
The innumerable caravan, which moves
To that mysterious realm, where each shall take
His chamber in the silent halls of death,
Thou go not, like the quarry-slave at night,
Scourged to his dungeon, but, sustained and soothed
By an unfaltering trust, approach thy grave
Like one who wraps the drapery of his couch
About him, and lies down to pleasant dreams.

William Burford

THE TOMBOY

The tomboy, unhelmeted, a blown-locks hero,
aimed into bluebonnets, intent to bee-bee
an imaginary monster; slay it; or at least
make it rear up from its lair wild-eyed,
high dinosaur in April's galed green meadow—
for her to fable to her elders, rocking
on their long veranda with a view of her,
small huntress in the deep scene. They licked
for teeth gone from their gums, to savor some
of their young one's wonder, or a tender meat.

The most she bagged was rabbit, not tall-eared
tough-legged jack, but the soft cottontail
that had looked at her. Midst the new blooms
its tiny twitching could not move memorially
more than the wind did, it lay with a red dot
where the shot, copper, struck between the eyes,
stunned the dumb heart into knowing that it must
keep beating to keep bright that slight beauty mark,
as though it were the final coal of the fire, life;
and its darkening, the deep chill of death.

Oh the tomboy, if still she had had the knack,
would have wept. She rushed the rabbit
in her hands up the earth's slow incline
she, stalking, had stepped painstakingly down;
rushed it to her elders who she'd heard knew
wondrous herbs and juices for health. But age,
and the grinning witch in the kitchen, prohibited
the spring's first sport to end so childishly;
insisted dinosaurs are dead. And cottontails?
A boy is told to eat his meal in silence.

THE FIRE

This winter day, we build our fire,
Two human beings making sacrifice.

For fuel, this cold day's news
Must serve: columns of men and words
In the dark place for fire to burn.

And then we gather, and gently lay
These shattered sticks, that to us remain,
Until we've raised a kind of pyre and grave

For the heavy thing. We lift it in our arms
Like an offering brought, or a child,
And set it down across the iron bars.

Now strike. The beast springs to life,
And we stand all bloodied in the light.

A CHRISTMAS TREE

Star,
If you are
A love compassionate,
You will walk with us this year.
We face a glacial distance, who are here
Huddl'd
At your feet.

Gelett Burgess

THE PURPLE COW

I never saw a Purple Cow,
I never hope to see one;
But I can tell you, anyhow,
I'd rather see than be one.

Robert Bhain Campbell

FINAL POEM

Bed-ridden, laid by an age's malady
    In the island of a room,
Made private by my purse, I'm priced to lie
Amid the system of the walls, to look
Past pillow, water-jar, dark basin, book,
    Fret, stare, stop, and resume,
At sill and frame, that great bright windowpane
Between me and a tree, an avenue, and man.

My contract gave me to the doctor's will,
    The anaesthesia of ease,
Here in the doctrine of this hospital
That by some further wounds my wounds could cure,
Yet travel is from wound to wound, to fear,
    Discussions of disease,
And I am given up to Latin terms
Which translate me into a dream's alarms.

Beyond, boughs dimly on an iron rail ring;
    Beyond, men, women walk.
Where do they walk? whence come? what bring?
Their traffic moves from right to left—to where—
Filling with incomprehensible sound the air,
    Like bird cries, horns, their talk.
Automobiles and men beyond the pane
Exist beyond this state, our rules, our reign.

Men may not ail, nor words, outside these halls—
    Yet what if I signal, shout?
So bright the light is where on them it falls
The pane is dark upon this company,
And though I see, they never will see me.
    But if dark come without,

If dark come, dark, then might I light this light
That they could see me here, come, let me out.

Yet, dark may to them be enemy, attack,
     And fled the avenue,
Or, else, my bright framed self seem maniac.
By dark and light that pane divides me, then,
The surgeon that shall cut my tongue from men—
     Unless my blood renew,
Rise up, stand tall, and bid the nurse go tell:
My will goes, surgeon, toward that windowsill.

Malcolm Cowley

THE LONG VOYAGE

Not that the pines were darker there,
nor mid-May dogwood brighter there,
nor swifts more swift in summer air;
    it was my own country,

having its thunderclap of spring,
its long midsummer ripening,
its corn hoar-stiff at harvesting,
    almost like any country,

yet being mine; its face, its speech,
its hills bent low within my reach,
its river birch and upland beech
    were mine, of my own country.

Now the dark waters at the bow
fold back, like earth against the plow;
foam brightens like the dogwood now
    at home, in my own country.

Hart Crane

EMBLEMS OF CONDUCT

By a peninsula the wanderer sat and sketched
The uneven valley graves. While the apostle gave
Alms to the meek the volcano burst
With sulphur and aureate rocks . . .
For joy rides in stupendous coverings
Luring the living into spiritual gates.

Orators follow the universe
And radio the complete laws to the people.
The apostle conveys thought through discipline.
Bowls and cups fill historians with adorations,—
Dull lips commemorating spiritual gates.

The wanderer later chose this spot of rest
Where marble clouds support the sea
And where was finally borne a chosen hero.
By that time summer and smoke were past.
Dolphins still played, arching the horizons,
But only to build memories of spiritual gates.

FOR THE MARRIAGE OF FAUSTUS AND HELEN

> "And so we may arrive by Talmud skill
> And profane Greek to raise the building up
> Of Helen's house against the Ismaelite,
> King of Thogarma, and his habergeons
> Brimstony, blue and fiery; and the force
> Of King Abaddon, and the beast of Cittim;
> Which Rabbi David Kimchi, Onkelos,
> And Aben Ezra do interpret Rome."
> —THE ALCHEMIST

I

The mind has shown itself at times
Too much the baked and labeled dough
Divided by accepted multitudes.

Across the stacked partitions of the day—
Across the memoranda, baseball scores,
The stenographic smiles and stock quotations
Smutty wings flash out equivocations.

The mind is brushed by sparrow wings;
Numbers, rebuffed by asphalt, crowd
The margins of the day, accent the curbs,
Convoying divers dawns on every corner
To druggist, barber and tobacconist,
Until the graduate opacities of evening
Take them away as suddenly to somewhere
Virginal perhaps, less fragmentary, cool.

> *There is the world dimensional for those un-*
> *twisted by the love of things irreconcilable . . .*

And yet, suppose some evening I forgot
The fare and transfer, yet got by that way
Without recall,—lost yet poised in traffic.
Then I might find your eyes across an aisle,
Still flickering with those prefigurations—
Prodigal, yet uncontested now,
Half-riant before the jerky window frame.

There is some way, I think, to touch
Those hands of yours that count the nights
Stippled with pink and green advertisements.
And now, before its arteries turn dark,
I would have you meet this bartered blood.
Imminent in his dream, none better knows
The white wafer cheek of love, or offers words
Lightly as moonlight on the eaves meets snow.

Reflective conversion of all things
At your deep blush, when ecstasies thread
The limbs and belly, when rainbows spread

Impinging on the throat and sides . . .
Inevitable, the body of the world
Weeps in inventive dust for the hiatus
That winks above it, bluet in your breasts.

The earth may glide diaphanous to death;
But if I lift my arms it is to bend
To you who turned away once, Helen, knowing
The press of troubled hands, too alternate
With steel and soil to hold you endlessly.
I meet you, therefore, in that eventual flame
You found in final chains, no captive then—
Beyond their million brittle, bloodshot eyes;
White, through white cities passed on to assume
That world which comes to each of us alone.

Accept a lone eye riveted to your plane,
Bent axle of devotion along companion ways
That beat, continuous, to hourless days—
One inconspicuous, glowing orb of praise.

II

Brazen hypnotics glitter here;
Glee shifts from foot to foot,
Magnetic to their tremolo.
This crashing opéra bouffe,
Blest excursion! this ricochet
From roof to roof—
Know, Olympians, we are breathless
While nigger cupids scour the stars!

A thousand light shrugs balance us
Through snarling hails of melody.
White shadows slip across the floor
Splayed like cards from a loose hand;
Rhythmic ellipses lead into canters
Until somewhere a rooster banters.

Greet naïvely—yet intrepidly
New soothings, new amazements
That cornets introduce at every turn—
And you may fall downstairs with me
With perfect grace and equanimity.
Or, plaintively scud past shores
Where, by strange harmonic laws
All relatives, serene and cool,
Sit rocked in patent armchairs.

O, I have known metallic paradises
Where cuckoos clucked to finches
Above the deft catastrophes of drums.
While titters hailed the groans of death
Beneath gyrating awnings I have seen
The incunabula of the divine grotesque.
This music has a reassuring way.

The siren of the springs of guilty song—
Let us take her on the incandescent wax
Striated with nuances, nervosities
That we are heir to: she is still so young,
We cannot frown upon her as she smiles,
Dipping here in this cultivated storm
Among slim skaters of the gardened skies.

III

Capped arbiter of beauty in this street
That narrows darkly into motor dawn,—
You, here beside me, delicate ambassador
Of intricate slain numbers that arise
In whispers, naked of steel;
                                        religious gunman!
Who faithfully, yourself, will fall too soon,
And in other ways than as the wind settles
On the sixteen thrifty bridges of the city:
Let us unbind our throats of fear and pity.

                              We even,
Who drove speediest destruction
In corymbulous formations of mechanics,—
Who hurried the hill breezes, spouting malice
Plangent over meadows, and looked down
On rifts of torn and empty houses
Like old women with teeth unjubilant
That waited faintly, briefly and in vain:

We know, eternal gunman, our flesh remembers
The tensile boughs, the nimble blue plateaus,
The mounted, yielding cities of the air!
That saddled sky that shook down vertical
Repeated play of fire—no hypogeum
Of wave or rock was good against one hour.

We did not ask for that, but have survived,
And will persist to speak again before
All stubble streets that have not curved
To memory, or known the ominous lifted arm
That lowers down the arc of Helen's brow
To saturate with blessing and dismay.

A goose, tobacco and cologne—
Three-winged and gold-shod prophecies of heaven,
The lavish heart shall always have to leaven
And spread with bells and voices, and atone
The abating shadows of our conscript dust.

Anchises' navel, dripping of the sea,—
The hands Erasmus dipped in gleaming tides,
Gathered the voltage of blown blood and vine;
Delve upward for the new and scattered wine,
O brother-thief of time, that we recall.
Laugh out the meager penance of their days
Who dare not share with us the breath released,
The substance drilled and spent beyond repair
For golden, or the shadow of gold hair.

Distinctly praise the years, whose volatile
Blamed bleeding hands extend and thresh the height
The imagination spans beyond despair,
Outpacing bargain, vocable and prayer.

AT MELVILLE'S TOMB

Often beneath the wave, wide from this ledge
The dice of drowned men's bones he saw bequeath
An embassy. Their numbers as he watched,
Beat on the dusty shore and were obscured.

And wrecks passed without sound of bells,
The calyx of death's bounty giving back
A scattered chapter, livid hieroglyph,
The portent wound in corridors of shells.

Then in the circuit calm of one vast coil,
Its lashings charmed and malice reconciled,
Frosted eyes there were that lifted altars;
And silent answers crept across the stars.

Compass, quadrant and sextant contrive

No farther tides . . . High in the azure steeps
Monody shall not wake the mariner.
This fabulous shadow only the sea keeps.

O CARIB ISLE!

The tarantula rattling at the lily's foot
Across the feet of the dead, laid in white sand
Near the coral beach—nor zigzag fiddler crabs
Side-stilting from the path (that shift, subvert
And anagrammatize your name)—No, nothing here
Below the palsy that one eucalyptus lifts
In wrinkled shadows—mourns.

And yet suppose
I count these nacreous frames of tropic death,
Brutal necklaces of shells around each grave
Squared off so carefully. Then

To the white sand I may speak a name, fertile
Albeit in a stranger tongue. Tree names, flower names
Deliberate, gainsay death's brittle crypt. Meanwhile
The wind that knots itself in one great death—
Coils and withdraws. So syllables want breath.

But where is the Captain of the doubloon isle
Without a turnstile? Who but catchword crabs
Patrols the dry groins of the underbrush?
What man, or What
Is Commissioner of the mildew throughout the ambushed
    senses?
His Carib mathematics web the eyes' baked lenses!

Under the poinciana, of a noon or afternoon
Let fiery blossoms clot the light, render my ghost
Sieved upward, white and black along the air
Until it meets the blue's comedian host.

Let not the pilgrim see himself again
For slow evisceration bound like those huge terrapin
Each daybreak on the wharf, their brine-caked eyes;
—Spiked, overturned; such thunder in their strain!

Slagged on the hurricane—I, cast within its flow,
Congeal by afternoons here, satin and vacant.
You have given me the shell, Satan,—carbonic amulet
Sere of the sun exploded in the sea.

TO BROOKLYN BRIDGE

How many dawns, chill from his rippling rest
The seagull's wings shall dip and pivot him,
Shedding white rings of tumult, building high
Over the chained bay waters Liberty—

Then, with inviolate curve, forsake our eyes
As apparitional as sails that cross
Some page of figures to be filed away;
—Till elevators drop us from our day . . .

I think of cinemas, panoramic sleights
With multitudes bent toward some flashing scene
Never disclosed, but hastened to again,
Foretold to other eyes on the same screen;

And Thee, across the harbor, silver-paced
As though the sun took step of thee, yet left
Some motion ever unspent in thy stride,—
Implicitly thy freedom staying thee!

Out of some subway scuttle, cell or loft
A bedlamite speeds to thy parapets,
Tilting there momently, shrill shirt ballooning,
A jest falls from the speechless caravan.

Down Wall, from girder into street noon leaks,
A rip-tooth of the sky's acetylene;
All afternoon the cloud-flown derricks turn . . .
Thy cables breathe the North Atlantic still.

And obscure as that heaven of the Jews,
Thy guerdon . . . Accolade thou dost bestow
Of anonymity time cannot raise:
Vibrant reprieve and pardon thou dost show.

O harp and altar, of the fury fused,
(How could mere toil align thy choiring strings!)

Terrific threshold of the prophet's pledge,
Prayer of pariah, and the lover's cry,—

Again the traffic lights that skim thy swift
Unfractioned idiom, immaculate sigh of stars,
Beading thy path—condense eternity:
And we have seen night lifted in thine arms.

Under thy shadow by the piers I waited;
Only in darkness is thy shadow clear.
The City's fiery parcels all undone,
Already snow submerges an iron year . . .

O Sleepless as the river under thee,
Vaulting the sea, the prairies' dreaming sod,
Unto us lowliest sometime sweep, descend
And of the curveship lend a myth to God.

AVE MARIA

Venient annis sæcula seris,
Quibus Oceanus vincula rerum
Laxet et ingens pateat tellus

Tethysque novos detegat orbes
Nec sit terris ultima Thule.
                              SENECA

Be with me, Luis de San Angel, now—
Witness before the tides can wrest away
The word I bring, O you who reined my suit
Into the Queen's great heart that doubtful day;
For I have seen now what no perjured breath
Of clown nor sage can riddle or gainsay:—
To you, too, Juan Perez, whose counsel fear
And greed adjourned,—I bring you back Cathay!

Columbus,
alone, gazing
toward Spain,
invokes the
presence of
two faithful
partisans of his
quest . . .

Here waves climb into dusk on gleaming mail;
Invisible valves of the sea,—locks, tendons
Crested and creeping, troughing corridors
That fall back yawning to another plunge.
Slowly the sun's red caravel drops light
Once more behind us. . . . It is morning there—

O where our Indian emperies lie revealed,
Yet lost, all, let this keel one instant yield!

I thought of Genoa; and this truth, now proved,
That made me exile in her streets, stood me
More absolute than ever—biding the moon
Till dawn should clear that dim frontier, first seen
—The Chan's great continent. . . . Then faith, not fear
Nigh surged me witless. . . . Hearing the surf near—
I, wonder-breathing, kept the watch,—saw
The first palm chevron the first lighted hill.

And lowered. And they came out to us crying,
"The Great White Birds!" (O Madre Maria, still
One ship of these thou grantest safe returning;
Assure us through thy mantle's ageless blue!)
And record of more, floating in a cask,
Was tumbled from us under bare poles scudding;
And later hurricanes may claim more pawn. . . .
For here between two worlds, another, harsh,

This third, of water, tests the word; lo, here
Bewilderment and mutiny heap whelming
Laughter, and shadow cuts sleep from the heart
Almost as though the Moor's flung scimitar
Found more than flesh to fathom in its fall.
Yet under tempest-lash and surfeitings
Some inmost sob, half-heard, dissuades the abyss,
Merges the wind in measure to the waves,

Series on series, infinite,—till eyes
Starved wide on blackened tides, accrete—enclose
This turning rondure whole, this crescent ring
Sun-cusped and zoned with modulated fire
Like pearls that whisper through the Doge's hands
—Yet no delirium of jewels! O Fernando,
Take of that eastern shore, this western sea,
Yet yield thy God's, thy Virgin's charity!

—Rush down the plenitude, and you shall see
Isaiah counting famine on this lee!

*

An herb, a stray branch among salty teeth,
The jellied weeds that drag the shore,—perhaps
Tomorrow's moon will grant us Saltes Bar—
Palos again,—a land cleared of long war.
Some Angelus environs the cordage tree;
Dark waters onward shake the dark prow free.

*

O Thou who sleepest on Thyself, apart
Like ocean athwart lanes of death and birth,
And all the eddying breath between dost search
Cruelly with love thy parable of man,—
Inquisitor! incognizable Word
Of Eden and the enchained Sepulchre,
Into thy steep savannahs, burning blue,
Utter to loneliness the sail is true.

Who grindest oar, and arguing the mast
Subscribest holocaust of ships, O Thou
Within whose primal scan consummately
The glistening seignories of Ganges swim;—
Who sendest greeting by the corposant,
And Teneriffe's garnet—flamed it in a cloud,
Urging through night our passage to the Chan;—
Te Deum laudamus, for thy teeming span!

Of all that amplitude that time explores,
A needle in the sight, suspended north,—
Yielding by inference and discard, faith
And true appointment from the hidden shoal:
This disposition that thy night relates
From Moon to Saturn in one sapphire wheel:
The orbic wake of thy once whirling feet,
Elohim, still I hear thy sounding heel!

White toil of heaven's cordons, mustering
In holy rings all sails charged to the far
Hushed gleaming fields and pendant seething wheat
Of knowledge,—round thy brows unhooded now
—The kindled Crown! acceded of the poles
And biassed by full sails, meridians reel
Thy purpose—still one shore beyond desire!
The sea's green crying towers a-sway, Beyond

And kingdoms
           naked in the
                      trembling heart—
Te Deum laudamus O Thou Hand of Fire

THE HARBOR DAWN

Insistently through sleep—a tide of voices—
They meet you listening midway in your dream,
The long, tired sounds, fog-insulated noises:
Gongs in white surplices, beshrouded wails,
Far strum of fog horns . . . signals dispersed in
    veils.

400 years and more . . . or is it from the soundless shore of sleep that time

And then a truck will lumber past the wharves
As winch engines begin throbbing on some deck;
Or a drunken stevedore's howl and thud below
Comes echoing alley-upward through dim snow.

And if they take your sleep away sometimes
They give it back again. Soft sleeves of sound
Attend the darkling harbor, the pillowed bay;
Somewhere out there in blankness steam

Spills into steam, and wanders, washed away
—Flurried by keen fifings, eddied
Among distant chiming buoys—adrift. The sky,
Cool feathery fold, suspends, distills
This wavering slumber. . . . Slowly—
Immemorially the window, the half-covered chair,
Ask nothing but this sheath of pallid air.

And you beside me, blessèd now while sirens   *recalls you to*
Sing to us, stealthily weave us into day—   *your love,*
                                                     there in a
Serenely now, before day claims our eyes   *waking dream*
Your cool arms murmurously about me lay.   *to merge your*
                                                     seed
While myriad snowy hands are clustering at the panes—

> *your hands within my hands are deeds;*
> *my tongue upon your throat—singing*
> *arms close; eyes wide, undoubtful*
> > *dark*
> > > *drink the dawn—*
> *a forest shudders in your hair!*

The window goes blond slowly. Frostily clears.   *—with whom?*
From Cyclopean towers across Manhattan waters
—Two—three bright window-eyes aglitter, disk   *Who is the*
                                                     woman with
The sun, released—aloft with cold gulls hither.   *us in the*
The fog leans one last moment on the sill.   *dawn? . . .*
                                                     whose is the
Under the mistletoe of dreams, a star—   *flesh our feet*
As though to join us at some distant hill—   *have moved*
                                                     upon?
Turns in the waking west and goes to sleep.

VOYAGES II

And yet this great wink of eternity,
Of rimless floods, unfettered leewardings,
Samite sheeted and processioned where
Her undinal vast belly moonward bends,
Laughing the wrapt inflections of our love;

Take this Sea, whose diapason knells
On scrolls of silver snowy sentences,
The sceptred terror of whose sessions rends
As her demeanors motion well or ill,
All but the pieties of lovers' hands.

And onward, as bells off San Salvador
Salute the crocus lustres of the stars,
In these poinsettia meadows of her tides,—
Adagios of islands, O my Prodigal,
Complete the dark confessions her veins spell.

Mark how her turning shoulders wind the hours,
And hasten while her penniless rich palms
Pass superscription of bent foam and wave,—
Hasten, while they are true,—sleep, death, desire,
Close round one instant in one floating flower.

Bind us in time, O Seasons clear, and awe.
O minstrel galleons of Carib fire,
Bequeath us to no earthly shore until
Is answered in the vortex of our grave
The seal's wide spindrift gaze toward paradise.

THE TUNNEL

To Find the Western path
Right thro' the Gates of Wrath.—BLAKE

Performances, assortments, résumés—
Up Times Square to Columbus Circle lights
Channel the congresses, nightly sessions,
Refractions of the thousand theatres, faces—
Mysterious kitchens. . . . You shall search them all.
Some day by heart you'll learn each famous sight
And watch the curtain lift in hell's despite;
You'll find the garden in the third act dead,
Finger your knees—and wish yourself in bed
With tabloid crime-sheets perched in easy sight.

Then let you reach your hat and go.
As usual, let you—also
walking down—exclaim
to twelve upward leaving

a subscription praise
for what time slays.

Or can't you quite make up your mind to ride;
A walk is better underneath the L a brisk
Ten blocks or so before? But you find yourself
Preparing penguin flexions of the arms,—
As usual you will meet the scuttle yawn:
The subway yawns the quickest promise home.

Be minimum, then, to swim the hiving swarms
Out of the Square, the Circle burning bright—
Avoid the glass doors gyring at your right,
Where boxed alone a second, eyes take fright
—Quite unprepared rush naked back to light:
And down beside the turnstile press the coin
Into the slot. The gongs already rattle.

And so
of cities you bespeak
subways, rivered under streets
and rivers. . . . In the car
the overtone of motion
underground, the monotone
of motion is the sound
of other faces, also underground—

"Let's have a pencil Jimmy—living now
at Floral Park
Flatbush—on the Fourth of July—
like a pigeon's muddy dream—potatoes
to dig in the field—travlin the town—too—
night after night—the Culver line—the
girls all shaping up—it used to be—"

Our tongues recant like beaten weather vanes.
This answer lives like verdigris, like hair
Beyond extinction, surcease of the bone;
And repetition freezes—"What

"what do you want? getting weak on the links?
fandaddle daddy don't ask for change—IS THIS
FOURTEENTH? it's half past six she said—if
you don't like my gate why did you
swing on it, why *didja*
swing on it anyhow—"

    And somehow anyhow swing—

The phonographs of hades in the brain
Are tunnels that re-wind themselves, and love
A burnt match skating in a urinal—
Somewhere above Fourteenth TAKE THE EXPRESS
To brush some new presentiment of pain—

"But I want service in this office SERVICE
I said—after
the show she cried a little afterwards but—"

Whose head is swinging from the swollen strap?
Whose body smokes along the bitten rails,
Bursts from a smoldering bundle far behind
In back forks of the chasms of the brain,—
Puffs from a riven stump far out behind
In interborough fissures of the mind . . . ?
And why do I often meet your visage here,
Your eyes like agate lanterns—on and on
Below the toothpaste and the dandruff ads?
—And did their riding eyes right through your side,
And did their eyes like unwashed platters ride?
And Death, aloft,—gigantically down
Probing through you—toward me, O evermore!
And when they dragged your retching flesh,
Your trembling hands that night through Baltimore—
That last night on the ballot rounds, did you
Shaking, did you deny the ticket, Poe?

For Gravesend Manor change at Chambers Street.
The platform hurries along to a dead stop.

The intent escalator lifts a serenade
Stilly
Of shoes, umbrellas, each eye attending its shoe, then
Bolting outright somewhere above where streets
Burst suddenly in rain. . . . The gongs recur:
Elbows and levers, guard and hissing door.
Thunder is galvothermic here below. . . . The car
Wheels off. The train rounds, bending to a scream,
Taking the final level for the dive
Under the river—
And somewhat emptier than before,
Demented, for a hitching second, humps; then
Lets go. . . . Toward corners of the floor
Newspapers wing, revolve and wing.
Blank windows gargle signals through the roar.
And does the Daemon take you home, also,
Wop washerwoman, with the bandaged hair?
After the corridors are swept, the cuspidors—
The gaunt sky-barracks cleanly now, and bare,
O Genoese, do you bring mother eyes and hands
Back home to children and to golden hair?
Daemon, demurring and eventful yawn!
Whose hideous laughter is a bellows mirth
—Or the muffled slaughter of a day in birth—
O cruelly to inoculate the brinking dawn
With antennæ toward worlds that glow and sink;—
To spoon us out more liquid than the dim
Locution of the eldest star, and pack
The conscience navelled in the plunging wind,
Umbilical to call—and straightway die!

O caught like pennies beneath soot and steam,
Kiss of our agony thou gatherest;
Condensed, thou takest all—shrill ganglia
Impassioned with some song we fail to keep.
And yet, like Lazarus, to feel the slope,
The sod and billow breaking,—lifting ground,

—A sound of waters bending astride the sky
Unceasing with some Word that will not die ...!

                ✲

A tugboat, wheezing wreaths of steam,
Lunged past, with one galvanic blare stove up the River.
I counted the echoes assembling, one after one,
Searching, thumbing the midnight on the piers.
Lights, coasting, left the oily tympanum of waters;
The blackness somewhere gouged glass on a sky.
And this thy harbor, O my City, I have driven under,
Tossed from the coil of ticking towers.... Tomorrow,
And to be.... Here by the River that is East—
Here at the waters' edge the hands drop memory;
Shadowless in that abyss they unaccounting lie.
How far away the star has pooled the sea—
Or shall the hands be drawn away, to die?
Kiss of our agony Thou gatherest,
                  O Hand of Fire
                        gatherest—

ATLANTIS

Music is then the knowledge of that which relates to love in harmony and system.—PLATO

Through the bound cable strands, the arching path
Upward, veering with light, the flight of strings,—
Taut miles of shuttling moonlight syncopate
The whispered rush, telepathy of wires.
Up the index of night, granite and steel—
Transparent meshes—fleckless the gleaming staves—
Sibylline voices flicker, waveringly stream
As though a god were issue of the strings....

And through that cordage, threading with its call
One arc synoptic of all tides below—
Their labyrinthine mouths of history
Pouring reply as though all ships at sea

Complighted in one vibrant breath made cry,—
"Make thy love sure—to weave whose song we ply!"
—From black embankments, moveless soundings hailed,
So seven oceans answer from their dream.

And on, obliquely up bright carrier bars
New octaves trestle the twin monoliths
Beyond whose frosted capes the moon bequeaths
Two worlds of sleep (O arching strands of song!)—
Onward and up the crystal-flooded aisle
White tempest nets file upward, upward ring
With silver terraces the humming spars,
The loft of vision, palladium helm of stars.

Sheerly the eyes, like seagulls stung with rime—
Slit and propelled by glistening fins of light—
Pick biting way up towering looms that press
Sidelong with flight of blade on tendon blade
—Tomorrows into yesteryear—and link
What cipher-script of time no traveller reads
But who, through smoking pyres of love and death,
Searches the timeless laugh of mythic spears.

Like hails, farewells—up planet-sequined heights
Some trillion whispering hammers glimmer Tyre:
Serenely, sharply up the long anvil cry
Of inchling aeons silence rivets Troy.
And you, aloft there—Jason! hesting Shout!
Still wrapping harness to the swarming air!
Silvery the rushing wake, surpassing call,
Beams yelling Æolus! splintered in the straits!

From gulfs unfolding, terrible of drums,
Tall Vision-of-the-Voyage, tensely spare—
Bridge, lifting night to cycloramic crest
Of deepest day—O Choir, translating time
Into what multitudinous Verb the suns
And synergy of waters ever fuse, recast

In myriad syllables,—Psalm of Cathay!
O Love, thy white, pervasive Paradigm . . . !

We left the haven hanging in the night—
Sheened harbor lanterns backward fled the keel.
Pacific here at time's end, bearing corn,—
Eyes stammer through the pangs of dust and steel.
And still the circular, indubitable frieze
Of heaven's meditation, yoking wave
To kneeling wave, one song devoutly binds—
The vernal strophe chimes from deathless strings!

O Thou steeled Cognizance whose leap commits
The agile precincts of the lark's return;
Within whose lariat sweep encinctured sing
In single chrysalis the many twain,—
Of stars Thou art the stitch and stallion glow
And like an organ, Thou, with sound of doom—
Sight, sound and flesh Thou leadest from time's realm
As love strikes clear direction for the helm.

Swift peal of secular light, intrinsic Myth
Whose fell unshadow is death's utter wound,—
O River-throated—iridescently upborne
Through the bright drench and fabric of our veins;
With white escarpments swinging into light,
Sustained in tears the cities are endowed
And justified conclamant with ripe fields
Revolving through their harvests in sweet torment.

Forever Deity's glittering Pledge, O Thou
Whose canticle fresh chemistry assigns
To rapt inception and beatitude,—
Always through blinding cables, to our joy,
Of thy white seizure springs the prophecy:
Always through spiring cordage, pyramids
Of silver sequel, Deity's young name
Kinetic of white choiring wings . . . ascends.

Migrations that must needs void memory,
Inventions that cobblestone the heart,—
Unspeakable Thou Bridge to Thee, O Love.
Thy pardon for this history, whitest Flower,
O Answerer of all,—Anemone,—
Now while thy petals spend the suns about us, hold—
(O Thou whose radiance doth inherit me)
Atlantis, hold thy floating singer late!

So to thine Everpresence, beyond time,
Like spears ensanguined of one tolling star
That bleeds infinity—the orphic strings,
Sidereal phalanxes, leap and converge:
—One Song, one Bridge of Fire! Is it Cathay,
Now pity steeps the grass and rainbows ring
The serpent with the eagle in the leaves . . . ?
Whispers antiphonal in azure swing.

Stephen Crane

I STOOD UPON A HIGH PLACE

I stood upon a high place,
And saw, below, many devils
Running, leaping,
And carousing in sin.
One looked up, grinning,
And said, "Comrade!
    Brother!"

I SAW A MAN PURSUING THE HORIZON

I saw a man pursuing the
    horizon;
Round and round they sped.
I was disturbed at this;
I accosted the man.
"It is futile," I said,
"You can never—"
"You lie," he cried,
And ran on.

THE WAYFARER

The wayfarer,
Perceiving the pathway to truth,
Was struck with astonishment.
It was thickly grown with weeds.
"Ha," he said,
"I see that no one has passed here
In a long time."
Later he saw that each weed
Was a singular knife.
"Well," he mumbled at last,
"Doubtless there are other roads."

A YOUTH IN APPAREL THAT GLITTERED

A youth in apparel that glittered
Went to walk in a grim forest.
There he met an assassin
Attired all in garb of old days;
He, scowling through the thickets,
And dagger poised quivering,
Rushed upon the youth.

"Sir," said this latter,
"I am enchanted, believe me,
To die, thus,
In this mediæval fashion,
According to the best legends;
Ah, what joy!"
Then took he the wound, smiling,
And died, content.

MANY WORKMEN

Many workmen
Built a huge ball of masonry
Upon a mountain-top.
Then they went to the valley below,
And turned to behold their work.
"It is grand," they said;

They loved the thing.

Of a sudden, it moved:
It came upon them swiftly;
It crushed them all to blood.
But some had opportunity to squeal.

A LEARNED MAN

A learned man came to me
once.
He said, "I know the way—
come."
And I was overjoyed at this.
Together we hastened.

Soon, too soon, were we
Where my eyes were useless,
And I knew not the ways
of my feet.
I clung to the hand of my
friend;
But at last he cried, "I am
lost."

A MAN SAW A BALL OF GOLD IN THE SKY

A man saw a ball of gold in
the sky;
He climbed for it,
And eventually he achieved
it—
It was clay.

Now this is the strange part:

When the man went to the
earth
And looked again,
Lo, there was the ball of gold.
Now this is the strange part:
It was a ball of gold.
Ay, by the heavens, it was a
ball of gold.

"IT WAS WRONG TO DO THIS," SAID THE ANGEL

"It was wrong to do this,"
said the angel.
"You should live like a flower,
Holding malice like a puppy,
Waging war like a lambkin."

"Not so," quoth the man

Who had no fear of spirits;
"It is only wrong for angels
Who can live like flowers,
Holding malice like the
puppies,
Waging war like the lamb-
kins."

THERE WAS A MAN WITH A TONGUE OF WOOD

There was a man with a
tongue of wood
Who essayed to sing,
And in truth it was lamen-
table.
But there was one who heard

The clip-clapper of this
tongue of wood
And knew what the man
Wished to sing,
And with that the singer was
content.

E. E. Cummings

SONNET ENTITLED HOW TO RUN THE WORLD)

sonnet entitled how to run the world)

A always don't there B being no such thing
for C can't casts no shadow D drink and

E eat of her voice in whose silence the music of spring
lives F feel opens but shuts understand
G gladly forget little having less

with every least each most remembering
H highest fly only the flag that's furled

(sestet entitled grass is flesh or swim
who can and bathe who must or any dream
means more than sleep as more than know means guess)

I item i immaculately owe
dying one life and will my rest to these

children building this rainman out of snow

ALL IN GREEN WENT MY LOVE RIDING

All in green went my love riding
on a great horse of gold
into the silver dawn.

four lean hounds crouched low and smiling
the merry deer ran before.

Fleeter be they than dappled dreams
the swift sweet deer
the red rare deer.

Four red roebuck at a white water
the cruel bugle sang before.

Horn at hip went my love riding
riding the echo down
into the silver dawn.

four lean hounds crouched low and smiling
the level meadows ran before.

Softer be they than slippered sleep
the lean lithe deer
the fleet flown deer.

Four fleet does at a gold valley
the famished arrow sang before.

Bow at belt went my love riding
riding the mountain down
into the silver dawn.

four lean hounds crouched low and smiling
the sheer peaks ran before.

Paler be they than daunting death
the sleek slim deer
the tall tense deer.

Four tall stags at a green mountain
the lucky hunter sang before.

All in green went my love riding
on a great horse of gold
into the silver dawn.

four lean hounds crouched low and smiling
my heart fell dead before.

SPRING IS LIKE A PERHAPS HAND

Spring is like a perhaps hand
(which comes carefully
out of Nowhere)arranging
a window,into which people look(while
people stare
arranging and changing placing
carefully there a strange
thing and a known thing here)and

changing everything carefully

spring is like a perhaps
Hand in a window
(carefully to
and fro moving New and
Old things,while
people stare carefully
moving a perhaps
fraction of flower here placing
an inch of air there)and

without breaking anything.

NO MAN, IF MEN ARE GODS

no man,if men are gods;but if gods must
be men,the sometimes only man is this
(most common,for each anguish is his grief;
and,for his joy is more than joy,most rare)

a fiend,if fiends speak truth;if angels burn

by their own generous completely light,
an angel;or(as various worlds he'll spurn
rather than fail immeasurable fate)
coward,clown,traitor,idiot,dreamer,beast—

such was a poet and shall be and is

—who'll solve the depths of horror to defend
a sunbeam's architecture with his life:
and carve immortal jungles of despair
to hold a mountain's heartbeat in his hand

WHAT IF A MUCH OF A WHICH OF A WIND

what if a much of a which of a wind
gives the truth to summer's lie;
bloodies with dizzying leaves the sun
and yanks immortal stars awry?
Blow king to beggar and queen to seem
(blow friend to fiend:blow space to time)
—when skies are hanged and oceans drowned,
the single secret will still be man

what if a keen of a lean wind flays
screaming hills with sleet and snow:
strangles valleys by ropes of thing
and stifles forests in white ago?
Blow hope to terror;blow seeing to blind
(blow pity to envy and soul to mind)
—whose hearts are mountains,roots are trees,
it's they shall cry hello to the spring

what if a dawn of a doom of a dream
bites this universe in two,
peels forever out of his grave
and sprinkles nowhere with me and you?
Blow soon to never and never to twice
(blow life to isn't:blow death to was)
—all nothing's only our hugest home;
the most who die,the more we live

NEXT TO OF COURSE GOD

"next to of course god america i
love you land of the pilgrims' and so forth oh
say can you see by the dawn's early my
country 'tis of centuries come and go
and are no more what of it we should worry
in every language even deafanddumb
thy sons acclaim your glorious name by gorry
by jingo by gee by gosh by gum
why talk of beauty what could be more beautiful than these heroic happy dead
who rushed like lions to the roaring slaughter
they did not stop to think they died instead
then shall the voice of liberty be mute?"

He spoke.   And drank rapidly a glass of water

MY SWEET OLD ETCETERA

my sweet old etcetera
aunt lucy during the recent

war could and what
is more did tell you just
what everybody was fighting

for,
my sister

isabel created hundreds
(and
hundreds)of socks not to
mention shirts fleaproof earwarmers

etcetera wristers etcetera,my
mother hoped that

i would die etcetera
bravely of course my father used
to become hoarse talking about how it was
a privilege and if only he
could meanwhile my

self etcetera lay quietly
in the deep mud et

cetera
(dreaming,
et
   cetera,of
Your smile
eyes knees and of your Etcetera)

BUFFALO BILL'S

Buffalo Bill's
defunct
         who used to
         ride a watersmooth-silver
                                    stallion
and break onetwothreefourfive pigeonsjustlikethat
                                                     Jesus

he was a handsome man
                       and what i want to know is
how do you like your blueeyed boy
Mister Death

ALWAYS BEFORE YOUR VOICE MY SOUL

Always before your voice my soul
half-beautiful and wholly droll
is as some smooth and awkward foal,
whereof young moons begin
the newness of his skin,

so of my stupid sincere youth
the exquisite failure uncouth
discovers a trembling and smooth
Unstrength, against the strong
silences of your song;

or as a single lamb whose sheen
of full unsheared fleece is mean
beside its lovelier friends, between
your thoughts more white than wool
My thought is sorrowful:

but my heart smote in trembling thirds
of anguish quivers to your words,
As to a flight of thirty birds
shakes with a thickening fright
the sudden fooled light.

it is the autumn of a year:
When through the thin air stooped with fear,
across the harvest whitely peer
empty of surprise
death's faultless eyes

(whose hand my folded soul shall know
while on faint hills do frailly go
The peaceful terrors of the snow,
and before your dead face
which sleeps, a dream shall pass)

and these my days their sounds and flowers
Fall in a pride of petaled hours,
like flowers at the feet of mowers
whose bodies strong with love
through meadows hugely move.

yet what am i that such and such
mysteries very simply touch

me, whose heart-wholeness overmuch
Expects of your hair pale,
a terror musical?

while in an earthless hour my fond
soul seriously yearns beyond
this fern of sunset frond on frond
opening in a rare
Slowness of gloried air . . .

The flute of morning stilled in noon—
noon the implacable bassoon—
now Twilight seeks the thrill of moon,
washed with a wild and thin
despair of violin

JEHOVAH BURIED, SATAN DEAD

Jehovah buried,Satan dead,
do fearers worship Much and Quick;
badness not being felt as bad,
itself thinks goodness what is meek;
obey says toc,submit says tic,
Eternity's a Five Year Plan:
if Joy with Pain shall hang in hock
who dares to call himself a man?

go dreamless knaves on Shadows fed,
your Harry's Tom,your Tom is Dick;
while Gadgets murder squawk and add,
the cult of Same is all the chic;
by instruments,both span and spic,
are justly measured Spic and Span:
to kiss the mike if Jew turn kike
who dares to call himself a man?

loudly for Truth have liars pled,
their heels for Freedom slaves will click;

where Boobs are holy,poets mad,
illustrious punks of Progress shriek;
when Souls are outlawed,Hearts are sick,
Hearts being sick,Minds nothing can:
if Hate's a game and Love's a φυκ
who dares to call himself a man?

King Christ,this world is all aleak;
and lifepreservers there are none:
and waves which only He may walk
Who dares to call Himself a man.

BEING TO TIMELESSNESS AS IT'S TO TIME

being to timelessness as it's to time,
love did no more begin than love will end;
where nothing is to breathe to stroll to swim
love is the air the ocean and the land

(do lovers suffer? all divinities
proudly descending put on deathful flesh:
are lovers glad? only their smallest joy's
a universe emerging from a wish)

love is the voice under all silences,
the hope which has no opposite in fear;
the strength so strong mere force seems feebleness:
the truth more first than sun more last than star

—do lovers love? why then to heaven with hell.
Whatever sages say and fools, all's well

YOU SHALL ABOVE ALL THINGS BE GLAD AND YOUNG

you shall above all things be glad and young.
For if you're young,whatever life you wear

it will become you;and if you are glad
whatever's living will yourself become.
Girlboys may nothing more than boygirls need:
i can entirely her only love

whose any mystery makes every man's
flesh put space on;and his mind take off time

that you should ever think,may god forbid
and(in his mercy)your true lover spare:
for that way knowledge lies,the foetal grave
called progress,and negation's dead undoom.

I'd rather learn from one bird how to sing
than teach ten thousand stars how not to dance

PITY THIS BUSY MONSTER, MANUNKIND

pity this busy monster,manunkind,

not. Progress is a comfortable disease:
your victim(death and life safely beyond)

plays with the bigness of his littleness
—electrons deify one razorblade
into a mountainrange;lenses extend

unwish through curving wherewhen till unwish
returns on its unself.
                    A world of made
is not a world of born—pity poor flesh

and trees,poor stars and stones,but never this
fine specimen of hypermagical

ultraomnipotence. We doctors know

a hopeless case if—listen:there's a hell
of a good universe next door;let's go

I SING OF OLAF

i sing of Olaf glad and big
whose warmest heart recoiled at war:
a conscientious object-or

his well-belovéd colonel(trig
westpointer most succinctly bred)
took erring Olaf soon in hand;
but—though an host of overjoyed
noncoms(first knocking on the head
him)do through icy waters roll
that helplessness which others stroke
with brushes recently employed
anent this muddy toiletbowl,
while kindred intellects evoke
allegiance per blunt instruments—
Olaf(being to all intents
a corpse and wanting any rag
upon what God unto him gave)
responds,without getting annoyed
"I will not kiss your f.ing flag"

straightway the silver bird looked grave
(departing hurriedly to shave)

but—though all kinds of officers
(a yearning nation's blueeyed pride)
their passive prey did kick and curse
until for wear their clarion
voices and boots were much the worse,
and egged the firstclassprivates on
his rectum wickedly to tease
by means of skilfully applied
bayonets roasted hot with heat—
Olaf(upon what were once knees)
does almost ceaselessly repeat
"there is some s. I will not eat"

our president,being of which
assertions duly notified
threw the yellowsonofabitch
into a dungeon,where he died

Christ(of His mercy infinite)
i pray to see;and Olaf,too

preponderatingly because
unless statistics lie he was
more brave than me:more blond than you.

Reuel Denney

THE LABORATORY MIDNIGHT

Science is what the world is, earth and water.
And what its seasons do. And what space fountained it.
It is forges hidden underground. It is the dawn's slow salvo.
It is in the closed retort. And it is not yet.

It looks up and counts the Perseids in August,
A fire from nowhere like signals overhead
And it looks for portents, as redmen on a hill,
In the white stream where Altair swims with the Andromedid.

Now you who know what to believe, who have God with you
By desk and bed, blue fire in the stove;
Whom the rains from the northeast alter but perfect
Into new powers, and new pities, and new love;

Go look in lava flows for newer elements,
And dismantle the electric shape of matter like a house;
And weigh the mountains in small sensitive scales;
Break buds; and test the senses of a mouse;

And if you are unpanicked, tell me what you find
On how the sun flies and the snow is spent,
What blasts and bessemers we live in, that dissolve
All the loam loaned to spine and ligament.

Gene Derwood

STAR

Star, star, shining bright,
With new spectrum in the night,
Telescope game gone earnest now,
Prophets down to '50 brought
And the method shoved to naught,
Puddentame remains my name.
Ask again, I'll say the same
And let you soon know how.

First star I've seen tonight,
When the grain admires the blight,
At the gate the farmer enters
While the shine on water feathers
These new colours will change weathers.
I'll say the name till Puddentame
Rings in your head the very same.
Spite and spike the bombish mentors.

Make your wish come out of you,
Struck in water, say it true.
Star and stars are overhead,
Now the night is purpling rich
Fertilizing our deep ditch,
First was written when my name
Answers you with Puddentame,
Star crack wings and raise dead.

IN COMMON

Here am I, this carrot eating—
Orange but hard common;
Out the window sun is treating,
Laying still its gold on;

The color still is yellow,
Red now, but a late hello.

Does this, living feel, and starting,
Cry when out of earth it's sucked?
Is there tear in every parting,
Even from loose earth when plucked?
The last day shall we be very
Terrorized or merry?

Health itself is bled from this
Wandering dynamic in my veins;
What can be the vegetable bliss
Compensatory for the pains?
Here's sweet carrot, here am I,
Souls immortal we descry.

THIRD MADRIGAL

My wand strikes me no joy till loosened weeping
Prints my blue air with clouded beauty lying
In milky pools of silk, the cipolin
Smooth floor his momentary couch, and sighing,
My throaty ocarina blows to win
His hearing, though his madder ear lies sleeping
Among the browny spirals of his curls.

My clouds are grey on black, grey unworn pearls,
No broody moonstone quiet for his sight.
His sun-tipped clouds fly with soft angel golds;
Weathers all raw roam through my cyclone night.
I have long hot skies and cold snows in folds,
No mild green light of spring to weave him laurels.
My future floods be such as angels ford!

Noble sport of the vain cells that overlord
This massive heart with double gorgeous spate,

Now dare I hurl the jewel that drives him far,
Earth moving under beauty's feet, for where I wait
Even that mouth, my music's gate, and war,
My clouds in rains hold mirrored, a wound a word
Struck on my gong my heart, while his live bell

Chimes as he sleeps in my clouds' citadel.
My sea rolled tremor pierce his heaven's ear,
Plunge to his dream my restless echo's flash,
And wandering draw this source of song more near,
Made of so known a substance as the flesh,
Quick with his dream, live from my vision's shell . .
His throat and eyes struck open in my room.

Curse my night mourning witch's power and doom!
His pinions stir with throbbing flowers for feathers,
My rains in haloes fall round beauty's head,
May noose my wrist, so a smile hovers and quivers,
Such blossoms blow, his white, his dark, his red,
What artist's steady hand could hold their bloom?
Unloose eyes stare! I breathe his dream's excess,

My clouds rain curtains, my vision's jewel is his.

SHELTER

While people hunt for what can satisfy their wants,
There is a watching and a sharp recording.
Both seekers and the watchers are the palpitants,
And much is said with no deep, ferny wording.

Under the various shelters sits the soul
Not necessarily in misty, devious hiding;
The body housed, the body's firm, pale bole
Clothed, the body's self a blank abiding.

There sometimes goes a woman, fur on neck,
A man with hands immersed in pockets,

An insect crouched behind a built-up speck,
Or memories enclosed in fastened lockets.

But cease! The peering sleight-of-sight
Probing behind such partial enclosures
Is more befooled, because the definite might
Is open, like water seen through osiers.

Walking or languid, through the night or day,
Something familiar for a hiding wall
We carry, as a glove, or stare, or play
Of lips and brows. That's just a stall

That balks no frankness of the essence,
The too lightning truth of what we are —
No man can hide the presence or the absence,
We've come too quickly and too far.

TO GEORGE BARKER

'O, who will speak from a womb or cloud,' and cloud,
But I? From the womb of iron, in hard cry,
In shudder and rudder-bent, very out loud
Whisper that breathes out lost, faster and faster?
From the artificial womb (Mourn its making!)
Open token, yet to all as all, such fester
Paint-fair tree (we so much perverted) shaking
Acid dews down, pitting all interview!
Us now, not together but alone, take vow,
Stammer we must, but not full tongue-tied die.

Like yesterday this is shock-day and sorrow,
Tell, have you read the heinous thing they do?
Good pours from bags, but not the bag they harrow.
My prairie is no more, those book-dressed hinds,
Researching minds a-tongue in laboratory,
Loose bag of idols and the work of hands,

Where probe-men rend and know not what they worry,
Splitting us into factions to test inventions.
Let resolution meet resolvent and quench true.

They plod the rut, shod with ill-gathered knowledge,
Talk: Perhaps, and use will presently be found,
The learned dull! They know not use's dodge,
The use that founders us, the tongue's abuse
That keeps dunged ground crosstreed with steel, unfertile
Matted with heavy waste, what men debase,
Rich soil that once struck mind from mould, wore myrtle,
Moulds now, will mound with later victims' weight:
Skies bend with bombs, will pass, unless we hate
Foul play with monstered matter, and sing sound.

Insinuant strong tongue I know, and mine,
Soda that vitriol, as strive I soon,
Tear with twice stronger books the mane,
Entrails and trails of Look! power-angled beast
Unconscious with his many addled minds aglow
In fuddled flower! let truth-shook poets at least
Equate it with stopped earthquakes struck from NO.
By God's echo, Barker, though you doubt it,
Write, before hate, gas and bomb indite it.
Must nightmares ride our foreheads past our noon?

That which feeds on cool water as on coal,
Predicted fire, now predicated close,
Already lit electric hell, end's kill,
That which is loosed, not mad, the curse of earth,
That feeds as war not yet has fed on flesh,
But eats dear mountain, sea and cloud, the dearth
Of death at last, what with unending flash
Burns beauty's planet, with ourselves, to sun,
Tongues off our blue-white sky to space-black, gun
Opens hell, as no man guns, yet as man sows.

Love has been sung, war cried, and prophets' woe
Shouted forever in men's ears tight-strung
On former hearing, now it is not so.
All ears are open to the drum, and tongues
Praising the probers as their goal is reached,
The atom breached, unleashed, while no strong lungs
Breathe clean-fired word, as once was teached
Makes hell-fire faint. We cannot read, but write,
Write, write, as atom-crease uncoils our night:
The burning grin of space, knelled hell, is sprung.

MAILED TO G. B.

Look, Barker, when you wrote me I lay cringing,
Wore grieving words, hung wreaths weighted down hopeless
In my lost English depth, full-dipt, broke, twinging
My nerves in words as here typewritten hapless.
My freshet's staled in this night's paupered way,
My twin eyes bleached with reading out a why.
Broke I with wringing thought about face brought
From nightmare brooding after my dream phoenix
Pyred on the poets' island now burnt bright
With bombish fires; mourned bird in an old fix—
His ash but catalyst for being born.
Can I bear phoenix drowned or wormy-worn?

My weary I is drawn again to reading,
Reading the poets over, the code around.
Their pulse persists in rhythm minus-seeding
These thoughts dug cold, below the stuttering runed
Gait-hobbled breathing. Can language recover,
Have earth its book, I lie in rent-free clover?
What haunts? These men-mad maundering cells
Of the corporate with tank-heavy foliage
Wasped with hard wings, smother true bird's code-calls,
The inside foes of our great body's holy age.

What care I in my sob for ruth or hap
(If still an English island sails my map?)

Above our wisdom jaws a spawning fool
(Not Will's), my art goes wrong, your passion's songs
Skin me alive, scalp my great thoughts. Which ghoul
Drives me awry as books become my thongs?
Your rich lament is more of me than mine
Though hunger wilts and whips me wandering mean
Toward money's fiction dead I broke to scorn,
Not seeing world's broke then, though shark I saw
When thistle-pure I stung. I song acorn
Force oak to grow, while isolate in law.
My thews grow for a wrestle, my lines relax,
Word-faint, yet must I wax to shore dream-locks.

Gradate my dream, let me down easy, easy,
Shunted from harm's way, do I lapse in vain?
Read; here the books begin, I pause nerve-queasy,
Beauty in snarls prints your read page, dream-pain
Not of myself, though self in me does choke.
The broken breath of print fades with what's broke.
My mentor jokes unborn, my saviour sighs,
As plasm natural armies avid eat,
Poems read grey, words broken have long soughs,
No candour shines, the sorry slur defeat,
Firefly our beams, organic lights show dim,
You light my page, but no light leaps its rim.

N. B., SYMMETRIANS

We, the symmetrians, seek justice here,
And asymmetric nature makes a drought.
We wrap up handouts for the martyred poor,
Making sure to put in books and tin-can beer.
Each man relieved goes home and gives a clout
To mrs man, or pal-man, and slams the door.

The speechful day in knowing languors goes,
We seek again for salt and summer sky.
The pure-blue meteor flares and falls unburnt;
We take to our heels standing on staunch tiptoes.
We read half-works of science for the why
And scheme to balance marxly with what's learnt.

Fastened and fasting in the bed-rock man
The assainted, snuffed-down halo strives to rise;
The unstabilized land still slips up out of ocean,—
Bears odd, imperilled flora built to plan.
A natural start is now no one's surmise,
To take things as presented, no one's notion.

They used to start a-fresh, but we try burdened,
Trimming the present's future with the past.
It's all the fault of inter-communication,
Mountains of dove-tailed pebbles and words wordened.
The newest prism is moulded from the last.
The simplest thing is: to laud the massive nation.

The moon still shines beside the daytime star,
The waters weave, rain cools, dunes move, grain grows,
Soft words bring soft replies, muscles expand.
Whether we say the stars are near or far,
The polar lights still paint the glacier floes,
The temperate zones are yet more fully manned.

CAMEL

Wild white camel, camel wild, what behind
Your odd-toed feet uncoils no visible trail?
Deep oases hid from the slow caravans:
You are two-humped, incredible moan's hound,
You kneel not nor know how dun camels quail.
Fill you your furred hump in full glare of bans?

Camel white, they mutter and say you previse
The hordes that will rush with some hot fierce simoon,
The holy mad desert horse-riding Riffs;
That your Indian neck in Africa will rise
In unseeable speed, will flash night and noon.
You anticipate, your smoked nostril sniffs.

Wild camel, the Tartar will uproll to the West,
Himalayas sink to scarps when you smoke
The explosive split air of the eastern plateaux,
Your undulant shape will lay the smoked waste.
You was it the low-smiling fakirs bespoke
And you the untold mystery under black snows?

Wild camel unborn reincarnate spore,
Why know we not all the legend of humps?
What!   White moves unseen against dark eastern light?
Unseen humps out a myriad in feral war?
Unheard your peculiar foot stamp stamps,
Thump against loud whiteness foreseeing no night.

SO, MAN?

Halloo to man, the pleasuring, lording creature,
Tooled wielder of the brain and pottering hand,
Lord of the hungering mind, fierce hunting breacher
Of fact, of complex number, multiplicand
Of life, with fabricant the multiplier—
Blunt animal master, world his trembling choir.

He thinks.   Can anything escape such danger?
The vegetable must swell at his command;
The cow yield bursting, with her calf a stranger;
Dazed hens lay day and night at his demand.

The trees pulp into paper as his speech
Requires their long-grown lives for reeling sheets

Of speedy words.   All beasts pant fast to reach
The far-receding haven where no man beats.

The hawking birds wilt down their startled crests
Meeting his vollied presence in their air;
The fishes thin; the heaving whale attests,
With mammoth suicide, his fatal care.

He rips earth open for her ancient veins
Of molten splendour; toppling floods give room
Faced by his dams; the lightning knows his chains. . . .
He loves his handicraft and. . . . scorns what doom?

Carver of soap and carrots, steel and flesh,
Biped of upright dust and throbbing head,
Hurling your wilding intellect in the mesh
Of its own webbing, left by right hand led,
You blade, you scythe, recoiling your own swathe,
Forget not the one potter and . . . the . . . lathe.

WITH GOD CONVERSING

Red paths that wander through the gray, and cells
Of strangeness, rutted mouldings in the brain,
Untempered fevers heated by old kills,
By the pampered word, by the pat printed rune,
Unbalanced coil under glaucous blooms of thought,
A turning mind, unmitigated thinking that
Feeds human hunger and eats us alive
While cringing to the death, expecting love,—
Such make the self we are. And do you make it?
And practice on us? For we cannot take it.

Listen. Grow mild before the flicking lash
Seems welded to your hand, self-wounder.
What are we, cry we, while our pain leaps lush,
Too jungle thick: the jungle where we wander,

No seeded faith before, nor after, miracle,
Of bidden faith in things unseen, no particle.
For we think only through our troubled selves,
We note the worm that in the apple delves,
See gibbous moons and spots upon the sun,
Speak gibberish, and keep the poor in sin.

Plus birth and death must war-lash winnow
While every pod-burst leaf of May sucks life?
Because we think shall we be less than minnow,
Cat, carrot, rat, bat and such from sense aloof?
What doorless maze is this we wander through
With fuming souls parched of our morning dew?
Reason confounds as it presents to NAUGHT:
Earth worn, man moving into self-made night.
Reason-begotten science sets war's pace
And, civil-mouthed, makes civilization pass.

Created in your image, made up of words,
Till words reduce you to a zero—O,
We, then, reflecting you, are less than birds,
Bugs, or empty dugs, still less than minus no.
There must be something wrong with being wise—
Talking we go, wondering and wandering with woes,
Big thoughts have got us, hence we organize,
Govern our heroes with unmeant yeas and nays,
And breathe in dungeons of our nervous mesh
An air too blank to snare meandering flesh.

Night melting dawn shall turn the renewed sky,
Aurora Borealis and Australis
Fanfaring leap the poles, the moon fall by;
But if our science does not quickly fail us
How long for us will space blue light the dun
Of populaces, while wonderers eye the sun?
The gloomy silhouettes of wings we forged
With reason reasonless, are now enlarged,
The falsified subconscious, beast-a-woken?
We-you? Post-suicides, shall we awaken?

ELEGY ON GORDON BARBER

Lamentably Drowned in his Eighteenth Year

When in the mirror of a permanent tear
Over the iris of your mother's eye
I beheld the dark tremor of your face, austere
With space of death, spun too benign for youth,
Icicle of the past to pierce her living sigh—
I saw you wish the last kiss of mother's mouth,
Who took the salted waters rather in the suck
Of seas, sighing yourself to fill and drench
With water the plum-rich glory of your breast
Where beat the heart escaping from war's luck.

Gordon, I mourn your wrist, your running foot,
Your curious brows, your thigh, your unborn daughters,
Yet mourn more deep the drought-caught war dry boy
Who goes, a killer, to join you in your sleep
And envy you what made you blench
Taking your purple back to drought-less waters.
What choke of terror filled you in the wet
What fierce surprise caught you when play turned fate
And all the rains you loved became your net,
Formlessly yielding, yet stronger than your breath?
Then did you dream of mother or hopes hatched
When the cold cramp held you from nape to foot
And time dissolved, promise dissolved, in Death?
Did you cry 'cruel' to all the hands that stretched
Not near, but played afar, when you sank down
Your sponge of lungs hurt to the quick
Till you had left the quick to join the dead,
Whom, now, your mother mourns, grief-sick.
You were too young to drown.

Never will you take bride to happy bed,
Who lay awash in water yet no laving
Needed, so pure so young for sudden leaving.

Gone, gone is Gordon, tall and brilliant lad
Whose mind was science. Now hollow his skull
A noble sculpture, is but sunken bone,
His cells from water come by water laid
Grave-deep, to water gone.
Lost, lost the hope he had
Washed to a cipher his splendour and his skill.

But Gordon's gone, it's other boys who live afraid.

Two years, and lads have grown to hold a gun.
In dust must splendid lads go down and choke,
Red dry their hands and dry their one day's sun
From which they earthward fall to fiery tomb
Bomb-weighted, from bloodying children's hair.

Never a boy but takes as cross Cain's crime
And goes to death by making death, to pass
Death's gate distorted with the dried brown grime—
Better the watery death than death by air
Or death by sand
Where fall hard fish of fear
Loud in unwetted dust.

Spun on a lucky wave, O early boy!
Now ocean's fish you are
As heretofore.
Perhaps you had sweet mercy's tenderness
To win so soon largesse of choice
That you, by grace, went gayly to the wave
And all our mourning should be to rejoice.

THE INNOCENT

Beautiful always the littoral line,
Jointure of ocean and earth where globe winds lean
Over the lace whence Venus rose, the sands
From which little-less-than-gods flung history's sail,
  Round wave, round shell, and myth-bound lands.

Pacific soft touches the gold beachhead,
Sand swells to a nectarine mound fringed with red,
The mound a shoulder freckle-fretted, pale
As sand, except for the pulse-ravished blood,
  A young lad simply, newly dead.

His skin dipped golden on last summer's shore
As far past now as light years; life's no more
To this fruit of land whereon Columbus stood
Proving the global arc of earth, and trade.
  The boy reached farther, and has stayed.

While on Atlantic shores a hotel fair
Most sumptuous lords it in the stern sea air,
Built for the kings of gold their richened gladness
Now houses it the surgeon laying knots
  In organs of pain and madness.

Here innocently a-thought the while he rots
An old man stone-set in the stoppéd sun
Counts nothing placid on his inside done,
The cones of light seared from his eaglet eyes
  Last year, when he was twenty-one.

Talk, talk, within his silent gullet whirrs
Like spider-netted, spider-bitten flies.
Now to his childhood cat, now to a *they*
Ghostly as iceberg space, worn boy avers
  'Great causes made night of my day.

'Morning's love was mine with sun-savage hair,
It was for love I trained to fight the best.
The turbulent harmonics of my rare,
My sexual-burnished youth in discord dumb
    Fail, but not to give me rest.

'O velvet kitten is it you who claw
My sutured throat or *they* who wood-like numb
Desire itself within my burnt out maw,
My war-sucked eyes; or you, what enemy?
    Let any cormorant seize the womb.

'Your god-lost hatred has what regimen
To hide from what you do? but helpful bid
Not us in dreams be hid for in dreams' sea
Can you conceal crime's personal origin
    And gorge, if so you did?

'O she, who was my second and my peace,
She who was my touch's wonder and shore,
Avower of high love that could not cease,
Conviction of my god and heaven's poor,
    Her death was of the wound of life.

'I pass a cipher from my night-dropped shade:
The terrible fertility of strife
That loves the unborn but wants the born unmade.
O she, whose womb was opened for my son,
    Died, split with shock, for nature's fun.

'A moment's marriage for a child and child,
The parade, a gun-burst and a telegram
Cry all the rocks of love's sierra falling
In pain the massive heart laboring and tolling,
    The startled dainty soul defiled.

'Defiled and dead. Worst pain soonest forgotten
They say, you do; melodious morning's crime
To learn from those who have the child begotten.
Heroes are always young, called up from gardens,
    It is innocence that hardens.

'After the wound, the softening fears, the love,
But late. The majesty of god is lost.
Treading the living flesh chaos from above
Mates with the demon chaos of below.
    We shine with unseasonable frost.

'The narrowing circle of the Azimuth
Tautens like rawhide round the human floe,
Insectuous fliers charge at the moon. My youth
In my child too will rise threatening the sun
    Till littorals of space are won.

'In rains of atomic fire my hope is forward,
This tainted race will burn as burnt my gold
My stamen's sunny dust, my sweetling word,
My withering arm and tired mouth struck old,
    The insect whirr on harmless sedge.

'But spring, but sunny beaches rich with girls!
Definite diver strong at the sea's edge,
O he who his peace-dappled body hurls
At all adventure, would that he were I.
    Life, life, you will not let me die.'

AFTER READING ST. JOHN THE DIVINE

Moon's glow by seven fold multiplied, turned red,
Burned fierce by the coronal limbs at last
Out-leaping insulating space, a-blast
The searing heat sheeting round earth ahead
Of the scorched geoid's course; and I a-bed
Watching that increased flame and holding fast
To pulse and pillow. Worse! No shadow cast
By chair or cat. All people waking dead . . .
Earth lurches spacial waste; my room is hot;
That moon waxes her monstrous, brimstone disk;
Thick fear stretches before the febrile light;
Green fires pierce at my clenching eye's blind spot . . .
My buried soul, rising to face the risk,
With one pure deed restores the natural night.

RIDES

So we ride, and ride through milked heaven
                    Above earth.
No more for us the housed and fatted standing still.
The train is carrier of us on the two-striped road-bed;
We sit in thunder over miles, calm as chairs,
                    At will?
Look again; we zoom in planes over the hill's head;
Motion, motion, our motion, up, down, and on,
                    World's girth.

And laughing under the town-world's crust,
                    Thus riding
At the open and rushed dark subway doors;
Swung singing and talking with the unnoticed horses;
Or unfoamed by the spray, on liners,
                    Changing lores
Of bored speed; or rivalling winds in their (our?) courses
In the air we flight, to air-pressure-up
                    Confiding.

Sometimes on the tumbled skin of laced seas,
Thus cresting
With staunch legs and opened hallooing, of surf
Making a race-shot thrill, on board with pair of reins,
Lengthened freedom of running covering the inland
Fraught turf. . . .
Ah, from riding, and the riding, who abstains?
In the cars, to the stars, waves, wars, riding
And questing.

WAR'S CLOWN IN THE PROSCENIUM

The night, too long illumined, comes a stranger
Driving to roof this audience hard-weathered
Through the play of rage and bitter luck of danger.
Born to these uniform seats, they claim
No hunter's pleasure, the historic name.

Long foundered is our prow that feathered
The warm archaic wave.

The limelight warns, the need to worship waits
A serious humour, the laud-lifted clown.
The lights are fluorescent,
Pale, pale and cold, ice flickering incessant
As at Asgärd's fall, were north gods' twilight
Ceaselessly from no star.
The nerveless curtain, like dead water, parts.
Increasing thousands raise their long slow stare
To the pacified shroud, our silver screen of fêtes.

No choral song arises, no drama starts.
This pantomime, like beauty, only lies
In the entrancèd eyes.
Our mask of shadow comes, there pantaloon
How massive stands, anabasis of stone
Toward the prickling cells: the final form of Gilles.

Quick with electric chill
All profiles right and left unending freeze
Not as at death's pole or Gorgon's locks,
But tight to one grounded wire, in paralysis.

Nothing will happen but fear's thrill on the nerve
Which makes the heart a nave.

If this were but enchantment or a dream
Even of solstice sacrifice, a rite
Of Druids moving with dark seasonal pace
Barefoot beneath Stonehenge's antique weight,
Endurance might ennoble the tranced face
Or quell emotion with a natural light.

But here projection worse than mirror's spell
Our clown's oiled paradox
Drips from his skull and sockets' peacock pride.
The last cry for justice dies.
The sterile form of megalomaniac woe
Is malice; violence at recurrent speed
Is death's boredom motionless, thus is hell
Gone vacant, and so mocks.
The fawn has horned the doe.

The old, below their naked eyeballs' trance,
Recall Pierrot, the dance,
The silken lips, the fluttering love whose lease
Was years, fountains of smiles, the tears' duet
Before the risk was hate, the vines' empurpled lace.
The young lack memory. They fiercely throw
From the blank iris gun-glances for Gilles,
At Gilles, whose mask has the strength they make grow.

Innocent are their eyes, as pure as cruel,
Innocent of compassion, innocent as rue.
For the tuberose scent of love
Takes time and time to breathe;

This is amusement, to see the skull heave
Hard on the plastic ruff of hardened milk.

Even the young remember Punch. They're tough.
Punch had these heavy hands, but not this bat-winged hulk.
They have two hands for sticks, and hands enough.
Tyros of flowers and veterans of flight,
Born without firmament
In the planetary prison with a ceiling for skies,
One hour for love, short days,
They may not wing like bees through hearts of flowers
But wing like ants in regiments
Capturing aphides.

The undecipherable fate of Cain,
His mark, may saturate us with clown's pain.

Gilles sates our hunger and bloats hypnotized
In the proscenium. But he'll burst
In the easy rain of bombs, our uranium sin.
The ascending dust will sift the son of Cain,
This generation dust, or lost, or dazed.

O animals were equal at the first.
We studied hunch of bison claw of cat
For duels. In the deep caves of the bat
Our risk was beautiful.
Now, at the slaughter pen, moans the young bull.

Christ's love! Who dreed our weird? Nobility
Troubles the heart in unexpected moments,
Heart's ease.
                    New Human creatures tranquilly
New seasons will inhabit, safe as the wren,
Like the lion the chicken the hyena,
Natural as the veronica and the verbena,
In agricultural health.

Emily Dickinson

THE SOUL SELECTS HER OWN SOCIETY

The soul selects her own society,
Then shuts the door;
On her divine majority
Obtrude no more.

Unmoved, she notes the chariot's pausing
At her low gate;
Unmoved, an emperor is kneeling
Upon her mat.

I've known her from an ample nation
Choose one;
Then close the valves of her attention
Like stone.

MY LIFE CLOSED TWICE BEFORE ITS CLOSE

My life closed twice before its close;
    It yet remains to see
If Immortality unveil
    A third event to me,

So huge, so hopeless to conceive,
    As these that twice befell.
Parting is all we know of heaven,
    And all we need of hell.

I NEVER SAW A MOOR

I never saw a moor,
I never saw the sea;
Yet know I how the heather
    looks,
And what a wave must be.

I never spoke with God,
Nor visited in heaven;
Yet certain am I of the spot
As if the chart were given.

BECAUSE I COULD NOT STOP FOR DEATH

Because I could not stop for Death,
He kindly stopped for me;
The carriage held but just ourselves
And Immortality.

We slowly drove, he knew no haste,
And I had put away
My labor, and my leisure too,
For his civility.

We passed the school where children played
At wrestling in a ring;
We passed the fields of gazing grain,
We passed the setting sun.

We paused before a house that seemed
A swelling of the ground;
The roof was scarcely visible,
The cornice but a mound.

Since then 't is centuries; but each
Feels shorter than the day
I first surmised the horses' heads
Were toward eternity.

I WENT TO HEAVEN

I went to heaven,—
'Twas a small town,
Lit with a ruby,
Lathed with down.
Stiller than the fields
At the full dew,
Beautiful as pictures
No man drew.
People like the moth,
Of mechlin frames,
Duties of gossamer,
And eider names.
Almost contented
I could be
'Mong such unique
Society.

THERE'S A CERTAIN SLANT OF LIGHT

There's a certain slant of light,
On winter afternoons,
That oppresses, like the weight
Of cathedral tunes.

Heavenly hurt it gives us;
We can find no scar,
But internal difference
Where the meanings are.

None may teach it anything,
'T is the seal, despair,—
An imperial affliction
Sent us of the air.

When it comes, the landscape listens,
Shadows hold their breath;
When it goes, 't is like the distance
On the look of death.

AFTER GREAT PAIN A FORMAL FEELING COMES

After great pain a formal feeling comes—
The nerves sit ceremonious like tombs;
The stiff Heart questions—was it He that bore?
And yesterday—or centuries before?

The feet mechanical
Go round a wooden way
Of ground or air or Ought, regardless grown,
A quartz contentment like a stone.

This is the hour of lead
Remembered if outlived,
As freezing persons recollect the snow—
First chill, then stupor, then the letting go.

A SHADY FRIEND FOR TORRID DAYS

A shady friend for torrid days
Is easier to find
Than one of higher temperature
For frigid hour of mind.

The vane a little to the east
Scares muslin souls away;
If broadcloth breasts are firmer
Than those of organdy,

Who is to blame? The weaver?
Ah! the bewildering thread!
The tapestries of paradise
So notelessly are made!

I HEARD A FLY BUZZ WHEN I DIED

I heard a fly buzz when I died;
The stillness in the room
Was like the stillness in the air
Between the heaves of storm.

The eyes around had wrung them dry,
And breaths were gathering firm
For that last onset, when the king
Be witnessed in the room.

I willed my keepsakes, signed away
What portion of me be
Assignable—and then it was
There interposed a fly,

With blue, uncertain, stumbling buzz,
Between the light and me;
And then the windows failed, and then
I could not see to see.

I TASTE A LIQUOR NEVER BREWED

I taste a liquor never brewed,
From tankards scooped in pearl;
Not all the vats upon the Rhine
Yield such an alcohol!

Inebriate of air am I,
And debauchee of dew,
Reeling, through endless summer days,
From inns of molten blue.

When landlords turn the drunken bee
Out of the foxglove's door,
When butterflies renounce their drams,
I shall but drink the more!

Till seraphs swing their snowy hats,
And saints to windows run,
To see the little tippler
Leaning against the sun!

THE MUSHROOM IS THE ELF OF PLANTS

The mushroom is the elf of
    plants,
At evening it is not;
At morning in a truffled hut
It stops upon a spot

As if it tarried always;
And yet its whole career
Is shorter than a snake's
    delay,
And fleeter than a tare.

'Tis vegetation's juggler,
The germ of alibi;

Doth like a bubble antedate,
And like a bubble hie.

I feel as if the grass were
    pleased
To have it intermit;
The surreptitious scion
Of summer's circumspect.

Had nature any outcast face,
Could she a son contemn,
Had nature an Iscariot,
That mushroom,—it is him.

A TRIUMPH MAY BE OF SEVERAL KINDS

A triumph may be of several kinds.
There's triumph in the room
When that old imperator, Death,
By faith is overcome.

There's triumph of the finer mind
When truth, affronted long,
Advances calm to her supreme,
Her God her only throng.

A triumph when temptation's bribe
Is slowly handed back,
One eye upon the heaven renounced
And one upon the rack.

Severer triumph, by himself
Experienced, who can pass
Acquitted from that naked bar,
Jehovah's countenance!

THEIR HEIGHT IN HEAVEN

Their height in heaven comforts not,
Their glory nought to me;
'Twas best imperfect, as it was;
I'm finite, I can't see.

The house of supposition,
The glimmering frontier
That skirts the acres of perhaps,
To me shows insecure.

The wealth I had contented me;
If 'twas a meaner size,
Then I had counted it until
It pleased my narrow eyes

Better than larger values,
However true their show;
This timid life of evidence
Keeps pleading, "I don't know."

I TOOK MY POWER IN MY HAND

I took my power in my hand
And went against the world;
'Twas not so much as David had,
But I was twice as bold.

I aimed my pebble, but myself
Was all the one that fell.
Was it Goliath was too large,
Or only I too small?

THERE IS A SHAME OF NOBLENESS

There is a shame of nobleness
Confronting sudden pelf,—
A finer shame of ecstasy
Convicted of itself.

A best disgrace a brave man feels,
Acknowledged of the brave,—
One more "Ye Blessed" to be told;
But this involves the grave.

THERE CAME A WIND LIKE A BUGLE

There came a wind like a bugle;
It quivered through the grass,
And a green chill upon the heat
So ominous did pass
We barred the windows and the doors
As from an emerald ghost;
The doom's electric moccasin
That very instant passed.
On a strange mob of panting trees,

And fences fled away,
And rivers where the houses ran
The living looked that day.
The bell within the steeple wild
The flying tidings whirled.
How much can come
And much can go,
And yet abide the world!

I KNOW A PLACE WHERE SUMMER STRIVES

I know a place where summer strives
With such a practised frost,
She each year leads her daisies back,
Recording briefly, "Lost."

But when the south wind stirs the pools
And struggles in the lanes,
Her heart misgives her for her vow,
And she pours soft refrains

Into the lap of adamant,
And spices, and the dew,
That stiffens quietly to quartz,
Upon her amber shoe.

IT SOUNDED AS IF THE STREETS WERE RUNNING

It sounded as if the streets were running,
And then the streets stood still.
Eclipse was all we could see at the window,
And awe was all we could feel.

By and by the boldest stole out of his covert,
To see if time was there.
Nature was in her beryl apron,
Mixing fresher air.

OF ALL THE SOULS THAT STAND CREATE

Of all the souls that stand create
I have elected one.
When sense from spirit files away,
And subterfuge is done;

When that which is and that which was
Apart, intrinsic, stand,
And this brief tragedy of flesh
Is shifted like a sand;

When figures show their royal front
And mists are carved away,—
Behold the atom I preferred
To all the lists of clay!

THE WIND TAPPED LIKE A TIRED MAN

The wind tapped like a tired
man,
And like a host, "Come in,"
I boldly answered; entered
then
My residence within

A rapid, footless guest,
To offer whom a chair
Were as impossible as hand
A sofa to the air.

No bone had he to bind him,
His speech was like the push

Of numerous humming-birds
at once
From a superior bush.

His countenance a billow,
His fingers, if he pass,
Let go a music, as of tunes
Blown tremulous in glass.

He visited, still flitting;
Then, like a timid man,
Again he tapped—'twas
flurriedly—
And I became alone.

HOW HAPPY IS THE LITTLE STONE

How happy is the little stone
That rambles in the road alone,
And doesn't care about careers,
And exigencies never fears;
Whose coat of elemental brown
A passing universe put on;
And independent as the sun,
Associates or glows alone,
Fulfilling absolute decree
In casual simplicity.

IN LANDS I NEVER SAW, THEY SAY

In lands I never saw, they say,
Immortal Alps look down,
Whose bonnets touch the firmament,
Whose sandals touch the town,—

Meek at whose everlasting feet
A myriad daisies play.
Which, sir, are you, and which am I,
Upon an August day?

THE ONLY GHOST I EVER SAW

The only ghost I ever saw
Was dressed in mechlin,—so;
He wore no sandal on his foot,
And stepped like flakes of snow.
His gait was soundless, like the bird,
But rapid, like the roe;
His fashions quaint, mosaic,
Or, haply, mistletoe.
His conversation seldom,
His laughter like the breeze
That dies away in dimples
Among the pensive trees.
Our interview was transient,—
Of me, himself was shy;
And God forbid I look behind
Since that appalling day!

I'VE SEEN A DYING EYE

I've seen a dying eye
Run round and round a room
In search of something, as it
  seemed,
Then cloudier become;

And then, obscure with fog,
And then be soldered down,
Without disclosing what it
  be,
'Twere blessed to have seen.

THE LAST NIGHT THAT SHE LIVED

The last night that she lived,
It was a common night,
Except the dying; this to us
Made nature different.

We noticed smallest things,—
Things overlooked before,
By this great light upon our
  minds
Italicized, as 'twere.

That others could exist
While she must finish
  quite,
A jealousy for her arose
So nearly infinite.

We waited while she passed;
It was a narrow time,
Too jostled were our souls to
  speak,
At length the notice came.

She mentioned, and forgot;
Then lightly as a reed
Bent to the water, shivered
  scarce,
Consented, and was dead.

And we, we placed the hair,
And drew the head erect;
And then an awful leisure
  was,
Our faith to regulate.

THE BUSTLE IN A HOUSE

The bustle in a house
The morning after death
Is solemnest of industries
Enacted upon earth,—

The sweeping up the heart,
And putting love away
We shall not want to use again
Until eternity.

WHAT INN IS THIS

What inn is this
Where for the night
Peculiar traveller comes?
Who is the landlord?
Where the maids?

Behold, what curious rooms!
No ruddy fires on the hearth,
No brimming tankards flow.
Necromancer, landlord,
Who are these below?

IT WAS NOT DEATH, FOR I STOOD UP

It was not death, for I stood
up,
And all the dead lie down;
It was not night, for all the
bells
Put out their tongues, for
noon.

It was not frost, for on my
flesh
I felt siroccos crawl,—
Nor fire, for just my marble
feet
Could keep a chancel cool.

And yet it tasted like them
all;
The figures I have seen
Set orderly, for burial,
Reminded me of mine,

As if my life were shaven
And fitted to a frame,
And could not breathe with-
out a key;
And 'twas like midnight,
some,

When everything that ticked
has stopped,
And space stares, all around,
Or grisly frosts, first autumn
morns,
Repeal the beating ground.

But most like chaos,—stop-
less, cool,—
Without a chance or spar,
Or even a report of land
To justify despair.

AS BY THE DEAD WE LOVE TO SIT

As by the dead we love to sit,
Become so wondrous dear,
As for the lost we grapple,
Though all the rest are here,—

In broken mathematics
We estimate our prize,
Vast, in its fading ratio,
To our penurious eyes!

STEP LIGHTLY ON THIS NARROW SPOT!

Step lightly on this narrow spot!
The broadest land that grows
Be not so ample as the breast
These emerald seams enclose.

Step lofty; for this name is told
As far as cannon dwell,
Or flag subsist, or fame export
Her deathless syllable.

LOVE IS THAT LATER THING THAN DEATH

Love is that later thing than death,
More previous than life,
Confirms it at its entrance and
Usurps it of itself;

Tastes death, the first to prove the sting,
The second, to its friend,
Disarms the little interval,
Deposits him with God.

Then hovers, an inferior guard,
Lest this belovéd charge
Need, once in an eternity,
A lesser than the large.

TELL ALL THE TRUTH

Tell all the truth but tell it
    slant,
Success in circuit lies,
Too bright for our infirm
    delight
The truth's superb surprise;

As lightning to the children
    eased
With explanation kind,
The truth must dazzle grad-
    ually
Or every man be blind.

I READ MY SENTENCE STEADILY

I read my sentence steadily,
Reviewed it with my eyes,
To see that I made no mistake
In its extremest clause,—

The date, and manner of the shame;
And then the pious form
That "God have mercy" on the soul
The jury voted him.

I made my soul familiar
With her extremity,
That at the last it should not be
A novel agony,

But she and Death, acquainted,
Meet tranquilly as friends,
Salute and pass without a hint—
And there the matter ends.

FLOSS WON'T SAVE YOU

Floss won't save you from
an abyss,
But a rope will,
Notwithstanding a rope for
a souvenir
Does not look as well.

But I tell you every step is
a sluice,
And every stop a well.
Now will you have the rope
or the floss?
Prices reasonable.

LOVE CAN DO ALL BUT RAISE THE DEAD

Love can do all but raise the dead;
I doubt if even that
From such a giant were withheld
Were flesh equivalent.

But love is tired and must sleep,
And hungry and must graze,
And so abets the shining fleet
Till it is out of gaze.

THE FINAL INCH

'Twas like a maelstrom, with a notch
That nearer every day
Kept narrowing its boiling wheel
Until the agony

Toyed coolly with the final inch
Of your delirious hem,
And you dropped, lost, when something broke
And let you from a dream

As if a goblin with a gauge
Kept measuring the hours,
Until you felt your second weigh
Helpless in his paws,

And not a sinew, stirred, could help,
And sense was setting numb,
When God remembered, and the fiend
Let go then, overcome;

As if your sentence stood pronounced,
And you were frozen led
From dungeon's luxury of doubt
To gibbets and the dead;

And when the film had stitched your eyes,
A creature gasped "Reprieve!"
Which anguish was the utterest then,
To perish, or to live?

Richard Eberhart

THE GROUNDHOG

In June, amid the golden fields,
I saw a groundhog lying dead.
Dead lay he; my senses shook,
And mind outshot our naked frailty.
There lowly in the vigorous summer
His form began its senseless change,
And made my senses waver dim
Seeing nature ferocious in him.
Inspecting close his maggots' might
And seething cauldron of his being,
Half with loathing, half with a strange love,
I poked him with an angry stick.
The fever arose, became a flame
And Vigour circumscribed the skies,
Immense energy in the sun,
And through my frame a sunless trembling.
My stick had done nor good nor harm.
Then stood I silent in the day
Watching the object, as before;
And kept my reverence for knowledge
Trying for control, to be still,
To quell the passion of the blood;
Until I had bent down on my knees
Praying for joy in the sight of decay.
And so I left; and I returned
In Autumn strict of eye, to see
The sap gone out of the groundhog,
But the bony sodden hulk remained.
But the year had lost its meaning,
And in intellectual chains
I lost both love and loathing,
Mured up in the wall of wisdom.
Another summer took the fields again

Massive and burning, full of life,
But when I chanced upon the spot
There was only a little hair left,
And bones bleaching in the sunlight
Beautiful as architecture;
I watched them like a geometer,
And cut a walking stick from a birch.
It has been three years, now.
There is no sign of the groundhog.
I stood there in the whirling summer,
My hand capped a withered heart,
And thought of China and of Greece,
Of Alexander in his tent;
Of Montaigne in his tower,
Of Saint Theresa in her wild lament.

THE ADVANTAGE OF THE OUTSIDE

There is a way, that sages tell,
Of sitting on the inside, looking out.
Like an Esquimau without an avalanche
All Heaven is a warm circularity.

It is the supposition of content.
Well-haled in hospitalities
Each gives a little, each takes a little.
Neither would suppose the other to outrage.

Some say the deepest way of all
Is through this socialistic sense.
Pat my back and I'll pat yours, Mack.
See the frightening stars through a handclasp

I hold with the rank outsiders
Who look in. Such freshness is theirs!

They voyage the skies' uncertainties;
They redeem ancient insecurities.

To throw away your fellow and depart
Into realms where Hell is on the rampage
Is only to find the brightest of all Ideas,
And walk upon your heavenly death.

ON A SQUIRREL CROSSING THE ROAD
IN AUTUMN, IN NEW ENGLAND

It is what he does not know,
Crossing the road under the elm trees,
About the mechanism of my car,
About the Commonwealth of Massachusetts,
About Mozart, India, Arcturus,

That wins my praise. I engage
At once in whirling squirrel-praise.

He obeys the orders of nature
Without knowing them.
It is what he does not know
That makes him beautiful.
Such a knot of little purposeful nature!

I who can see him as he cannot see himself
Repose in the ignorance that is his blessing.

It is what man does not know of God
Composes the visible poem of the world.

.... Just missed him!

THE FORGOTTEN ROCK

Tawny in a pasture by the true sea
Ship-shaped it stood, the never realizable
Rock.

It was the awe placed on this natural object,
When looking at one thing, another world was seen,
He remembered.

Even this rock, sun-stroked, high-fashioned,
Peopling dream, enticing him completely,
Was never itself.

With such subtlety the blood, blue-watery source,
Leaped from one thing to something other,
A double escape,

A paragon of sight was posed upon
The blue rock; the excitation of the world
Glanced off.

This was nothing but the world itself;
A voyage in blue distance under tawny charges
Vividly known,

As a ship like a jewel of sense, come to
With boundless appetite, is yet unknown,
And is forgotten,

As we forget time that is thoroughly gone,
But was so certainly there. We annihilate time
To remember,

And what we remember is the duality of time.
The rock was never known as it was,
But as we are.

It had a cave with an obscure dome
A hawk flew into heading home,
Killed instantly.

THE WISDOM OF INSECURITY

The endless part of disintegration
Is that it will build again;

Of a robin,
That he will become a memory;

Of a hand-great August moth,
With eyes in his wings, so fine

As to represent himself as a fable,
That he will be tried again in a poem;

Of a petal-departed rose,
That it is its loving grandparents;

Of the evil of man to man,
That it is the tenacity of mankind

To put it out of mind in the long time
And commit to the heart new fidelities;

Of the broken music of silence,
That it will be brought together,

Renaming poetry; of the days's colors,
That they make the painter's paradigm;

Of immeasurable fallibility,
That it becomes art, by authority;

That the disintegration of time
Becomes the enrichment of timelessness,

So that nothing is destroyed, but finds
Its truth in the eternal mind;

That death provides nowise no escape.
Man becomes some other shape.

I must have come down from Adam
And am his metropolitan.

The leaves are falling and the rain.
Mystery is palpable. Sameness ever the same,

Ever different, where I look
Is through the fish to the fish-hook.

The strangeness of the poet's dream
Will set what is, not what seems.

When you see destruction itself
You see form out of the formless

As I recall in the Campo Santo, at Pisa,
The work of medieval Giovanni

Who painted an old man, prone and dead,
An infant, the soul, springing from his head.

WORDS

First a word was fuzzy, and was nothing.
It had all India in fee.
It had to do with illusion's very self
And nothing to do with me.

Then a word was mighty, and flew away,
An eagle on a rocky shelf;
It glowered over our America,
Depleting the inner self.

Finally a word was elegant and sheer,
Like the fabric of a stuff
Durable with the fate of things,
When I had lived enough.

Then I had a total myth
Sounding on an eternal shore.
It was the world-memory alone
When I was dead and gone.

THE HORSE CHESTNUT TREE

Boys in sporadic but tenacious droves
Come with sticks, as certainly as Autumn,
To assault the great horse chestnut tree.

There is a law governs their lawlessness.
Desire is in them for a shining amulet
And the best are those that are highest up.

They will not pick them easily from the ground.
With shrill arms they fling to the higher branches,
To hurry the work of nature for their pleasure.

I have seen them trooping down the street
Their pockets stuffed with chestnuts shucked, unshucked.
It is only evening keeps them from their wish.

Sometimes I run out in a kind of rage
To chase the boys away; I catch an arm,
Maybe, and laugh to think of being the lawgiver.

I was once such a young sprout myself
And fingered in my pocket the prize and trophy.
But still I moralize upon the day

And see that we, outlaws on God's property,
Fling out imagination beyond the skies
Wishing a tangible good from the unknown.

And likewise death will drive us from the scene
With the great flowering world unbroken yet,
Which we held in idea, a little handful.

T. S. Eliot

THE LOVE SONG OF J. ALFRED PRUFROCK

S'io credesse che mia risposta fosse
A persona che mai tornasse al mondo,
Questa fiamma staria senza piu scosse.
Ma perciocche giammai di questo fondo
Non torno vivo alcun, s'i'odo il vero,
Senza tema d'infamia ti rispondo.

Let us go then, you and I,
When the evening is spread out against the sky
Like a patient etherised upon a table;
Let us go, through certain half-deserted streets,
The muttering retreats
Of restless nights in one-night cheap hotels
And sawdust restaurants with oyster-shells:
Streets that follow like a tedious argument
Of insidious intent
To lead you to an overwhelming question. . .
Oh, do not ask, "What is it?"
Let us go and make our visit.

In the room the women come and go
Talking of Michelangelo.

The yellow fog that rubs its back upon the window-panes,
The yellow smoke that rubs its muzzle on the window-panes
Licked its tongue into the corners of the evening,
Lingered upon the pools that stand in drains,
Let fall upon its back the soot that falls from chimneys,
Slipped by the terrace, made a sudden leap,
And seeing that it was a soft October night,
Curled once about the house, and fell asleep.

And indeed there will be time
For the yellow smoke that slides along the street,
Rubbing its back upon the window-panes;
There will be time, there will be time
To prepare a face to meet the faces that you meet;
There will be time to murder and create,
And time for all the works and days of hands
That lift and drop a question on your plate;
Time for you and time for me,
And time yet for a hundred indecisions,
And for a hundred visions and revisions,
Before the taking of a toast and tea.

    In the room the women come and go
Talking of Michelangelo.

    And indeed there will be time
To wonder, "Do I dare?" and, "Do I dare?"
Time to turn back and descend the stair,
With a bald spot in the middle of my hair—
[They will say: "How his hair is growing thin!"]
My morning coat, my collar mounting firmly to the chin,
My necktie rich and modest, but asserted by a simple pin—
[They will say: "But how his arms and legs are thin!"]
Do I dare
Disturb the universe?
In a minute there is time
For decisions and revisions which a minute will reverse.

    For I have known them all already, known them all:—
Have known the evenings, mornings, afternoons,
I have measured out my life with coffee spoons;
I know the voices dying with a dying fall
Beneath the music from a farther room.
    So how should I presume?

    And I have known the eyes already, known them all—
The eyes that fix you in a formulated phrase,
And when I am formulated, sprawling on a pin,

When I am pinned and wriggling on the wall,
Then how should I begin
To spit out all the butt-ends of my days and ways?
    And how should I presume?

And I have known the arms already, known them all—
Arms that are braceleted and white and bare
[But in the lamplight, downed with light brown hair!]
Is it perfume from a dress
That makes me so digress?
Arms that lie along a table, or wrap about a shawl.
    And should I then presume?
    And how should I begin?

                    . . . . .

Shall I say, I have gone at dusk through narrow streets
And watched the smoke that rises from the pipes
Of lonely men in shirt-sleeves, leaning out of windows? . . .

    I should have been a pair of ragged claws
Scuttling across the floors of silent seas.

                    . . . . .

And the afternoon, the evening, sleeps so peacefully!
Smoothed by long fingers,
Asleep . . . tired . . . or it malingers,
Stretched on the floor, here beside you and me.
Should I, after tea and cakes and ices,
Have the strength to force the moment to its crisis?
But though I have wept and fasted, wept and prayed,
Though I have seen my head [grown slightly bald] brought
        in upon a platter,
I am no prophet—and here's no great matter;
I have seen the moment of my greatness flicker,
And I have seen the eternal Footman hold my coat, and
        snicker,
And in short, I was afraid.

And would it have been worth it, after all,
After the cups, the marmalade, the tea,
Among the porcelain, among some talk of you and me,
Would it have been worth while,
To have bitten off the matter with a smile,
To have squeezed the universe into a ball
To roll it toward some overwhelming question,
To say: "I am Lazarus, come from the dead,
Come back to tell you all, I shall tell you all"—
If one, settling a pillow by her head,
    Should say: "That is not what I meant at all.
    That is not it, at all."

And would it have been worth it, after all,
Would it have been worth while,
After the sunsets and the dooryards and the sprinkled streets,
After the novels, after the teacups, after the skirts that trail
    along the floor—
And this, and so much more?—
It is impossible to say just what I mean!
But as if a magic lantern threw the nerves in patterns on a
    screen:
Would it have been worth while
If one, settling a pillow or throwing off a shawl,
And turning toward the window, should say:
    "That is not it at all,
    That is not what I meant, at all."

    . . . . .

No! I am not Prince Hamlet, nor was meant to be;
Am an attendant lord, one that will do
To swell a progress, start a scene or two,
Advise the prince; no doubt, an easy tool,
Deferential, glad to be of use,
Politic, cautious, and meticulous;
Full of high sentence, but a bit obtuse;
At times, indeed, almost ridiculous—
Almost, at times, the Fool.

I grow old . . . I grow old . . .
I shall wear the bottoms of my trousers rolled.

Shall I part my hair behind? Do I dare to eat a peach?
I shall wear white flannel trousers, and walk upon the beach.
I have heard the mermaids singing, each to each.

I do not think that they will sing to me.

I have seen them riding seaward on the waves
Combing the white hair of the waves blown back
When the wind blows the water white and black.

We have lingered in the chambers of the sea
By sea-girls wreathed with seaweed red and brown
Till human voices wake us, and we drown.

MORNING AT THE WINDOW

They are rattling breakfast plates in basement kitchens,
And along the trampled edges of the street
I am aware of the damp souls of housemaids
Sprouting despondently at area gates.

The brown waves of fog toss up to me
Twisted faces from the bottom of the street,
And tear from a passer-by with muddy skirts
An aimless smile that hovers in the air
And vanishes along the level of the roofs.

THE *BOSTON EVENING TRANSCRIPT*

The readers of the *Boston Evening Transcript*
Sway in the wind like a field of ripe corn.

When evening quickens faintly in the street,
Wakening the appetites of life in some
And to others bringing the *Boston Evening Transcript,*
I mount the steps and ring the bell, turning
Wearily, as one would turn to nod good-bye to Rochefoucauld,
If the street were time and he at the end of the street,
And I say, "Cousin Harriet, here is the *Boston Evening Tran-
script.*"

THE WIND SPRANG UP AT FOUR O'CLOCK

The wind sprang up at four o'clock
The wind sprang up and broke the bells
Swinging between life and death
Here, in death's dream kingdom
The waking echo of confusing strife
Is it a dream or something else
When the surface of the blackened river
Is a face that sweats with tears?
I saw across the blackened river
The camp fire shake with alien spears.
Here, across death's other river
The Tartar horsemen shake their spears.

GERONTION

> *Thou hast nor youth nor age*
> *But as it were an after dinner sleep*
> *Dreaming of both.*

Here I am, an old man in a dry month,
Being read to by a boy, waiting for rain.
I was neither at the hot gates
Nor fought in the warm rain
Nor knee deep in the salt marsh, heaving a cutlass,
Bitten by flies, fought.
My house is a decayed house,
And the jew squats on the window sill, the owner,
Spawned in some estaminet of Antwerp,
Blistered in Brussels, patched and peeled in London.
The goat coughs at night in the field overhead;
Rocks, moss, stonecrop, iron, merds.
The woman keeps the kitchen, makes tea,
Sneezes at evening, poking the peevish gutter.
                I an old man,
A dull head among windy spaces.

Signs are taken for wonders. "We would see a sign!"
The word within a word, unable to speak a word,
Swaddled with darkness. In the juvescence of the year
Came Christ the tiger

In depraved May, dogwood and chestnut, flowering judas,
To be eaten, to be divided, to be drunk
Among whispers; by Mr. Silvero
With caressing hands, at Limoges
Who walked all night in the next room;

By Hakagawa, bowing among the Titians;
By Madame de Tornquist, in the dark room
Shifting the candles; Fräulein von Kulp
Who turned in the hall, one hand on the door.

Vacant shuttles
Weave the wind. I have no ghosts,
An old man in a draughty house
Under a windy knob.

After such knowledge, what forgiveness? Think now
History has many cunning passages, contrived corridors
And issues, deceives with whispering ambitions,
Guides us by vanities. Think now
She gives when our attention is distracted
And what she gives, gives with such supple confusions
That the giving famishes the craving. Gives too late
What's not believed in, or if still believed,
In memory only, reconsidered passion. Gives too soon
Into weak hands, what's thought can be dispensed with
Till the refusal propagates a fear. Think
Neither fear nor courage saves us. Unnatural vices
Are fathered by our heroism. Virtues
Are forced upon us by our impudent crimes.
These tears are shaken from the wrath-bearing tree.

The tiger springs in the new year. Us he devours. Think at
          last
We have not reached conclusion, when I
Stiffen in a rented house. Think at last
I have not made this show purposelessly
And it is not by any concitation
Of the backward devils.
I would meet you upon this honestly.
I that was near your heart was removed therefrom
To lose beauty in terror, terror in inquisition.
I have lost my passion: why should I need to keep it
Since what is kept must be adulterated?
I have lost my sight, smell, hearing, taste and touch:
How should I use them for your closer contact?

These with a thousand small deliberations
Protract the profit of their chilled delirium,

Excite the membrane, when the sense has cooled,
With pungent sauces, multiply variety
In a wilderness of mirrors. What will the spider do,
Suspend its operations, will the weevil
Delay? De Bailhache, Fresca, Mrs. Cammel, whirled
Beyond the circuit of the shuddering Bear
In fractured atoms. Gull against the wind, in the windy straits
Of Belle Isle, or running on the Horn,
White feathers in the snow, the Gulf claims,
And an old man driven by the Trades
To a sleepy corner.

                              Tenants of the house,
Thoughts of a dry brain in a dry season.

SWEENEY AMONG THE NIGHTINGALES

ὤμοι, πέπληγμαι καιρίαν πληγὴν ἔσω.

Apeneck Sweeney spreads his knees
Letting his arms hang down to laugh,
The zebra stripes along his jaw
Swelling to masculate giraffe.

The circles of the stormy moon
Slide westward toward the River Plate,
Death and the Raven drift above
And Sweeney guards the hornèd gate.

Gloomy Orion and the Dog
Are veiled; and hushed the shrunken seas;
The person in the Spanish cape
Tries to sit on Sweeney's knees

Slips and pulls the table cloth
Overturns a coffee-cup,

Reorganized upon the floor
She yawns and draws a stocking up;

The silent man in mocha brown
Sprawls at the window-sill and gapes;
The waiter brings in oranges
Bananas figs and hothouse grapes;

The silent vertebrate in brown
Contracts and concentrates, withdraws;
Rachel *née* Rabinovitch
Tears at the grapes with murderous paws;

She and the lady in the cape
Are suspect, thought to be in league;
Therefore the man with heavy eyes
Declines the gambit, shows fatigue,

Leaves the room and reappears
Outside the window, leaning in,
Branches of wistaria
Circumscribe a golden grin;

The host with someone indistinct
Converses at the door apart,
The nightingales are singing near
The Convent of the Sacred Heart,

And sang within the bloody wood
When Agamemnon cried aloud,
And let their liquid siftings fall
To stain the stiff dishonoured shroud.

JOURNEY OF THE MAGI

'A cold coming we had of it,
Just the worst time of the year
For a journey, and such a long journey:
The ways deep and the weather sharp,
The very dead of winter.'
And the camels galled, sore-footed, refractory,
Lying down in the melting snow.
There were times we regretted
The summer palaces on slopes, the terraces,
And the silken girls bringing sherbet.
Then the camel men cursing and grumbling
And running away, and wanting their liquor and women,
And the night-fires going out, and the lack of shelters,
And the cities hostile and the towns unfriendly
And the villages dirty and charging high prices:
A hard time we had of it.
At the end we preferred to travel all night,
Sleeping in snatches,
With the voices singing in our ears, saying
That this was all folly.

Then at dawn we came down to a temperate valley,
Wet, below the snow line, smelling of vegetation;
With a running stream and a water-mill beating the darkness,
And three trees on the low sky,
And an old white horse galloped away in the meadow.
Then we came to a tavern with vine-leaves over the lintel,
Six hands at an open door dicing for pieces of silver,
And feet kicking the empty wine-skins.
But there was no information, and so we continued
And arrived at evening, not a moment too soon
Finding the place; it was (you may say) satisfactory.

All this was a long time ago, I remember,
And I would do it again, but set down

This set down
This: were we led all that way for
Birth or Death? There was a Birth, certainly,
We had evidence and no doubt. I had seen birth and death,
But had thought they were different; this Birth was
Hard and bitter agony for us, like Death, our death.
We returned to our places, these Kingdoms,
But no longer at ease here, in the old dispensation,
With an alien people clutching their gods.
I should be glad of another death.

WHISPERS OF IMMORTALITY

Webster was much possessed by death
And saw the skull beneath the skin;
And breathless creatures under ground
Leaned backward with a lipless grin.

Daffodil bulbs instead of balls
Stared from the sockets of the eyes!
He knew that thought clings round dead limbs
Tightening its lusts and luxuries.

Donne, I suppose, was such another
Who found no substitute for sense,
To seize and clutch and penetrate;
Expert beyond experience,

He knew the anguish of the marrow
The ague of the skeleton;
No contact possible to flesh
Allayed the fever of the bone.

. . . . . .

Grishkin is nice: her Russian eye
Is underlined for emphasis;
Uncorseted, her friendly bust
Gives promise of pneumatic bliss.

The couched Brazilian jaguar
Compels the scampering marmoset
With subtle effluence of cat;
Grishkin has a maisonette;

The sleek Brazilian jaguar
Does not in its arboreal gloom
Distil so rank a feline smell
As Grishkin in a drawing-room.

And even the Abstract Entities
Circumambulate her charm;
But our lot crawls between dry ribs
To keep our metaphysics warm.

THE WASTE LAND

1922

*"Nam Sibyllam quidem Cumis ego ipse oculis meis vidi
in ampulla pendere, et cum illi pueri dicerent: Σίβυλλα
τί θέλεις; respondebat illa: ἀποθανεῖν θέλω."*

For Ezra Pound
il miglior fabbro.

I

THE BURIAL OF THE DEAD

April is the cruellest month, breeding
Lilacs out of the dead land, mixing
Memory and desire, stirring
Dull roots with spring rain.
Winter kept us warm, covering
Earth in forgetful snow, feeding
A little life with dried tubers.
Summer surprised us, coming over the Starnbergersee
With a shower of rain; we stopped in the colonnade,
And went on in sunlight, into the Hofgarten,   10

And drank coffee, and talked for an hour.
Bin gar keine Russin, stamm' aus Litauen, echt deutsch.
And when we were children, staying at the archduke's,
My cousin's, he took me out on a sled,
And I was frightened. He said, Marie,
Marie, hold on tight. And down we went.
In the mountains, there you feel free.
I read, much of the night, and go south in the winter.

What are the roots that clutch, what branches grow
Out of this stony rubbish? Son of man,   20
You cannot say, or guess, for you know only
A heap of broken images, where the sun beats,
And the dead tree gives no shelter, the cricket no relief,
And the dry stone no sound of water. Only
There is shadow under this red rock,
(Come in under the shadow of this red rock),
And I will show you something different from either
Your shadow at morning striding behind you
Or your shadow at evening rising to meet you;
I will show you fear in a handful of dust.   30

            Frisch weht der Wind
            Der Heimat zu
            Mein Irisch Kind,
            Wo weilest du?
"You gave me hyacinths first a year ago;
"They called me the hyacinth girl."
—Yet when we came back, late, from the Hyacinth garden,
Your arms full, and your hair wet, I could not
Speak, and my eyes failed, I was neither
Living nor dead, and I knew nothing,   40
Looking into the heart of light, the silence.
Oed' und leer das Meer.

Madame Sosostris, famous clairvoyante,
Had a bad cold, nevertheless
Is known to be the wisest woman in Europe,
With a wicked pack of cards. Here, said she,

Is your card, the drowned Phoenician Sailor,
(Those are pearls that were his eyes. Look!)
Here is Belladonna, the Lady of the Rocks,
The lady of situations.   50
Here is the man with three staves, and here the Wheel,
And here is the one-eyed merchant, and this card,
Which is blank, is something he carries on his back,
Which I am forbidden to see. I do not find
The Hanged Man. Fear death by water.
I see crowds of people, walking around in a ring.
Thank you. If you see dear Mrs. Equitone,
Tell her I bring the horoscope myself:
One must be so careful these days.

  Unreal City,   60
Under the brown fog of a winter dawn,
A crowd flowed over London Bridge, so many,
I had not thought death had undone so many.
Sighs, short and infrequent, were exhaled,
And each man fixed his eyes before his feet.
Flowed up the hill and down King William Street,
To where Saint Mary Woolnoth kept the hours
With a dead sound on the final stroke of nine.
There I saw one I knew, and stopped him, crying: "Stetson!
"You who were with me in the ships at Mylae!   70
"That corpse you planted last year in your garden,
"Has it begun to sprout? Will it bloom this year?
"Or has the sudden frost disturbed its bed?
"Oh keep the Dog far hence, that's friend to men,
"Or with his nails he'll dig it up again!
"You! hypocrite lecteur!—mon semblable,—mon frère!"

II

A GAME OF CHESS

The Chair she sat in, like a burnished throne,
Glowed on the marble, where the glass
Held up by standards wrought with fruited vines

From which a golden Cupidon peeped out 80
(Another hid his eyes behind his wing)
Doubled the flames of sevenbranched candelabra
Reflecting light upon the table as
The glitter of her jewels rose to meet it,
From satin cases poured in rich profusion;
In vials of ivory and coloured glass
Unstoppered, lurked her strange synthetic perfumes,
Unguent, powdered, or liquid—troubled, confused
And drowned the sense in odours; stirred by the air
That freshened from the window, these ascended 90
In fattening the prolonged candle-flames,
Flung their smoke into the laquearia,
Stirring the pattern on the coffered ceiling.
Huge sea-wood fed with copper
Burned green and orange, framed by the coloured stone,
In which sad light a carvèd dolphin swam.
Above the antique mantel was displayed
As though a window gave upon the sylvan scene
The change of Philomel, by the barbarous king
So rudely forced; yet there the nightingale 100
Filled all the desert with inviolable voice
And still she cried, and still the world pursues,
"Jug Jug" to dirty ears.
And other withered stumps of time
Were told upon the walls; staring forms
Leaned out, leaning, hushing the room enclosed.
Footsteps shuffled on the stair.
Under the firelight, under the brush, her hair
Spread out in fiery points
Glowed into words, then would be savagely still. 110

"My nerves are bad to-night. Yes, bad. Stay with me.
"Speak to me. Why do you never speak. Speak.
"What are you thinking of? What thinking? What?
"I never know what you are thinking. Think."

I think we are in rats' alley
Where the dead men lost their bones.

"What is that noise?"
> The wind under the door.
"What is that noise now? What is the wind doing?"
> Nothing again nothing.   120

> > "Do
"You know nothing? Do you see nothing? Do you remember
"Nothing?"

> I remember
Those are pearls that were his eyes.
"Are you alive, or not? Is there nothing in your head?"

> > But

O O O O that Shakespeherian Rag—
It's so elegant
So intelligent   130
"What shall I do now? What shall I do?"
"I shall rush out as I am, and walk the street
"With my hair down, so. What shall we do to-morrow?
"What shall we ever do?"
> The hot water at ten.
And if it rains, a closed car at four.
And we shall play a game of chess,
Pressing lidless eyes and waiting for a knock upon the door.

> When Lil's husband got demobbed, I said—
I didn't mince my words, I said to her myself,   140
HURRY UP PLEASE ITS TIME
Now Albert's coming back, make yourself a bit smart.
He'll want to know what you done with that money he gave
> you
To get yourself some teeth. He did, I was there.
You have them all out, Lil, and get a nice set,
He said, I swear, I can't bear to look at you.
And no more can't I, I said, and think of poor Albert,
He's been in the army four years, he wants a good time,
And if you don't give it him, there's others will, I said.
Oh is there, she said. Something o' that, I said.   150
Then I'll know who to thank, she said, and give me a
> straight look.

HURRY UP PLEASE ITS TIME
If you don't like it you can get on with it, I said.
Others can pick and choose if you can't.
But if Albert makes off, it won't be for lack of telling.
You ought to be ashamed, I said, to look so antique.
(And her only thirty-one.)
I can't help it, she said, pulling a long face,
It's them pills I took, to bring it off, she said.
(She's had five already, and nearly died of young George.) 160
The chemist said it would be all right, but I've never been
    the same.
You are a proper fool, I said.
Well, if Albert won't leave you alone, there it is, I said,
What you get married for if you don't want children?
HURRY UP PLEASE ITS TIME
Well, that Sunday Albert was home, they had a hot gammon,
And they asked me in to dinner, to get the beauty of it hot—
HURRY UP PLEASE ITS TIME
HURRY UP PLEASE ITS TIME
Goonight Bill. Goonight Lou. Goonight May. Goonight. 170
Ta ta. Goonight. Goonight.
Good night, ladies, good night, sweet ladies, good night,
    good night.

III

THE FIRE SERMON

The river's tent is broken: the last fingers of leaf
Clutch and sink into the wet bank. The wind
Crosses the brown land, unheard. The nymphs are departed.
Sweet Thames, run softly, till I end my song.
The river bears no empty bottles, sandwich papers,
Silk handkerchiefs, cardboard boxes, cigarette ends
Or other testimony of summer nights. The nymphs are de-
    parted.
And their friends, the loitering heirs of city directors; 180
Departed, have left no addresses.
By the waters of Leman I sat down and wept . . .

Sweet Thames, run softly till I end my song,
Sweet Thames, run softly, for I speak not loud or long.
But at my back in a cold blast I hear
The rattle of the bones, and chuckle spread from ear to ear.
A rat crept softly through the vegetation
Dragging its slimy belly on the bank
While I was fishing in the dull canal
On a winter evening round behind the gashouse   190'
Musing upon the king my brother's wreck
And on the king my father's death before him.
White bodies naked on the low damp ground
And bones cast in a little low dry garret,
Rattled by the rat's foot only, year to year.
But at my back from time to time I hear
The sound of horns and motors, which shall bring
Sweeney to Mrs. Porter in the spring.
O the moon shone bright on Mrs. Porter
And on her daughter   200
They wash their feet in soda water
Et O ces voix d'enfants, chantant dans la coupole!

    Twit twit twit
Jug jug jug jug jug jug
So rudely forc'd.
Tereu

    Unreal City
Under the brown fog of a winter noon
Mr. Eugenides, the Smyrna merchant
Unshaven, with a pocket full of currants   210
C.i.f. London: documents at sight,
Asked me in demotic French
To luncheon at the Cannon Street Hotel
Followed by a weekend at the Metropole.

    At the violet hour, when the eyes and back
Turn upward from the desk, when the human engine waits
Like a taxi throbbing waiting,

I Tiresias, though blind, throbbing between two lives,
Old man with wrinkled female breasts, can see
At the violet hour, the evening hour that strives   220
Homeward, and brings the sailor home from sea,
The typist home at teatime, clears her breakfast, lights
Her stove, and lays out food in tins.
Out of the window perilously spread
Her drying combinations touched by the sun's last rays,
On the divan are piled (at night her bed)
Stockings, slippers, camisoles, and stays.
I Tiresias, old man with wrinkled dugs
Perceived the scene, and foretold the rest—
I too awaited the expected guest.   230
He, the young man carbuncular, arrives,
A small house agent's clerk, with one bold stare,
One of the low on whom assurance sits
As a silk hat on a Bradford millionaire.
The time is now propitious, as he guesses,
The meal is ended, she is bored and tired,
Endeavours to engage her in caresses
Which still are unreproved, if undesired.
Flushed and decided, he assaults at once;
Exploring hands encounter no defence;   240
His vanity requires no response,
And makes a welcome of indifference.
(And I Tiresias have foresuffered all
Enacted on this same divan or bed;
I who have sat by Thebes below the wall
And walked among the lowest of the dead.)
Bestows one final patronising kiss,
And gropes his way, finding the stairs unlit . . .

She turns and looks a moment in the glass,
Hardly aware of her departed lover;   250
Her brain allows one half-formed thought to pass:
"Well now that's done: and I'm glad it's over."
When lovely woman stoops to folly and
Paces about her room again, alone,

She smoothes her hair with automatic hand,
And puts a record on the gramophone.

"This music crept by me upon the waters"
And along the Strand, up Queen Victoria Street.
O City city, I can sometimes hear
Beside a public bar in Lower Thames Street,   260
The pleasant whining of a mandoline
And a clatter and a chatter from within
Where fishmen lounge at noon: where the walls
Of Magnus Martyr hold
Inexplicable splendour of Ionian white and gold.

        The river sweats
        Oil and tar
        The barges drift
        With the turning tide
        Red sails   270
        Wide
        To leeward, swing on the heavy spar.
        The barges wash
        Drifting logs
        Down Greenwich reach
        Past the Isle of Dogs.
                Weialala leia
                Wallala leialala

        Elizabeth and Leicester
        Beating oars   280
        The stern was formed
        A gilded shell
        Red and gold
        The brisk swell
        Rippled both shores
        Southwest wind
        Carried down stream
        The peal of bells
        White towers

Weialala leia   290
Wallala leialala

"Trams and dusty trees.
Highbury bore me. Richmond and Kew
Undid me. By Richmond I raised my knees
Supine on the floor of a narrow canoe."

"My feet are at Moorgate, and my heart
Under my feet. After the event
He wept. He promised 'a new start.'
I made no comment. What should I resent?"

"On Margate Sands.   300
I can connect
Nothing with nothing.
The broken fingernails of dirty hands.
My people humble people who expect
Nothing."
                    la la

To Carthage then I came

Burning burning burning burning
O Lord Thou pluckest me out
O Lord Thou pluckest   310

burning

IV

DEATH BY WATER

Phlebas the Phoenician, a fortnight dead,
Forgot the cry of gulls, and the deep sea swell
And the profit and loss.
                    A current under sea
Picked his bones in whispers. As he rose and fell

He passed the stages of his age and youth
Entering the whirlpool.
                    Gentile or Jew
O you who turn the wheel and look to windward,   319
Consider Phlebas, who was once handsome and tall as you.

                              v

                    WHAT THE THUNDER SAID

After the torchlight red on sweaty faces
After the frosty silence in the gardens
After the agony in stony places
The shouting and the crying
Prison and palace and reverberation
Of thunder of spring over distant mountains
He who was living is now dead
We who were living are now dying
With a little patience   330

    Here is no water but only rock
Rock and no water and the sandy road
The road winding above among the mountains
Which are mountains of rock without water
If there were water we should stop and drink
Amongst the rock one cannot stop or think
Sweat is dry and feet are in the sand
If there were only water amongst the rock
Dead mountain mouth of carious teeth that cannot spit
Here one can neither stand nor lie nor sit   340
There is not even silence in the mountains
But dry sterile thunder without rain
There is not even solitude in the mountains
But red sullen faces sneer and snarl
From doors of mudcracked houses
                              If there were water

And no rock
If there were rock
And also water
And water   350
A spring
A pool among the rock
If there were the sound of water only
Not the cicada
And dry grass singing
But sound of water over a rock
Where the hermit-thrush sings in the pine trees
Drip drop drip drop drop drop drop
But there is no water

Who is the third who walks always beside you?
When I count, there are only you and I together   360
But when I look ahead up the white road
There is always another one walking beside you
Gliding wrapt in a brown mantle, hooded
I do not know whether a man or a woman
—But who is that on the other side of you?

What is that sound high in the air
Murmur of maternal lamentation
Who are those hooded hordes swarming
Over endless plains, stumbling in cracked earth
Ringed by the flat horizon only   370
What is the city over the mountains
Cracks and reforms and bursts in the violet air
Falling towers
Jerusalem Athens Alexandria
Vienna London
Unreal

A woman drew her long black hair out tight
And fiddled whisper music on those strings
And bats with baby faces in the violet light
Whistled, and beat their wings   380

And crawled head downward down a blackened wall
And upside down in air were towers
Tolling reminiscent bells, that kept the hours
And voices singing out of empty cisterns and exhausted wells.

In this decayed hole among the mountains
In the faint moonlight, the grass is singing
Over the tumbled graves, about the chapel
There is the empty chapel, only the wind's home.
It has no windows, and the door swings,
Dry bones can harm no one.   390
Only a cock stood on the rooftree
Co co rico co co rico
In a flash of lightning. Then a damp gust
Bringing rain

Ganga was sunken, and the limp leaves
Waited for rain, while the black clouds
Gathered far distant, over Himavant.
The jungle crouched, humped in silence.
Then spoke the thunder
DA   400
Datta: what have we given?
My friend, blood shaking my heart
The awful daring of a moment's surrender
Which an age of prudence can never retract
By this, and this only, we have existed
Which is not to be found in our obituaries
Or in memories draped by the beneficent spider
Or under seals broken by the lean solicitor
In our empty rooms
DA   410
Dayadhvam: I have heard the key
Turn in the door once and turn once only
We think of the key, each in his prison
Thinking of the key, each confirms a prison
Only at nightfall, aethereal rumours
Revive for a moment a broken Coriolanus

D A
Damyata: The boat responded
Gaily, to the hand expert with sail and oar
The sea was calm, your heart would have responded 420
Gaily, when invited, beating obedient
To controlling hands

I sat upon the shore
Fishing, with the arid plain behind me
Shall I at least set my lands in order?
London Bridge is falling down falling down falling down
Poi s'ascose nel foco che gli affina
Quando fiam uti chelidon—O swallow swallow
Le Prince d'Aquitaine à la tour abolie
These fragments I have shored against my ruins 430
Why then Ile fit you. Hieronymo's mad againe.
Datta. Dayadhvam. Damyata.
Shantih   shantih   shantih

EAST COKER

I

In my beginning is my end. In succession
Houses rise and fall, crumble, are extended,
Are removed, destroyed, restored, or in their place
Is an open field, or a factory, or a by-pass.
Old stone to new building, old timber to new fires,
Old fires to ashes, and ashes to the earth
Which is already flesh, fur and faeces,
Bone of man and beast, cornstalk and leaf.
Houses live and die: there is a time for building
And a time for living and for generation
And a time for the wind to break the loosened pane
And to shake the wainscot where the field-mouse trots
And to shake the tattered arras woven with a silent motto.

In my beginning is my end. Now the light falls
Across the open field, leaving the deep lane

Shuttered with branches, dark in the afternoon,
Where you lean against a bank while a van passes,
And the deep lane insists on the direction
Into the village, in the electric heat
Hypnotised. In a warm haze the sultry light
Is absorbed, not refracted, by grey stone.
The dahlias sleep in the empty silence.
Wait for the early owl.

In that open field

If you do not come too close, if you do not come too close,
On a Summer midnight, you can hear the music
Of the weak pipe and the little drum
And see them dancing around the bonfire
The association of man and woman
In daunsinge, signifying matrimonie—
A dignified and commodious sacrament.
Two and two, necessarye coniunction,
Holding eche other by the hand or the arm
Whiche betokeneth concorde. Round and round the fire
Leaping through the flames, or joined in circles,
Rustically solemn or in rustic laughter
Lifting heavy feet in clumsy shoes,
Earth feet, loam feet, lifted in country mirth
Mirth of those long since under earth
Nourishing the corn. Keeping time,
Keeping the rhythm in their dancing
As in their living in the living seasons
The time of the seasons and the constellations
The time of milking and the time of harvest
The time of the coupling of man and woman
And that of beasts. Feet rising and falling.
Eating and drinking. Dung and death.

Dawn points, and another day
Prepares for heat and silence. Out at sea the dawn wind
Wrinkles and slides. I am here
Or there, or elsewhere. In my beginning.

II

What is the late November doing
With the disturbance of the spring
And creatures of the summer heat,
And snowdrops writhing under feet
And hollyhocks that aim too high
Red into grey and tumble down
Late roses filled with early snow?
Thunder rolled by the rolling stars
Simulates triumphal cars
Deployed in constellated wars
Scorpion fights against the Sun
Until the Sun and Moon go down
Comets weep and Leonids fly
Hunt the heavens and the plains
Whirled in a vortex that shall bring
The world to that destructive fire
Which burns before the ice-cap reigns.

    That was a way of putting it—not very satisfactory:
A periphrastic study in a worn-out poetical fashion,
Leaving one still with the intolerable wrestle
With words and meanings. The poetry does not matter.
It was not (to start again) what one had expected.
What was to be the value of the long looked forward to,
Long hoped for calm, the autumnal serenity
And the wisdom of age? Had they deceived us
Or deceived themselves, the quiet-voiced elders,
Bequeathing us merely a receipt for deceit?
The serenity only a deliberate hebetude,
The wisdom only the knowledge of dead secrets
Useless in the darkness into which they peered
Or from which they turned their eyes. There is, it seems to us,
At best, only a limited value
In the knowledge derived from experience.
The knowledge imposes a pattern, and falsifies,

For the pattern is new in every moment
And every moment is a new and shocking
Valuation of all we have been. We are only undeceived
Of that which, deceiving, could no longer harm.
In the middle, not only in the middle of the way
But all the way, in a dark wood, in a bramble,
On the edge of a grimpen, where is no secure foothold,
And menaced by monsters, fancy lights,
Risking enchantment. Do not let me hear
Of the wisdom of old men, but rather of their folly,
Their fear of fear and frenzy, their fear of possession,
Of belonging to another, or to others, or to God.
The only wisdom we can hope to acquire
Is the wisdom of humility: humility is endless.

The houses are all gone under the sea.

The dancers are all gone under the hill.

III

O dark dark dark. They all go into the dark,
The vacant interstellar spaces, the vacant into the vacant,
The captains, merchant bankers, eminent men of letters,
The generous patrons of art, the statesmen and the rulers,
Distinguished civil servants, chairmen of many committees,
Industrial lords and petty contractors, all go into the dark,
And dark the Sun and Moon, and the Almanach de Gotha
And the Stock Exchange Gazette, the Directory of Directors,
And cold the sense and lost the motive of action.
And we all go with them, into the silent funeral,
Nobody's funeral, for there is no one to bury.
I said to my soul, be still, and let the dark come upon you
Which shall be the darkness of God.   As, in a theatre,
The lights are extinguished, for the scene to be changed
With a hollow rumble of wings, with a movement of darkness
     on darkness,

And we know that the hills and the trees, the distant panorama
And the bold imposing facade are all being rolled away—
Or as, when an underground train, in the tube, stops too long
    between stations
And the conversation rises and slowly fades into silence
And you see behind every face the mental emptiness deepen
Leaving only the growing terror of nothing to think about;
Or when, under ether, the mind is conscious but conscious of
    nothing—
I said to my soul, be still, and wait without hope
For hope would be hope for the wrong thing; wait without
    love
For love would be love of the wrong thing; there is yet faith
But the faith and the love and the hope are all in the waiting.
Wait without thought, for you are not ready for thought:
So the darkness shall be the light, and the stillness the
    dancing.

    Whisper of running streams, and winter lightning.
The wild thyme unseen and the wild strawberry,
The laughter in the garden, echoed ecstasy
Not lost, but requiring, pointing to the agony
Of death and birth.
              You say I am repeating
Something I have said before. I shall say it again.
Shall I say it again? In order to arrive there,
To arrive where you are, to get from where you are not,
    You must go by a way wherein there is no ecstasy.
In order to arrive at what you do not know
    You must go by a way which is the way or ignorance.
In order to possess what you do not possess
    You must go by the way of dispossession.
In order to arrive at what you are not
    You must go through the way in which you are not.
And what you do not know is the only thing you know
And what you own is what you do not own
And where you are is where you are not.

IV

The wounded surgeon plies the steel
That questions the distempered part;
Beneath the bleeding hands we feel
The sharp compassion of the healer's art
Resolving the enigma of the fever chart.

Our only health is the disease
If we obey the dying nurse
Whose constant care is not to please
But to remind of our, and Adam's curse,
And that, to be restored, our sickness must grow worse.

The whole earth is our hospital
Endowed by the ruined millionaire,
Wherein, if we do well, we shall
Die of the absolute paternal care
That will not leave us, but prevents us everywhere.

The chill ascends from feet to knees,
The fever sings in mental wires.
If to be warmed, then I must freeze
And quake in frigid purgatorial fires
Of which the flame is roses, and the smoke is briars.

The dripping blood our only drink,
The bloody flesh our only food:
In spite of which we like to think
That we are sound, substantial flesh and blood—
Again, in spite of that, we call this Friday good.

V

So here I am, in the middle way, having had twenty years—
Twenty years largely wasted, the years of *l'entre deux
    guerres*—
Trying to learn to use words, and every attempt
Is a wholly new start, and a different kind of failure

Because one has only learnt to get the better of words
For the thing one no longer has to say, or the way in which
One is no longer disposed to say it. And so each venture
Is a new beginning, a raid on the inarticulate
With shabby equipment always deteriorating
In the general mess of imprecision of feeling,
Undisciplined squads of emotion. And what there is to conquer
By strength and submission, has already been discovered
Once or twice, or several times, by men whom one cannot hope
To emulate—but there is no competition—
There is only the fight to recover what has been lost
And found and lost again and again: and now, under conditions
That seem unpropitious. But perhaps neither gain nor loss.
For us, there is only the trying. The rest is not our business.

    Home is where one starts from. As we grow older
The world becomes stranger, the pattern more complicated
Of dead and living. Not the intense moment
Isolated, with no before and after,
But a lifetime burning in every moment
And not the lifetime of one man only
But of old stones that cannot be deciphered.
There is a time for the evening under starlight,
A time for the evening under lamplight
(The evening with the photograph album).
Love is most nearly itself
When here and now cease to matter.
Old men ought to be explorers
Here and there does not matter
We must be still and still moving
Into another intensity
For a further union, a deeper communion
Through the dark cold and the empty desolation,
The wave cry, the wind cry, the vast waters
Of the petrel and the porpoise.   In my end is my beginning.

Ralph Waldo Emerson

CONCORD HYMN

Sung at the completion of the Battle Monument, July 4, 1837

By the rude bridge that arched the flood,
    Their flag to April's breeze unfurled,
Here once the embattled farmers stood
    And fired the shot heard round the world.

The foe long since in silence slept;
    Alike the conqueror silent sleeps;
And Time the ruined bridge has swept
    Down the dark stream which seaward creeps.

On this green bank, by this soft stream,
    We set to-day a votive stone;
That memory may their deed redeem,
    When, like our sires, our sons are gone.

Spirit, that made those heroes dare
    To die, and leave their children free,
Bid Time and Nature gently spare
    The shaft we raise to them and thee.

EACH AND ALL

Little thinks, in the field, yon red-cloaked clown
Of thee from the hill-top looking down;
The heifer that lows in the upland farm,
Far-heard, lows not thine ear to charm;
The sexton, tolling his bell at noon,
Deems not that great Napoleon
Stops his horse, and lists with delight,
Whilst his files sweep round yon Alpine height;

Nor knowest thou what argument
Thy life to thy neighbor's creed has lent.
All are needed by each one;
Nothing is fair or good alone.
I thought the sparrow's note from heaven,
Singing at dawn on the alder bough;
I brought him home, in his nest, at even;
He sings the song, but it cheers not now,
For I did not bring home the river and sky;—
He sang to my ear,—they sang to my eye.
The delicate shells lay on the shore;
The bubbles of the latest wave
Fresh pearls to their enamel gave,
And the bellowing of the savage sea
Greeted their safe escape to me.
I wiped away the weeds and foam,
I fetched my sea-born treasures home;
But the poor, unsightly, noisome things
Had left their beauty on the shore
With the sun and the sand and the wild uproar.
The lover watched his graceful maid,
As 'mid the virgin train she strayed,
Nor knew her beauty's best attire
Was woven still by the snow-white choir.
At last she came to his hermitage,
Like the bird from the woodlands to the cage;—
The gay enchantment was undone,
A gentle wife, but fairy none.
Then I said, 'I covet truth;
Beauty is unripe childhood's cheat;
I leave it behind with the games of youth:'—
As I spoke, beneath my feet
The ground-pine curled its pretty wreath,
Running over the club-moss burrs;
I inhaled the violet's breath;
Around me stood the oaks and firs;
Pine-cones and acorns lay on the ground;
Over me soared the eternal sky,

Full of light and of deity;
Again I say, again I heard,
The rolling river, the morning bird;—
Beauty through my senses stole;
I yielded myself to the perfect whole.

THE PROBLEM

I like a church; I like a cowl;
I love a prophet of the soul;
And on my heart monastic aisles
Fall like sweet strains, or pensive smiles;
Yet not for all his faith can see
Would I that cowlèd churchman be.

Why should the vest on him allure,
Which I could not on me endure?

Not from a vain or shallow thought
His awful Jove young Phidias brought;
Never from lips of cunning fell
The thrilling Delphic oracle;
Out from the heart of nature rolled
The burdens of the Bible old;
The litanies of nations came,
Like the volcano's tongue of flame
Up from the burning core below,—
The canticles of love and woe:
The hand that rounded Peters dome
And groined the aisles of Christian Rome
Wrought in a sad sincerity;
Himself from God he could not free;
He builded better than he knew;—
The conscious stone to beauty grew.

Know'st thou what wove yon woodbird's nest
Of leaves, and feathers from her breast?

Or how the fish outbuilt her shell,
Painting with morn each annual cell?
Or how the sacred pine-tree adds
To her old leaves new myriads?
Such and so grew these holy piles,
Whilst love and terror laid the tiles.
Earth proudly wears the Parthenon,
As the best gem upon her zone,
And Morning opes with haste her lids
To gaze upon the Pyramids;
O'er England's abbeys bends the sky,
As on its friends, with kindred eye;
For out of Thought's interior sphere
These wonders rose to upper air;
And Nature gladly gave them place,
Adopted them into her race,
And granted them an equal date
With Andes and with Ararat.

These temples grew as grows the grass;
Art might obey, but not surpass.
The passive Master lent his hand
To the vast soul that o'er him planned;
And the same power that reared the shrine
Bestrode the tribes that knelt within.
Ever the fiery Pentecost
Girds with one flame the countless host,
Trances the heart through chanting choirs,
And through the priest the mind inspires.
The word unto the prophet spoken
Was writ on tables yet unbroken;
The word by seers or sibyls told,
In groves of oak, or fanes of gold,
Still floats upon the morning wind,
Still whispers to the willing mind.
One accent of the Holy Ghost
The heedless world hath never lost.

I know what say the fathers wise,—
The Book itself before me lies,
Old *Chrysostom*, best Augustine,
And he who blent both in his line.
The younger *Golden Lips* or mines,
Taylor, the Shakspeare of divines.
His words are music in my ear.
I see his cowlèd portrait dear;
And yet, for all his faith could see,
I would not the good bishop be.

URIEL

It fell in the ancient periods
    Which the brooding soul surveys,
Or ever the wild Time coined itself
    Into calendar months and days.

This was the lapse of Uriel,
Which in Paradise befell.
Once, among the Pleiads walking,
Seyd overheard the young gods talking;
And the treason, too long pent,
To his ears was evident.
The young deities discussed
Laws of form, and metre just,
Orb, quintessence, and sunbeams,
What subsisteth, and what seems.
One, with low tones that decide,
And doubt and reverend use defied,
With a look that solved the sphere,
And stirred the devils everywhere,
Gave his sentiment divine
Against the being of a line.
'Line in nature is not found;
Unit and universe are round;
In vain produced, all rays return;

Evil will bless, and ice will burn.'
As Uriel spoke with piercing eye,
A shudder ran around the sky;
The stern old war-gods shook their heads,
The seraphs frowned from myrtle-beds;
Seemed to the holy festival
The rash word boded ill to all;
The balance-beam of Fate was bent;
The bounds of good and ill were rent;
Strong Hades could not keep his own,
But all slid to confusion.

A sad self-knowledge, withering, fell
On the beauty of Uriel;
In heaven once eminent, the god
Withdrew, that hour, into his cloud;
Whether doomed to long gyration
In the sea of generation,
Or by knowledge grown too bright
To hit the nerve of feebler sight.
Straightway, a forgetting wind
Stole over the celestial kind,
And their lips the secret kept,
If in ashes the fire-seed slept.
But now and then, truth-speaking things
Shamed the angels' veiling wings;
And, shrilling from the solar course,
Or from fruit of chemic force,
Procession of a soul in matter,
Or the speeding change of water,
Or out of the good of evil born,
Came Uriel's voice of cherub scorn,
And a blush tinged the upper sky,
And the gods shook, they knew not why.

WOODNOTES

When the pine tosses its cones
To the song of its waterfall tones,
Who speeds to the woodland walks?
To birds and trees who talks?
Cæsar of his leafy Rome,
There the poet is at home.
He goes to the river-side,—
Not hook nor line hath he;
He stands in the meadows wide,—
Nor gun nor scythe to see.
Sure some god his eye enchants:
What he knows nobody wants.
In the wood he travels glad,
Without better fortune had,
Melancholy without bad.

Knowledge this man prizes best
Seems fantastic to the rest:
Pondering shadows, colors, clouds,
Grass-buds and caterpillar-shrouds,
Boughs on which the wild bees settle,
Tints that spot the violet's petal,
Why Nature loves the number five,
And why the star-form she repeats:
Lover of all things alive,
Wonderer at all he meets,
Wonderer chiefly at himself,
Who can tell him what he is?
Or how meet in human elf
Coming and past eternities?

And such I knew, a forest seer,
A minstrel of the natural year,
Foreteller of the vernal ides,
Wise harbinger of spheres and tides,
A lover true, who knew by heart
Each joy the mountain dales impart;

It seemed that Nature could not raise
A plant in any secret place,
In quaking bog, on snowy hill,
Beneath the grass that shades the rill,
Under the snow, between the rocks,
In damp fields known to bird and fox.
But he would come in the very hour
It opened in its virgin bower,
As if a sunbeam showed the place,
And tell its long-descended race.

It seemed as if the breezes brought him,
It seemed as if the sparrows taught him;
As if by secret sight he knew
Where, in far fields, the orchis grew.
Many haps fall in the field
Seldom seen by wishful eyes,
But all her shows did Nature yield,
To please and win this pilgrim wise.
He saw the partridge drum in the woods;
He heard the woodcock's evening hymn;
He found the tawny thrushes' broods;
And the shy hawk did wait for him;
What others did at distance hear,
And guessed within the thicket's gloom,
Was shown to this philosopher,
And at his bidding seemed to come.

In unploughed Maine he sought the lumberers' gang
Where from a hundred lakes young rivers sprang;
He trode the unplanted forest floor, whereon
The all-seeing sun for ages hath not shone;
Where feeds the moose, and walks the surly bear,
And up the tall mast runs the woodpecker.
He saw beneath dim aisles, in odorous beds,
The slight Linnæa hang its twin-born heads,
And blessed the monument of the man of flowers,
Which breathes his sweet fame through the northern bowers.

He heard, when in the grove, at intervals,
With sudden roar the aged pine-tree falls,—
One crash, the death-hymn of the perfect tree,
Declares the close of its green century.
Low lies the plant to whose creation went
Sweet influence from every element;
Whose living towers the years conspired to build,
Whose giddy top the morning loved to gild.
Through these green tents, by eldest Nature dressed,
He roamed, content alike with man and beast.
Where darkness found him he lay glad at night;
There the red morning touched him with its light.
Three moons his great heart him a hermit made,
So long he roved at will the boundless shade.
The timid it concerns to ask their way,
And fear what foe in caves and swamps can stray,
To make no step until the event is known,
And ills to come as evils past bemoan.
Not so the wise; no coward watch he keeps
To spy what danger on his pathway creeps;
Go where he will, the wise man is at home,
His hearth the earth,—his hall the azure dome;
Where his clear spirit leads him, there's his road
By God's own light illumined and foreshowed.

'T was one of the charmèd days
When the genius of God doth flow;
The wind may alter twenty ways,
A tempest cannot blow;
It may blow north, it still is warm;
Or south, it still is clear;
Or east, it smells like a clover-farm;
Or west, no thunder fear.
The musing peasant, lowly great,
Beside the forest water sate;
The rope-like pine-roots crosswise grown
Composed the network of his throne;
The wide lake, edged with sand and grass,

Was burnished to a floor of glass,
Painted with shadows green and proud
Of the tree and of the cloud.
He was the heart of all the scene;
On him the sun looked more serene;
To hill and cloud his face was known,—
It seemed the likeness of their own;
They knew by secret sympathy
The public child of earth and sky.
'You ask,' he said, 'what guide
Me through trackless thickets led,
Through thick-stemmed woodlands rough and wide.
I found the water's bed.
The watercourses were my guide;
I travelled grateful by their side,
Or through their channel dry;
They led me through the thicket damp,
Through brake and fern, the beavers' camp,
Through beds of granite cut my road,
And their resistless friendship showed.
The falling waters led me,
The foodful waters fed me,
And brought me to the lowest land,
Unerring to the ocean sand.
The moss upon the forest bark
Was pole-star when the night was dark;
The purple berries in the wood
Supplied me necessary food;
For Nature ever faithful is
To such as trust her faithfulness.
When the forest shall mislead me,
When the night and morning lie,
When sea and land refuse to feed me,
'T will be time enough to die;
Then will yet my mother yield
A pillow in her greenest field,
Nor the June flowers scorn to cover
The clay of their departed lover.'

GIVE ALL TO LOVE

Give all to love;
Obey thy heart;
Friends, kindred, days,
Estate, good-fame,
Plans, credit, and the Muse,—
Nothing refuse.

'Tis a brave master;
Let it have scope:
Follow it utterly,
Hope beyond hope:
High and more high
It dives into noon,
With wing unspent,
Untold intent;
But it is a god,
Knows its own path,
And the outlets of the sky.

It was never for the mean;
It requireth courage stout,
Souls above doubt,
Valor unbending;
It will reward,—
They shall return
More than they were,
And ever ascending

Leave all for love;
Yet, hear me, yet,

One word more thy heart
    behoved,
One pulse more of firm
    endeavor,—
Keep thee to-day
To-morrow, forever,
Free as an Arab
Of thy beloved.

Cling with life to the maid;
But when the surprise,
First vague shadow of
    surmise
Flits across her bosom young
Of a joy apart from thee,
Free be she, fancy-free;
Nor thou detain her vesture's
    hem,
Nor the palest rose she flung
From her summer diadem.

Though thou loved her as
    thyself,
As a self of purer clay,
Though her parting dims
    the day,
Stealing grace from all alive;
Heartily know,
When half-gods go,
The gods arrive.

BRAHMA

If the red slayer think he slays,
  Or if the slain think he is slain,
They know not well the subtle ways
  I keep, and pass, and turn again.

Far or forgot to me is near;
  Shadow and sunlight are the same;
The vanquished gods to me appear;
  And one to me are shame and fame.

They reckon ill who leave me out;
  When me they fly, I am the wings;
I am the doubter and the doubt,
  And I the hymn the Brahmin sings.

The strong gods pine for my abode,
  And pine in vain the sacred Seven;
But thou, meek lover of the good!
  Find me, and turn thy back on heaven.

FABLE

The mountain and the
    squirrel
Had a quarrel,
And the former called the
    latter "Little Prig";
Bun replied,
"You are doubtless very big;
But all sorts of things and
    weather
Must be taken in together,
To make up a year
And a sphere.
And I think it no disgrace
To occupy my place.
If I'm not so large as you,
You are not so small as I,
And not half so spry.
I'll not deny you make
A very pretty squirrel track;
Talents differ; all is well and
    wisely put;
If I cannot carry forests on
    my back,
Neither can you crack a nut."

THE SNOW-STORM

Announced by all the trumpets of the sky,
Arrives the snow, and, driving o'er the fields,
Seems nowhere to alight: the whited air
Hides hills and woods, the river, and the heaven,
And veils the farm-house at the garden's end.
The sled and traveller stopped, the courier's feet
Delayed, all friends shut out, the housemates sit
Around the radiant fireplace, enclosed
In a tumultuous privacy of storm.

Come see the north wind's masonry.
Out of an unseen quarry evermore
Furnished with tile, the fierce artificer
Curves his white bastions with projected roof
Round every windward stake, or tree, or door.
Speeding, the myriad-handed, his wild work
So fanciful, so savage, nought cares he
For number or proportion. Mockingly,
On coop or kennel he hangs Parian wreaths;
A swan-like form invests the hidden thorn;
Fills up the farmer's lane from wall to wall,
Maugre the farmer's sighs; and at the gate
A tapering turret overtops the work.
And when his hours are numbered, and the world
Is all his own, retiring, as he were not,
Leaves, when the sun appears, astonished Art
To mimic in slow structures, stone by stone,
Built in an age, the mad wind's night-work,
The frolic architecture of the snow.

Anthony Euwer

MY FACE

As a beauty I am not a great star,
There are others more handsome, by far,
    But my face—I don't mind it
    For I am behind it,—
It's the people in front get the jar!

John Gould Fletcher

FROM "IRRADIATIONS"

I

Over the roof-tops race the shadows of clouds;
Like horses the shadows of clouds charge down the street.

Whirlpools of purple and gold,
Winds from the mountains of cinnabar,
Lacquered mandarin moments, palanquins swaying and
    balancing
Amid vermilion pavilions, against the jade balustrades,
Glint of the glittering wings of dragon-flies in the light:
Silver filaments, golden flakes settling downwards,
Rippling, quivering flutters, repulse and surrender,
The sun broidered upon the rain,
The rain rustling with the sun.

Over the roof-tops race the shadows of clouds;
Like horses the shadows of clouds charge down the street.

II

Flickering of incessant rain
On flashing pavements:
Sudden scurry of umbrellas:
Bending, recurved blossoms of the storm.

The winds come clanging and clattering
From long white highroads whipping in ribbons up summits:
They strew upon the city gusty wafts of apple-blossom,
And the rustling of innumerable translucent leaves.

Uneven tinkling, the lazy rain
Dripping from the eaves.

III

The trees, like great jade elephants,
Chained, stamp and shake 'neath the gadflies of the breeze;
The trees lunge and plunge, unruly elephants:
The clouds are their crimson howdah-canopies,
The sunlight glints like the golden robe of a Shah.
Would I were tossed on the wrinkled backs of those trees.

IV

O seeded grass, you army of little men
Crawling up the long slope with quivering, quick blades of
    steel:
You who storm millions of graves, tiny green tentacles of
    Earth,
Interlace yourselves tightly over my heart,
And do not let me go:
For I would lie here forever and watch with one eye
The pilgrimaging ants in your dull, savage jungles,
The while with the other I see the stiff lines of the slope
Break in mid-air, a wave surprisingly arrested,—
And above them, wavering, dancing, bodiless, colorless,
    unreal,
The long thin lazy fingers of the heat.

v

The morning is clean and blue and the wind blows up the
    clouds:
Now my thoughts gathered from afar
Once again in their patched armor, with rusty plumes and
    blunted swords,
Move out to war.

Smoking our morning pipes we shall ride two and two
Through the woods,
For our old cause keeps us together,
And our hatred is so precious not death or defeat can break it.

God willing, we shall this day meet that old enemy
Who has given us so many a good beating.
Thank God we have a cause worth fighting for,
And a cause worth losing and a good song to sing.

Philip Freneau

THE INDIAN BURYING GROUND

In spite of all the learned have said,
    I still my old opinion keep;
The posture, that we give the dead,
    Points out the soul's eternal sleep.

Not so the ancients of these lands—
    The Indian, when from life released,
Again is seated with his friends,
    And shares again the joyous feast.

His imaged birds, and painted bowl,
    And venison, for a journey dressed,
Bespeak the nature of the soul,
    Activity, that knows no rest.

His bow, for action ready bent,
  And arrows, with a head of stone,
Can only mean that life is spent,
  And not the old ideas gone.

Thou, stranger, that shalt come this way,
  No fraud upon the dead commit—
Observe the swelling turf, and say
  They do not lie, but here they sit.

Here still a lofty rock remains,
  On which the curious eye may trace
(Now wasted, half, by wearing rains)
  The fancies of a ruder race.

Here still an aged elm aspires,
  Beneath whose far-projecting shade
(And which the shepherd still admires)
  The children of the forest played!

There oft a restless Indian queen
  (Pale Shebah, with her braided hair)
And many a barbarous form is seen
  To chide the man that lingers there.

By midnight moons, o'er moistening dews;
  In habit for the chase arrayed,
The hunter still the deer pursues,
  The hunter and the deer, a shade!

And long shall timorous fancy see
  The painted chief, and pointed spear,
And Reason's self shall bow the knee
  To shadows and delusions here.

Robert Frost

FIRE AND ICE

Some say the world will end in fire,
Some say in ice.
From what I've tasted of desire
I hold with those who favor fire.
But if it had to perish twice,
I think I know enough of hate
To say that for destruction ice
Is also great
And would suffice.

ACQUAINTED WITH THE NIGHT

I have been one acquainted with the night.
I have walked out in rain—and back in rain.
I have outwalked the further city light.

I have looked down the saddest city lane.
I have passed by the watchman on his beat
And dropped my eyes, unwilling to explain.

I have stood still and stopped the sound of feet
When far away an interrupted cry
Came over houses from another street,

But not to call me back or say good-bye;
And further still at an unearthly height,
One luminary clock against the sky

Proclaimed the time was neither wrong nor right
I have been one acquainted with the night.

THE HILL WIFE

The Impulse

It was too lonely for her there,
    And too wild,
And since there were but two of them,
    And no child,

And work was little in the house,
    She was free,
And followed where he furrowed field,
    Or felled tree.

She rested on a log and tossed
    The fresh chips,
With a song only to herself
    On her lips.

And once she went to break a bough
    Of black alder.
She strayed so far she scarcely heard
    When he called her—

And didn't answer—didn't speak—
    Or return.
She stood, and then she ran and hid
    In the fern.

He never found her, though he looked
    Everywhere,
And he asked at her mother's house
    Was she there.

Sudden and swift and light as that
    The ties gave,
And he learned of finalities
    Besides the grave.

TO EARTHWARD

Love at the lips was touch
As sweet as I could bear;
And once that seemed too
　much;
I lived on air

That crossed me from sweet
　things,
The flow of—was it musk
From hidden grapevine
　springs
Down hill at dusk?

I had the swirl and ache
From sprays of honeysuckle
That when they're gathered
　shake
Dew on the knuckle.

I craved strong sweets, but
　those
Seemed strong when I was
　young;

The petal of the rose
It was that stung.

Now no joy but lacks salt
That is not dashed with pain
And weariness and fault;
I crave the stain

Of tears, the aftermark
Of almost too much love,
The sweet of bitter bark
And burning clove.

When stiff and sore scarred
I take away my hand
From leaning on it hard
In grass and sand,

The hurt is not enough:
I long for weight and
　strength
To feel the earth as rough
To all my length.

ONCE BY THE PACIFIC

The shattered water made a misty din.
Great waves looked over others coming in,
And thought of doing something to the shore
That water never did to land before.
The clouds were low and hairy in the skies,
Like locks blown forward in the gleam of eyes.
You could not tell, and yet it looked as if
The shore was lucky in being backed by cliff,
The cliff in being backed by continent;
It looked as if a night of dark intent

Was coming, and not only a night, an age.
Someone had better be prepared for rage.
There would be more than ocean-water broken
Before God's last *Put out the Light* was spoken.

A BLUE RIBBON AT AMESBURY

Such a fine pullet ought to go
All coiffured to a winter show,
And be exhibited, and win.
The answer is this one has been—

And come with all her honors home.
Her golden leg, her coral comb,
Her fluff of plumage, white as chalk,
Her style, were all the fancy's talk.

It seems as if you must have heard.
She scored an almost perfect bird.
In her we make ourselves acquainted
With one a Sewell might have painted.

Here common with the flock again,
At home in her abiding pen,
She lingers feeding at the trough,
The last to let night drive her off.

The one who gave her ankle-band,
Her keeper, empty pail in hand,
He lingers too, averse to slight
His chores for all the wintry night.

He leans against the dusty wall,
Immured almost beyond recall,
A depth past many swinging doors
And many litter-muffled floors.

He meditates the breeder's art.
He has a half a mind to start,
With her for Mother Eve, a race
That shall all living things displace.

'Tis ritual with her to lay
The full six days, then rest a day;
At which rate barring broodiness
She well may score an egg-success.

The gatherer can always tell
Her well-turned egg's brown sturdy shell,
As safe a vehicle of seed
As is vouchsafed to feathered breed.

No human spectre at the feast
Can scant or hurry her the least.
She takes her time to take her fill.
She whets a sleepy sated bill.

She gropes across the pen alone
To peck herself a precious stone.
She waters at the patent fount.
And so to roost, the last to mount.

The roost is her extent of flight.
Yet once she rises to the height,
She shoulders with a wing so strong
She makes the whole flock move along.

The night is setting in to blow.
It scours the windowpane with snow,
But barely gets from them or her
For comment a complacent chirr.

The lowly pen is yet a hold
Against the dark and wind and cold
To give a prospect to a plan
And warrant prudence in a man.

TREE AT MY WINDOW

Tree at my window, window tree,
My sash is lowered when night comes on;
But let there never be curtain drawn
Between you and me.

Vague dream-head lifted out of the ground,
And thing next most diffuse to cloud,
Not all your light tongues talking aloud
Could be profound.

But tree, I have seen you taken and tossed,
And if you have seen me when I slept,
You have seen me when I was taken and swept
And all but lost.

That day she put our heads together,
Fate had her imagination about her,
Your head so much concerned with outer,
Mine with inner, weather.

TWO TRAMPS IN MUD TIME

Out of the mud two strangers came
And caught me splitting wood in the yard,
And one of them put me off my aim
By hailing cheerily 'Hit them hard!'
I knew pretty well why he dropped behind
And let the other go on a way.
I knew pretty well what he had in mind:
He wanted to take my job for pay.

Good blocks of beech it was I split,
As large around as the chopping block;
And every piece I squarely hit
Fell splinterless as a cloven rock.

The blows that a life of self-control
Spares to strike for the common good
That day, giving a loose to my soul,
I spent on the unimportant wood.

The sun was warm but the wind was chill.
You know how it is with an April day
When the sun is out and the wind is still,
You're one month on in the middle of May.
But if you so much as dare to speak,
A cloud comes over the sunlit arch,
A wind comes off a frozen peak,
And you're two months back in the middle of March.

A bluebird comes tenderly up to alight
And fronts the wind to unruffle a plume
His song so pitched as not to excite
A single flower as yet to bloom.
It is snowing a flake: and he half knew
Winter was only playing possum.
Except in color he isn't blue,
But he wouldn't advise a thing to blossom.

The water for which we may have to look
In summertime with a witching-wand,
In every wheelrut's now a brook,
In every print of a hoof a pond.
Be glad of water, but don't forget
The lurking frost in the earth beneath
That will steal forth after the sun is set
And show on the water its crystal teeth.

The time when most I loved my task
These two must make me love it more
By coming with what they came to ask.
You'd think I never had felt before
The weight of an ax-head poised aloft,
The grip on earth of outspread feet.

The life of muscles rocking soft
And smooth and moist in vernal heat.

Out of the woods two hulking tramps
(From sleeping God knows where last night,
But not long since in the lumber camps).
They thought all chopping was theirs of right.
Men of the woods and lumberjacks,
They judged me by their appropriate tool.
Except as a fellow handled an ax,
They had no way of knowing a fool.

Nothing on either side was said.
They knew they had but to stay their stay
And all their logic would fill my head:
As that I had no right to play
With what was another man's work for gain.
My right might be love but theirs was need.
And where the two exist in twain
Theirs was the better right—agreed.

But yield who will to their separation,
My object in living is to unite
My avocation and my vocation
As my two eyes make one in sight.
Only where love and need are one,
And the work is play for mortal stakes,
Is the deed ever really done
For Heaven and the future's sakes.

A RECORD STRIDE

In a Vermont bedroom closet
With a door of two broad boards
And for back wall a crumbling old chimney
(And that's what their toes are towards),

I have a pair of shoes standing,
Old rivals of sagging leather,
Who once kept surpassing each other,
But now live even together.

They listen for me in the bedroom
To ask me a thing or two
About who is too old to go walking,
With too much stress on the who.

I wet one last year at Montauk
For a hat I had to save.
The other I wet at the Cliff House
In an extra-vagant wave.

Two entirely different grandchildren
Got me into my double adventure.
But when they grow up and can read this
I hope they won't take it for censure.

I touch my tongue to the shoes now
And unless my sense is at fault,
On one I can taste Atlantic,
On the other Pacific, salt.

One foot in each great ocean
Is a record stride or stretch.
The authentic shoes it was made in
I should sell for what they would fetch.

But instead I proudly devote them
To my museum and muse;
So the thick-skins needn't act thin-skinned
About being past-active shoes.

And I ask all to try to forgive me
For being as over-elated
As if I had measured the country
And got the United States stated.

MENDING WALL

Something there is that doesn't love a wall,
That sends the frozen-ground-swell under it,
And spills the upper boulders in the sun;
And makes gaps even two can pass abreast.
The work of hunters is another thing:
I have come after them and made repair
Where they have left not one stone on a stone,
But they would have the rabbit out of hiding,
To please the yelping dogs. The gaps I mean,
No one has seen them made or heard them made,
But at spring mending-time we find them there.
I let my neighbour know beyond the hill;
And on a day we meet to walk the line
And set the wall between us once again.
We keep the wall between us as we go.
To each the boulders that have fallen to each.
And some are loaves and some so nearly balls
We have to use a spell to make them balance:
'Stay where you are until our backs are turned!'
We wear our fingers rough with handling them.
Oh, just another kind of out-door game,
One on a side. It comes to little more:
There where it is we do not need the wall:
He is all pine and I am apple orchard.
My apple trees will never get across
And eat the cones under his pines, I tell him.
He only says, 'Good fences make good neighbours.'
Spring is the mischief in me, and I wonder
If I could put a notion in his head:
'*Why* do they make good neighbours? Isn't it
Where there are cows? But here there are no cows.
Before I built a wall I'd ask to know
What I was walling in or walling out,
And to whom I was like to give offence.
Something there is that doesn't love a wall,
That wants it down.' I could say 'Elves' to him,

But it's not elves exactly, and I'd rather
He said it for himself. I see him there
Bringing a stone grasped firmly by the top
In each hand, like an old-stone savage armed.
He moves in darkness as it seems to me,
Not of woods only and the shade of trees.
He will not go behind his father's saying,
And he likes having thought of it so well
He says again, 'Good fences make good neighbours.'

THE ROAD NOT TAKEN

Two roads diverged in a yellow wood,
And sorry I could not travel both
And be one traveler, long I stood
And looked down one as far as I could
To where it bent in the undergrowth;

Then took the other, as just as fair,
And having perhaps the better claim,
Because it was grassy and wanted wear;
Though as for that the passing there
Had worn them really about the same,

And both that morning equally lay
In leaves no step had trodden black.
Oh, I kept the first for another day!
Yet knowing how way leads on to way,
I doubted if I should ever come back.

I shall be telling this with a sigh
Somewhere ages and ages hence:
Two roads diverged in a wood, and I—
I took the one less traveled by,
And that has made all the difference.

STOPPING BY WOODS ON A SNOWY EVENING

Whose woods these are I think I know.
His house is in the village though;
He will not see me stopping here
To watch his woods fill up with snow.

My little horse must think it queer
To stop without a farmhouse near
Between the woods and frozen lake
The darkest evening of the year.

He gives his harness bells a shake
To ask if there is some mistake.
The only other sound's the sweep
Of easy wind and downy flake.

The woods are lovely, dark and deep.
But I have promises to keep,
And miles to go before I sleep,
And miles to go before I sleep.

DIRECTIVE

Back out of all this now too much for us,
Back in a time made simple by the loss
Of detail, burned, dissolved, and broken off
Like graveyard marble sculpture in the weather,
There is a house that is no more a house
Upon a farm that is no more a farm
And in a town that is no more a town.
The road there, if you'll let a guide direct you
Who only has at heart your getting lost,
May seem as if it should have been a quarry—
Great monolithic knees the former town
Long since gave up pretence of keeping covered.
And there's a story in a book about it:

Besides the wear of iron wagon wheels
The ledges show lines ruled southeast northwest,
The chisel work of an enormous Glacier
That braced his feet against the Arctic Pole.
You must not mind a certain coolness from him
Still said to haunt this side of Panther Mountain.
Nor need you mind the serial ordeal
Of being watched from forty cellar holes
As if by eye pairs out of forty firkins.
As for the woods' excitement over you
That sends light rustle rushes to their leaves,
Charge that to upstart inexperience.
Where were they all not twenty years ago?
They think too much of having shaded out
A few old pecker-fretted apple trees.
Make yourself up a cheering song of how
Someone's road home from work this once was,
Who may be just ahead of you on foot
Or creaking with a buggy load of grain.
The height of the adventure is the height
Of country where two village cultures faded
Into each other. Both of them are lost.
And if you're lost enough to find yourself
By now, pull in your ladder road behind you
And put a sign up CLOSED to all but me.
Then make yourself at home. The only field
Now left's no bigger than a harness gall.
First there's the children's house of make believe,
Some shattered dishes underneath a pine,
The playthings in the playhouse of the children.
Weep for what little things could make them glad.
Then for the house that is no more a house,
But only a belilaced cellar hole,
Now slowly closing like a dent in dough.
This was no playhouse but a house in earnest.
Your destination and your destiny's
A brook that was the water of the house,
Cold as a spring as yet so near its source,

Too lofty and original to rage.
(We know the valley streams that when aroused
Will leave their tatters hung on barb and thorn.)
I have kept hidden in the instep arch
Of an old cedar at the waterside
A broken drinking goblet like the Grail
Under a spell so the wrong ones can't find it,
So can't get saved, as Saint Mark says they mustn't.
(I stole the goblet from the children's playhouse.)
Here are your waters and your watering place.
Drink and be whole again beyond confusion.

ALL REVELATION

A head thrusts in as for the view,
But where it is it thrusts in from
Or what it is it thrusts into
By that Cyb'laean avenue,
And what can of its coming come,

And whither it will be withdrawn,
And what take hence or leave behind,
These things the mind has pondered on
A moment and still asking gone.
Strange apparition of the mind!

But the impervious geode
Was entered, and its inner crust
Of crystals with a ray cathode
At every point and facet glowed
In answer to the mental thrust.

Eyes seeking the response of eyes
Bring out the stars, bring out the flowers,
Thus concentrating earth and skies
So none need be afraid of size.
All revelation has been ours.

THE SILKEN TENT

She is as in a field a silken tent
At midday when a sunny summer breeze
Has dried the dew and all its ropes relent,
So that in guys it gently sways at ease,
And its supporting central cedar pole,
That is its pinnacle to heavenward
And signifies the sureness of the soul,
Seems to owe naught to any single cord,
But strictly held by none, is loosely bound
By countless silken ties of love and thought
To everything on earth the compass round,
And only by one's going slightly taut
In the capriciousness of summer air
Is of the slightest bondage made aware.

ON LOOKING UP BY CHANCE AT THE CONSTELLATIONS

You'll wait a long, long time for anything much
To happen in heaven beyond the floats of cloud
And the Northern Lights that run like tingling nerves.
The sun and moon get crossed, but they never touch,
Nor strike out fire from each other, nor crash out loud.
The planets seem to interfere in their curves,
But nothing ever happens, no harm is done.
We may as well go patiently on with our life,
And look elsewhere than to stars and moon and sun
For the shocks and changes we need to keep us sane.
It is true the longest drouth will end in rain,
The longest peace in China will end in strife.
Still it wouldn't reward the watcher to stay awake
In hopes of seeing the calm of heaven break
On his particular time and personal sight.
That calm seems certainly safe to last tonight.

A SOLDIER

He is that fallen lance that lies as hurled,
That lies unlifted now, come dew, come rust,
But still lies pointed as it plowed the dust.
If we who sight along it round the world,
See nothing worthy to have been its mark,
It is because like men we look too near,
Forgetting that as fitted to the sphere,
Our missiles always make too short an arc.
They fall, they rip the grass, they intersect
The curve of earth, and striking, break their own;
They make us cringe for metal-point on stone.
But this we know, the obstacle that checked
And tripped the body, shot the spirit on
Further than target ever showed or shone.

THE MOST OF IT

He thought he kept the universe alone;
For all the voice in answer he could wake
Was but the mocking echo of his own
From some tree-hidden cliff across the lake.
Some morning from the boulder-broken beach
He would cry out on life, that what it wants
Is not its own love back in copy speech,
But counter-love, original response.
And nothing ever came of what he cried
Unless it was the embodiment that crashed
In the cliff's talus on the other side,
And then in the far distant water splashed,
But after a time allowed for it to swim,
Instead of proving human when it neared
And someone else additional to him,
As a great buck it powerfully appeared,
Pushing the crumpled water up ahead,
And landed pouring like a waterfall,
And stumbled through the rocks with horny tread,
And forced the underbrush—and that was all.

THE LESSON FOR TODAY

If this uncertain age in which we dwell
Were really as dark as I hear sages tell,
And I convinced that they were really sages,
I should not curse myself with it to hell,
But leaving not the chair I long have sat in,
I should betake me back ten thousand pages
To the world's undebatably dark ages,
And getting up my mediaeval Latin,
Seek converse common cause and brotherhood
(By all that's liberal—I should, I should)
With poets who could calmly take the fate
Of being born at once too early and late,
And for these reasons kept from being great.
Yet singing but Dione in the wood
And *ver aspergit terram floribus*
They slowly led old Latin verse to rhyme
And to forget the ancient lengths of time,
And so began the modern world for us.

I'd say, O Master of the Palace School,
You were not Charles' nor anybody's fool:
Tell me as pedagogue to pedagogue,
You did not know that since King Charles did rule
You had no chance but to be minor, did you?
Your light was spent perhaps as in a fog
That at once kept you burning low and hid you.
The age may very well have been to blame
For your not having won to Virgil's fame.
But no one ever heard you make the claim.
You would not think you knew enough to judge
The age when full upon you. That's my point.
We have to-day and I could call their name
Who know exactly what is out of joint
To make their verse and their excuses lame.
They've tried to grasp with too much social fact
Too large a situation. You and I

Would be afraid if we should comprehend
And get outside of too much bad statistics
Our muscles never could again contract:
We never could recover human shape,
But must live lives out mentally agape,
Or die of philosophical distension.
That's how we feel—and we're no special mystics.

We can't appraise the time in which we act.
But for the folly of it, let's pretend
We know enough to know it for adverse.
One more millennium's about to end.
Let's celebrate the event, my distant friend,
In publicly disputing which is worse,
The present age or your age. You and I
As schoolmen of repute should qualify
To wage a fine scholastical contention
As to whose age deserves the lower mark,
Or should I say the higher one, for dark.
I can just hear the way you make it go:
There's always something to be sorry for,
A sordid peace or an outrageous war.
Yes, yes, of course. We have the same convention.
The groundwork of all faith is human woe.
It was well worth preliminary mention.
There's nothing but injustice to be had,
No choice is left a poet, you might add,
But how to take the curse, tragic or comic.
It was well worth preliminary mention.
But let's get on to where our cases part,
If part they do. Let me propose a start.
(We're rivals in the badness of our case,
Remember, and must keep a solemn face.)
Space ails us moderns: we are sick with space.
Its contemplation makes us out as small
As a brief epidemic of microbes
That in a good glass may be seen to crawl

The patina of this the least of globes.
But have we there the advantage after all?
You were belittled into vilest worms
God hardly tolerated with his feet;
Which comes to the same thing in different terms.
We both are the belittled human race.
One as compared with God and one with space.
I had thought ours the more profound disgrace;
But doubtless this was only my conceit.
The cloister and the observatory saint
Take comfort in about the same complaint.
So science and religion really meet.

I can just hear you call your Palace class:
Come learn the Latin Eheu for alas.
You may not want to use it and you may.
O paladins, the lesson for to-day
Is how to be unhappy yet polite.
And at the summons Roland, Olivier,
And every sheepish paladin and peer,
Being already more than proved in fight,
Sits down in school to try if he can write
Like Horace in the true Horatian vein,
Yet like a Christian disciplined to bend
His mind to thinking always of the end.
Memento Mori and obey the Lord.
Art and religion love the somber chord.
Earth's a hard place in which to save the soul,
And could it be brought under state control,
So automatically we all were saved,
Its separateness from Heaven could be waived;
It might as well at once be kingdom-come.
(Perhaps it will be next millennium.)

But these are universals, not confined
To any one time, place, or human kind.
We're either nothing or a God's regret.

As ever when philosophers are met,
No matter where they stoutly mean to get,
Nor what particulars they reason from,
They are philosophers, and from old habit
They end up in the universal Whole
As unoriginal as any rabbit.

One age is like another for the soul.
I'm telling you. You haven't said a thing,
Unless I put it in your mouth to say.
I'm having the whole argument my way—
But in your favor—please to tell your King—
In having granted you all ages shine
With equal darkness, yours as dark as mine.
I'm liberal. You, you aristocrat
Won't know exactly what I mean by that.
I mean so altruistically moral
I never take my own side in a quarrel.
I'd lay my hand on his hand on his staff,
Lean back and have my confidential laugh,
And tell him I had read his Epitaph.

It sent me to the graves the other day.
The only other there was far away
Across the landscape with a watering pot
As his devotions in a special plot.
And he was there resuscitating flowers
(Make no mistake about its being bones);
But I was only there to read the stones
To see what on the whole they had to say
About how long a man may think to live,
Which is becoming my concern of late.
And very wide the choice they seemed to give;
The ages ranging all the way from hours
To months and years and many many years.
One man had lived one hundred years and eight.
But though we all may be inclined to wait
And follow some development of state,

Or see what comes of science and invention,
There is a limit to our time extension.
We all are doomed to broken-off careers,
And so's the nation, so's the total race.
The earth itself is liable to the fate
Of meaninglessly being broken off.
(And hence so many literary tears
At which my inclination is to scoff.)
I may have wept that any should have died
Or missed the chance, or not have been their best,
Or been their riches, fame, or love denied;
On me as much as any is the jest.
I take my incompleteness with the rest.
God bless himself can no one else be blessed.

I hold your doctrine of Memento Mori.
And were an epitaph to be my story
I'd have a short one ready for my own.
I would have written of me on my stone:
I had a lover's quarrel with the world.

THE WITCH OF COÖS

I staid the night for shelter at a farm
Behind the mountain, with a mother and son,
Two old-believers. They did all the talking.

MOTHER. Folks think a witch who has familiar spirits
She could call up to pass a winter evening,
But won't, should be burned at the stake or something.
Summoning spirits isn't 'Button, button,
Who's got the button,' I would have them know.

SON. Mother can make a common table rear
And kick with two legs like an army mule.

MOTHER. And when I've done it, what good have I done?
Rather than tip a table for you, let me

Tell you what Ralle the Sioux Control once told me.
He said the dead had souls, but when I asked him
How could that be—I thought the dead were souls,
He broke my trance. Don't that make you suspicious
That there's something the dead are keeping back?
Yes, there's something the dead are keeping back.

SON. You wouldn't want to tell him what we have
Up attic, mother?

MOTHER. Bones—a skeleton.

SON. But the headboard of mother's bed is pushed
Against the attic door: the door is nailed.
It's harmless. Mother hears it in the night
Halting perplexed behind the barrier
Of door and headboard. Where it wants to get
Is back into the cellar where it came from.

MOTHER. We'll never let them, will we, son! We'll never!

SON. It left the cellar forty years ago
And carried itself like a pile of dishes
Up one flight from the cellar to the kitchen,
Another from the kitchen to the bedroom,
Another from the bedroom to the attic,
Right past both father and mother, and neither stopped it
Father had gone upstairs; mother was downstairs.
I was a baby: I don't know where I was.

MOTHER. The only fault my husband found with me—
I went to sleep before I went to bed,
Especially in winter when the bed
Might just as well be ice and the clothes snow.
The night the bones came up the cellar-stairs
Toffile had gone to bed alone and left me,
But left an open door to cool the room off
So as to sort of turn me out of it.
I was just coming to myself enough
To wonder where the cold was coming from,

When I heard Toffile upstairs in the bedroom
And thought I heard him downstairs in the cellar.
The board we had laid down to walk dry-shod on
When there was water in the cellar in spring
Struck the hard cellar bottom. And then someone
Began the stairs, two footsteps for each step,
The way a man with one leg and a crutch,
Or a little child, comes up. It wasn't Toffile:
It wasn't anyone who could be there.
The bulkhead double-doors were double-locked
And swollen tight and buried under snow.
The cellar windows were banked up with sawdust
And swollen tight and buried under snow.
It was the bones. I knew them—and good reason.
My first impulse was to get to the knob
And hold the door. But the bones didn't try
The door; they halted helpless on the landing,
Waiting for things to happen in their favor.
The faintest restless rustling ran all through them.
I never could have done the thing I did
If the wish hadn't been too strong in me
To see how they were mounted for this walk.
I had a vision of them put together
Not like a man, but like a chandelier.
So suddenly I flung the door wide on him.
A moment he stood balancing with emotion,
And all but lost himself. (A tongue of fire
Flashed out and licked along his upper teeth.
Smoke rolled inside the sockets of his eyes.)
Then he came at me with one hand outstretched,
The way he did in life once; but this time
I struck the hand off brittle on the floor,
And fell back from him on the floor myself.
The finger-pieces slid in all directions.
(Where did I see one of those pieces lately?
Hand me my button-box—it must be there.)
I sat up on the floor and shouted, 'Toffile,
It's coming up to you.' It had its choice

Of the door to the cellar or the hall.
It took the hall door for the novelty,
And set off briskly for so slow a thing,
Still going every which way in the joints, though,
So that it looked like lightning or a scribble,
From the slap I had just now given its hand.
I listened till it almost climbed the stairs
From the hall to the only finished bedroom,
Before I got up to do anything;
Then ran and shouted, 'Shut the bedroom door,
Toffile, for my sake!' 'Company?' he said,
'Don't make me get up; I'm too warm in bed.'
So lying forward weakly on the handrail
I pushed myself upstairs, and in the light
(The kitchen had been dark) I had to own
I could see nothing. 'Toffile, I don't see it.
It's with us in the room though. It's the bones.'
'What bones?' 'The cellar bones—out of the grave.'
That made him throw his bare legs out of bed
And sit up by me and take hold of me.
I wanted to put out the light and see
If I could see it, or else mow the room,
With our arms at the level of our knees,
And bring the chalk-pile down. 'I'll tell you what—
It's looking for another door to try.
The uncommonly deep snow has made him think
Of his old song, *The Wild Colonial Boy*,
He always used to sing along the tote-road.
He's after an open door to get out-doors.
Let's trap him with an open door up attic.'
Toffile agreed to that, and sure enough,
Almost the moment he was given an opening,
The steps began to climb the attic stairs.
I heard them. Toffile didn't seem to hear them.
'Quick!' I slammed to the door and held the knob,
'Toffile, get nails.' I made him nail the door shut,
And push the headboard of the bed against it.
Then we asked was there anything

Up attic that we'd ever want again.
The attic was less to us than the cellar.
If the bones liked the attic, let them have it.
Let them stay in the attic. When they sometimes
Come down the stairs at night and stand perplexed
Behind the door and headboard of the bed,
Brushing their chalky skull with chalky fingers,
With sounds like the dry rattling of a shutter,
That's what I sit up in the dark to say—
To no one any more since Toffile died.
Let them stay in the attic since they went there.
I promised Toffile to be cruel to them
For helping them be cruel once to him.

SON. We think they had a grave down in the cellar.

MOTHER. We know they had a grave down in the cellar.

SON. We never could find out whose bones they were.

MOTHER. Yes, we could too, son. Tell the truth for once
They were a man's his father killed for me.
I mean a man he killed instead of me.
The least I could do was to help dig their grave.
We were about it one night in the cellar.
Son knows the story: but 'twas not for him
To tell the truth, suppose the time had come.
Son looks surprised to see me end a lie
We'd kept all these years between ourselves
So as to have it ready for outsiders.
But tonight I don't care enough to lie—
I don't remember why I ever cared.
Toffile, if he were here, I don't believe
Could tell you why he ever cared himself . . .
She hadn't found the finger-bone she wanted
Among the buttons poured out in her lap.
I verified the name next morning: Toffile.
The rural letter-box said Toffile Lajway.

Isabella Gardner

THE MILKMAN

The door was bolted and the windows of my porch
were screened to keep invaders out, the mesh of rust-
proof wire sieved the elements. Did my throat parch
then sat I at my table there and ate with lust
most chaste, the raw red apples; juice, flesh, rind and core.

One still and summer noon while dining in the sun
I was poulticing my thirst with apples, slaking care,
when suddenly I felt a whir of dread. Soon, soon,
stiff as a bone, I listened for the Milkman's tread.
I heard him softly bang the door of the huge truck
and then his boots besieged my private yard. I tried
to keep my eyes speared to the table, but the suck
of apprehension milked my force. At last he mounted
my backstairs, climbed to the top, and there he stood still
outside the bolted door. The sun's colour fainted.
I felt the horror of his quiet melt me, steal
into my sockets, and seduce me to him from
my dinner. His hand clung round the latch like rubber.
I felt him ooze against the screen and shake the frame.
I had to slide the bolt; and thus I was the robber
of my porch. Breathing smiling shape of fright,
the Milkman made his entrance; insistent donor,
he held in soft bleached hands the bottled sterile fruit,
and gave me this fatal, this apostate dinner.

Now in winter I have retreated from the porch
into the house and the once red apples rot where
I left them on the table. Now if my throat parch
for fruit the Milkman brings a quart for my despair.

THAT 'CRANING OF THE NECK'

The primary word is I-Thou. The primary word I-Thou can only be spoken with the whole being. The primary word I-It can never be spoken with the whole being.   MARTIN BUBER

Birthdays from the ocean one desert april noon
I rode through the untouching and no-odored air
astride an english saddle on a western mare
through the resisting tow-colored grass and the dune-
less sand. Under me swam a stream strange in that dried
country. A 'great blue heron' stood still in the tide-
less water and when I saw him there my heart dazzled. I whispered the mare to move quietly as
Indians move, I reined her with a catpaw hand
and my breathless feet crouched into the stirrups and
I prayed her through cactus mesquite and cattlebones
to the water's edge where the tall bird fished the stones.
The listening heron expanded with despair
unloosed unwilling wings, heaved from water into air.
O he hated to fly he flapped with a splayed painful motion. Deliberate as a weathervane
he plodded through the air that touched the fishful water.
I followed him silently giving no quarter
all that afternoon. He never flew far from me
we kept meeting past each cape and estuary
but he always heaved doggedly out of touch. I
only wanted to stare myself into him to try
and thou him till we recognized and became each
other. We were both fishing. But I could not reach
his eye. He fled in puzzled ponderous pain
and I at last rode home, conspicuous as Cain,
yet ashamed of a resigned demeaning pity
that denied us both. I returned to the city
and visited the zoo, fished on a concrete shore,
took children to aquariums, and rode no more.

I found that the encyclopedia says 'A
gregarious bird . . .' No one spoke that desert day,
not one word. That fisher who heaved to dodge my eye
has damned himself on It and I shall never fly.

WHEN A WARLOCK DIES

For Dylan Thomas

When a warlock dies his rout of lemans, demons, fallen angels
and Familiars bend to the brewing of elegiac potions, fruity
runes
plummed with their dead's distinctive spells,
mournful marketable meads composted of his rich remains.

As an apprentice witch, a mere familiar of Familiars, my
sunday-go-to-funeral broomstick (wreathed with mistletoe)
is handy to bestride in a cortege, to stir the baked meats, or to
fly
a'wake-ing. Surely this deft-dirged, over-o-
ded, buzzard-hungry, heron-lonely, phoenix-hearted, gull-
lunged
hummingbird-pulsed, falcon-winged and lark-tongued
Chanticleer has crowed his own Farewells and Hails.
And not all the ink and drink and spunk from Wichita to
Wales
will wake this cock. The homage of our elegies whistles against
the night
that looms too close for comfort since his death and our
uncomfortable respite.

The roaring riming of this most mourned Merlin canticles his
praise, and His, and ours,
and Jerichos the walls of heaven with a surfing shout of love,
and blasts of flowers.

Brewster Ghiselin

TO THE SOUTH

The umber slant lands under the Apennines
Clouded their sunward dust with pluffs and plumes,
Rust of peaches, pale of almonds and plums,
And lower yet a still green mist of vines;
These passed the slow train sliding down from the pines
And the winter rocks and the smoke-gray ravines.

Over the tiles of noon I saw upstart
The domes and pistil tower, as in a kiln:
Not like those shut steel buds of sleep at Köln
That close eternal winter on the heart
Nor like the April-folded stone of Chartres
Whose waiting is the unsummered spirit's hurt.

I came as from the ignominy of dream
Into the precincts of the sun's renown,
To feel the cycle of the night and noon,
To see on the shadowy river noonfire teem
And on the terra-cotta hills the gleam
Of fruit boughs whitening, a foam of time.

Samuel Greenberg

ESSENCE

The opera singer softly sang
Like the pellucid birds of Australian
Thicket. Anatomy's lace wrung
The cells of thousand feelings
And tastes, centigrade's power
Told climates revelations

The Psychologist felt the Heart
The poet's instinct slumber apart
Through the parks. The Forest
Filled the air of incense pure
The painter bent his brush
Through sensation's quest
Time weeps in patience duration
Through scepters create emotional resist.

THE PHILOSOPHIC APOLOGY

I still bear in mind the picture of the globe
That palpitates in absorbed fear, in thought.
O sweltering dew, what chaos doth ruminate
Upon zone's firmament, what perfection in
Such listlessness, a rock of earth doth float;
Tempests' call to balance its fees,
Its unseen course through the infinite walls.
The virtue of the sulphur sun that shades
The night, that clears the heaven from reveries—
O Heavenly Father thou hast in plea
Mankind's thirsty juggle, to upheave its concept,
Who shares thy width of love and all
Whose palm holds the shadow of fear
That judgment soothes, thy dusty heart-speck's tear.

THE GLASS BUBBLES

The motion of gathering loops of water
Must either burst or remain in a moment.
The violet colors through the glass
Throw up little swellings that appear
And spatter as soon as another strikes
And is born; so pure are they of colored
Hues, that we feel the absent strength
Of its power. When they begin they gather
Like sand on the beach: each bubble
Contains a complete eye of water.

Louis Grudin

CITIZEN

Hairless beast in old clothes
Dry-eyed, whispering as he moved:
Forty years paying the rent
Sending the boy to school
Saying amen, voting for president,
Gone with a tremor of the lip.

In the half octave of his sound
A hundred words, to pass the time of day
And thirty ciphers
To count his change and make his way
But not one word to tell his tale
Or hear the meaning of his name:
Or mark him once, whose warm cloaked heart
Played with all its might a little chime
While in the weed topped skull
The protean lenses turned to slime.

Donald Hall

EXILE

Each of us waking to the window's light
Has found the curtains changed, our pictures gone;
Our furniture has vanished in the night
And left us to an unfamiliar dawn.
Even the contours of our room are strange
And everything is change.
Waking, our minds construct of memory
What figure stretched beside us, or what voice
Shouted to pull us from our luxury—
And all the mornings leaning to our choice.

To put away—both child and murderer—
The toys we played with just a month ago,
That wisdom come, and make our moving sure,
Began our exile with our lust to grow.
(Remembering a train I tore apart,
Because it knew my heart.)
We move and move, but our perversity
Betrays us into love of what is lost.
We search our minds for childhood, and we see
Only the parting struggle and its cost.

Not only from the intellectual child
Time has removed us, but unyieldingly
Cuts down the groves in which our Indians filed
And where the sleep of pines was mystery.
(I walked the streets of where I lived and grew,
And all the streets were new.)
The room of love is always rearranged.
Someone has torn the corner of a chair
So that the past we cultivate is changed,
The scene deprived by an intruding tear.

Exiled by death from men that we have known,
We are betrayed again by years, and try
To call them back and clothe the barren bone,
Not to admit a man can ever die.
(A boy who talked and read and grew with me,
Fell from a maple tree.)
But we are still alone, who love the dead,
And always miss their action's character,
Trapped in our cells of living, visited
By no sweet ghosts, by no sad men that were.

In years, and in the numbering of space
Thousands of miles from what we grew to know,
We stray like paper blown from place to place,
Impelled by every element to go.
(I think of haying on an August day,

Forking the stacks of hay.)
We can remember trees and attitudes
That foreign landscapes do not imitate;
They grow distinct within the interludes
Of memory beneath a stranger state.

The favorite toy was banished, and our act
Was banishment of the self; then growing, we
Murdered the girls we loved, for our love lacked
Self-knowledge of its real perversity.
(I loved her, but I told her I did not,
And grew, and then forgot.)
It was mechanical, and in our age,
That cruelty should be our way of speech;
Our movement is a single pilgrimage,
Never returning; action does not teach.

In isolation from our present love
We spell her out in daily memory,
Thinking these images we practice move
On human avenues across a sea.
(All day I see her simple figure stand,
Out of the reach of hand.)
Each door and window is a spectral frame
In which her ghost is for the moment found.
Each lucky scrap of paper bears her name,
And half-heard phrases imitate its sound.

Imagining, by exile kept from fact,
We build of distance mental rock and tree,
And make of memory creative act,
Persons and worlds no waking eye can see.
(From lacking her, I built her new again,
And loved the image then.)
The manufactured country is so green
The eyes of sleep are blinded by its shine;
We spend our lust in that imagined scene
But never wake to cross its borderline.

No man can knock his human fist upon
The door built by his mind, or hear the voice
He meditated come again if gone;
We live outside the country of our choice.
Leaning toward harvest, fullness as our end,
Our habits will not mend.
Our humanness betrays us to the cage
Within whose limits each is free to walk,
But where no man can hear our prayers or rage,
And none of us can break the walls to talk.

Exiled by years, by death the present end,
By worlds that must remain unvisited,
And by the wounds that growing does not mend,
We are as solitary as the dead,
Wanting to king it in that perfect land
We make and understand.
And in this world whose pattern is unmade,
Phases of splintered light and shapeless sand,
We shatter through our motions and evade
Whatever hand might reach and touch our hand.

Anthony Hecht

UPON THE DEATH OF GEORGE SANTAYANA

Down every passage of the cloister hung
A dark wood cross on a white plaster wall;
But in the court were roses, not as tongue
Might have them, something of Christ's blood grown small,
But just as roses, and at three o'clock
Their essences, inseparably bouqueted,
Seemed more than Christ's last breath, and rose to mock
An elderly man for whom the Sisters prayed.

What heart can know itself? The Sibyl speaks
Mirthless and unbedizened things, but who
Can fathom her intent? Loving the Greeks,
He whispered to a nun who strove to woo
His spirit unto God by prayer and fast,
'Pray that I go to Limbo, if it please
Heaven to let my soul regard at last
Democritus, Plato and Socrates.'

And so it was. The river, as foretold,
Ran darkly by; under his tongue he found
Coin for the passage; the ferry tossed and rolled;
The sages stood on their appointed ground,
Sighing, all as foretold. The mind was tasked;
He had not dreamed that so many had died.
'But where is Alcibiades,' he asked,
'The golden roisterer, the animal pride?'

Those sages who had spoken of the love
And enmity of things, how all things flow,
Stood in a light no life is witness of,
And Socrates, whose wisdom was to know
He did not know, spoke with a solemn mien,
And all his wonderful ugliness was lit,
'He whom I loved for what he might have been
Freezes with traitors in the ultimate pit.'

OSTIA ANTICA

Given this light,
The departing thunderhead in its anger
Off to one side, and given
These ancient stones in their setting, themselves refreshed
And rendered strangely younger
By wetness alive with the wriggling brass of heaven,
Where is the spirit's part unwashed
Of all poor spite?

The cypress thrust,
Greened in the glass of air as never
Since the first greenness offered,
Not to desire our prayer: "To ghostly creatures,
Peace, and an end of fever
Till all this dust assemble," but delivered
To their resistless lives and natures,
Rise as they must.

And the broken wall
Is only itself, deeply accepting
The sun's warmth to its bricks.
The puddles blink; a snail marches the Roman
Road of its own adopting.
The marble nymph is stripped to the flush of sex
As if in truth this timeless, human
Instant were all.

Is it the bird's
Voice, the delicious voice of water,
Addresses us on the splendid
Topic of love? And promises to youth
Still livelier forms and whiter?
Here are quick freshes, here is the body suspended
In its firm blessing, here the mouth
Finds out its words.

See, they arise
In the sign of ivy, the young males
To their strength, the meadows restored;
Concupiscence of eye, and the world's pride;
Of love, the naked skills.
At the pool's edge, the rippled image cleared,
That face set among leaves is glad,
Noble and wise.

What was begun,
The mastered force, breeds and is healing.

Pebbles and clover speak.
Each hanging waterdrop burns with a fierce
     Bead of the sun's instilling.
But softly, beneath the flutesong and volatile shriek
     Of birds, are to be heard discourse
          Mother and son.

          "If there were hushed
To us the images of earth, its poles
     Hushed, and the waters of it,
And hushed the tumult of the flesh, even
     The voice intrinsic of our souls,
Each tongue and token hushed and the long habit
     Of thought, if that first light, the given
          To us were hushed,

          So that the washed
Object, fixed in the sun, were dumb,
     And to the mind its brilliance
Were from beyond itself, and the mind were clear
     As the unclouded dome
Wherein all things diminish, in that silence
     Might we not confidently hear
          God as he wished?"

          Then from the grove
Suddenly falls a flight of bells.
     A figure moves from the wood,
Darkly approaching at the hour of vespers
     Along the ruined walls.
And bearing heavy articles of blood
     And symbols of endurance, whispers,
          "This is love."

Daniel G. Hoffman

IN HUMBLENESS

Neither malt nor Milton can
Explain to God the ways of Man:
Hobnailed troops have ever trod
Upon the flocks who know that God
Has a passion, plan, or mind,
Or that the Universe is kind.

Come flood, come war, come pestilence,
Come Man at last to Common Sense:
At last admit, in humbleness,
Whatever spire he dares erect
Of either faith or intellect
Can be but his sarcophagus;

Yet even in that iron tomb
Man stirs again, as in the womb:
Tunnels free, then, word by word,
Rebuilds, and is again interred.
Read this in the histories:
Newsweek, or Thucydides.

AN ARMADA OF THIRTY WHALES

(Galleons in sea-pomp) sails
over the emerald ocean.

The ceremonial motion
of their ponderous race is

given dandiacal graces
in the ballet of their geysers.

Eyes deep-set in whalebone vizors
have found a Floridian beach;

they leave their green world to fish.
Like the Pliocene midge, they declare

their element henceforth air.
What land they walk upon

becomes their Holy Land;
when these pilgrims have all found tongue

how their canticles shall be sung!
They nudge the beach with their noses,

eager for hedgerows and roses;
they raise their great snouts from the sea

and exulting gigantically
each trumpets a sousaphone wheeze

and stretches his finfitted knees.
But they who won't swim and can't stand

lie mired in mud and in sand,
And the sea and the wind and the worms

will contest the last will of the Sperms.

Oliver Wendell Holmes

THE CHAMBERED NAUTILUS

This is the ship of pearl, which, poets feign,
   Sails the unshadowed main,—
   The venturous bark that flings
On the sweet summer wind its purpled wings
In gulfs enchanted, where the Siren sings,
   And coral reefs lie bare,
Where the cold sea-maids rise to sun their streaming hair.

Its webs of living gauze no more unfurl;
   Wrecked is the ship of pearl!
   And every chambered cell,

Where its dim dreaming life was wont to dwell,
As the frail tenant shaped his growing shell,
   Before thee lies revealed,—
Its irised ceiling rent, its sunless crypt unsealed!

Year after year beheld the silent toil
   That spread his lustrous coil;
     Still, as the spiral grew,
He left the past year's dwelling for the new,
Stole with soft step its shining archway through,
     Built up its idle door,
Stretched in his last-found home, and knew the old no more.

Thanks for the heavenly message brought by thee,
   Child of the wandering sea,
     Cast from her lap, forlorn!
From thy dead lips a clearer note is born
Than ever Triton blew from wreathèd horn!
     While on mine ear it rings,
Through the deep caves of thought I hear a voice that sings:—

Build thee more stately mansions, O my soul,
   As the swift seasons roll!
     Leave thy low-vaulted past!
Let each new temple, nobler than the last,
Shut thee from heaven with a dome more vast,
     Till thou at length art free,
Leaving thine outgrown shell by life's unresting sea!

THE DEACON'S MASTERPIECE
OR, THE WONDERFUL 'ONE-HOSS SHAY'

A Logical Story

Have you heard of the wonderful one-hoss shay,
That was built in such a logical way
It ran a hundred years to a day,
And then, of a sudden, it—ah, but stay,

I'll tell you what happened without delay,
Scaring the parson into fits,
Frightening people out of their wits,—
Have you ever heard of that, I say?

Seventeen hundred and fifty-five.
Georgius Secundus was then alive,—
Snuffy old drone from the German hive.
That was the year when Lisbon-town
Saw the earth open and gulp her down,
And Braddock's army was done so brown,
Left without a scalp to its crown.
It was on the terrible Earthquake-day
That the Deacon finished the one-hoss shay.

Now in building of chaises, I tell you what,
There is always *somewhere* a weakest spot,—
In hub, tire, felloe, in spring or thill,
In panel, or crossbar, or floor, or sill,
In screw, bolt, thoroughbrace,—lurking still,
Find it somewhere you must and will,—
Above or below, or within or without,—
And that's the reason, beyond a doubt,
That a chaise *breaks down,* but doesn't *wear out.*

But the Deacon swore (as Deacons do,
With an 'I dew vum,' or an 'I tell *yeou*')
He would build one shay to beat the taown
'n' the keounty 'n' all the kentry raoun';
It should be so built that it *couldn'* break daown:
'Fur,' said the Deacon, ''t 's mighty plain
Thut the weakes' place mus' stan' the strain;
'n' the way t' fix it, uz I maintain, Is only jest
T' make that place uz strong uz the rest.'

So the Deacon inquired of the village folk
Where he could find the strongest oak,
That couldn't be split nor bent nor broke,—

That was for spokes and floor and sills;
He sent for lancewood to make the thills;
The crossbars were ash, from the straightest trees,
The panels of white-wood, that cuts like cheese,
But lasts like iron for things like these;
The hubs of logs from the 'Settler's ellum,'—
Last of its timber,—they couldn't sell 'em,
Never an axe had seen their chips,
And the wedges flew from between their lips,
Their blunt ends frizzled like celery-tips;
Step and prop-iron, bolt and screw,
Spring, tire, axle, and linchpin too,
Steel of the finest, bright and blue;
Thoroughbrace bison-skin, thick and wide;
Boot, top, dasher, from tough old hide
Found in the pit when the tanner died.
That was the way he 'put her through.'
'There!' said the Deacon, 'naow she'll dew!'

Do! I tell you, I rather guess
She was a wonder, and nothing less!
Colts grew horses, beards turned gray,
Deacon and deaconess dropped away,
Children and grandchildren—where were they?
But there stood the stout old one-hoss shay
As fresh as on Lisbon-earthquake-day!

EIGHTEEN HUNDRED;—it came and found
The Deacon's masterpiece strong and sound.
Eighteen hundred increased by ten;—
'Hahnsum kerridge' they called it then.
Eighteen hundred and twenty came;—
Running as usual; much the same.
Thirty and forty at last arrive,
And then come fifty, and FIFTY-FIVE.

Little of all we value here
Wakes on the morn of its hundredth year

Without both feeling and looking queer.
In fact, there's nothing that keeps its youth,
So far as I know, but a tree and truth.
(This is a moral that runs at large;
Take it.—You're welcome.—No extra charge.)

FIRST OF NOVEMBER,—the Earthquake-day,—
There are traces of age in the one-hoss shay,
A general flavor of mild decay,
But nothing local, as one may say.
There couldn't be,—for the Deacon's art
Had made it so like in every part
That there wasn't a chance for one to start.
For the wheels were just as strong as the thills,
And the floor was just as strong as the sills,
And the panels just as strong as the floor,
And the whipple-tree neither less nor more,
And the back-crossbar as strong as the fore,
And spring and axle and hub *encore.*
And yet, *as a whole,* it is past a doubt
In another hour it will be *worn out!*

First of November, fifty-five!
This morning the parson takes a drive.
Now, small boys, get out of the way!
Here comes the wonderful one-hoss shay,
Drawn by a rat-tailed, ewe-necked bay.
'Huddup!' said the parson.—Off went they.
The parson was working his Sunday's text,—
Had got to *fifthly,* and stopped perplexed
At what the—Moses—was coming next.
All at once the horse stood still,
Close by the meet'n'-house on the hill.
First a shiver, and then a thrill,
Then something decidedly like a spill,—
And the parson was sitting upon a rock,
At half past nine by the meet'n'-house clock,—
Just the hour of the Earthquake shock!

What do you think the parson found,
When he got up and stared around?
The poor old chaise in a heap or mound,
As if it had been to the mill and ground!
You see, of course, if you're not a dunce,
How it went to pieces all at once,—
All at once, and nothing first,—
Just as bubbles do when they burst.

End of the wonderful one-hoss shay.
Logic is logic. That's all I say.

Edwin Honig

HAPPENING

Behind me the house was asleep.
I could hear it relax and breathe,
Tied to its summer thick hill.
A bird or a chipmunk scraped
Through the eaves or a hollow hand
Roamed in its paintless hide,
Tinkled a pane in the upper storey
While I walked and the house
Slept on. And it breathed,
I know, because it was then
The highest perturbable trees
Shook down a wind like a lash,
The road fell down a ravine,
And all that wide blue summer
Grew narrow and turned on itself
Like a fan. When I turned, the house
Had opened its face, gray as a man's.

**W
A
L
WHITMAN**

Prophet of the body's roving
Magnitude, he still commands a hope
Elusive as the Jewish Savior—not dying,
Not yet born, but always imminent: coming in
A blaze one sunny afternoon, defying winter, to
Everyone's distinct advantage, then going on to Eden,
Half sham, half hearsay, like California or Miami, golden.
All his life was squandered in his
Poverty when he became the body's
Prime   reunionist,   bankrupt   exploiter,
From early middle age, of the nation's largest
Unexploited   enterprise—baggy,   queer,   a   Johnny
Appleseed freely planting selves the future mashes into
Commonplaces, lops off as flourishes, an unweaned appetite.
Yet   who   can   shape   his
Mouth's beard-brimming bubble,
That violent honey sound? Afterwards
They   just   blew   hard,   Tarzans   hamming
Through the swampy lots. His patent, never
Filed, was being man quixotically alive against the
Hoax of sin and dying. Paradise is now. America, whose
Greatest war was civil, must be born from Abel's wound,
& Cain be
Welcomed home by Adam
—Father   Abraham   opening
His blood to continents, all armies,
Lovers, tramps. A time for heroes, but the
Captains, shot or dowdy, died. (Had old Abe
Really smiled & tipped his hat or had he merely gri-
maced? Ulysses, finished, promptly sighed & chomped
Cigars & toured the capitals.) The people yea'd & shambled
To the great-
est fortunes made, while he
Conveyed the lippy cop, the whistling

Streetcar man, the ferry pilot billowing
Upon the apron of his praise. Nakedly at last
He flailed his own paralysis with mud and flesh-
Brush. A man, all men himself alone, a rugged blue-eyed
Testament, his looks in Brady's lens are calm with after-rages.

"The real war
Will never get
In the books."
Below the ragged
Line he signed
His chummy name.

THE TALL TOMS

All told the gray world
sponges hopelessly on swift
tall Toms, fliers in the
howling highways, scorchers
of the lush long countries.

Hats on or off they
head through glass,
through bowls of
winter roses, through
women hard as diamonds.

Floods and crosses
kiss their shoes, and
trolleys late for work
pray like snails till
sirens swill the streets.

Their failure is success
in the eye highballing
white and black, and if
they end, even grim lids in
grass jaws ponder over them.

Robert Horan

LITTLE CITY

Spider, from his flaming sleep,
staggers out into the window frame;
swings out from the red den where he slept
to nest in the gnarled glass.
Fat hero, burnished cannibal
lets down a frail ladder and ties a knot,
sways down to a landing with furry grace.

By noon this corner is a bullet-colored city
and the exhausted architect sleeps in his pale wheel,
waits without pity for a gold visitor
or coppery captive, his aerial enemies
spinning headlong down the window to the trap.

The street of string shakes now and announces
a surprised angel in the tunnel of thread,
Spider dances down his wiry heaven to taste the moth.
A little battle begins and the prison trembles.
The round spider hunches like a judge.
The wheel glistens.
But this transparent town that caves in at a breath
is paved with perfect steel.
The victim hangs by his feet, and the spider
circles invisible avenues, weaving a grave.

By evening the web is heavy with monsters,
bright constellation of wasps and bees,
breathless, surrendered.
Bronze skeletons dangle on the wires
and a thin wing flutters.
The medieval city hangs in its stars.

Spider lumbers down the web
and the city stretches with the weight of his walking.
By night we cannot see the flies' faces
and the spider, rocking.

Julia Ward Howe

BATTLE-HYMN OF THE REPUBLIC

Mine eyes have seen the glory of the coming of the Lord:
He is trampling out the vintage where the grapes of wrath are
    stored;
He hath loosed the fateful lightning of his terrible swift sword:
    His truth is marching on.

I have seen him in the watch-fires of a hundred circling
    camps;
They have builded him an altar in the evening dews and
    damps;
I can read his righteous sentence by the dim and flaring lamps:
    His day is marching on.

I have read a fiery gospel, writ in burnished rows of steel:
"As ye deal with my contemners, so with you my grace shall
    deal;
Let the Hero, born of woman, crush the serpent with his heel,
    Since God is marching on."

He has sounded forth the trumpet that shall never call retreat;
He is sifting out the hearts of men before his judgment-seat:
O, be swift, my soul, to answer him! be jubilant, my feet!
    Our God is marching on.

In the beauty of the lilies Christ was born across the sea,
With a glory in his bosom that transfigures you and me;
As he died to make men holy, let us die to make men free,
    While God is marching on.

He is coming like the glory of the morning on the wave,
He is wisdom to the mighty, he is honor to the brave,
So the world shall be his footstool, the soul of wrong his slave,
    Our God is marching on!

Robinson Jeffers

THE STARS GO OVER THE LONELY OCEAN

Unhappy about some far off things
That are not my affair, wandering
Along the coast and up the lean ridges,
I saw in the evening
The stars go over the lonely ocean,
And a black-maned wild boar
Plowing with his snout on Mal Paso Mountain.

The old monster snuffled, "Here are sweet roots,
Fat grubs, slick beetles and sprouted acorns.
The best nation in Europe has fallen,
And that is Finland,
But the stars go over the lonely ocean,"
The old black-bristled boar,
Tearing the sod on Mal Paso Mountain.

"The world's in a bad way, my man,
And bound to be worse before it mends;
Better lie up in the mountain here
Four or five centuries,
While the stars go over the lonely ocean,"
Said the old father of wild pigs,
Plowing the fallow on Mal Paso Mountain.

"Keep clear of the dupes that talk democracy
And the dogs that bark revolution,
Drunk with talk, liars and believers.
I believe in my tusks.
Long live freedom and damn the ideologies,"
Said the gamey black-maned wild boar
Tusking the turf on Mal Paso Mountain.

PROMISE OF PEACE

The heads of strong old age are beautiful
Beyond all grace of youth. They have strange quiet,
Integrity, health, soundness, to the full
They've dealt with life and been attempered by it.
A young man must not sleep; his years are war
Civil and foreign but the former's worse;
But the old can breathe in safety now that they are
Forgetting what youth meant, the being perverse,
Running the fool's gauntlet and being cut
By the whips of the five senses. As for me,
If I should wish to live long it were but
To trade those fevers for tranquillity,
Thinking though that's entire and sweet in the grave
How shall the dead taste the deep treasure they have?

THE BLOODY SIRE

It is not bad. Let them play.
Let the guns bark and the bombing-plane
Speak his prodigious blasphemies.
It is not bad, it is high time,
Stark violence is still the sire of all the world's values.

What but the wolf's tooth chiseled so fine
The fleet limbs of the antelope?
What but fear winged the birds and hunger
Gemmed with such eyes the great goshawk's head?
Violence has been the sire of all the world's values.

Who would remember Helen's face
Lacking the terrible halo of spears?
Who formed Christ but Herod and Caesar,
The cruel and bloody victories of Caesar?
Violence has been the sire of all the world's values.

Never weep, let them play,
Old violence is not too old to beget new values.

MAY-JUNE, 1940

Foreseen for so many years: these evils, this monstrous
   violence, these massive agonies: no easier to bear.
We saw them with slow stone strides approach, everyone saw
   them; we closed our eyes against them, we looked
And they had come nearer. We ate and drank and slept, they
   came nearer. Sometimes we laughed, they were nearer. Now
They are here. And now a blind man foresees what follows
   them: degradation, famine, recovery and so forth, and the
Epidemic manias: but not enough death to serve us, not
   enough death. It would be better for men
To be few and live far apart, where none could infect another;
   then slowly the sanity of field and mountain
And the cold ocean and glittering stars might enter their
   minds.
Another dream, another dream.
We shall have to accept certain limitations
In future, and abandon some humane dreams; only hard-
   minded, sleepless and realist, can ride this rock-slide
To new fields down the dark mountain; and we shall have to
   perceive that these insanities are normal;
We shall have to perceive that battle is a burning flower or
   like a huge music, and the dive-bomber's screaming orgasm
As beautiful as other passions; and that death and life are not
   serious alternatives. One has known all these things
For many years: there is greater and darker to know
In the next hundred.
               And why do you cry, my dear, why do you cry?
It is all in the whirling circles of time.
If millions are born millions must die,
If England goes down and Germany up
The stronger dog will still be on top,
All in the turning of time.
If civilization goes down, that
Would be an event to contemplate.
It will not be in our time, alas, my dear,
It will not be in our time.

BLACK-OUT

The war that we have carefully for years provoked
Comes on us unprepared, amazed and indignant. Our war-
    ships are shot
Like sitting ducks and our planes like nest-birds, both our
    coasts ridiculously panicked,
And our leaders make orations. This is the people
That hopes to impose on the whole planetary world
An American peace.
    (Oh, we'll win our war. My money on amazed Gulliver
And his horse-pistols.)
                    Meanwhile our prudent officers
Have cleared the coast-long ocean of ships and fishing craft,
    the sky of planes, the windows of light: these clearings
Make a strange beauty. Watch the wide sea, there is nothing
    human, the gulls have it. Watch the wide sky,
All day clean of machines, only at dawn and dusk a military
    hawk passes
High on patrol. Walk at night on the shore,
The pretty firefly spangle that used to line it
Perfectly silent, shut are the shops, mouse-dark the houses.
    Here the prehuman dignity of night
Stands, as it was and will be again. Oh beautiful
Darkness and silence, the two eyes that see God. Great staring
    eyes.

CASSANDRA

The mad girl with the staring eyes and long white fingers
Hooked in the stones of the wall,
The storm-wrack hair and the screeching mouth: does it
    matter, Cassandra,
Whether the people believe
Your bitter fountain? Truly men hate the truth, they'd liefer
Meet a tiger on the road.
Therefore the poets honey their truth with lying; but religion-

Venders and political men
Pour from the barrel, new lies on the old, and are praised for
    kindly
Wisdom. Poor bitch be wise.
No: you'll still mumble in a corner a crust of truth, to men
And gods disgusting. —You and I, Cassandra.

SHINE, PERISHING REPUBLIC

While this America settles in the mold of its vulgarity, heavily
    thickening to empire,
And protest, only a bubble in the molten mass, pops and sighs
    out, and the mass hardens,

I sadly smiling remember that the flower fades to make fruit,
    the fruit rots to make earth.
Out of the mother; and through the spring exultances, ripe-
    ness and decadence; and home to the mother.

You, making haste, haste on decay: not blameworthy; life is
    good, be it stubbornly long or suddenly
A mortal splendor: meteors are not needed less than moun-
    tains: shine, perishing republic.

But for my children, I would have them keep their distance
    from the thickening center; corruption
Never has been compulsory, when the cities lie at the mon-
    ster's feet there are left the mountains.

And boys, be in nothing so moderate as in love of man, a
    clever servant, insufferable master.
There is the trap that catches noblest spirits, that caught—
    they say—God, when he walked on earth.

THE WORLD'S WONDERS

Being now three or four years more than sixty,
I have seen strange things in my time. I have seen a merman
standing waist-deep in the ocean off my rock shore,

Unmistakably human and unmistakably a sea-beast: he submerged and never came up again,
While we stood watching. I do not know what he was, and I
have no theory: but this was the least of wonders.

I have seen the United States grow up the strongest and
wealthiest of nations, and swim in the wind over bank-
ruptcy.
I have seen Europe, for twenty-five hundred years the crown
of the world, become its beggar and cripple.

I have seen my people, fooled by ambitious men and a froth
of sentiment, waste themselves on three wars.
None was required, all futile, all grandly victorious. A fourth
is forming.

I have seen the invention of human flight; a chief desire of
man's dreaming heart for ten thousand years;
And men have made it the chief of the means of massacre.

I have seen the far stars weighed and their distance measured,
and the powers that make the atom put into service—
For what?—To kill. To kill half a million flies—men I should
say—at one slap.

I have also seen doom. You can stand up and struggle or lie
down and sleep—you are doomed as Oedipus.
A man and a civilization grow old, grow fatally—as we say—
ill: courage and the will are bystanders.

It is easy to know the beauty of inhuman things, sea, storm
and mountain; it is their soul and their meaning.
Humanity has its lesser beauty, impure and painful; we have
to harden our hearts to bear it.

I have hardened my heart only a little: I have learned that
happiness is important, but pain *gives* importance.
The use of tragedy: Lear becomes as tall as the storm he
crawls in; and a tortured Jew became God.

Josephine W. Johnson

FINAL AUTUMN

End will come swiftly in an early autumn,
Forewarned by blooded rising of the moon,
Its great arc swollen like a hill of fire, —
And long continuous lightning in the north,
Portent of that unearthly rain whose knives
Shall slash the hard integument of earth
Down to its unknown core.
And man, having ravaged earth's beauty and outlived her
prime,
Strained from her hands all mystery and dark,
Shall hear
The far wasp-whispering of the flames to come
Over the outworn cities and infertile soil;
Shall know the fierce increasing sound
Of iron cities' great volcanic death,
The roar of oak fire and the straining steel,
The quivering to and fro of towers
Like fiery grass stems in a wind.
And over the broken face of earth shall sear
Iron of the cauterizing flame,
Over the unclean, crying mouths
The clean sound of the flame.

And some men in this hour of death shall know
More heat and glory than had ever come
Into the spare and cautious veins of life,
And cry out with the tardy grief of those who find
Night of a great and unreturning day
In which they had no part.
And some by light of this flame-opened hour
Shall face
The knotted fabric of their lives

—Woven in darkness and unseen till now,
And will be glad to die.

But there shall be no grief so bitter,
Nor any anguish on the earth that can compare
With the intolerable bitterness of those voices that shall cry—
Not out of fear of this great tidal flame—
Not for the ashless bodies of the dead,
But out of the knowledge that this burning means
The long ritual of life brought to a close
In the high horror and red pageantry of death,
    With still the face of God unseen,
    His great confessional unread.

Francis Scott Key

THE STAR-SPANGLED BANNER

Oh, say, can you see, by the dawn's early light,
    What so proudly we hailed at the twilight's last gleaming,
Whose broad stripes and bright stars through the perilous
        fight,
    O'er the ramparts we watched were so gallantly streaming?
And the rockets' red glare, the bombs bursting in air,
Gave proof through the night that our flag was still there.
Oh, say, does that star-spangled banner yet wave
O'er the land of the free, and the home of the brave?

On the shore, dimly seen through the mists of the deep,
    Where the foe's haughty host in dread silence reposes,
What is that which the breeze, o'er the towering steep,
    As it fitfully blows, half conceals, half discloses?
Now it catches the gleam of the morning's first beam,
In full glory reflected, now shines on the stream.
'Tis the star-spangled banner; oh, long may it wave
O'er the land of the free, and the home of the brave!

And where is that band who so vauntingly swore
    That the havoc of war and the battle's confusion
A home and a country should leave us no more?
    Their blood has washed out their foul footsteps' pollution.
No refuge could save the hireling and slave
From the terror of flight, or the gloom of the grave:
And the star-spangled banner in triumph doth wave
O'er the land of the free, and the home of the brave!

Oh! thus be it ever when freemen shall stand
    Between their loved homes and the war's desolation!
Blest with victory and peace, may the heaven-rescued land
    Praise the Power that hath made and preserved us a nation!
Then conquer we must, for our cause it is just,
And this be our motto: "In God is our trust!"
And the star-spangled banner in triumph shall wave,
O'er the land of the free, and the home of the brave!

V. R. Lang

WAITING AND PEEKING

"The Tongue is a Great Magnifier, Mrs. DuBois." MY SISTER'S DENTIST

Nobody believes in Fate any more, nobody listens to the
    Norns.
Nobody solicits garlic or white of egg, or fears effigies.
But Things go on anyway, arranging everything that happens.

People think unkindly of others, and these in particular
Break out into horrible rashes, or die in convulsions.
Spirits sift and creep, and stones see back.

Trees and rocks and water and objects in public Parks
All go secretly, knowingly on, and every quiet, heavy Thing
Maintains its own life and its powers, peeking at us as it does.

Sidney Lanier

THE RAVEN DAYS

Our hearths are gone out, and our hearts are broken,
    And but the ghosts of homes to us remain,
And ghostly eyes and hollow sighs give token
    From friend to friend of an unspoken pain.

O, Raven Days, dark Raven Days of sorrow,
    Bring to us, in your whetted ivory beaks,
Some sign out of the far land of To-morrow,
    Some strip of sea-green dawn, some orange streaks.

Ye float in dusky files, forever croaking—
    Ye chill our manhood with your dreary shade.
Pale, in the dark, not even God invoking,
    We lie in chains, too weak to be afraid.

O Raven Days, dark Raven Days of sorrow,
    Will ever any warm light come again?
Will ever the lit mountains of To-morrow
    Begin to gleam across the mournful plain?

FROM THE FLATS

What heartache—ne'er a hill!
Inexorable, vapid, vague, and chill
The drear sand-levels drain my spirit low.
With one poor word they tell me all they know;
Whereat their stupid tongues, to tease my pain,
Do drawl it o'er again and o'er again.
They hurt my heart with griefs I cannot name:
    Always the same, the same.

    Nature hath no surprise,
No ambuscade of beauty 'gainst mine eyes

From brake or lurking dell or deep defile;
No humors, frolic forms—this mile, that mile;
No rich reserves or happy-valley hopes
Beyond the bends of roads, the distant slopes.
Her fancy fails, her wild is all run tame:
　　Ever the same, the same.

Oh, might I through these tears
But glimpse some hill my Georgia high uprears,
Where white the quartz and pink the pebble shine,
The hickory heavenward strives, the muscadine
Swings o'er the slope, the oak's far-falling shade
Darkens the dogwood in the bottom glade,
And down the hollow from a ferny nook
　　Bright leaps a living brook!

THE MARSHES OF GLYNN

Glooms of the live-oaks, beautiful-braided and woven
With intricate shades of the vines that myriad-cloven
　　Clamber the forks of the multiform boughs,—
　　　　Emerald twilights,—
　　　　Virginal shy lights,
Wrought of the leaves to allure to the whisper of vows,
When lovers pace timidly down through the green colonnades
Of the dim sweet woods, of the dear dark woods,
　　Of the heavenly woods and glades,
That run to the radiant marginal sand-beach within
　　The wide sea-marshes of Glynn;—

Beautiful glooms, soft dusks in the noon-day fire,—
Wildwood privacies, closets of lone desire,
Chamber from chamber parted with wavering arras of leaves,—
Cells for the passionate pleasure of prayer to the soul that
　　grieves,
Pure with a sense of the passing of saints through the wood,
Cool for the dutiful weighing of ill with good;—

O braided dusks of the oak and woven shades of the vine,
While the riotous noon-day sun of the June-day long did shine,
Ye held me fast in your heart and I held you fast in mine;
But now when the noon is no more, and riot is rest,
And the sun is a-wait at the ponderous gate of the West,
And the slant yellow beam down the wood-aisle doth seem
Like a lane into heaven that leads from a dream,—
Ay, now, when my soul all day hath drunken the soul of the
    oak,
And my heart is at ease from men, and the wearisome sound
    of the stroke
Of the scythe of time and the trowel of trade is low,
And belief overmasters doubt, and I know that I know,
And my spirit is grown to a lordly great compass within,
That the length and the breadth and the sweep of the marshes
    of Glynn
Will work me no fear like the fear they have wrought me of
    yore
When length was fatigue, and when breadth was but bitter-
    ness sore,
And when terror and shrinking and dreary unnamable pain
Drew over me out of the merciless miles of the plain,—
    Oh, now, unafraid, I am fain to face
    The vast sweet visage of space.
To the edge of the wood I am drawn, I am drawn,
    Where the gray beach glimmering runs, as a belt of the
    dawn,
    For a mete and a mark
    To the forest-dark:—
    So:
Affable live-oak, leaning low,—
Thus—with your favor—soft, with a reverent hand,
(Not lightly touching your person, Lord of the land!)
Bending your beauty aside, with a step I stand
    On the firm-packed sand,
        Free
    By a world of marsh that borders a world of sea.

Sinuous southward and sinuous northward the shimmering
band
Of the sand-beach fastens the fringe of the marsh to the folds
of the land.
Inward and outward to northward and southward the beach-
lines linger and curl
As a silver-wrought garment that clings to and follows the
firm sweet limbs of a girl.
Vanishing, swerving, evermore curving again into sight,
Softly the sand-beach wavers away to a dim gray looping of
light.
And what if behind me to westward the wall of the woods
stands high?
The world lies east: how ample, the marsh and the sea and
the sky!
A league and a league of marsh-grass, waist-high, broad in the
blade,
Green, and all of a height, and unflecked with a light or a
shade,
    Stretch leisurely off, in a pleasant plain,
    To the terminal blue of the main.

Oh, what is abroad in the marsh and the terminal sea?
    Somehow my soul seems suddenly free
From the weighing of fate and the sad discussion of sin,
By the length and the breadth and the sweep of the marshes
of Glynn.
Ye marshes, how candid and simple and nothing-withholding
and free
Ye publish yourselves to the sky and offer yourselves to the
sea!
Tolerant plains, that suffer the sea and the rains and the sun,
Ye spread and span like the catholic man who hath mightily
won
God out of knowledge and good out of infinite pain
And sight out of blindness and purity out of a stain.

As the marsh-hen secretly builds on the watery sod,
Behold I will build me a nest on the greatness of God:
I will fly in the greatness of God as the marsh-hen flies
In the freedom that fills all the space 'twixt the marsh and the
skies:
By so many roots as the marsh-grass sends in the sod
I will heartily lay me a-hold on the greatness of God:
Oh, like to the greatness of God is the greatness within
The range of the marshes, the liberal marshes of Glynn.

And the sea lends large, as the marsh: lo, out of his plenty the
sea
Pours fast: full soon the time of the flood-tide must be:
Look how the grace of the sea doth go
About and about through the intricate channels that flow
Here and there,
Everywhere,
Till his waters have flooded the uttermost creeks and the low-
lying lanes,
And the marsh is meshed with a million veins,
That like as with rosy and silvery essences flow
In the rose-and-silver evening glow.
Farewell, my lord Sun!
The creeks overflow: a thousand rivulets run
'Twixt the roots of the sod; the blades of the marsh-grass stir;
Passeth a hurrying sound of wings that westward whirr;
Passeth, and all is still; and the currents cease to run;
And the sea and the marsh are one.
How still the plains of the waters be!
The tide is in his ecstasy.
The tide is at his highest height:
And it is night.

And now from the Vast of the Lord will the waters of sleep
Roll in on the souls of men,
But who will reveal to our waking ken
The forms that swim and the shapes that creep

Under the waters of sleep?
And I would I could know what swimmeth below when the
   tide comes in
On the length and the breadth of the marvellous marshes of
   Glynn.

SONG OF THE CHATTAHOOCHEE

Out of the hills of Habersham,
   Down the valleys of Hall,
I hurry amain to reach the plain,
Run the rapid and leap the fall,
Split at the rock and together again,
Accept my bed, or narrow or wide,
And flee from folly on every side
With a lover's pain to attain the plain
   Far from the hills of Habersham,
   Far from the valleys of Hall.

All down the hills of Habersham,
   All through the valleys of Hall,
The rushes cried *Abide, abide,*
The willful waterweeds held me thrall,
The laving laurel turned my tide,
The ferns and the fondling grass said *Stay,*
The dewberry dipped for to work delay,
And the little reeds sighed *Abide, abide,*
   Here in the hills of Habersham,
   Here in the valleys of Hall.

High o'er the hills of Habersham,
   Veiling the valleys of Hall,
The hickory told me manifold
Fair tales of shade, the poplar tall
Wrought me her shadowy self to hold,
The chestnut, the oak, the walnut, the pine,

Overleaning, with flickering meaning and sign,
Said, *Pass not, so cold, these manifold*
Deep shades of the hills of Habersham,
These glades in the valleys of Hall.

And oft in the hills of Habersham,
And oft in the valleys of Hall,
The white quartz shone, and the smooth brook-stone
Did bar me of passage with friendly brawl,
And many a luminous jewel lone
—Crystals clear or a-cloud with mist,
Ruby, garnet and amethyst—
Made lures with the lights of streaming stone
In the clefts of the hills of Habersham,
In the beds of the valleys of Hall.

But oh, not the hills of Habersham,
And oh, not the valleys of Hall
Avail: I am fain for to water the plain.
Downward the voices of Duty call—
Downward, to toil and be mixed with the main,
The dry fields burn, and the mills are to turn,
And a myriad flowers mortally yearn,
And the lordly main from beyond the plain
Calls o'er the hills of Habersham,
Calls through the valleys of Hall.

Vachel Lindsay

THE LEADEN-EYED

Let not young souls be smothered out before
They do quaint deeds and fully flaunt their pride.
It is the world's one crime its babes grow dull,
Its poor are ox-like, limp and leaden-eyed.
Not that they starve, but starve so dreamlessly;
Not that they sow, but that they seldom reap;
Not that they serve, but have no gods to serve;
Not that they die, but that they die like sheep.

THE UNPARDONABLE SIN

This is the sin against the Holy Ghost:—
To speak of bloody power as right divine,
And call on God to guard each vile chief's house,
And for such chiefs, turn men to wolves and swine:—

To go forth killing in White Mercy's name,
Making the trenches stink with spattered brains,
Tearing the nerves and arteries apart,
Sowing with flesh the unreaped golden plains.

In any Church's name, to sack fair towns,
And turn each home into a screaming sty,
To make the little children fugitive,
And have their mothers for a quick death cry,—

This is the sin against the Holy Ghost:
This is the sin no purging can atone:—
To send forth rapine in the name of Christ:—
To set the face, and make the heart a stone.

SIMON LEGREE—A NEGRO SERMON

(To be read in your own variety of negro dialect.)

Legree's big house was white and green.
His cotton-fields were the best to be seen.
He had strong horses and opulent cattle,
And bloodhounds bold, with chains that would rattle.
His garret was full of curious things:
Books of magic, bags of gold,
And rabbits' feet on long twine strings.
But he went down to the Devil.

Legree, he sported a brass-buttoned coat,
A snake-skin necktie, a blood-red shirt.
Legree he had a beard like a goat,
And a thick hairy neck, and eyes like dirt.
His puffed-out cheeks were fish-belly white,
He had great long teeth, and an appetite.
He ate raw meat, 'most every meal,
And rolled his eyes till the cat would squeal.
His fist was an enormous size
To mash poor niggers that told him lies:
He was surely a witch-man in disguise.
But he went down to the Devil.

He wore hip boots, and would wade all day
To capture his slaves that had fled away.
But he went down to the Devil.

He beat poor Uncle Tom to death
Who prayed for Legree with his last breath.
Then Uncle Tom to Eva flew,
To the high sanctoriums bright and new;
And Simon Legree stared up beneath,
And cracked his heels, and ground his teeth:
And went down to the Devil.

He crossed the yard in the storm and gloom;
He went into his grand front room.

He said, "I liked him, and I don't care."
He kicked a hound, he gave a swear;
He tightened his belt, he took a lamp,
Went down cellar to the webs and damp.
There in the middle of the mouldy floor
He heaved up a slab, he found a door—
And went down to the Devil.

His lamp blew out, but his eyes burned bright.
Simon Legree stepped down all night—
Down, down to the Devil.
Simon Legree he reached the place,
He saw one half of the human race,
He saw the Devil on a wide green throne,
Gnawing the meat from a big ham-bone,
And he said to Mister Devil:
    "I see that you have much to eat—
    A red ham-bone is surely sweet.
    I see that you have lion's feet;
    I see your frame is fat and fine,
    I see you drink your poison wine—
    Blood and burning turpentine."

And the Devil said to Simon Legree:
    "I like your style, so wicked and free.
    Come sit and share my throne with me,
    And let us bark and revel."
And there they sit and gnash their teeth,
And each one wears a hop-vine wreath.
They are matching pennies and shooting craps,
They are playing poker and taking naps.
And old Legree is fat and fine:
He heats the fire, he drinks the wine—
Blood and burning turpentine—
        Down, down with the Devil;
          Down, down with the Devil;
            Down, down with the Devil.

THE EAGLE THAT IS FORGOTTEN

John P. Altgeld. Born December 30, 1847; Died March 12, 1902

Sleep softly . . . eagle forgotten . . . under the stone,
Time has its way with you there, and the clay has its own.
'We have buried him now,' thought your foes, and in secret
rejoiced.
They made a brave show of their mourning, their hatred un-
voiced.
They had snarled at you, barked at you, foamed at you, day
after day,
Now you were ended. They praised you, . . . and laid you
away.

The others that mourned you in silence and terror and truth,
The widow bereft of her pittance, the boy without youth,
The mocked and the scorned and the wounded, the lame and
the poor
That should have remembered forever, . . . remember no more.

Where are those lovers of yours, on what name do they call
The lost, that in armies wept over your funeral pall?
They call on the names of a hundred high-valiant ones,
A hundred white eagles have risen, the sons of your sons,
The zeal in their wings is a zeal that your dreaming began,
The valor that wore out your soul in the service of man.

Sleep softly, . . . eagle forgotten, . . . under the stone,
Time has its way with you there, and the clay has its own.
Sleep on, O brave hearted, O wise man, that kindled the
flame—
To live in mankind is far more than to live in a name,
To live in mankind, far, far more . . . than to live in a name.

THE BRONCHO THAT WOULD NOT BE BROKEN

A little colt—broncho, loaned to the farm
To be broken in time without fury or harm,
Yet black crows flew past you, shouting alarm,
Calling 'Beware,' with lugubrious singing . . .
The butterflies there in the bush were romancing,
The smell of the grass caught your soul in a trance,
So why be a-fearing the spurs and the traces,
O broncho that would not be broken of dancing?

You were born with the pride of the lords great and olden
Who danced, through the ages, in corridors golden.
In all the wide farm-place the person most human.
You spoke out so plainly with squealing and capering,
With whinnying, snorting contorting and prancing,
As you dodged your pursuers, looking askance,
With Greek-footed figures, and Parthenon paces,
O broncho that would not be broken of dancing.

The grasshoppers cheered. 'Keep whirling,' they said.
The insolent sparrows called from the shed
'If men will not laugh, make them wish they were dead.'
But arch were your thoughts, all malice displacing,
Though the horse-killers came, with snake-whips advancing.
You bantered and cantered away your last chance.
And they scourged you, with Hell in their speech and their
     faces,
O broncho that would not be broken of dancing.

'Nobody cares for you,' rattled the crows,
As you dragged the whole reaper, next day, down the rows.
The three mules held back, yet you danced on your toes.
You pulled like a racer, and kept the mules chasing.
You tangled the harness with bright eyes side-glancing,
While the drunk driver bled you—a pole for a lance—
And the giant mules bit at you—keeping their places,
O broncho that would not be broken of dancing.

In that last afternoon your boyish heart broke.
The hot wind came down like a sledge-hammer stroke.
The blood-sucking flies to a rare feast awoke.
And they searched out your wounds, your death-warrant
    tracing.
And the merciful men, their religion enhancing,
Stopped the red reaper, to give you a chance.
Then you died on the prairie, and scorned all disgraces,
O broncho that would not be broken of dancing.

THE GHOSTS OF THE BUFFALOES

Last night at black midnight I woke with a cry,
The windows were shaking, there was thunder on high,
The floor was atremble, the door was ajar,
White fires, crimson fires, shone from afar.
I rushed to the dooryard. The city was gone.
My home was a hut without orchard or lawn.
It was mud-smear and logs near a whispering stream,
Nothing else built by man could I see in my dream . . .

Then . . .
Ghost-kings came headlong, row upon row,
Gods of the Indians, torches aglow.
They mounted the bear and the elk and the deer,
And eagles gigantic, agèd and sere,
They rode long-horn cattle, they cried 'A-la-la.'
They lifted the knife, the bow, and the spear,
They lifted ghost-torches from dead fires below,
The midnight made grand with the cry 'A-la-la.'
The midnight made grand with a red-god charge,
A red-god show,
A red-god show,
'A-la-la, a-la-la, a-la-la, a-la-la.'

With bodies like bronze, and terrible eyes
Came the rank and the file, with catamount cries,

Gibbering, yipping, with hollow-skull clacks,
Riding white bronchos with skeleton backs,
Scalp-hunters, beaded and spangled and bad,
Naked and lustful and foaming and mad,
Flashing primeval demoniac scorn,
Blood-thirst and pomp amid darkness reborn,
Power and glory that sleep in the grass
While the winds and the snows and the great rains pass.
They crossed the gray river, thousands abreast,
They rode out in infinite lines to the west,
Tide upon tide of strange fury and foam,
Spirits and wraiths, the blue was their home,
The sky was their goal where the star-flags are furled,
And on past those far golden splendors they whirled.
They burned to dim meteors, lost in the deep,
And I turned in dazed wonder, thinking of sleep.

And the wind crept by
Alone, unkempt, unsatisfied,
The wind cried and cried—
Muttered of massacres long past,
Buffaloes in shambles vast . . .
An owl said, 'Hark, what is a-wing?'
I heard a cricket caroling,
I heard a cricket caroling,
I heard a cricket caroling.

Then . . .
Snuffing the lightning that crashed from on high
Rose royal old buffaloes, row upon row.
The lords of the prairie came galloping by.
And I cried in my heart 'A-la-la, a-la-la.
A red-god show,
A red-god show,
A-la-la, a-la-la, a-la-la.'
Buffaloes, buffaloes, thousands abreast,
A scourge and amazement, they swept to the west.
With black bobbing noses, with red rolling tongues,

Coughing forth steam from their leather-wrapped lungs,
Cows with their calves, bulls big and vain,
Goring the laggards, shaking the mane,
Stamping flint feet, flashing moon eyes,
Pompous and owlish, shaggy and wise.

Like sea-cliffs and caves resounded their ranks
With shoulders like waves, and undulant flanks.
Tide upon tide of strange fury and foam,
Spirits and wraiths, the blue was their home,
The sky was their goal where the star-flags are furled,
And on past those far golden splendors they whirled.
They burned to dim meteors, lost in the deep,
And I turned in dazed wonder, thinking of sleep.

I heard a cricket's cymbals play,
A scarecrow lightly flapped his rags,
And a pan that hung by his shoulder rang,
Rattled and thumped in a listless way,
And now the wind in the chimney sang,
The wind in the chimney,
The wind in the chimney,
The wind in the chimney,
Seemed to say:—   'Dream, boy, dream,
                    If you anywise can.
                    To dream is the work
                    Of beast or man.
Life is the west-going dream-storm's breath,
Life is a dream, the sigh of the skies,
The breath of the stars, that nod on their pillows
With their golden hair mussed over their eyes.'
The locust played on his musical wing,
Sang to his mate of love's delight.
I heard the whippoorwill's soft fret.
I heard a cricket caroling,
I heard a cricket caroling,
I heard a cricket say: 'Good-night, good-night,
Good-night, good-night, . . . good-night.'

FACTORY WINDOWS ARE ALWAYS BROKEN

Factory windows are always broken.
Somebody's always throwing bricks,
Somebody's always heaving cinders,
Playing ugly Yahoo tricks.

Factory windows are always broken.
Other windows are let alone.
No one throws through the chapel-window
The bitter, snarling, derisive stone.

Factory windows are always broken.
Something or other is going wrong.
Something is rotten—I think, in Denmark.
End of the factory-window song.

THE PONTOON BRIDGE MIRACLE

Prophets, preaching in new stars,
Have come in ships of sleep
And built a ghostly pontoon bridge that Michigan Avenue
Can keep.
Have built a causeway bright with sails
Where hares and tortoises may creep,
Where burbling bullfinches, laughing hyenas, whinnying
    Shetlands
Climb the steep.

Oh the harp-song of our sand-dunes
Up this arching avenue,
Oh the voices in the prophet-sails
Oh the lovers strolling slowly, two and two!

Though every Yankee patents some iron animals at last,
And does invent his own World's Fair,

And World's Fair tunes to cheer the air,
This is wild America, not orderly Timbuctoo.
So Barnum's old procession holds proud Michigan Avenue,
Again moves by up the pontoon bridge
To the Prophet Avenue.
The thought goes again through the night so dark,
Going up to the North-star ark,
Ostriches two and two,
Kangaroos two and two, behemoths two and two,
Hippogriffs two and two, chimeras two and two.

Oh Radio, Oh Saxophone, Oh Slide Trombone, Oh Horns that
    moan:—
The lion, the lion, goes roaring from his cage,
Ten thousand years before your jazz he roared a deeper rage.
And Jumbo, great Jumbo, goes swaying left and right,
Ten thousand years before your jazz his trumpet shook the
    night.
But Jenny Lind outsings him still upon the heaven-born wind,
Stands up in Barnum's carriage on that bridge across the vast,
That pontoon span of comet-boats arching above the past,
That silvery bridge of dawn across the cold.
In the rigging of their ships the prophets old
Sing with her their songs across the cold.

So, come let us forget our ivory-towers, brothers,
Come let us be bold with our songs.

THE CHINESE NIGHTINGALE

(A Song in Chinese Tapestries)

"How, how," he said. "Friend Chang," I said,
"San Francisco sleeps as the dead—
Ended license, lust and play:
Why do you iron the night away?
Your big clock speaks with a deadly sound,
With a tick and a wail till dawn comes round,

While the monster shadows glower and creep,
What can be better for man than sleep?"

"I will tell you a secret," Chang replied;
"My breast with vision is satisfied,
And I see green trees and fluttering wings,
And my deathless bird from Shanghai sings."
Then he lit five firecrackers in a pan,
"Pop, pop," said the firecrackers, "cra-cra-crack."
He lit a joss stick long and black.
Then the proud gray joss in the corner stirred;
On his wrist appeared a gray small bird,
And this was the song of the gray small bird:
"Where is the princess, loved forever,
Who made Chang first of the kings of men?"

And the joss in the corner stirred again;
And the carved dog, curled in his arms, awoke,
Barked forth a smoke-cloud that whirled and broke.
It piled in a maze round the ironing-place,
And there on the snowy table wide
Stood a Chinese lady of high degree,
With a scornful, witching, tea-rose face. . . .
Yet she put away all form and pride,
And laid her glimmering veil aside
With a childlike smile for Chang and me.

The walls fell back, night was aflower,
The table gleamed in a moonlit bower,
While Chang, with a countenance carved of stone,
Ironed and ironed, all alone.
And thus she sang to the busy man Chang:
"Have you forgotten . . .
Deep in the ages, long, long ago,
I was your sweetheart, there on the sand—
Storm-worn beach of the Chinese land?
We sold our grain in the peacock town—
Built on the edge of the sea-sands brown—
Built on the edge of the sea-sands brown. . . .

When all the world was drinking blood
From the skulls of men and bulls
And all the world had swords and clubs of stone,
We drank our tea in China beneath the sacred spice-trees,
And heard the curled waves of the harbor moan.
And this gray bird, in Love's first spring,
With a bright-bronze breast and a bronze-brown wing,
Captured the world with his caroling.
Do you remember, ages after,
At last the world we were born to own?
You were the heir of the yellow throne—
The world was the field of the Chinese man
And we were the pride of the Sons of Han?
We copied deep books and we carved in jade,
And wove blue silks in the mulberry shade...."

"I remember, I remember
That Spring came on forever,
That Spring came on forever,"
Said the Chinese nightingale.

My heart was filled with marvel and dream,
Though I saw the western street-lamps gleam,
Though dawn was bringing the western day,
Though Chang was a laundryman ironing away....
Mingled there with the streets and alleys,
The railroad-yard and the clock-tower bright,
Demon clouds crossed ancient valleys;
Across wide lotus-ponds of light
I marked a giant firefly's flight.

And the lady, rosy-red,
Flourished her fan, her shimmering fan,
Stretched her hand toward Chang, and said:
"Do you remember, Ages after,
Our palace of heart-red stone?
Do you remember
The little doll-faced children
With their lanterns full of moon-fire,
That came from all the empire

Honoring the throne?—
The loveliest fête and carnival
Our world had ever known?
The sages sat about us
With their heads bowed in their beards,
With proper meditation on the sight.
Confucius was not born;
We lived in those great days
Confucius later said were lived aright. . . .
And this gray bird, on that day of spring,
With a bright-bronze breast and a bronze-brown wing,
Captured the world with his caroling.
Late at night his tune was spent.
Peasants, Sages, Children, Homeward went,
And then the bronze bird sang for you and me.
We walked alone. Our hearts were high and free.
I had a silvery name, I had a silvery name,
I had a silvery name—do you remember
The name you cried beside the tumbling sea?"

Chang turned not to the lady slim—
He bent to his work, ironing away;
But she was arch, and knowing and glowing,
For the bird on his shoulder spoke for him.

"Darling . . . darling . . . darling . . . darling . . ."
Said the Chinese nightingale.

The great gray joss on the rustic shelf,
Rakish and shrewd, with his collar awry,
Sang impolitely, as though by himself,
Drowning with his bellowing the nightingale's cry:
"Back through a hundred, hundred years
Hear the waves as they climb the piers,
Hear the howl of the silver seas,
Hear the thunder.
Hear the gongs of holy China
How the waves and tunes combine
In a rhythmic clashing wonder,
Incantation old and fine:

'Dragons, dragons, Chinese dragons,
    Red firecrackers, and green firecrackers
    And dragons, dragons, Chinese dragons.' "

Then the lady, rosy-red,
Turned to her lover Chang and said:
"Dare you forget that turquoise dawn
When we stood in our mist-hung velvet lawn,
And worked a spell this great joss taught
Till a God of the Dragons was charmed and caught?
From the flag high over our palace home
He flew to our feet in rainbow-foam—
A king of beauty and tempest and thunder
Panting to tear our sorrows asunder.
A dragon of fair adventure and wonder.
We mounted the back of that royal slave
With thoughts of desire that were noble and grave.
We swam down the shore to the dragon-mountains,
We whirled to the peaks and the fiery fountains.
To our secret ivory house we were borne.
We looked down the wonderful wind-filled regions
Where the dragons darted in glimmering legions.
Right by my breast the nightingale sang;
The old rhymes rang in the sunlit mist
That we this hour regain— Song-fire for the brain.
When my hands and my hair and my feet you kissed,
When you cried for your heart's new pain,
What was my name in the dragon-mist,
In the rings of the rainbowed rain?"

"Sorrow and love, glory and love,"
        Sang the Chinese nightingale,
"Sorrow and love, glory and love,"
        Said the Chinese nightingale.

And now the joss broke in with his song:
"Dying ember, bird of Chang,
Soul of Chang, do you remember?—
Ere you returned to the shining harbor
There were pirates by ten thousand

Descended on the town
In vessels mountain-high and red and brown,
Moon-ships that climbed the storms and cut the skies.
On their prows were painted terrible bright eyes.
But I was then a wizard and a scholar and a priest;
I stood upon the sand;
With lifted hand I looked upon them
And sunk their vessels with my wizard eyes,
And the stately lacquer-gate made safe again.
Deep, deep below the bay, the seaweed and the spray,
Embalmed in amber every pirate lies,
Embalmed in amber every pirate lies."

Then this did the noble lady say:
"Bird, do you dream of our home-coming day
When you flew like a courier on before
From the dragon-peak to our palace-door,
And we drove the steed in your singing path—
The ramping dragon of laughter and wrath:
And found our city all aglow,
And knighted this joss that decked it so?
There were golden fishes in the purple river
And silver fishes and rainbow fishes.
There were golden junks in the laughing river,
And silver junks and rainbow junks:
There were golden lilies by the bay and river,
And silver lilies and tiger-lilies,
And tinkling wind-bells in the gardens of the town
By the black-lacquer gate Where walked in state
The kind king Chang And his sweetheart mate. . . .
With his flag-born dragon And his crown of pearl . . . and . . .
    jade,
And his nightingale reigning in the mulberry shade,
And sailors and soldiers on the sea-sands brown,
And priests who bowed them down to your song—
By the city called Han, the peacock town,
By the city called Han, the nightingale town,
The nightingale town."

Then sang the bird, so strangely gay,
Fluttering, fluttering, ghostly and gray,
A vague, unraveling, final tune,
Like a long unwinding silk cocoon;
Sang as though for the soul of him
Who ironed away in that bower dim:—
   "I have forgotten
   Your dragons great,
   Merry and mad and friendly and bold.
Dim is your proud lost palace-gate.
I vaguely know
There were heroes of old,
Troubles more than the heart could hold,
There were wolves in the woods
Yet lambs in the fold,
Nests in the top of the almond tree. . . .
The evergreen tree . . . and the mulberry tree. . . .
Life and hurry and joy forgotten,
Years and years I but half-remember . . .
Man is a torch, then ashes soon,
May and June, then dead December,
Dead December, then again June.
Who shall end my dream's confusion?
Life is a loom, weaving illusion. . . .
I remember, I remember
There were ghostly veils and laces. . . .
In the shadowy bowery places. . . .
With lovers' ardent faces Bending to one another,
Speaking each his part.
They infinitely echo In the red cave of my heart,
'Sweetheart, sweetheart, sweetheart,'
They said to one another.
They spoke, I think, of perils past.
They spoke, I think, of peace at last.
One thing I remember:
Spring came on forever,
Spring came on forever,"
Said the Chinese nightingale.

Henry Wadsworth Longfellow

HYMN TO THE NIGHT

I heard the trailing garments of the Night
   Sweep through her marble halls!
I saw her sable skirts all fringed with light
   From the celestial walls!

I felt her presence, by its spell of might,
   Stoop o'er me from above;
The calm, majestic presence of the Night,
   As of the one I love.

I heard the sounds of sorrow and delight,
   The manifold, soft chimes,
That fill the haunted chambers of the Night,
   Like some old poet's rhymes.

From the cool cisterns of the midnight air
   My spirit drank repose;
The fountain of perpetual peace flows there,—
   From those deep cisterns flows.

O holy Night! from thee I learn to bear
   What man has borne before!
Thou layest thy finger on the lips of Care,
   And they complain no more.

Peace! Peace! Orestes-like I breathe this prayer!
   Descend with broad-winged flight,
The welcome, the thrice-prayed for, the most fair,
   The best-beloved Night!

THE TIDE RISES, THE TIDE FALLS

The tide rises, the tide falls,
The twilight darkens, the curlew calls;
Along the sea-sands damp and brown
The traveller hastens toward the town,
    And the tide rises, the tide falls.

Darkness settles on roofs and walls,
But the sea, the sea in the darkness calls;
The little waves, with their soft, white hands,
Efface the footprints in the sands,
    And the tide rises, the tide falls.

The morning breaks; the steeds in their stalls
Stamp and neigh, as the hostler calls;
The day returns, but nevermore
Returns the traveller to the shore,
    And the tide rises, the tide falls.

CHAUCER

An old man in a lodge within a park;
The chamber walls depicted all around
With portraitures of huntsman, hawk, and hound,
And the hurt deer. He listeneth to the lark,
Whose song comes with the sunshine through the dark
Of painted glass in leaden lattice bound;
He listeneth and he laugheth at the sound,
Then writeth in a book like any clerk.
He is the poet of the dawn, who wrote
The Canterbury Tales, and his old age
Made beautiful with song; and as I read
I hear the crowing cock, I hear the note
Of lark and linnet, and from every page
Rise odors of ploughed field or flowery mead.

DIVINA COMMEDIA

I

Oft have I seen at some cathedral door
A laborer, pausing in the dust and heat,
Lay down his burden, and with reverent feet
Enter, and cross himself, and on the floor
Kneel to repeat his paternoster o'er;
Far off the noises of the world retreat;
The loud vociferations of the street
Become an undistinguishable roar.
So, as I enter here from day to day,
And leave my burden at this minster gate,
Kneeling in prayer, and not ashamed to pray,
The tumult of the time disconsolate
To inarticulate murmurs dies away,
While the eternal ages watch and wait.

II

How strange the sculptures that adorn these towers!
This crowd of statues, in whose folded sleeves
Birds build their nests; while canopied with leaves
Parvis and portal bloom like trellised bowers,
And the vast minster seems a cross of flowers!
But fiends and dragons on the gargoyled eaves
Watch the dead Christ between the living thieves,
And, underneath, the traitor Judas lowers!
Ah! from what agonies of heart and brain,
What exultations trampling on despair,
What tenderness, what tears, what hate of wrong,
What passionate outcry of a soul in pain,
Uprose this poem of the earth and air,
This mediæval miracle of song!

III

I enter, and I see thee in the gloom
Of the long aisles, O poet saturnine!

And strive to make my steps keep pace with thine.
The air is filled with some unknown perfume;
The congregation of the dead make room
For thee to pass; the votive tapers shine;
Like rooks that haunt Ravenna's groves of pine
The hovering echoes fly from tomb to tomb.
From the confessionals I hear arise
Rehearsals of forgotten tragedies,
And lamentations from the crypts below;
And then a voice celestial that begins
With the pathetic words, 'Although your sins
As scarlet be,' and ends with 'as the snow.'

IV

With snow-white veil and garments as of flame,
She stands before thee, who so long ago
Filled thy young heart with passion and the woe
From which thy song and all its splendors came;
And while with stern rebuke she speaks thy name,
The ice about thy heart melts as the snow
On mountain heights, and in swift overflow
Comes gushing from thy lips in sobs of shame.
Thou makest full confession; and a gleam,
As of the dawn on some dark forest cast,
Seems on thy lifted forehead to increase;
Lethe and Eunoë—the remembered dream
And the forgotten sorrow—bring at last
That perfect pardon which is perfect peace.

V

I lift mine eyes, and all the windows blaze
With forms of Saints and holy men who died,
Here martyred and hereafter glorified;
And the great Rose upon its leaves displays
Christ's Triumph, and the angelic roundelays,
With splendor upon splendor multiplied;
And Beatrice again at Dante's side

No more rebukes, but smiles her words of praise.
And then the organ sounds, and unseen choirs
Sing the old Latin hymns of peace and love
And benedictions of the Holy Ghost;
And the melodious bells among the spires
O'er all the house-tops and through heaven above
Proclaim the elevation of the Host!

VI

O star of morning and of liberty!
O bringer of the light, whose splendor shines
Above the darkness of the Apennines,
Forerunner of the day that is to be!
The voices of the city and the sea,
The voices of the mountains and the pines,
Repeat thy song, till the familiar lines
Are footpaths for the thought of Italy!
Thy flame is blown abroad from all the heights,
Through all the nations, and a sound is heard,
As of a mighty wind, and men devout,
Strangers of Rome, and the new proselytes,
In their own language hear thy wondrous word,
And many are amazed and many doubt.

MY LOST YOUTH

Often I think of the beautiful town
    That is seated by the sea;
Often in thought go up and down
The pleasant streets of that dear old town,
    And my youth comes back to me.
        And a verse of a Lapland song
        Is haunting my memory still:
        'A boy's will is the wind's will,
And the thoughts of youth are long, long thoughts.'

I can see the shadowy lines of its trees,
    And catch, in sudden gleams,
The sheen of the far-surrounding seas,
And islands that were the Hesperides
    Of all my boyish dreams.
        And the burden of that old song,
        It murmurs and whispers still:
        'A boy's will is the wind's will,
And the thoughts of youth are long, long thoughts.'

I remember the black wharves and the slips,
    And the sea-tides tossing free;
And Spanish sailors with bearded lips,
And the beauty and mystery of the ships,
    And the magic of the sea.
        And the voice of that wayward song
        Is singing and saying still:
        'A boy's will is the wind's will,
And the thoughts of youth are long, long thoughts.'

I remember the bulwarks by the shore,
    And the fort upon the hill;
The sunrise gun, with its hollow roar,
The drum-beat repeated o'er and o'er,
    And the bugle wild and shrill.
        And the music of that old song
        Throbs in my memory still:
        'A boy's will is the wind's will,
And the thoughts of youth are long, long thoughts.'

I remember the sea-fight far away,
    How it thundered o'er the tide!
And the dead captains, as they lay
In their graves, o'erlooking the tranquil bay
    Where they in battle died.
        And the sound of that mournful song
        Goes through me with a thrill:

'A boy's will is the wind's will,
And the thoughts of youth are long, long thoughts.'

I can see the breezy dome of groves,
     The shadows of Deering's Woods;
And the friendships old and the early loves
Come back with a Sabbath sound, as of doves
     In quiet neighborhoods.
          And the verse of that sweet old song,
               It flutters and murmurs still:
               'A boy's will is the wind's will,
And the thoughts of youth are long, long thoughts.'

I remember the gleams and glooms that dart
     Across the school-boy's brain;
The song and the silence in the heart,
That in part are prophecies, and in part
     Are longings wild and vain.
          And the voice of that fitful song
               Sings on, and is never still:
               'A boy's will is the wind's will,
And the thoughts of youth are long, long thoughts.'

There are things of which I may not speak;
     There are dreams that cannot die;
There are thoughts that make the strong heart weak,
And bring a pallor into the cheek,
     And a mist before the eye.
          And the words of that fatal song
               Come over me like a chill:
               'A boy's will is the wind's will,
And the thoughts of youth are long, long thoughts.'

Strange to me now are the forms I meet
     When I visit the dear old town;
But the native air is pure and sweet,
And the trees that o'ershadow each well-known street,

As they balance up and down,
Are singing the beautiful song,
Are sighing and whispering still:
'A boy's will is the wind's will,
And the thoughts of youth are long, long thoughts.'

And Deering's Woods are fresh and fair,
And with joy that is almost pain
My heart goes back to wander there,
And among the dreams of the days that were,
I find my lost youth again.
And the strange and beautiful song,
The groves are repeating it still:
'A boy's will is the wind's will,
And the thoughts of youth are long, long thoughts.'

MILTON

I pace the sounding sea-beach and behold
How the voluminous billows roll and run,
Upheaving and subsiding, while the sun
Shines through their sheeted emerald far unrolled
And the ninth wave, slow gathering fold on fold
All its loose-flowing garments into one,
Plunges upon the shore, and floods the dun
Pale reach of sands, and changes them to gold.
So in majestic cadence rise and fall
The mighty undulations of thy song,
O sightless bard, England's Maeonides!
And ever and anon, high over all
Uplifted, a ninth wave superb and strong,
Floods all the soul with its melodious seas.

David Lougée

A SESTINA FOR CYNTHIA

You whom the waters make fierce and the moon quiets,
In whose white body's book I read an owlish tale
And to whose sacred wood I sent a houndsman riding,
Receive what I have built in the night's quarry;
See, as in a mirror, what I have always known;
Trace the flesh's wonder in its changing image.

It was as crying sea-gales carved your image
That green birds came, as when a cool wind quiets
Bothered sleep, and spelled out what I had not known
Before, how lightest birds can buff a weather's tale
And hold back winter from a blackened quarry,
Though on the coldest waters they are riding.

And wild in the wet wood, tuned to a houndsman's riding
And a bird's cry steady mounting, I traced the image
In your tussled hair, and in my dark stone quarry,
And caught the raging spell no rude mouth quiets
And found that of your name is knelled the water's tale.
So do bells relate what chimed rock has known.

Harking to those bells, a red-capped prince has known
The wonder of a princess, prim and coy; and of her riding
In the hidden wood. Hearing loud the flail-winds' tale,
Marking long those hills where blows your image
And called to by a houndsman whom no hard night quiets,
That anxious prince strayed past my silent quarry.

Held in that constant season, autumn round my quarry,
I sought what chiseled note a princess would have known;
Told the carrying wind how a grave surge quiets,
Let ring the lasting vision of those light birds riding.
And saw as my reply the rock-sprung curling of your image
Through bending grasses where began the wild tale.

And waters leapt to that reply, mirroring the tale
Knelled in the waves' top reaches; and joyous in my quarry,
There rose in utter bloom the white blaze of your image,
Spread through swelling light what a worn wood had known,
Fast before the houndsman the proud prince riding
Seeking straight that clamor which a soft rain quiets.

You whose smile quiets night and the knelling tale,
To whom a high prince riding and the poet in his quarry
Bow, know what love has known, this shifting image.

Amy Lowell

PATTERNS

I walk down the garden paths,
And all the daffodils
Are blowing, and the bright blue squills.
I walk down the patterned garden-paths
In my stiff, brocaded gown.
With my powdered hair and jewelled fan,
I too am a rare
Pattern. As I wander down
The garden paths.

My dress is richly figured,
And the train
Makes a pink and silver stain
On the gravel, and the thrift
Of the borders.
Just a plate of current fashion,
Tripping by in high-heeled, ribboned shoes.
Not a softness anywhere about me,
Only whalebone and brocade.
And I sink on a seat in the shade
Of a lime tree. For my passion
Wars against the stiff brocade.

The daffodils and squills
Flutter in the breeze
As they please.
And I weep;
For the lime-tree is in blossom
And one small flower has dropped upon my bosom.

And the plashing of waterdrops
In the marble fountain
Comes down the garden-paths.
The dripping never stops.
Underneath my stiffened gown
Is the softness of a woman bathing in a marble basin,
A basin in the midst of hedges grown
So thick, she cannot see her lover hiding,
But she guesses he is near,
And the sliding of the water
Seems the stroking of a dear
Hand upon her.
What is Summer in a fine brocaded gown!
I should like to see it lying in a heap upon the ground.
All the pink and silver crumpled up on the ground.

I would be the pink and silver as I ran along the paths,
And he would stumble after,
Bewildered by my laughter.
I should see the sun flashing from his sword-hilt and the
        buckles on his shoes.
I would choose
To lead him in a maze along the patterned paths,
A bright and laughing maze for my heavy-booted lover.
Till he caught me in the shade,
And the buttons of his waistcoat bruised my body as he
        clasped me,
Aching, melting, unafraid.
With the shadows of the leaves and the sundrops,
And the plopping of the waterdrops,
All about us in the open afternoon—

I am very like to swoon
With the weight of this brocade,
For the sun sifts through the shade.

Underneath the fallen blossom
In my bosom,
Is a letter I have hid.
It was brought to me this morning by a rider from the Duke.
'Madam, we regret to inform you that Lord Hartwell
Died in action Thursday se'nnight.'
As I read it in the white, morning sunlight,
The letters squirmed like snakes.
'Any answer, Madam,' said my footman.
'No,' I told him.
'See that the messenger takes some refreshment.
No, no answer.'
And I walked into the garden,
Up and down the patterned paths,
In my stiff, correct brocade.
The blue and yellow flowers stood up proudly in the sun,
Each one.
I stood upright too,
Held rigid to the pattern
By the stiffness of my gown.
Up and down I walked,
Up and down.

In a month he would have been my husband.
In a month, here, underneath this lime,
We would have broke the pattern;
He for me, and I for him,
He as Colonel, I as Lady,
On this shady seat.
He had a whim
That sunlight carried blessing.
And I answered, 'It shall be as you have said.'
Now he is dead.

In Summer and in Winter I shall walk
Up and down
The patterned garden-paths
In my stiff, brocaded gown.
The squills and daffodils
Will give place to pillared roses, and to asters, and to snow.
I shall go
Up and down,
In my gown.
Gorgeously arrayed,
Boned and stayed.
And the softness of my body will be guarded from embrace
By each button, hook, and lace.
For the man who should loose me is dead,
Fighting with the Duke in Flanders,
In a pattern called a war.
Christ! What are patterns for?

James Russell Lowell

NOT ONLY AROUND OUR INFANCY

Not only around our infancy
Doth heaven with all its splendors lie;
Daily, with souls that cringe and plot,
We Sinais climb and know it not.

Over our manhood bend the skies;
　　Against our fallen and traitor lives
The great winds utter prophecies;
　　With our faint hearts the mountain strives;
Its arms outstretched, the druid wood
　　Waits with its benedicite;
And to our age's drowsy blood
　　Still shouts the inspiring sea.

Earth gets its price for what Earth gives us;
  The beggar is taxed for a corner to die in,
The priest hath his fee who comes and shrives us.
  We bargain for the graves we lie in;
At the Devil's booth are all things sold,
Each ounce of dross costs its ounce of gold;
  For a cap and bells our lives we pay,
Bubbles we buy with a whole soul's tasking:
  'Tis heaven alone that is given away,
'Tis only God may be had for the asking.

From *The Vision of Sir Launfal*

WHAT IS SO RARE AS A DAY IN JUNE?

No price is set on the lavish summer,
And June may be had by the poorest comer.
And what is so rare as a day in June?
  Then, if ever, come perfect days;
Then Heaven tries the earth if it be in tune,
  And over it softly her warm ear lays:
Whether we look, or whether we listen,
We hear life murmur, or see it glisten;
Every clod feels a stir of might,
  An instinct within it that reaches and towers
And, groping blindly above it for light,
  Climbs to a soul in grass and flowers;
The flush of life may well be seen
  Thrilling back over hills and valleys;
The cowslip startles in meadows green,
  The buttercup catches the sun in its chalice
And there's never a leaf or a blade too mean
  To be some happy creature's palace;
The little bird sits at his door in the sun,
  Atilt like a blossom among the leaves,
And lets his illumined being o'errun
  With the deluge of summer it receives;
His mate feels the eggs beneath her wings,

And the heart in her dumb breast flutters and sings;
He sings to the wide world, and she to her nest,—
In the nice ear of Nature, which song is the best?

Now is the high-tide of the year,
    And whatever of life hath ebbed away
Comes flooding back, with a ripply cheer,
    Into every bare inlet and creek and bay;
Now the heart is so full that a drop overfills it,
We are happy now because God wills it;
No matter how barren the past may have been,
'Tis enough for us now that the leaves are green;
We sit in the warm shade and feel right well
How the sap creeps up and the blossoms swell;
We may shut our eyes, but we cannot help knowing
That skies are clear and grass is growing;
That breeze comes whispering in our ear,
That dandelions are blossoming near,
    That maize has sprouted, that streams are flowing,
That the river is bluer than the sky,
That the robin is plastering his house hard by;
And if the breeze kept the good news back,
For other couriers we should not lack;
    We could guess it all by yon heifer's lowing,—
And hark! how clear bold chanticleer,
Warmed with the new wine of the year,
    Tells all in his lusty crowing!

Joy comes, grief goes, we know not how;
Everything is happy now,
    Everything is upward striving;
'Tis as easy now for the heart to be true
As for grass to be green or skies to be blue,—
    'Tis the natural way of living:
Who knows whither the clouds have fled?
    In the unscarred heaven they leave no wake,
And the eyes forget the tears they have shed,

The heart forgets its sorrow and ache;
The soul partakes the season's youth,
    And the sulphurous rifts of passion and woe
Lie deep 'neath a silence pure and smooth,
    Like burnt-out craters healed with snow.

From *The Vision of Sir Launfal*

AUSPEX

My heart, I cannot still it,
Nest that had song-birds in it;
And when the last shall go,
The dreary days, to fill it,
Instead of lark or linnet,
Shall whirl dead leaves and
    snow.

Had they been swallows
    only,
Without the passion stronger
That skyward longs and sings,—

Woe's me, I shall be lonely
When I can feel no longer
The impatience of their
    wings!

A moment, sweet delusion,
Like birds the brown leaves
    hover;
But it will not be long
Before their wild confusion
Fall wavering down to cover
The poet and his song.

Robert Lowell

AS A PLANE TREE BY THE WATER

Darkness has called to darkness, and disgrace
Elbows about our windows in this planned
Babel of Boston where our money talks
And multiplies the darkness of a land
Of preparation where the Virgin walks
And roses spiral her enamelled face
Or fall to splinters on unwatered streets.
Our Lady of Babylon, go by, go by,

I was once the apple of your eye;
Flies, flies are on the plane tree, on the streets.

The flies, the flies, the flies of Babylon
Buzz in my ear-drums while the devil's long
Dirge of the people detonates the hour
For floating cities where his golden tongue
Enchants the masons of the Babel Tower
To raise tomorrow's city to the sun
That never sets upon these hell-fire streets
Of Boston, where the sunlight is a sword
Striking at the withholder of the Lord:
Flies, flies are on the plane tree, on the streets.

Flies strike the miraculous waters of the iced
Atlantic and the eyes of Bernadette
Who saw Our Lady standing in the cave
At Massabielle, saw her so squarely that
Her vision put out reason's eyes. The grave
Is open-mouthed and swallowed up in Christ.
O walls of Jericho! And all the streets
To our Atlantic wall are singing: 'Sing,
Sing for the resurrection of the King.'
Flies, flies are on the plane tree, on the streets.

CHRISTMAS EVE UNDER HOOKER'S STATUE

Tonight a blackout. Twenty years ago
I hung my stocking on the tree, and hell's
Serpent entwined the apple in the toe
To sting the child with knowledge. Hooker's heels
Kicking at nothing in the shifting snow,
A cannon and a cairn of cannon balls
Rusting before the blackened Statehouse, know
How the long horn of plenty broke like glass
In Hooker's gauntlets. Once I came from Mass;

Now storm-clouds shelter Christmas, once again
Mars meets his fruitless star with open arms,
His heavy saber flashes with the rime,
The war-god's bronzed and empty forehead forms
Anonymous machinery from raw men;
The cannon on the Common cannot stun
The blundering butcher as he rides on Time—
The barrel clinks with holly. I am cold:
I ask for bread, my father gives me mould;

His stocking is full of stones. Santa in red
Is crowned with wizened berries. Man of war,
Where is the summer's garden? In its bed
The ancient speckled serpent will appear,
And black-eyed susan with her frizzled head.
When Chancellorsville mowed down the volunteer,
'All wars are boyish,' Herman Melville said;
But we are old, our fields are running wild:
Till Christ again turn wanderer and child.

THE EXILE'S RETURN

There mounts in squalls a sort of rusty mire,
Not ice, not snow, to leaguer the Hôtel
De Ville, where braced pig-iron dragons grip
The blizzard to their rigor mortis. A bell
Grumbles when the reverberations strip
The thatching from its spire,
The search-guns click and spit and split up timber
And nick the slate roofs on the Holstenwall
Where torn-up tilestones crown the victor. Fall
And winter, spring and summer, guns unlimber
And lumber down the narrow gabled street
Past your gray, sorry and ancestral house
Where the dynamited walnut tree
Shadows a squat, old, wind-torn gate and cows
The bristling podestà. You will not see
Strutting children or meet

The peg-leg and reproachful chancellor
With a forget-me-not in his button-hole
When the unseasoned liberators roll
Into the Market Square, ground arms before
The Rathaus; but already lily-stands
Burgeon the risen Rhineland, and a rough
Cathedral lifts its eye. Pleasant enough,
Voi ch'entrate, and your life is in your hands.

THE DEAD IN EUROPE

After the planes unloaded, we fell down
Buried together, unmarried men and women;
Not crown of thorns, not iron, not Lombard crown,
Not grilled and spindle spires pointing to heaven
Could save us. Raise us, Mother, we fell down
Here hugger-mugger in the jellied fire:
Our sacred earth in our day was our curse.

Our Mother, shall we rise on Mary's day
In Maryland, wherever corpses married
Under the rubble, bundled together? Pray
For us whom the blockbusters marred and buried;
When Satan scatters us on Rising-day,
O Mother, snatch our bodies from the fire:
Our sacred earth in our day was our curse.

Mother, my bones are trembling and I hear
The earth's reverberations and the trumpet
Bleating into my shambles. Shall I bear,
(O Mary!) unmarried man and powder-puppet,
Witness to the Devil? Mary, hear,
O Mary, marry earth, sea, air and fire;
Our sacred earth in our day is our curse.

THE QUAKER GRAVEYARD IN NANTUCKET

(For Warren Winslow, Dead at Sea)

Let man have dominion over the fishes of the sea and the fowls of the air and the beasts and the whole earth, and every creeping creature that moveth upon the earth.

I

A brackish reach of shoal off Madaket,—
The sea was still breaking violently and night
Had steamed into our North Atlantic Fleet,
When the drowned sailor clutched the drag-net. Light
Flashed from his matted head and marble feet,
He grappled at the net
With the coiled, hurdling muscles of his thighs:
The corpse was bloodless, a botch of reds and whites,
Its open, staring eyes
Were lustreless dead-lights
Or cabin-windows on a stranded hulk
Heavy with sand. We weight the body, close
Its eyes and heave it seaward whence it came,
Where the heel-headed dogfish barks its nose
On Ahab's void and forehead; and the name
Is blocked in yellow chalk.
Sailors, who pitch this portent at the sea
Where dreadnaughts shall confess
Its hell-bent deity,
When you are powerless
To sand-bag this Atlantic bulwark, faced
By the earth-shaker, green, unwearied, chaste
In his steel scales: ask for no Orphean lute
To pluck life back. The guns of the steeled fleet
Recoil and then repeat
The hoarse salute.

II

Whenever winds are moving and their breath
Heaves at the roped-in bulwarks of this pier,
The terns and sea-gulls tremble at your death

In these home waters. Sailor, can you hear
The Pequod's sea wings, beating landward, fall
Headlong and break on our Atlantic wall
Off 'Sconset, where the yawing S-boats splash
The bellbuoy, with ballooning spinnakers,
As the entangled, screeching mainsheet clears
The blocks: off Madaket, where lubbers lash
The heavy surf and throw their long lead squids
For blue-fish? Sea-gulls blink their heavy lids
Seaward. The winds' wings beat upon the stones,
Cousin, and scream for you and the claws rush
At the sea's throat and wring it in the slush
Of this old Quaker graveyard where the bones
Cry out in the long night for the hurt beast
Bobbing by Ahab's whaleboats in the East.

III

All you recovered from Poseidon died
With you, my cousin, and the harrowed brine
Is fruitless on the blue beard of the god,
Stretching beyond us to the castles in Spain,
Nantucket's westward haven. To Cape Cod
Guns, cradled on the tide,
Blast the eelgrass about a waterclock
Of bilge and backwash, roil the salt and sand
Lashing earth's scaffold, rock
Our warships in the hand
Of the great God, where time's contrition blues
Whatever it was these Quaker sailors lost
In the mad scramble of their lives. They died
When time was open-eyed,
Wooden and childish; only bones abide
There, in the nowhere, where their boats were tossed
Sky-high, where mariners had fabled news
Of Is, the swashing castle. What it cost
Them is their secret. In the monster's slick
I see the Quakers drown and hear their cry:

'If God himself had not been on our side,
If God himself had not been on our side,
When the Atlantic rose against us, why,
Then it had swallowed us up quick.'

IV

This is the end of the whaleroad and the whale
Who spewed Nantucket bones on the thrashed swell
And stirred the troubled waters to whirlpools
To send the Pequod packing off to hell:
This is the end of them, three-quarters fools,
Snatching at straws to sail
Seaward and seaward on the turntail whale,
Spouting out blood and water as it rolls,
Sick as a dog to these Atlantic shoals:
Clamavimus, O depths. Let the sea-gulls wail

For water, for the deep where the high tide
Mutters to its hurt self, mutters and ebbs.
Waves wallow in their wash, go out and out,
Leave only the death-rattle of the crabs,
The beach increasing, its enormous snout
Sucking the ocean's side.
This is the end of running on the waves;
We are poured out like water. Who will dance
The mast-lashed master of Leviathans
Up from this field of Quakers in their unstoned graves?

V

When the whale's viscera go and the roll
Of its corruption overruns this world
Beyond tree-swept Nantucket and Wood's Hole
And Martha's Vineyard, Sailor, will your sword
Whistle and fall and sink into the fat?
In the great ash-pit of Jehoshaphat
The bones cry for the blood of the white whale,
The fat flukes arch and whack about its ears,

The death-lance churns into the sanctuary, tears
The gun-blue swingle, heaving like a flail,
And hacks the coiling life out: it works and drags
And rips the sperm-whale's midriff into rags,
Gobbets of blubber spill to wind and weather,
Sailor, and gulls go round the stoven timbers
Where the morning stars sing out together
And thunder shakes the white surf and dismembers
The red flag hammered in the mast-head. Hide,
Our steel, Jonas Messias, in Thy side.

VI

Our Lady of Walsingham

There once the penitents took off their shoes
And then walked barefoot the remaining mile;
And the small trees, a stream and hedgerows file
Slowly along the munching English lane,
Like cows to the old shrine, until you lose
Track of your dragging pain.
The stream flows down under the druid tree,
Shiloah's whirlpools gurgle and make glad
The castle of God. Sailor, you were glad
And whistled Sion by that stream. But see:

Our Lady, too small for her canopy,
Sits near the altar. There's no comeliness
At all or charm in that expressionless
Face with its heavy eyelids. As before,
This face, for centuries a memory,
Non est species, neque decor,
Expressionless, expresses God: it goes
Past castled Sion. She knows what God knows,
Not Calvary's Cross nor crib at Bethlehem
Now, and the world shall come to Walsingham.

VII

The empty winds are creaking and the oak
Splatters and splatters on the cenotaph,
The boughs are trembling and a gaff
Bobs on the untimely stroke
Of the greased wash exploding on a shoal-bell
In the old mouth of the Atlantic. It's well;
Atlantic, you are fouled with the blue sailors,
Sea-monsters, upward angel, downward fish:
Unmarried and corroding, spare of flesh
Mart once of supercilious, wing'd clippers,
Atlantic, where your bell-trap guts its spoil
You could cut the brackish winds with a knife
Here in Nantucket, and cast up the time
When the Lord God formed man from the sea's slime
And breathed into his face the breath of life,
And blue-lung'd combers lumbered to the kill.
The Lord survives the rainbow of His will.

Willard Maas

ON READING GENE DERWOOD'S 'THE INNOCENT'

Death of the innocent by the innocent
Endured! Poet, asking for Death who asked for Life,
Rare as rose by savage new-spring sent,
Warm welcome to the bursting eyes, O living leaf!
Over us all the act we all repent,
Over all the pall, the deed, this grief.
Dare the tongue cry out but what *our* guilt repents?

Everyone being the cause of everyone's pain,
Under star, under war, under the look of joy
Great as the marble smile from Greece, everyone
Endures the mutual crime. The flying-boy
Nightward to murder lifted, in his heart-stone,
In which like the thunder-rock the amethysts lay,
All acts in their secret core bear the violet jewel then.

Archibald MacLeish

THE SILENT SLAIN

We too, we too, descending once again
The hills of our own land, we too have heard
Far off—Ah, que ce cor a longue haleine—
The horn of Roland in the passages of Spain,
The first, the second blast, the failing third,
And with the third turned back and climbed once more
The steep road southward, and heard faint the sound
Of swords, of horses, the disastrous war,
And crossed the dark defile at last, and found
At Roncevaux upon the darkening plain
The dead against the dead and on the silent ground
The silent slain—

L'AN TRENTIESME DE MON EAGE

And I have come upon this place
By lost ways, by a nod, by words,
By faces, by an old man's face
At Morlaix lifted to the birds,

By hands upon the tablecloth
At Aldebori's, by the thin
Child's hands that opened to the moth
And let the flutter of the moonlight in,

By hands, by voices, by the voice
Of Mrs. Whitman on the stair,
By Margaret's "If we had the choice
To choose or not—" through her thick hair,

By voices, by the creak and fall
Of footsteps on the upper floor,

By silence waiting in the hall
Between the doorbell and the door,

By words, by voices, a lost way—
And here above the chimney stack
The unknown constellations sway—
And by what way shall I go back?

EVER SINCE

What do you remember thinking back?
What do you think of at dusk in the slack
Evening when the mind refills
With the cool past as a well fills in
Darkness from forgotten rains?

Do you think of waking in the all-night train,
The curtains drawn, the Mediterranean
Blue, blue, and the sellers of oranges
Holding heaped up morning toward you?

Do you think of Kumomoto-Ken
And the clogs going by in the night and the scent of
Clean mats, the sound of the peepers,
The wind in the pines, the dark sleep?

Do you think how Santiago stands at
Night under its stars, under its Andes:
Its bells like heavy birds that climb
Widening circles out of time?

I saw them too. I know those places.
There are no mountains—scarcely a face
Of all the faces you have seen,
Or a town or a room, but I have seen it.

Even at dusk in the deep chair
Letting the long past take you, bear you—

Even then you never leave me, never can.
Your eyes close, your small hands
Keep their secrets in your lap:
Wherever you are we two were happy.

I wonder what those changing lovers do,
Watching each other in the darkening room,
Whose world together is the night they've shared:
Whose past is parting: strangers side by side.

POLE STAR FOR THIS YEAR

Where the wheel of light is turned:
Where the axle of the night is
Turned: is motionless: where holds
And has held ancient sureness always:

Where of faring men the eyes
At oar bench at the rising bow
Have seen—torn shrouds between—the Wain
And that star's changelessness: not changing:

There upon that intent star:
Trust of wandering men: of truth
The most reminding witness: we
Fix our eyes also: waylost: the wanderers:

We too turn now to that star:
We too in whose trustless hearts
All truth alters and the lights
Of earth are out now turn to that star:

Liberty of man and mind
That once was mind's necessity
And made the West blaze up has burned
To bloody embers and the lamp's out:

Hope that was a noble flame
Has fanned to violence and feeds

On cities and the flesh of men
And chokes where unclean smoke defiles it:

Even the small spark of pride
That taught the tyrant once is dark
Where gunfire rules the starving street
And justice cheats the dead of honor:

Liberty and pride and hope
And every guide-mark of the mind
That led our blindness once has vanished.
This star will not. Love's star will not.

Love that has beheld the face
A man has with a man's eyes in it
Bloody from the slugger's blows
Or heard the cold child cry for hunger—

Love that listens where the good:
The virtuous: the men of faith:
Proclaim the paradise on earth
And murder starve and burn to make it—

Love that cannot either sleep
Or keep rich music in the ear
Or lose itself for the wild beat
The anger in the blood makes raging—

Love that hardens into hate—
Love like hatred and as bright—
Love is that one waking light
That leads now when all others darken.

SPEECH TO A CROWD

Tell me, my patient friends, awaiters of messages,
From what other shore, from what stranger,
Whence, was the word to come? Who was to lesson you?

Listeners under a child's crib in a manger,
Listeners once by the oracles, now by the transoms,
Whom are you waiting for? Who do you think will explain?

Listeners thousands of years and still no answer—
Writers at night to Miss Lonely-Hearts, awkward spellers,
Open your eyes! There is only earth and the man!

There is only you. There is no one else on the telephone:
No one else is on the air to whisper:
No one else but you will push the bell.

No one knows if you don't: neither ships
Nor landing-fields decode the dark between.
You have your eyes and what your eyes see, is.

The earth you see is really the earth you are seeing.
The sun is truly excellent, truly warm,
Women are beautiful as you have seen them—

Their breasts (believe it) like cooing of doves in a portico.
They bear at their breasts tenderness softly. Look at them!
Look at yourselves. You are strong. You are well formed.

Look at the world—the world you never took!
It is really true you may live in the world heedlessly.
Why do you wait to read it in a book then?

Write it yourselves! Write to yourselves if you need to!
Tell yourselves there is sun and the sun will rise.
Tell yourselves the earth has food to feed you.

Let the dead men say that men must die!
Who better than you can know what death is?
How can a bone or a broken body surmise it?

Let the dead shriek with their whispering breath.
Laugh at them! Say the murdered gods may wake

But we who work have end of work together.

Tell yourselves the earth is yours to take!

Waiting for messages out of the dark you were poor.
The world was always yours: you would not take it.

HYPOCRITE AUTEUR

mon semblable, mon frère

(1)

Our epoch takes a voluptuous satisfaction
In that perspective of the action
Which pictures us inhabiting the end
Of everything with death for only friend.

Not that we love death,
Not truly, not the fluttering breath,
The obscene shudder of the finished act—
What the doe feels when the ultimate fact
Tears at her bowels with its jaws.

Our taste is for the opulent pause
Before the end comes. If the end is certain
All of us are players at the final curtain:
All of us, silence for a time deferred,
Find time before us for one sad last word.
Victim, rebel, convert, stoic—
Every role but the heroic—
We turn our tragic faces to the stalls
To wince our moment till the curtain falls.

(2)

A world ends when its metaphor has died.

An age becomes an age, all else beside,
When sensuous poets in their pride invent

Emblems for the soul's consent
That speak the meanings men will never know
But man-imagined images can show:
It perishes when those images, though seen,
No longer mean.

(3)
A world was ended when the womb
Where girl held God became the tomb
Where God lies buried in a man:
Botticelli's image neither speaks nor can
To our kind. His star-guided stranger
Teaches no longer, by the child, the manger,
The meaning of the beckoning skies.

Sophocles, when his reverent actors rise
To play the king with bleeding eyes,
No longer shows us on the stage advance
God's purpose in the terrible fatality of chance.

No woman living, when the girl and swan
Embrace in verses, feels upon
Her breast the awful thunder of that breast
Where God, made beast, is by the blood confessed.

Empty as conch shell by the waters cast
The metaphor still sounds but cannot tell,
And we, like parasite crabs, put on the shell
And drag it at the sea's edge up and down.

This is the destiny we say we own.

(4)
But are we sure
The age that dies upon its metaphor
Among these Roman heads, these mediaeval towers,
Is ours?—
Or ours the ending of that story?

The meanings in a man that quarry

Images from blinded eyes
And white birds and the turning skies
To make a world of were not spent with these
Abandoned presences.

The journey of our history has not ceased:
Earth turns us still toward the rising east,
The metaphor still struggles in the stone,
The allegory of the flesh and bone
Still stares into the summer grass
That is its glass,
The ignorant blood
Still knocks at silence to be understood.

Poets, deserted by the world before,
Turn round into the actual air:
Invent the age! Invent the metaphor!

THE END OF THE WORLD

Quite unexpectedly as Vasserot
The armless ambidextrian was lighting
A match between his great and second toe
And Ralph the lion was engaged in biting
The neck of Madame Sossman while the drum
Pointed, and Teeny was about to cough
In waltz-time swinging Jocko by the thumb—
Quite unexpectedly the top blew off:

And there, there overhead, there, there, hung over
Those thousands of white faces, those dazed eyes,
There in the starless dark the poise, the hover,
There with vast wings across the canceled skies,
There in the sudden blackness the black pall
Of nothing, nothing, nothing—nothing at all.

REASONS FOR MUSIC

for Wallace Stevens

Why do we labor at the poem
Age after Age—even an age like
This one, when the living rock
No longer lives and the cut stone perishes?—

Hölderlin's question. Why be poet
Now when the meanings do not mean?—
When the stone shape is shaped stone?—
Dürftiger Zeit?—time without inwardness?

Why lie upon our beds at night
Holding a mouthful of words, exhausted
Most by the absence of the adversary?

Why be poet? Why be man!

Far out in the uttermost Andes
Mortised enormous stones are piled.
What is man? Who founds a poem
In the rubble of wild world—wilderness.

The acropolis of eternity that crumbles
Time and again is mine—my task.
The heart's necessity compels me:
Man I am: poet must be.

The labor of order has no rest:
To impose on the confused, fortuitous
Flowing away of the world, Form—
Still, cool, clean, obdurate,

Lasting forever, or at least
Lasting: a precarious monument
Promising immortality, for the wing
Moves and in the moving balances.

Why do we labor at the poem?
Out of the turbulence of the sea,

Flower by brittle flower, rises
The coral reef that calms the water.

Generations of the dying
Fix the sea's dissolving salts
In stone, still trees, their branches immovable,
Meaning
        the movement of the sea.

VICISSITUDES OF THE CREATOR

Fish has laid her succulent eggs
Safe in Sargasso weed
So wound and bound that crabbed legs
Nor clattering claws can find and feed.

Thus fish commits unto the sea
Her infinite future and the Trade
Blows westward toward eternity
The universe her love has made.

But when, upon this leeward beach,
The measureless sea journey ends
And ball breaks open, from the breach
A deft, gold, glossy crab extends

In ring-side ritual of self-applause
The small ironic silence of his claws.

MY NAKED AUNT

Who puts off shift
Has love's concealment left.

Who puts off skin
Has pain to wind her in.

Who puts off flesh
Wears soul's enormous wish.

Who puts off bone
Has all of death for gown.

None go naked who have
    drawn this breath
Till love's put off and pain
    and wish and death.

WORDS IN TIME

Bewildered with the broken tongue
Of wakened angels in our sleep—
Then, lost the music that was sung
And lost the light time cannot keep!

There is a moment when we lie
Bewildered, wakened out of sleep,
When light and sound and all reply:
That moment time must tame and keep.

That moment, like a flight of birds
Flung from the branches where they sleep,
The poet with a beat of words
Flings into time for time to keep.

WHAT THE SERPENT SAID TO ADAM

Which is you, old two-in-one?
Which is which, old one of two?
When the doubling is undone
Which one is you?

Is it you that so delights
By that woman in her bed?
Or you the glimmering sky afrights,
Vast overhead?

Are you body, are you ghost?
Were you got or had no father?
Is this you—the guest?—the host?
Who then's the other?

That woman says, old one-of-two,
In body was the soul begun:
Now two are one and one is you:—
Which one? Which one?

Edgar Lee Masters

THE HILL

Where are Elmer, Herman, Bert, Tom and Charley,
The weak of will, the strong of arm, the clown, the boozer, the
　　fighter?
All, all, are sleeping on the hill.

One passed in a fever,
One was burned in a mine,
One was killed in a brawl,
One died in a jail,
One fell from a bridge toiling for children and wife—
All, all are sleeping, sleeping, sleeping on the hill.

Where are Ella, Kate, Mag, Lizzie and Edith,
The tender heart, the simple soul, the loud, the proud, the
　　happy one?—
All, all, are sleeping on the hill.

One died in shameful child-birth,
One of a thwarted love,
One at the hands of a brute in a brothel,
One of a broken pride, in the search for heart's desire,
One after life in far-away London and Paris
Was brought to her little space by Ella and Kate and Mag—
All, all are sleeping, sleeping, sleeping on the hill.

Where are Uncle Isaac and Aunt Emily,
And old Towny Kincaid and Sevigne Houghton,
And Major Walker who had talked
With venerable men of the revolution?—
All, all, are sleeping on the hill.

They brought them dead sons from the war,
And daughters whom life had crushed,

And their children fatherless, crying—
All, all are sleeping, sleeping, sleeping on the hill.

Where is Old Fiddler Jones
Who played with life all his ninety years,
Braving the sleet with bared breast,
Drinking, rioting, thinking neither of wife nor kin,
Nor gold, nor love, nor heaven?
Lo! he babbles of the fish-frys of long ago,
Of the horse-races of long ago at Clary's Grove,
Of what Abe Lincoln said
One time at Springfield.

SEXSMITH THE DENTIST

Do you think that odes and sermons,
And the ringing of church bells,
And the blood of old men and young men,
Martyred for the truth they saw
With eyes made bright by faith in God,
Accomplished the world's great reformations?
Do you think the Battle Hymn of the Republic
Would have been heard if the chattel slave
Had crowned the dominant dollar,
In spite of Whitney's cotton gin,
And steam and rolling mills and iron
And telegraphs and white free labour?
Do you think that Daisy Fraser
Had been put out and driven out
If the canning works had never needed
Her little house and lot?
Or do you think the poker room
Of Johnnie Taylor, and Burchard's bar
Had been closed up if the money lost
And spent for beer had not been turned,
By closing them, to Thomas Rhodes
For larger sale of shoes and blankets,

And children's cloaks and gold-oak cradles?
Why, a moral truth is a hollow tooth
Which must be propped with gold.

'BUTCH' WELDY

After I got religion and steadied down
They gave me a job in the canning works,
And every morning I had to fill
The tank in the yard with gasoline,
That fed the blow-fires in the sheds
To heat the soldering irons.
And I mounted a rickety ladder to do it,
Carrying buckets full of the stuff.
One morning, as I stood there pouring,
The air grew still and seemed to heave,
And I shot up as the tank exploded,
And down I came with both legs broken,
And my eyes burned crisp as a couple of eggs.
For someone left a blow-fire going,
And something sucked the flame in the tank.
The Circuit Judge said whoever did it
Was a fellow-servant of mine, and so
Old Rhodes' son didn't have to pay me.
And I sat on the witness stand as blind
As Jack the Fiddler, saying over and over,
'I didn't know him at all.'

ANNE RUTLEDGE

Out of me unworthy and unknown
The vibrations of deathless music;
'With malice toward none, with charity for all.'
Out of me the forgiveness of millions toward millions,
And the beneficent face of a nation
Shining with justice and truth.

I am Anne Rutledge who sleep beneath these weeds,
Beloved in life of Abraham Lincoln,
Wedded to him, not through union,
But through separation.
Bloom forever, O Republic,
From the dust of my bosom!

Esther Mathews

SONG

I can't be talkin' of love, dear,
I can't be talkin' of love.
If there be one thing I can't talk of
That one thing do be love.

But that's not sayin' that I'm not lovin'—
Still water, you know, runs deep,
An' I do be lovin' so deep, dear,
I be lovin' you in my sleep.

But I can't be talkin' of love, dear,
I can't be talkin' of love,
If there be one thing I can't talk of
That one thing do be love.

Claire McAllister

AENEID

Creüsa cried for, through the tomb of Troy
When the bright town changed like a May dandelion,
Her golden dome turned powder gray;
Creüsa cried for; with stumbling step,
Eyes as if slapped, in his great quick loss,
Aeneas, retracing the empty streets, said
As we, too, once said, that it could not be thus,

Only to scatter his hope like the down
Of a late May dandelion.
And since, after leaving behind spring and home,
I have known the small golden hopes change so,
I wonder how he could still turn to show
All those men their tired way.
O round bright dome that was blown gray.

JULY IN THE JARDIN DES PLANTES

The summer days moved with the pace of a caged lion.
To stroll through crowds by the parkgates at dusk was a game:
O could we snatch out of that dusk a moment
That memory might, as food or whip-lash, tame.

To take what shape of cloud or smile was given
Was to stroll no longer the lost one's eyes
Upon us except obliquely, like next Autumn,
Last Spring that peered at Summer now through bars.

Mist rising up from the morning-warmed grass was a spectre
That muffled the noise of nurses and nursed by sand.
Sycamore branches stuck outside the nightmare;
I traced them like the lines in the palm of my hand

Thinking someday under a sycamore I shall watch summers
Remembering with pride, with shame, the streets of Youth,

The cities that hummed with the din of their ruined lovers,
Traffic lights that shattered the dreaming dusk.

Truth that we look for in lilacs each spring changes color
When love is but a longing for something not said.
Often the telling of dreams is the great error:
The dream, like a perfect crime, must remain in the head.

And as the pace of summer quickened I thought of what
    hovered
Outside the simple joys till I knew that the knot,
The knots in dreams haven't come from defeat, but desire;
It is not within nightmares we walk alone, but without.

Sun hung high in the yellow six o'clock darkness;
Motorcars and crowds swam in that light.
We still had the rest of July and all of August,
But the summerdusk darkens; leaves turn red overnight.

Herman Melville

MISGIVINGS

When ocean-clouds over inland hills
    Sweep storming in late autumn brown,
And horror the sodden valley fills,
    And the spire falls crashing in the town,
I muse upon my country's ills—
The tempest bursting from the waste of Time
On the world's fairest hope linked with man's foulest crime.

Nature's dark side is heeded now—
    (Ah! optimist-cheer disheartened flown)—
A child may read the moody brow
    Of yon black mountain lone.
With shouts the torrents down the gorges go,
    And storms are formed behind the storm we feel:
The hemlock shakes in the rafter, the oak in the driving keel.

THE MALDIVE SHARK

About the Shark, phlegmatical one,
Pale sot of the Maldive sea,
The sleek little pilot-fish, azure and slim,
How alert in attendance be.
From his saw-pit of mouth, from his charnel of maw
They have nothing of harm to dread,
But liquidly glide on his ghastly flank
Or before his Gorgonian head;
Or lurk in the port of serrated teeth
In white triple tiers of glittering gates,
And there find a haven when peril's abroad,
An asylum in jaws of the Fates!
They are friends; and friendly they guide him to prey,
Yet never partake of the treat—
Eyes and brains to the dotard lethargic and dull,
Pale ravener of horrible meat.

W. S. Merwin

VARIATION ON A LINE BY EMERSON

In May, when sea-winds pierced our solitudes,
In the May winds not yet warmed out of malice,
At a certain doorway once I stood, my face
Leaning westward, a little before evening—
Oh, though all breath be seasonal, who can tell
A story like new grass blown in sunlight?

In May when winds blow westward into the light
As though both would depart our solitudes,
Though the door be different, what can I tell,
Feeling the sun thus fail from all life and malice?
But once the measure and sight of day, at evening,
Died in the shadows, so, of a cold face.

You that have forsaken the door, the face,
Burgeon, body, decrease, the turning light,
Who keep such single quiet both morning and evening
That approach but multiplies your solitudes,
Whether the bodily death is death to malice
Not the intrusions of sea-wind tell.

Let a kind diction out of the shadows tell,
Now toward my slumber, a legend unto my face
Of sleep as a quiet garden without malice
Where body moves, after the bitter light,
A staid dance among innocent solitudes;
So let me lie in a story, heavy with evening.

But I dream of distances where at evening
Ghost begins (as no migrant birds can tell)
A journey through outlandish solitudes,
Hair all ways lifted, leaves wild against face,
Feet trammeled among dune grass, with spent light,
And finds no roof at last against wind or malice.

Sir, who have locked your doors, but without malice,
Or madam, who draw your shawl against evening,
By the adumbrations of your thin light
What but this poor contention can you tell:
Ceaseless intruders have demeaned your face
And contrived homesteads in your solitudes.

Tell me who keeps infrangible solitudes
But the evening's dead on whose decided face
Morning repeats the malice and the light.

TWO HORSES

Oh in whose grove have we wakened, the bees
Still droning under the carved wall, the fountain playing
Softly to itself, and the gold light, muted,
Moving long over the olives; and whose,

Stamping the shadowy grass at the end of the garden,
Are these two wild horses tethered improbably
To the withes of a young quince? No rider
Is to be seen; they bear neither saddle nor bridle;
Their brute hooves splash the knee-high green
Without sound, and their flexed tails like flags float,
Whipping, their brows down like bulls. Yet the small tree
Is not shaken; and the broken arches
Of their necks in the dim air are silent
As the doorways of ruins. Birds flit in the garden:
Jay and oriole, blades in the hanging shadows,
Small cries confused. And dawn would be eastward
Over the dark neck a red mane tossed high
Like flame, and the dust brightening along the wall.
These have come up from Egypt, from the dawn countries,
Syria, and the land between the rivers,
Have ridden at the beaks of vessels, by Troy neighed,
And along the valley of the Danube, and to Etruria;
And all dust was of their making; and passion
Under their hooves puffed into flight like a sparrow
And died down when they departed. The haze of summer
Blows south over the garden terraces,
Vague through the afternoon, remembering rain;
But in the night green with beasts as April with grass
Orion would hunt high from southward, over the hill,
And the blood of beasts herald morning. Where these have
    passed,
Tramping white roads, their ears drinking the sword-crash,
The chariots are broken, bright battle-cars
Shambles under earth; whether by sharp bronze
Or the years' ebbing, all blood has flowed into the ground;
There was wailing at sundown, mourning for kings,
Weeping of widows, but these went faint, were forgotten.
And the columns have fallen like shadows. Crickets
Sing under the stones; and beyond the carved wall
Westward, fires drifting in darkness like the tails
Of jackals flaring, no hounds heard at their hunting,
Float outward into the dark. And these horses stamp

Before us now in this garden; and northward
Beyond the terraces the misted sea
Swirls endless, hooves of the gray wind forever
Thundering, churning the ragged spume-dusk
High that there be no horizons nor stars, and there
Are white islands riding, ghost-guarded, twisted waves flash-
ing,
Porpoises plunging like the necks of horses.

TORO

Black, black, the sheen of his back and shoulders
Blazing, his brawn and wide forehead plunging
On, on into wrath, hooves detonating the dust
Under his rushing darkness, the green and white
Streamers fixed in the hump of his anger rattling
And snapping behind like slaver from a mad mouth, and
The high-shaken lances of his tossing horns seeking
Bodies for shock, his wrath like a ghost seeking
Bodies to sink in, to house in, destruction to be wrought,
Out of the starving dark, daring headlong
The one-way doors of day, he hurls himself now
Into the orange light, and lunging down
Like judgment erupting or a dark planet he crashes
Across the spread glare and becomes the raging centre
Of these flickering faces ranged in rings, who thirst
For his darkness, who stare like blains
In the sun-blaze. They thought it was they
Who for their thirst's sake, and that their black fear might be
Loosed and defeated in the familiar light, conceived
A darkness and set him there. But all black
Is the abyss brooding, and he brings into the day
The one dark, that was there before the world was. Low
In his own shadow deep as a mountain he waited
Till they said, "Now we are all together
And seem brave in the light, let the challenging shadow
Show itself among us; now, that we may shame it,

Let there be dark." And he heard the first day
Of Creation banging on the barrier, and, ravenous,
His red eyes saw the light. And, look: he became
The black sun and burst among them, and the sun has horns
As the moon has, whereby all dawns shall be bloody
And all wests ripped with crimson! Bull. And legs,
Spoke-flashing of knees, even thunder of hooves seem as
    nothing
To pillar and propel that bulk and fury. His belly gulping
For breath sucks up and drops like a blast-shaken
Floor; between his flanks censer and tassel
Of generation swing and lurch, and nothing in the profound
    world
Blares deep as now his maddened bellow. What torment is it
That baits him, that wrings forth this roar: for the men
Performing with bright darts are toys merely,
Masquers playing with emblems, signifying far off
The one faceless pain, momentary puppets
Of the infliction he tolls. The blood and burning
In his eyes are not blindness, but bring the world's rage
To be seen red as it is. And oh do not suppose
Because a thin blade may empty him suddenly
Of fury, and his black become the colour of quiet,
That it means that the known earth is broad world enough
To be his battling-ground. His death, though dedicated,
May end much, but will fulfill nothing; will be adequate
Neither to sate the size and lust of his fury
Nor to gather and bless with acceptable sacrifice
Those faces so small, so faint and far that still
They sit and sway in a world where such things
As danger are. But he, for all fear's reasons
Worshipful, slumps back into fear's secret
And abyss, more terrible, for his rage disdains now
All that they know of pain, and looks like infinite
Gentleness, waiting, forever patient,
Black, with long horns. What trouble is it
That baits them now, since the shape they made of their fear
Is dead? The light is different. And they are alone.

CAMEL

Remember that we are dust. It is said
That this place of our passage is prone to mirages:
That the waves of the drifting desert, the heat-daft
Air playing like water-light, the horizon
Swirling slow as a shadow and laying up
To itself all their unearthly shiftings,
Or simply the salt tides working
Of need or desire, out of some fold
Of their flowing raise often visions
As of white cities like walled clouds, agleam
On their hills, so clear that you can see the tiered
Buildings glint still in the rocking daylight,
Or again of trees even whose shadows
Seem green and to breathe, or merely of pools
Of simple water on that same dry surge borne,
That will ride nearer, nearer, like elusive
Aphrodite; and these are nothing
But the playing of the heated light teasing
Like pain over this dust. In truth, it may
Be nothing but ourselves, this that is
All about us for our eyes to see: this dust
That we cannot see beyond. Remember
That we are dust, dust and a little breath,
As the sand dervishes the wind lifts
Whirling and sends over the sea-shaped dunes;
As does their dancing, we wind between breathless
Dust and breathless dust, and our passage
Even as theirs, may be no more
Than a casual sport of the air gliding
To no depth over the delusive surface
Of our breathless selves. But speaking of virtues
We think of water; moving, we think
Of arrival as of water, of virtue
As the means of arrival. And we have named
For water him who is visibly
Our practice of virtue, beast of our motion,

Calling him "Ship of the Desert." Who rolls
When he walks; whose going also
Has strangely the gait of a cradle. He too is dust,
Yet not as we, save as that figure
Of what our faring is, for his breath is speechless,
His back that bears us has a wave's shape
Drawn by a child; or hill's lurching
As he strides; when he runs, his shadow
Over the rippling dust is a wind's
Shudder across modelled bay-water,
Curved gust across grain-field, or storm silvering
Fast as some hastening angel over
Hillsides of olive trees, darkness
Of rain-cloud chasing the sunlight
On carved hills, or wave-crest over
Far reef flung, its main strength still racing
For shore. Even as these
It would seem our progress is, in itself bearing
Its own sustenance for long waste-wending;
A power that may be, in event of all
Arrival failing, other resources
Parched, our water of desperation; that is not
Ourselves; whose capacities may not be
Arrived at even by prayer, patient study
And deprivation, yet whose presence we have known
To affect us so that even in places of water,
Of pleasure, repose, abode, when we had thought
To escape the sense of it, it will sometimes break
From where it was tethered and find us out,
Intruding its ungainly ill-smelling head
Over our shoulders. A creature that can shut
Both eyes and nostrils against the lash
Of dust risen suddenly savage. That if not
Drained at last dry as a white bone,
Exhausted beyond sense, or buried
In the capricious cruelty of
Its own condition, can sense more surely than we
Over the dust-driven horizon the green

Places where the roots grope trusting
Down into the dark breathlessness, the trees
Sway and give shade, dew falls early,
Stones drip in the mossed shadow, and the motes
Seem to dance to a falling cadence
That mortal ears might apprehend. Catching, as we,
At phantoms, breaking into a dangerous
Rocking-horse sprint at false visions, nevertheless
When we are despairing, drawn it would seem
By deceptions only, working to wean
Our minds from arrival, staring vacantly
At the tormented air, while the enraged sun
Careens in white circles about a sky
The blood-orange of an eyelid, he can with no warning
Lift the furred neck swinging there
Like a winter serpent, flare divining nostrils,
Even from far off smell the true water.

Edna St. Vincent Millay

ON HEARING A SYMPHONY OF BEETHOVEN

Sweet sounds, oh, beautiful music, do not cease!
Reject me not into the world again.
With you alone is excellence and peace,
Mankind made plausible, his purpose plain.
Enchanted in your air benign and shrewd,
With limbs a-sprawl and empty faces pale,
The spiteful and the stingy and the rude
Sleep like the scullions in the fairy-tale.

This moment is the best the world can give:
The tranquil blossom on the tortured stem.
Reject me not, sweet sounds; oh, let me live,
Till Doom espy my towers and scatter them,
A city spell-bound under the aging sun.
Music my rampart, and my only one.

DIRGE WITHOUT MUSIC

I am not resigned to the shutting away of loving hearts in the
    hard ground.
So it is, and so it will be, for so it has been, time out of mind:
Into the darkness they go, the wise and the lovely. Crowned
With lilies and with laurel they go; but I am not resigned.

Lovers and thinkers, into the earth with you.
Be one with the dull, the indiscriminate dust.
A fragment of what you felt, of what you knew,
A formula, a phrase remains,—but the best is lost.

The answers quick & keen, the honest look, the laughter, the
    love,
They are gone. They have gone to feed the roses. Elegant and
    curled
Is the blossom. Fragrant is the blossom. I know. But I do not
    approve.
More precious was the light in your eyes than all the roses in
    the world.

Down, down, down into the darkness of the grave
Gently they go, the beautiful, the tender, the kind;
Quietly they go, the intelligent, the witty, the brave.
I know. But I do not approve. And I am not resigned.

RENASCENCE

All I could see from where I stood
Was three long mountains and a wood;
I turned and looked another way,
And saw three islands in a bay.
So with my eyes I traced the line
Of the horizon, thin and fine,
Straight around till I was come
Back to where I'd started from;

And all I saw from where I stood
Was three long mountains and a wood.
Over these things I could not see;
These were the things that bounded me;
And I could touch them with my hand,
Almost, I thought, from where I stand.
And all at once things seemed so small
My breath came short, and scarce at all
But, sure, the sky is big, I said;
Miles and miles above my head;
So here upon my back I'll lie
And look my fill into the sky.
And so I looked, and, after all,
The sky was not so very tall.
The sky, I said, must somewhere stop,
And—sure enough!—I see the top!
The sky, I thought, is not so grand;
I 'most could touch it with my hand!
And, reaching up my hand to try,
I screamed to feel it touch the sky.

I screamed, and—lo!—Infinity
Came down and settled over me;
Forced back my scream into my chest,
Bent back my arm upon my breast,
And, pressing of the Undefined
The definition on my mind,
Held up before my eyes a glass
Through which my shrinking sight did pass
Until it seemed I must behold
Immensity made manifold;
Whispered to me a word whose sound
Deafened the air for worlds around,
And brought unmuffled to my ears
The gossiping of friendly spheres,
The creaking of the tented sky,
The ticking of Eternity.

I saw and heard, and knew at last
The How and Why of all things, past,
And present, and forevermore.
The universe, cleft to the core,
Lay open to my probing sense
That, sickening, I would fain pluck thence
But could not,—nay! But needs must suck
At the great wound, and could not pluck
My lips away till I had drawn
All venom out.—Ah, fearful pawn!
For my omniscience I paid toll
In infinite remorse of soul.
All sin was of my sinning, all
Atoning mine, and mine the gall
Of all regret. Mine was the weight
Of every brooded wrong, the hate
That stood behind each envious thrust,
Mine every greed, mine every lust.
And all the while for every grief,
Each suffering, I craved relief
With individual desire,—
Craved all in vain! And felt fierce fire
About a thousand people crawl;
Perished with each,—then mourned for all!
A man was starving in Capri;
He moved his eyes and looked at me;
I felt his gaze, I heard his moan,
And knew his hunger as my own.
I saw at sea a great fog-bank
Between two ships that struck and sank;
A thousand screams the heavens smote;
And every scream tore through my throat;
No hurt I did not feel, no death
That was not mine; mine each last breath
That, crying, met an answering cry
From the compassion that was I.
All suffering mine, and mine its rod;
Mine, pity like the pity of God.

Ah, awful weight! Infinity
Pressed down upon the finite me!
My anguished spirit, like a bird,
Beating against my lips I heard;
Yet lay the weight so close about
There was no room for it without.
And so beneath the weight lay I
And suffered death, but could not die.

Long had I lain thus, craving death,
When quietly the earth beneath
Gave way, and inch by inch, so great
At last had grown the crushing weight,
Into the earth I sank till I
Full six feet under ground did lie,
And sank no more,—there is no weight
Can follow here, however great.
From off my breast I felt it roll,
And as it went my tortured soul
Burst forth and fled in such a gust
That all about me swirled the dust.

Deep in the earth I rested now;
Cool is its hand upon the brow
And soft its breast beneath the head
Of one who is so gladly dead.
And all at once, and over all,
The pitying rain began to fall.
I lay and heard each pattering hoof
Upon my lowly, thatchèd roof.
And seemed to love the sound far more
Than ever I had done before.
For rain it hath a friendly sound
To one who's six feet underground;
And scarce the friendly voice or face:
A grave is such a quiet place.

The rain, I said, is kind to come
And speak to me in my new home.

I would I were alive again
To kiss the fingers of the rain,
To drink into my eyes the shine
Of every slanting silver line,
To catch the freshened, fragrant breeze
From drenched and dripping apple-trees.
For soon the shower will be done,
And then the broad face of the sun
Will laugh above the rain-soaked earth
Until the world with answering mirth
Shakes joyously, and each round drop
Rolls, twinkling, from its grass-blade top.
How can I bear it; buried here,
While overhead the sky grows clear
And blue again after the storm?
O, multi-colored, multiform,
Belovèd beauty over me,
That I shall never, never see
Again! Spring-silver, autumn-gold,
That I shall never more behold!
Sleeping your myriad magics through,
Close-sepulchered away from you!
O God, I cried, give me new birth,
And put me back upon the earth!
Upset each cloud's gigantic gourd
And let the heavy rain, down-poured
In one big torrent, set me free,
Washing my grave away from me!

I ceased; and, through the breathless hush
That answered me, the far-off rush
Of herald wings came whispering
Like music down the vibrant string
Of my ascending prayer, and—crash!
Before the wild wind's whistling lash
The startled storm-clouds reared on high
And plunged in terror down the sky,

And the big rain in one black wave
Fell from the sky and struck my grave.

I know not how such things can be,
I only know there came to me
A fragrance such as never clings
To aught save happy living things;
A sound as of some joyous elf
Singing sweet songs to please himself,
And, through and over everything,
A sense of glad awakening.
The grass, a tip-toe at my ear,
Whispering to me I could hear;
I felt the rain's cool finger-tips
Brushed tenderly across my lips,
Laid gently on my sealèd sight,
And all at once the heavy night
Fell from my eyes and I could see,—
A drenched and dripping apple-tree,
A last long line of silver rain,
A sky grown clear and blue again.
And as I looked a quickening gust
Of wind blew up to me and thrust
Into my face a miracle
Of orchard-breath, and with the smell,—
I know not how such things can be!—
I breathed my soul back into me.

Ah! Up then from the ground sprang I
And hailed the earth with such a cry
As is not heard save from a man
Who has been dead and lives again.
About the trees my arms I wound;
Like one gone mad I hugged the ground;
I raised my quivering arms on high;
I laughed and laughed into the sky,
Till at my throat a strangling sob
Caught fiercely, and a great heart-throb

Sent instant tears into my eyes;
O God, I cried, no dark disguise
Can e'er hereafter hide from me
Thy radiant identity!
Thou canst not move across the grass
But my quick eyes will see Thee pass,
Nor speak, however silently,
But my hushed voice will answer Thee.
I know the path that tells Thy way
Through the cool eve of every day;
God, I can push the grass apart
And lay my finger on Thy heart!

The world stands out on either side
No wider than the heart is wide;
Above the world is stretched the sky,—
No higher than the soul is high.
The heart can push the sea and land
Farther away on either hand;
The soul can split the sky in two,
And let the face of God shine through.
But East and West will pinch the heart
That cannot keep them pushed apart;
And he whose soul is flat—the sky
Will cave in on him by and by.

THE POET AND HIS BOOK

Down, you mongrel, Death!
  Back into your kennel!
I have stolen breath
  In a stalk of fennel!
You shall scratch and you shall whine
  Many a night, and you shall worry
  Many a bone, before you bury
One sweet bone of mine!

When shall I be dead?
  When my flesh is withered,
And above my head
  Yellow pollen gathered
All the empty afternoon?
  When sweet lovers pause and wonder
  Who am I that lie thereunder,
Hidden from the moon?

This my personal death?—
  That my lungs be failing
To inhale the breath
  Others are exhaling?
This my subtle spirit's end?—
  Ah, when the thawed winter splashes
  Over these chance dust and ashes,
Weep not me, my friend!

Me, by no means dead
  In that hour, but surely
When this book, unread,
  Rots to earth obscurely,
And no more to any breast,
  Close against the clamorous swelling
  Of the thing there is no telling,
Are these pages pressed!

When this book is mold,
  And a book of many
Waiting to be sold
  For a casual penny,
In a little open case,
  In a street unclean and cluttered,
  Where a heavy mud is spattered
From the passing drays,

Stranger, pause and look;
  From the dust of ages

Lift this little book,
  Turn the tattered pages,
Read me, do not let me die!
  Search the fading letters, finding
  Steadfast in the broken binding
All that once was I!

When these veins are weeds,
  When these hollowed sockets
Watch the rooty seeds
  Bursting down like rockets,
And surmise the spring again,
  Or, remote in that black cupboard,
  Watch the pink worms writhing upward
At the smell of rain,

Boys and girls that lie
  Whispering in the hedges,
Do not let me die,
  Mix me in your pledges;
Boys and girls that slowly walk
  In the woods, and weep, and quarrel,
  Staring past the pink wild laurel,
Mix me with your talk.

Do not let me die!
  Farmers at your raking,
When the sun is high,
  While the hay is making,
When, along the stubble strewn,
  Withering on their stalks uneaten,
  Strawberries turn dark and sweeten
In the lapse of noon;

Shepherds on the hills,
  In the pastures, drowsing
To the tinkling bells
  Of the brown sheep browsing;

Sailors crying through the storm;
　　Scholars at your study; hunters
　　Lost amid the whirling winter's
Whiteness uniform;

Men that long for sleep;
　　Men that wake and revel;—
If an old song leap
　　To your senses' level
At such moments, may it be
　　Sometimes, though a moment only,
　　Some forgotten, quaint and homely
Vehicle of me!

Women at your toil,
　　Women at your leisure
Till the kettle boil,
　　Snatch of me your pleasure,
Where the broom-straw marks the leaf;
　　Women quiet with your weeping
　　Lest you wake a workman sleeping,
Mix me with your grief!

Boys and girls that steal
　　From the shocking laughter
Of the old, to kneel
　　By a dripping rafter
Under the discolored eaves,
　　Out of trunks with hingeless covers
　　Lifting tales of saint and lovers,
Travelers, goblins, thieves,

Suns that shine by night,
　　Mountains made from valleys,—
Bear me to the light,
　　Flat upon your bellies
By the webby window lie,
　　Where the little flies are crawling,—
　　Read me, margin me with scrawling,
Do not let me die!

Sexton, ply your trade!
    In a shower of gravel
Stamp upon your spade!
    Many a rose shall ravel,
Many a metal wreath shall rust
    In the rain, and I go singing
        Through the lots where you are flinging
Yellow clay on dust!

SPRING

To what purpose, April, do you return again?
Beauty is not enough.
You can no longer quiet me with the redness
Of little leaves opening stickily.
I know what I know.
The sun is hot on my neck as I observe
The spikes of the crocus.
The smell of the earth is good.
It is apparent that there is no death.
But what does that signify?
Not only under ground are the brains of men
Eaten by maggots.
Life in itself
Is nothing,
An empty cup, a flight of uncarpeted stairs,
It is not enough that yearly, down this hill,
April
Comes like an idiot, babbling and strewing flowers.

PITY ME NOT

Pity me not because the light of day
At close of day no longer walks the sky;
Pity me not for beauties passed away
From field and thicket as the year goes by;

Pity me not the waning of the moon,
Nor that the ebbing tide goes out to sea,
Nor that a man's desire is hushed so soon,
And you no longer look with love on me.

This have I known always: love is no more
Than the wide blossom which the wind assails;
Than the great tide that treads the shifting shore
Strewing fresh wreckage gathered in the gales.
Pity me that the heart is slow to learn
What the swift mind beholds at every turn.

ELEGY

Let them bury your big eyes
In the secret earth securely,
Your thin fingers, and your fair,
Soft, indefinite-colored hair,—
All of these in some way, surely,
From the secret earth shall rise.
Not for these I sit and stare,
Broken and bereft completely;
Your young flesh that sat so neatly
On your little bones will sweetly
Blossom in the air.

But your voice,—never the rushing
Of a river underground,
Not the rising of the wind
In the trees before the rain,
Not the woodcock's watery call,
Not the note the white-throat utters,
Not the feet of children pushing
Yellow leaves along the gutters
In the blue and bitter fall,
Shall content my musing mind
For the beauty of that sound

That in no new way at all
Ever will be heard again.

Sweetly through the sappy stalk
Of the vigorous weed,
Holding all it held before,
Cherished by the faithful sun,
On and on eternally
Shall your altered fluid run,
Bud and bloom and go to seed;
But your singing days are done;
But the music of your talk
Never shall the chemistry
Of the secret earth restore.
All your lovely words are spoken.
Once the ivory box is broken,
Beats the golden bird no more.

I SHALL GO BACK

I shall go back again to the bleak shore
And build a little shanty on the sand
In such a way that the extremest band
Of brittle seaweed will escape my door
But by a yard or two, and nevermore
Shall I return to take you by the hand;
I shall be gone to what I understand
And happier than I ever was before.

The love that stood a moment in your eyes,
The words that lay a moment on your tongue,
Are one with all that in a moment dies,
A little under-said and over-sung;
But I shall find the sullen rocks and skies
Unchanged from what they were when I was young.

Marianne Moore

POETRY

I, too, dislike it: there are things that are important
      beyond all this fiddle.
Reading it, however, with a perfect contempt for it, one
      discovers in
it after all, a place for the genuine.
   Hands that can grasp, eyes
   that can dilate, hair that can rise
     if it must, these things are important not because a

high-sounding interpretation can be put upon them but
      because they are
useful. When they become so derivative as to become
      unintelligible,
the same thing may be said for all of us, that we
   do not admire what
   we cannot understand: the bat
     holding on upside down or in quest of something to

eat, elephants pushing, a wild horse taking a roll, a tireless
      wolf under
a tree, the immovable critic twitching his skin like a
      horse that feels a flea, the base—
ball fan, the statistician—
   nor is it valid
     to discriminate against 'business documents and

school-books'; all these phenomena are important. One
      must make a distinction
however: when dragged into prominence by half poets,
      the result is not poetry,
nor till the poets among us can be
   'literalists of the imagination'—above
   insolence and triviality and can present
for inspection, 'imaginary gardens with real toads in them,'*

     *Author's Note: A quotation from W. B. Yeats' 'Ideas of Good and Evil.'

shall we have
it. In the meantime, if you demand on the one hand,
the raw material of poetry in
all its rawness and
that which is on the other hand
genuine, then you are interested in poetry.

CRITICS AND CONNOISSEURS

There is a great amount of poetry in unconscious
fastidiousness. Certain Ming
products, imperial floor-coverings of coach-
wheel yellow, are well enough in their way but I have
seen something
that I like better—a
mere childish attempt to make an imperfectly
ballasted animal stand up,
similar determination to make a pup
eat his meat from the plate.

I remember a swan under the willows in Oxford,
with flamingo-coloured, maple-
leaflike feet. It reconnoitred like a battle-
ship. Disbelief and conscious fastidiousness were the staple
ingredients in its
disinclination to move. Finally its hardihood was not
proof against its
proclivity to more fully appraise such bits
of food as the stream

bore counter to it; it made away with what I gave it
to eat. I have seen this swan and
I have seen you; I have seen ambition without
understanding in a variety of forms. Happening to stand
by an ant-hill, I have
seen a fastidious ant carrying a stick north, south,
east, west, till it turned on
itself, struck out from the flower-bed into the lawn
and returned to the point

from which it had started. Then abandoning the stick as
  useless and overtaxing its
    jaws with a particle of whitewash—pill-like but
heavy—it again went through the same course of
              procedure. What is
        there in being able
          to say that one has dominated the stream in an
              attitude of self-defence;
          in proving that one has had the experience
              of carrying a stick?

HIS SHIELD

        The pin-swin or spine-swine
(the edgehog miscalled hedgehog) with
        all his edges out,
  echidna and echinoderm in distressed-
pincushion thorn-fur coats,
        the spiny pig or porcupine,
            the rhino with horned snout,—
everything is battle-dressed.

            Pig-fur won't do, I'll wrap
myself in salamander-skin
        like Presbyter John.
A lizard in the midst of flames, a firebrand
that is life, asbestos-
            eyed asbestos-eared with tattooed nap
              and permanent pig on
        the instep; he can withstand

        fire and won't drown. In his
unconquerable country of
            unpompous gusto,
    gold was so common none considered it; greed
and flattery were

unknown. Though rubies large as tennis-
balls conjoined in streams so
that the mountain seemed to bleed,

the inextinguishable
salamander styled himself but
presbyter. His shield
was his humility. In Carpasian
linen coat, flanked by his
household lion-cubs and sable
retinue, he revealed
a formula safer than

an armorer's: the power of relinquishing
what one would keep; that is freedom.
Become dinosaur-
skulled, quilled or salamander-wooled, more ironshod
and javelin-dressed than
a hedgehog battalion of steel; but be
dull. Don't be envied or
armed with a measuring-rod.

A CARRIAGE FROM SWEDEN

They say there is a sweeter air
where it was made, than we have here;
a Hamlet's castle atmosphere.
At all events there is in Brooklyn
something that makes me feel at home.

No one may see this put-away
museum-piece, this country cart
that inner happiness made art;
and yet, in this city of freckled
integrity it is a vein

of resined straightness from north-wind
hardened Sweden's once-opposed-to-
compromise archipelago

of rocks. Washington and Gustavus
Adolphus, forgive our decay.

Seats, dashboard and sides of smooth gourd-
    rind texture, a flowered step, swan-
      dart brake, and swirling crustacean-
tailed equine amphibious creatures
that garnish the axle-tree! What

a fine thing! What unannoying
    romance; And how beautiful, she
      with the natural stoop of the
snowy egret, gray-eyed and straight-haired,
for whom it should come to the door,—

of whom it reminds me. The split
    pine fair hair, steady gannet-clear
      eyes and the pine-needled-path deer-
swift step; that is Sweden—land of the
free and the soil for a spruce-tree—

vertical though a seedling—all
    needles: from a green trunk, green shelf
      on shelf fanning out by itself.
The deft white-stockinged dance in thick-soled
shoes! Denmark's sanctuaried Jews!

The puzzle-jugs and hand-spun rugs,
    the root-legged kracken shaped like dogs,
      the hanging buttons and the frogs
that edge the Sunday jackets! Sweden,
you have a runner called the Deer, who

when he's won a race, likes to run
    more; you have the sun-right gable-
      ends due east and west, the table
spread as for a banquet; and the put-
in twin vest-pleats with a fish-fin

effect when you need none. Sweden,
    what makes the people dress that way

and those who see you wish to stay?
The runner, not too tired to run more
at the end of the race? And that

cart, dolphin-graceful? A Dalgrén
      lighthouse, self-lit? responsive and
      responsible, I understand;
it's not pine-needle-paths that give spring
when they're run on, it's a Sweden

of moated white castles,—the bed
      of densely grown flowers in an S
      meaning Sweden and stalwartness,
skill, and a surface that says
Made in Sweden: carts are my trade.

IN DISTRUST OF MERITS

Strengthened to live, strengthened to die for
      medals and positioned victories?
They're fighting, fighting, fighting the blind
      man who thinks he sees,—
who cannot see that the enslaver is
enslaved; the hater, harmed. O shining O
      firm star, O tumultuous
      ocean lashed till small things go
      as they will, the mountainous
      wave makes us who look, know

depth. Lost at sea before they fought! O
      star of David, star of Bethlehem,
O Black imperial lion
      of the Lord—emblem
of a risen world—be joined at last, be
joined. There is hate's crown beneath which all is
      death; there's love's without which none
      is king; the blessed deeds bless
      the halo. As contagion
      of sickness makes sickness,

contagion of trust can make trust. They're
    fighting in deserts and caves, one by
one, in battalions and squadrons;
    they're fighting that I
may yet recover from the disease, *my
self;* some have it lightly, some will die. "Man's
        wolf to man?" And we devour
          ourselves? The enemy could not
      have made a greater breach in our
      defenses. One pilot-

ing a blind man can escape him, but
    Job disheartened by false comfort knew,
that nothing is so defeating
    as a blind man who
can see. O alive who are dead, who are
proud not to see, O small dust of the earth
        that walks so arrogantly,
          trust begets power and faith is
      an affectionate thing. We
      vow, we make this promise

to the fighting—it's a promise—"We'll
    never hate black, white, red, yellow, Jew,
Gentile, Untouchable." We are
    not competent to
make our vows. With set jaw they are fighting,
fighting, fighting,—some we love whom we know,
        some we love but know not—that
          hearts may feel and not be numb.
      It cures me; or am I what
      I can't believe in? Some

in snow, some on crags, some in quicksands,
    little by little, much by much, they
are fighting fighting fighting that where
    there was death there may
be life. "When a man is prey to anger,

he is moved by outside things; when he holds
  his ground in patience patience
       patience, that is action or
  beauty," the soldier's defense
  and hardest armor for

the fight. The world's an orphans' home. Shall
  we never have peace without sorrow?
without pleas of the dying for
  help that won't come? O
quiet form upon the dust, I cannot
look and yet I must. If these great patient
    dyings—all these agonies
       and woundbearings and blood shed—
  can teach us how to live, these
    dyings were not wasted.

Hate-hardened heart, O heart of iron,
  iron is iron till it is rust.
There never was a war that was
  not inward; I must
fight till I have conquered in myself what
causes war, but I would not believe it.
    I inwardly did nothing.
      O Iscariotlike crime!
    Beauty is everlasting
      and dust is for a time.

SPENSER'S IRELAND

Has not altered;—
    the kindest place I've never been,
    the greenest place I've never seen.
Every name is a tune.
Denunciations do not affect
    the culprit;   nor blows, but it
is torture to him to not be spoken to.
They're natural,—

the coat, like Venus'
mantle lined with stars,
buttoned close at the neck,—the
    sleeves new from disuse.

If in Ireland
    they play the harp backward at need,
    and gather at midday the seed
of the fern, eluding
their "giants all covered with iron," might
    there be fern   seed for unlearn-
ing obduracy and for reinstating
the enchantment?
    Hindered characters
seldom have mothers—
in Irish stories—
    but they all have grandmothers.

It was Irish;
    a match not a marriage was made
    when my great great grandmother'd said
with native genius for
disunion, "although your suitor be
    perfection,   one objection
is enough; he is not
Irish." Outwitting
    the fairies, befriending the furies,
whoever again
and again says, "I'll never
    give in," never sees

that you're not free
    until you've been made captive by
    supreme belief,—credulity
you say? When large dainty
fingers tremblingly divide the wings
    of the fly   for mid-July

with a needle and wrap it with peacock-tail,
or tie wool and
        buzzard's wing, their pride,
like the enchanter's
is in care, not madness. Con-
        curring hands divide

flax for damask
    that when bleached by Irish weather
    has the silvered chamois-leather
water-tightness of a
skin. Twisted torcs and gold new-moon-shaped
      lunulae   aren't jewelry
like the purple-coral fuchsia-tree's. If Eire—
"the guillemot
      so neat" and the hen
of the heath and "the
linnet spinet-sweet"—bespeak
      relentlessness, then

they are to me
    like enchanted Earl Gerald who
    changed himself into a stag, to
a great green-eyed cat of
the mountain. Discommodity makes
      then invis   ible; they've dis-
appeared. The Irish say "Your trouble is their
trouble and your
      joy their joy?" I wish
I could believe it;
I am troubled, I'm dissat-
      isfied, I'm Irish.

Howard Moss

WATERWALL BLUES

I gnarled me where the spinster tree
Unwound its green hosanna
And built its sorrow, leaf by knee,
A lachrymal cabana.

The selfsame night I cracked my cowl,
Unwound myself with Anna:
Speech by speech and howl by howl
O don't you cry Susanna.

I left my childhood sadness near
The winder of blue water,
Walking in the windmill year
With his summer daughter.

That very night I spoke my piece,
Unwound my heigh-ho merry;
Started my newfangledness
Across her downtown ferry.

But when my halfway laughing gulls
Despair the death of her,
Dumb sorrow rides the same old hulls
With his mad mariner.

CHALK FROM EDEN

Doctrine has wound of lovers' limbs
A sulphurous wreath of antonyms,
And strung its gnomes of hell and damn
On wiry thoughts throughout all time,

And taken a stick to the naked couple,
Cursing the moonlight, the river bend,
Music and dark—and the world goes round.

For virgins will come, all green thumb,
Into the garden of their martyrdom,
And dilly-dally in the orchard air
And say to holy doctrine, "Less we care
For the black commandments of your lasting scruple
Than we do for a dancer who is supple;
Hell is not heaven, and go to the devil."

Doctrine has turned pilgrims of pleasure
Into dull spinsters of meanest measure,
Made of pure angels infidels,
And hauled wet witches out of dry wells.
There is a warning in the steeple,
Spelling a lesson for good people,
Which leads us back to the garden's apple.

But time and again, in every season,
Love is a meeting mating reason,
And young and old walk in their park
And spin in their skins from light to dark.
The sheets of time have a common wrinkle
For youngsters will take their flaking chalk
And write of love on wall and sidewalk.

UNDERWOOD

From the thin slats of the Venetian blinds
The sun has plucked a sudden metaphor:
A harp of light, reflected on the floor,
Disorients the chair and desk and door.
Those much too delicate hands still tapping
The Underwood seem now Hindu dancers

Or five or ten young Balinese children
Hopping up and down in a clearing where
The striped light scrapes through bamboo seedlings
And moves from skinny shade to thin veneer
And changes as the harp of light is changing
Its twanging image on the office floor,
Being so remarkably the blinding heir
Of something that is not, and yet is, there.

Once I watched at the water cooler
A face bent over the jet-thin water:
The iris of the bent eye changed its color
As if the water jet had stained it green;
I saw the animal head's slight shudder,
Lifted from the surface of that running stream.
Tall branches then grew green in the hallway,
Arching above a green-ferned pathway;
A screen of green leaves hung in the doorway.
Was that a mirror where I saw the beaked birds,
The sluggish coffin of the alligator,
The monkeys climbing up the sunlit tree trunks?
Or did imagination, in that corridor,
Create, like the harp, its sudden metaphor?

Inside that drawer, among the blotters, folders,
Memos, carbons, pencils, papers,
Is the youngest animal of all awaking
In that coarse nest where he's been sleeping?
If I should reach into that dangerous drawer,
What singular teeth might pierce my skin?
Or if he should leap, should I then kill him,
And watch, where the harp had set its lightness,
The marvellous animal blood go thin?

Ogden Nash

OH, STOP BEING THANKFUL ALL OVER THE PLACE

In the glittering collection of paste diamonds one in particular
ranks very high,

And that is the often-quoted remark of the prominent and
respectable dignitary who on seeing a condemned man
on his way to the scaffold crashed into a thousand anthologies by remarking, There but for the grace of God
go I.

Here is a deplorable illustration

Of sloppy ratiocination;

Here is a notable feat

Of one-way thinking on a two-way street.

It must certainly have been the speaker's lucky day,

Or otherwise he would have been run over by his speech
turning around and coming back the other way,

Because did he stop to work out his premise to its logical
conclusion? Ah no,

He just got it off and let it go,

And now whenever people are with people they want to im-
press with their combined greateartedness and book-
learning they cry

Oh look at that condemned man on his way to the scaffold,
there but for the grace of God go I.

Which is so far so good, but they neglect to continue with
the heretofore unspoken balance of the theme, which is
equally true,

That there but for the grace of God goes Jimmy Durante
or the Prince of Wales or Aimee Semple McPherson or
Dr. Wellington Koo,

Or Moses or Napoleon or Cleopatra or King Midas,

Or a man named Harris who is just getting over an attack of
tonsilidas.

So away with you, all you parrot-like repeaters of high-sound-

ing phrases that you never stop to consider what they
actually mean,
I wouldn't allow you to stay in any college of which I was the
Dean.
I can never listen to you without thinking Oh my,
There but for the grace of God speak I.

THE TERRIBLE PEOPLE

People who have what they want are very fond of telling
people who haven't what they want that they really
don't want it,
And I wish I could afford to gather all such people into a
gloomy castle on the Danube and hire half a dozen
capable Draculas to haunt it.
I don't mind their having a lot of money, and I don't care
how they employ it,
But I do think that they damn well ought to admit they
enjoy it.
But no, they insist on being stealthy
About the pleasures of being wealthy,
And the possession of a handsome annuity
Makes them think that to say how hard it is to make both
ends meet is their bounden duity.
You cannot conceive of an occasion
Which will find them without some suitable evasion.
Yes indeed, with arguments they are very fecund;
Their first point is that money isn't everything, and that they
have no money anyhow is their second.
Some people's money is merited,
And other people's is inherited,
But wherever it comes from,
They talk about it as if it were something you got pink gums
from.
This may well be,
But if so, why do they not relieve themselves of the burden
by transferring it to the deserving poor or to me?

Perhaps indeed the possession of wealth is constantly
distressing,
But I should be quite willing to assume every curse of
wealth if I could at the same time assume every blessing.
The only incurable troubles of the rich are the troubles that
money can't cure,
Which is a kind of trouble that is even more troublesome if
you are poor.
Certainly there are lots of things in life that money won't buy,
but it's very funny—
Have you ever tried to buy them without money?

AND THREE HUNDRED AND SIXTY-SIX IN LEAP YEAR

Some people shave before bathing,
And about people who bathe before shaving they are scathing,
While those who bathe before shaving,
Well, they imply that those who shave before bathing are
misbehaving.
Suppose you shave before bathing, well the advantage is
that you don't have to make a special job of washing the
lather off afterwards, it just floats off with the rest of
your accumulations in the tub,
But the disadvantage is that before bathing your skin is hard
and dry and your beard confronts the razor like a grizzly
bear defending its cub.
Well then, suppose you bathe before shaving, well the advantage is that after bathing your skin is soft and moist,
and your beard positively begs for the blade,
But the disadvantage is that to get the lather off you have to
wash your face all over again at the basin almost immediately after washing it in the tub, which is a dupli-
cation of effort that leaves me spotless but dismayed.
The referee reports, gentlemen, that Fate has loaded the dice,
Since your only choice is between walking around all day
with a sore chin or washing your face twice,
So I will now go and get a shave from a smug man in a crisp
white coat,

And I will disrupt his smugness by asking him about his private life, does he bathe before shaving or shave before
bathing, and then I will die either of laughing or of a
clean cut throat.

OH, PLEASE DON'T GET UP!

There is one form of life to which I unconditionally surrender,
Which is the feminine gender.
Like lightning and thunder, women are awe-inspiring
phenomena,
And they have a custom which many men might well adopt,
which is to gird themselves in devices that reduce or at
least repress their abdomena,
And they have a traditional rite which is handed down from
mother to daughter,
Which is that they always have to wash their face with cold
cream instead of water.
Also, I think there must be some great difference in the way
men and women are built,
Because women walk around all day wearing shoes that a man
would break his neck the first step he took in them because where a man's shoe has a heel a woman's shoe has
a stilt,
So I often wonder who started this rumor about woman being
the clinging vine and man the mighty oak or elm,
And I have an idea that the phrase "weaker sex" was coined
by some woman to disarm some man she was preparing
to overwhelm,
Because certainly a man shod like a woman would just have
to sit down all day, and yet my land!
Women not only don't have to sit, but prefer to stand,
Because their pleasure in standing up is exquisite,
As everybody knows who has ever watched a woman pay a
call or a visit,
Because at first they will sit in a chair,
And their heart may be in the highlands, but it certainly isn't
there,

And their conversation is unspontaneous,
And their topics are trifling and miscellaneous,
But finally, after an uncomfortable while,
Their faces brighten with the well-I-must-be-running-along-
now smile,
And they get to their feet and the front door,
And the Old Mother of Waters surges over the levee with a
roar,
Because the proportions of feminine social chitchat are con-
stant, always;
One part of sitting down in the sitting room to four parts
standing up saying good-by in foyers and hallways,
Which is why I think that when it comes to physical prowess,
Why woman is a wow, or should I say a wowess.

THE SEA-GULL

Hark to the whimper of the sea-gull;
He weeps because he's not an ea-gull.
Suppose you were, you silly sea-gull,
Could you explain it to your she-gull?

THE TURTLE

The turtle lives 'twixt plated decks
Which practically conceal its sex.
I think it clever of the turtle
In such a fix to be so fertile.

REFLECTIONS ON ICE-BREAKING

Candy
Is dandy

But liquor
Is quicker.

THIRD LIMICK

Two nudists of Dover,
Being purple all over,

Were munched by a cow
When mistaken for clover.

BENJAMIN

There was a brave girl of Connecticut
Who flagged the express with her pecticut,
Which critics defined
As presence of mind,
But deplorable absence of ecticut.

THE PARSNIP

The parsnip, children, I repeat,
Is simply an anemic beet.
Some people call the parsnip edible;
Myself, I find this claim incredible.

THE OCTOPUS

Tell me, O Octopus, I begs,
Is those things arms, or is they legs?
I marvel at thee, Octopus;
If I were thou, I'd call me Us.

EDOUARD

A bugler named Dougal MacDougal
Found ingenious ways to be frugal.
He learned how to sneeze
In various keys,
Thus saving the price of a bugle.

THE PHŒNIX

Deep in the study
Of eugenics
We find that fabled
Fowl, the Phœnix.
The wisest bird
As ever was,
Rejecting other
Mas and Pas,
It lays one egg,
Not ten or twelve,
And when it's hatched,
Out pops itselve.

A CAUTION TO EVERYBODY

Consider the auk;
Becoming extinct because he forgot how to fly, and could
    only walk.
Consider man, who may well become extinct
Because he forgot how to walk and learned how to fly before
    he thinked.

PORTRAIT OF THE ARTIST AS A PREMATURELY OLD MAN

It is common knowledge to every schoolboy and even every
    Bachelor of Arts,
That all sin is divided into two parts.
One kind of sin is called a sin of commission, and that is very
    important,
And it is what you are doing when you are doing something
    you ortant,
And the other kind of sin is just the opposite and is called a
    sin of omission and is equally bad in the eyes of all right-
    thinking people, from Billy Sunday to Buddha,
And it consists of not having done something you shudda.
I might as well give you my opinion of these two kinds of sin
    as long as, in a way, against each other we are pitting them,
And that is, don't bother your head about sins of commission
    because however sinful, they must at least be fun or else
    you wouldn't be committing them.
It is the sin of omission, the second kind of sin,
That lays eggs under your skin.
The way you get really painfully bitten
Is by the insurance you haven't taken out and the checks you
    haven't added up the stubs of and the appointments you
    haven't kept and the bills you haven't paid and the letters
    you haven't written.
Also, about sins of omission there is one particularly painful
    lack of beauty,
Namely, it isn't as though it had been a riotous red letter day
    or night every time you neglected to do your duty;

You didn't get a wicked forbidden thrill
Every time you let a policy lapse or forgot to pay a bill;
You didn't slap the lads in the tavern on the back and loudly
cry Whee,
Let's all fail to write just one more letter before we go home,
and this round of unwritten letters is on me.
No, you never get any fun
Out of the things you haven't done,
But they are the things that I do not like to be amid,
Because the suitable things you didn't do give you a lot more
trouble than the unsuitable things you did.
The moral is that it is probably better not to sin at all, but if
some kind of sin you must be pursuing,
Well, remember to do it by doing rather than by not doing.

Howard Nemerov

REDEPLOYMENT

They say the war is over. But water still
Comes bloody from the taps, and my pet cat
In his disorder vomits worms which crawl
Swiftly away. Maybe they leave the house.
These worms are white, and flecked with the cat's blood.

The war may be over. I know a man
Who keeps a pleasant souvenir, he keeps
A soldier's dead blue eyeballs that he found
Somewhere—hard as chalk, and blue as slate.
He clicks them in his pocket while he talks.

And now there are cockroaches in the house,
They get slightly drunk on DDT,
Are fast, hard, shifty—can be drowned but not
Without you hold them under quite some time.
People say the Mexican kind can fly.

The end of the war. I took it quietly
Enough. I tried to wash the dirt out of
My hair and from under my fingernails,
I dressed in clean white clothes and went to bed.
I heard the dust falling between the walls.

THE PHOENIX

The Phoenix comes of flame and dust
He bundles up his sire in myrrh
A solar and unholy lust
Makes a cradle of his bier

In the City of the Sun
He dies and rises all divine
There is never more than one
Genuine

By incest, murder, suicide
Survives the sacred purple bird
Himself his father, son and bride
And his own Word

DANDELIONS

These golden heads, these common suns
Only less multitudinous
Than grass itself that gluts
The market of the world with green,
They shine as lovely as they're mean,
Fine as the daughters of the poor
Who go proudly in spangles of brass;
Light-headed, then headless, stalked for a salad.

Inside a week they will be seen
Stricken and old, ghosts in the field
To be picked up at the lightest breath,
With brazen tops all shrunken in

And swollen green gone withered white.
You'll say it's nature's price for beauty
That goes cheap; that being light
Is justly what makes girls grow heavy;
And that the wind, bearing their death,
Whispers the second kingdom come.
—You'll say, the fool of piety,
By resignations hanging on
Until, still justified, you drop.
But surely the thing is sorrowful,
At evening, when the light goes out
Slowly, to see those ruined spinsters,
All down the field their ghostly hair,
Dry sinners waiting in the valley
For the last word and the next life
And the liberation from the lion's mouth.

I ONLY AM ESCAPED ALONE TO TELL THEE

I tell you that I see her still
At the dark entrance of the hall.
One gas lamp burning near her shoulder
Shone also from her other side
Where hung the long inaccurate glass
Whose pictures were as troubled water.
An immense shadow had its hand
Between us on the floor, and seemed
To hump the knuckles nervously,
A giant crab readying to walk,
Or a blanket moving in its sleep.

You will remember, with a smile
Instructed by movies to reminisce,
How strict her corsets must have been,
How the huge arrangements of her hair
Would certainly betray the least
Impassionate displacement there.
It was no rig for dallying,

And maybe only marriage could
Derange that queenly scaffolding—
As when a great ship, coming home,
Coasts in the harbor, dropping sail
And loosing all the tackle that had laced
Her in the long lanes. . . .

                I know
We need not draw this figure out.
But all that whalebone came from whales.
And all the whales lived in the sea,
In calm beneath the troubled glass,
Until the needle drew their blood.

I see her standing in the hall,
Where the mirror's lashed to blood and foam,
And the black flukes of agony
Beat at the air till the light blows out.

Helen Neville

BODY'S FREEDOM

From body's self the body
cries release;
itself to shed
in unbodied space:

but weighed with its blood,
  dragging
a pulse like a chain;
breath drawn up and pressed
  back
on itself again;

limbs that ebb and flow:
in this wilderness,
the pulse may run, the blood
  leap, the body
find its egress;

swell to its ends, flooding
sinew and thigh and
  breast:
the body released, to
  fathom
the body released.

For body's freedom
is bodied yet:
the absolute flesh
goes to defeat:

the crescent flesh
weighs like a stone:
the body flies
within the bone.

Elder Olson

PLOT IMPROBABLE, CHARACTER UNSYMPATHETIC

I was born in a bad slum
Where no one had to die
To show his skeleton.
The wind came through the walls,
A three-legged rat and I
Fought all day for swill.
My father was crazed, my mother cruel,
My brothers chopped the stairs for fuel,
I tumbled my sisters in a broken bed
And jiggled them till all were dead,
Then I ran away and lived with my lice
On my wits, a knife, and a pair of dice,
Slept like a rat in the river reeds,
Got converted fifty times
To fifty different creeds
For bowls of mission-broth,
Till I killed the grocer and his wife
With a stove-poker and a carving-knife.

The mayor said, Hang him high,
The merchants said, He won't buy or sell,
The bishop said, He won't pay to pray.
They flung me into a jail.
But I, I broke out,
Beat my bars to a bell,
Ran all around the town
Dingling my sweet bell,
And the mayor wanted it for his hall,
The merchants wanted to buy it,
The bishop wanted it for his church,
But I broke my bell in two,
Of one half a huge bullet made,
Of the other an enormous gun,
Took all the people of all the world
And rolled them into one,
And when the World went by
With a monocle in his eye
With a silk hat on his head,
Took aim and shot him dead.

THE NIGHT THERE WAS DANCING IN THE STREETS

More paper blackened with more signatures;
Top-hats and handshakes, smiles of marble-toothed diplomats,
Crowds, drums, flags, cannon, fireworks, torchlight processions.
Truce, peace, alliance,
What matter, what matter? Close the windows, now,
Light the lamp, and read Thucydides.

Who knew that passion and character of a nation
Stemmed from far causes; poverty of the soil
Brought safety; safety, growth, eventual greatness;
Habit of growth, ambition; the quick Athenian
Was his own land's best harvest, and so flourished.
Conversely, now, richness of earth brought war,
Stunting increase, and the sullen Spartan
Sank man in soldier; the armor moulded the man.
Thus power and fear of power grew side by side,
Contrary blossoms out of contrary earths;
There lay the principles of war; meanwhile, let run,
Let rhetors roar and heralds strut, let town
Quibble with town; the tough root turns all axes,
The fruits of Necessity ripen in all weathers.

JACK-IN-THE-BOX

Devil sprang from box,
Frightening the children, who would not be quieted.
In vain they were wooed with all the other toys;
Expecting new terror, they would not look or listen; like an
   angry demon
Their fear ran round the house, from room to room.
At last their mother bore them off to bed.

Blakely lit his pipe,
Let it go out again with thinking; something more had been
   released

Than long-necked Punch, nodding and leering still.
As in the ancient casuistry of Eden,
Falsehood, accepted, falsified all truth;
All the old pleasant truths now fell away,
Flimsy as Christmas papers; there was the house, now,
Pretty with snows, with candy roofs and sills,
Sparkling and false as the house in the fairy tale;
As if in a haunted forest shone the tree
With fruits—pear, apple, plum—all poison-bright.
Outside, the wind swept away the Christmas illusion, raising
   a white fog
Where toys like Martians stalked, destroying all.

He thought: how simply terror can enter a house;
The angel, treed, was trembling, that had promised peace.

Robert Pack

ANECDOTE OF THE SPARROW

The modern house, with great glass eye,
Stared like an idol at the sun.
Such judgment singed the air that one
Could almost hear the flowers cry
Down in the garden below the glass:
There the broken sparrow lay.
What silent force will block our way
Or smash us as we darkly pass
On some bright noon, to seek a place?
Prepare, since even gods are blind,
For things unseen. Be of the kind;
Or in the glass come see your face.

Edgar Allan Poe

THE HAPPIEST DAY, THE HAPPIEST HOUR

The happiest day, the happiest hour
  My sear'd and blighted heart hath known,
The highest hope of pride and power,
  I feel hath flown.

Of power! said I? yes! such I ween;
  But they have vanish'd long, alas!
The visions of my youth have been—
  But let them pass.

And, pride, what have I now with thee?
  Another brow may ev'n inherit
The venom thou hast pour'd on me—
  Be still, my spirit!

The happiest day, the happiest hour
  Mine eyes shall see, have ever seen,
The brightest glance of pride and power,
  I feel—have been:

But were that hope of pride and power
  Now offer'd, with the pain
Ev'n *then* I felt—that brightest hour
  I would not live again:

For on its wing was dark alloy,
  And as it flutter'd, fell
An essence—powerful to destroy
A soul that knew it well.

SONNET—TO SCIENCE

Science! true daughter of Old Time thou art!
Who alterest all things with thy peering eyes.
Why preyest thou thus upon the poet's heart,
Vulture, whose wings are dull realities?
How should he love thee? or how deem thee wise,
Who wouldst not leave him in his wandering
To seek for treasure in the jewelled skies,
Albeit he soared with an undaunted wing?
Hast thou not dragged Diana from her car,
And driven the Hamadryad from the wood
To seek a shelter in some happier star?
Hast thou not torn the Naiad from her flood,
The Elfin from the green grass, and from me
The summer dream beneath the tamarind tree?

SONG FROM "AL AARAAF"

'Neath blue-bell or streamer—
  Or tufted wild spray
That keeps from the dreamer
  The moonbeam away—
Bright beings! that ponder,
  With half closing eyes,
On the stars which your
    wonder
  Hath drawn from the skies,
Till they glance thro' the
    shade, and
  Come down to your brow
Like—eyes of the maiden
  Who calls on you now—
Arise! from your dreaming
  In violet bowers,
To duty beseeming
  These star-litten hours—
And shake from your tresses,
  Encumber'd with dew,
The breath of those kisses
  That cumber them too
(O, how, without you, Love!
  Could angels be blest?)—
Those kisses of true love
  That lull'd ye to rest!
Up!—shake from your wing
  Each hindering thing:
The dew of the night—
  It would weigh down your
    flight;
And true love caresses—
  O! leave them apart:
They are light on the tresses,
  But lead on the heart.

Ligeia! Ligeia!
  My beautiful one!
Whose harshest idea
  Will to melody run,
O! is it thy will
  On the breezes to toss?
Or, capriciously still,
  Like the lone Albatross,
Incumbent on night
  (As she on the air)
To keep watch with delight
  On the harmony there?
Ligeia! wherever
  Thy image may be,
No magic shall sever
  Thy music from thee.
Thou hast bound many eyes
  In a dreamy sleep—
But the strains still arise
  Which *thy* vigilance keep:
The sound of the rain
  Which leaps down to the
    flower,
And dances again
  In the rhythm of the
    shower—
The murmur that springs
  From the growing of grass
Are the music of things—
  But are modell'd, alas!—
Away, then, my dearest,

O! hie thee away
To springs that lie clearest
  Beneath the moon-ray—
To lone lake that smiles,
  In its dream of deep rest,
At the many star-isles
  That enjewel its breast—
Where wild flowers, creep-
    ing,
  Have mingled their shade,
On its margin is sleeping
  Full many a maid—
Some have left the cool glade,
    and
  Have slept with the bee—
Arouse them, my maiden,
  On moorland and lea—
Go! Breathe on their slumber,
  All softly in ear,
The musical number
  They slumber'd to hear—
For what can awaken
  An angel so soon,
Whose sleep hath been taken
  Beneath the cold moon,
As the spell which no
    slumber
  Of witchery may test,
The rhythmical number
  Which lull'd him to rest?

ROMANCE

Romance, who loves to nod and sing,
With drowsy head and folded wing,
Among the green leaves as they shake
Far down within some shadowy lake,
To me a painted paroquet
Hath been—a most familiar bird—
Taught me my alphabet to say,
To lisp my very earliest word,
While in the wild wood I did lie,
A child—with a most knowing eye.

Of late, eternal Condor years
So shake the very Heaven on high
With tumult as they thunder by,
I have no time for idle cares
Through gazing on the unquiet sky.
And when an hour with calmer wings
Its down upon my spirit flings—
That little time with lyre and rhyme
To while away—forbidden things!
My heart would feel to be a crime
Unless it trembled with the strings.

TO HELEN

Helen, thy beauty is to me
    Like those Nicéan barks of yore,
That gently, o'er a perfumed sea,
    The weary, way-worn wanderer bore
    To his own native shore.

On desperate seas long wont to roam,
    Thy hyacinth hair, thy classic face,
Thy Naiad airs have brought me home
    To the glory that was Greece
And the grandeur that was Rome.

Lo! in yon brilliant window-niche
   How statue-like I see thee stand,
   The agate lamp within thy hand!
Ah, Psyche, from the regions which
   Are Holy Land!

DREAM-LAND

By a route obscure and lonely,
Haunted by ill angels only,
Where an Eidolon, named NIGHT,
On a black throne reigns upright,
I have reached these lands but newly
From an ultimate dim Thule—
From a wild weird clime that lieth, sublime,
   Out of SPACE—out of TIME.

Bottomless vales and boundless floods,
And chasms, and caves, and Titan woods,
With forms that no man can discover
For the tears that drip all over;
Mountains toppling evermore
Into seas without a shore;
Seas that restlessly aspire,
Surging, unto skies of fire;
Lakes that endlessly outspread
Their lone waters, lone and dead,—
Their still waters, still and chilly
With the snows of the lolling lily.

By the lakes that thus outspread
Their lone waters, lone and dead,—
Their sad waters, sad and chilly
With the snows of the lolling lily,—
By the mountains—near the river
Murmuring lowly murmuring ever,—
By the grey woods,—by the swamp

Where the toad and the newt encamp,—
By the dismal tarns and pools
  Where dwell the Ghouls,—
By each spot the most unholy—
In each nook most melancholy,—
There the traveller meets, aghast,
Sheeted Memories of the Past—
Shrouded forms that start and sigh
As they pass the wanderer by—
White-robed forms of friends long given,
In agony, to the Earth—and Heaven.

For the heart whose woes are legion
'T is a peaceful, soothing region—
For the spirit that walks in shadow
'T is—oh, 't is an Eldorado!
But the traveller, travelling through it,
May not—dare not openly view it;
Never its mysteries are exposed
To the weak human eye unclosed;
So wills its King, who hath forbid
The uplifting of the fringéd lid;
And thus the sad Soul that here passes
Beholds it but through darkened glasses.

By a route obscure and lonely,
Haunted by ill angels only,
Where an Eidolon, named NIGHT,
On a black throne reigns upright,
I have wandered home but newly
From this ultimate dim Thule.

ANNABEL LEE

It was many and many a year ago,
    In a kingdom by the sea,
That a maiden there lived whom you may know
    By the name of Annabel Lee;—
And this maiden she lived with no other thought
    Than to love and be loved by me.

She was a child and *I* was a child,
    In this kingdom by the sea,
But we loved with a love that was more than love—
    I and my Annabel Lee—
With a love that the wingéd seraphs of Heaven
    Coveted her and me.

And this was the reason that, long ago,
    In this kingdom by the sea,
A wind blew out of a cloud by night
    Chilling my Annabel Lee;
So that her highborn kinsmen came
    And bore her away from me,
To shut her up in a sepulchre
    In this kingdom by the sea.

The angels, not half so happy in Heaven,
    Went envying her and me:—
Yes! that was the reason (as all men know,
    In this kingdom by the sea)
That the wind came out of the cloud, chilling
    And killing my Annabel Lee.

But our love it was stronger by far than the love
    Of those who were older than we—
    Of many far wiser than we—
And neither the angels in Heaven above

Nor the demons down under the sea,
Can ever dissever my soul from the soul
   Of the beautiful Annabel Lee:—

For the moon never beams without bringing me dreams
   Of the beautiful Annabel Lee;
And the stars never rise but I see the bright eyes
   Of the beautiful Annabel Lee;
And so, all the night-tide, I lie down by the side
Of my darling, my darling, my life and my bride,
   In her sepulchre there by the sea—
   In her tomb by the side of the sea.

TO MY MOTHER

Because I feel that, in the Heavens above,
The angels, whispering to one another,
Can find, among their burning terms of love,
None so devotional as that of 'Mother,'
Therefore by that dear name I long have called you—
You who are more than mother unto me,
And fill my heart of hearts, where Death installed you
In setting my Virginia's spirit free.
My mother—my own mother, who died early,
Was but the mother of myself; but you
Are mother to the one I loved so dearly,
And thus are dearer than the mother I knew
By that infinity with which my wife
Was dearer to my soul than its soul-life.

ULALUME—A BALLAD

The skies they were ashen and sober;
    The leaves they were crispéd and sere—
    The leaves they were withering and sere:
It was night, in the lonesome October
    Of my most immemorial year:
It was hard by the dim lake of Auber,
    In the misty mid region of Weir—
It was down by the dank tarn of Auber,
    In the ghoul-haunted woodland of Weir.

Here once, through an alley Titanic,
    Of cypress, I roamed with my Soul—
    Of cypress, with Psyche, my Soul.
These were days when my heart was volcanic
    As the scoriac rivers that roll—
    As the lavas that restlessly roll
Their sulphurous currents down Yaanek
    In the ultimate climes of the Pole—
That groan as they roll down Mount Yaanek
    In the realms of the Boreal Pole.

Our talk had been serious and sober,
    But our thoughts they were palsied and sere—
    Our memories were treacherous and sere;
For we knew not the month was October,
    And we marked not the night of the year
    (Ah, night of all nights in the year!)—
We noted not the dim lake of Auber
    (Though once we had journeyed down here)—
We remembered not the dank tarn of Auber,
    Nor the ghoul-haunted woodland of Weir.

And now, as the night was senescent
    And star-dials pointed to morn—
    As the star-dials hinted of morn—
At the end of our path a liquescent
    And nebulous lustre was born,

Out of which a miraculous crescent
　　Arose with a duplicate horn—
Astarte's bediamonded crescent
　　　Distinct with its duplicate horn.

And I said: 'She is warmer than Dian;
　　She rolls through an ether of sighs—
　　She revels in a region of sighs.
She has seen that the tears are not dry on
　　These cheeks, where the worm never dies,
And has come past the stars of the Lion,
　　To point us the path to the skies—
　　To the Lethean peace of the skies—
Come up, in despite of the Lion,
　　To shine on us with her bright eyes—
Come up through the lair of the Lion,
　　With love in her luminous eyes.'

But Psyche, uplifting her finger,
　　Said: 'Sadly this star I mistrust—
　　Her pallor I strangely mistrust:
Ah, hasten!—ah, let us not linger.
　　Ah, fly!—let us fly!—for we must.'
In terror she spoke, letting sink her
　　Wings till they trailed in the dust—
In agony sobbed, letting sink her
　　Plumes till they trailed in the dust—
　　Till they sorrowfully trailed in the dust.

I replied: 'This is nothing but dreaming:
　　Let us on by this tremulous light!
　　Let us bathe in this crystalline light!
Its Sibyllic splendor is beaming
　　With Hope and in Beauty to-night:—
　　See!—it flickers up the sky through the night!
Ah, we safely may trust to its gleaming,
　　And be sure it will lead us aright—
We surely may trust to a gleaming,

That cannot but guide us aright,
Since it flickers up to Heaven through the night.'

Thus I pacified Psyche and kissed her,
    And tempted her out of her gloom—
    And conquered her scruples and gloom;
And we passed to the end of the vista,
    But were stopped by the door of a tomb—
    By the door of a legended tomb;
And I said: 'What is written, sweet sister,
    On the door of this legended tomb?'
    She replied: 'Ulalume—Ulalume!—
    'T is the vault of thy lost Ulalume!'

Then my heart it grew ashen and sober
    As the leaves that were crispéd and sere—
    As the leaves that were withering and sere;
And I cried: 'It was surely October
    On *this* very night of last year
    That I journeyed—I journeyed down here!—
    That I brought a dread burden down here—
    On this night of all nights in the year,
    Ah, what demon hath tempted me here?
Well I know, now, this dim lake of Auber—
    This misty mid region of Weir—
Well I know, now, this dank tarn of Auber,
    This ghoul-haunted woodland of Weir.'

Said we, then—the two, then: 'Ah, can it
    Have been that the woodlandish ghouls—
    The pitiful, the merciful ghouls—
To bar up our way and to ban it
    From the secret that lies in these wolds—
    From the thing that lies hidden in these wolds—
Have drawn up the spectre of a planet
    From the limbo of lunary souls—
This sinfully scintillant planet
    From the Hell of the planetary souls?'

ELDORADO

Gaily bedight,
A gallant knight,
In sunshine and in shadow,
Had journeyed long,
Singing a song,
In search of Eldorado.

But he grew old—
This knight so bold—
And o'er his heart a shadow
Fell as he found
No spot of ground
That looked like Eldorado.

And, as his strength
Failed him at length,
He met a pilgrim shadow—
'Shadow,' said he,
'Where can it be—
This land of Eldorado?'

'Over the Mountains
Of the Moon,
Down the Valley of the
Shadow,
Ride, boldly ride,'
The shade replied,—
'If you seek for Eldorado!'

FOR ANNIE

Thank Heaven! the crisis,
The danger, is past,
And the lingering illness
Is over at last—
And the fever called 'Living'
Is conquered at last.

Sadly, I know
I am shorn of my strength,
And no muscle I move
As I lie at full length—
But no matter!—I feel
I am better at length.

And I rest so composedly,
Now, in my bed,
That any beholder

Might fancy me dead—
Might start at beholding me,
Thinking me dead.

The moaning and groaning,
The sighing and sobbing,
Are quieted now, with
That horrible throbbing
At heart:—ah, that horrible,
Horrible throbbing!

The sickness—the nausea—
The pitiless pain—
Have ceased, with the fever
That maddened my brain—
With the fever called 'Living'
That burned in my brain.

And oh! of all tortures
   That torture the worst
Has abated—the terrible
   Torture of thirst
For the naphthaline river
   Of Passion accurst:—
I have drank of a water
   That quenches all thirst:—

Of a water that flows,
   With a lullaby sound,
From a spring but a very few
   Feet under ground—
From a cavern not very far
   Down under ground.

And ah! let it never
   Be foolishly said
That my room it is gloomy
   And narrow my bed;
For man never slept
   In a different bed—
And, to *sleep*, you must slumber
   In just such a bed.

My tantalized spirit
   Here blandly reposes,
Forgetting, or never
   Regretting, its roses—
Its old agitations
   Of myrtles and roses:

For now, while so quietly
   Lying, it fancies
A holier odor
   About it, of pansies—

A rosemary odor,
   Commingled with pansies—
With rue and the beautiful
   Puritan pansies.

And so it lies happily,
   Bathing in many
A dream of the truth
   And the beauty of Annie—
Drowned in a bath
   Of the tresses of Annie.

She tenderly kissed me,
   She fondly caressed,
And then I fell gently
   To sleep on her breast—
Deeply to sleep
   From the heaven of her breast.

When the light was extinguished,
   She covered me warm,
And she prayed to the angels
   To keep me from harm—
To the queen of the angels
   To shield me from harm.

And I lie so composedly,
   Now, in my bed
(Knowing her love),
   That you fancy me dead—
And I rest so contentedly,
   Now, in my bed
(With her love at my breast),
   That you fancy me dead—
That you shudder to look at me,
   Thinking me dead:—

But my heart it is brighter
  Than all of the many
Stars in the sky,
  For it sparkles with
    Annie—

It glows with the light
  Of the love of my Annie—
With the thought of the light
  Of the eyes of my Annie.

ISRAFEL

*And the angel Israfel, whose heart-strings are a lute, and who has the
sweetest voice of all God's creatures.*—KORAN

In Heaven a spirit doth dwell
  "Whose heart-strings are a lute";
None sing so wildly well
As the angel Israfel,
And the giddy stars (so legends tell),
Ceasing their hymns, attend the spell
  Of his voice, all mute.

Tottering above
  In her highest noon,
  The enamored moon
Blushes with love,
  While, to listen, the red levin
  (With the rapid Pleiads, even,
  Which were seven,)
  Pauses in Heaven.

And they say (the starry choir
  And the other listening things)
That Israfeli's fire
Is owing to that lyre
  By which he sits and sings—
The trembling living wire
  Of those unusual strings.

But the skies that angel trod,
  Where deep thoughts are a duty,
Where Love's a grown-up God,

Where the Houri glances are
Imbued with all the beauty
Which we worship in a star.

Therefore, thou art not wrong,
Israfeli, who despisest
An unimpassioned song;
To thee the laurels belong,
Best bard, because the wisest.
Merrily live, and long!

The ecstasies above
With thy burning measures suit—
Thy grief, thy joy, thy hate, thy love,
With the fervor of thy lute—
Well may the stars be mute!

Yes, Heaven is thine; but this
Is a world of sweets and sours;
Our flowers are merely—flowers,
And the shadow of thy perfect bliss
Is the sunshine of ours.

If I could dwell
Where Israfel
Hath dwelt, and he where I,
He might not sing so wildly well
A mortal melody,
While a bolder note than this might swell
From my lyre within the sky.

FROM CHILDHOOD'S HOUR

From childhood's hour I have not been
As others were; I have not seen
As others saw; I could not bring
My passions from a common spring.

From the same source I have not taken
My sorrow; I could not awaken
My heart to joy at the same tone;
And all I loved, I loved alone.
Then—in my childhood, in the dawn
Of a most stormy life—was drawn
From every depth of good and ill
The mystery which binds me still:
From the torrent or the fountain,
From the red cliff of the mountain,
From the sun that round me rolled
In its autumn tint of gold,
From the lightning in the sky
As it passed me flying by,
From the thunder and the storm,
And the cloud that took the form
(When the rest of Heaven was blue)
Of a demon in my view.

THE CITY IN THE SEA

Lo! Death has reared himself a throne
In a strange city lying alone
Far down within the dim West,
Where the good and the bad and the worst and the best
Have gone to their eternal rest.
There shrines and palaces and towers
(Time-eaten towers that tremble not!)
Resemble nothing that is ours.
Around, by lifting winds forgot,
Resignedly beneath the sky
The melancholy waters lie.

No rays from the holy heaven come down
On the long night-time of that town;
But light from out the lurid sea
Streams up the turrets silently—

Gleams up the pinnacles far and free—
Up domes—up spires—up kingly halls—

Up fanes—up Babylon-like walls—
Up shadowy long-forgotten bowers
Of sculptured ivy and stone flowers—
Up many and many a marvellous shrine
Whose wreathéd friezes intertwine
The viol, the violet, and the vine.

Resignedly beneath the sky
The melancholy waters lie.
So blend the turrets and shadows there
That all seem pendulous in air,
While from a proud tower in the town
Death looks gigantically down.

There open fanes and gaping graves
Yawn level with the luminous waves;
But not the riches there that lie
In each idol's diamond eye—
Not the gaily-jewelled dead
Tempt the waters from their bed;
For no ripples curl, alas!
Along that wilderness of glass—
No swellings tell that winds may be
Upon some far-off happier sea—
No heavings hint that winds have been
On seas less hideously serene.

But lo, a stir is in the air!
The wave—there is a movement there!
As if the towers had thrust aside,
In slightly sinking, the dull tide—
As if their tops had feebly given
A void within the filmy Heaven.
The waves have now a redder glow—

The hours are breathing faint and low—
And when, amid no earthly moans,
Down, down that town shall settle hence,
Hell, rising from a thousand thrones,
Shall do it reverence.

THE SLEEPER

At midnight, in the month of June,
I stand beneath the mystic moon.
An opiate vapor, dewy, dim,
Exhales from out her golden rim,
And softly dripping, drop by drop,
Upon the quiet mountain top,
Steals drowsily and musically
Into the universal valley.
The rosemary nods upon the grave;
The lily lolls upon the wave;
Wrapping the fog about its breast,
The ruin moulders into rest;
Looking like Lethe, see! the lake
A conscious slumber seems to take,
And would not, for the world, awake.
All Beauty sleeps!—and lo! where lies
Irene, with her Destinies!

Oh, lady bright! can it be right—
This window open to the night?
The wanton airs, from the tree-top,
Laughingly through the lattice drop—
The bodiless airs, a wizard rout,
Flit through thy chamber in and out,
And wave the curtain canopy
So fitfully—so fearfully—
Above the closed and fringéd lid
'Neath which thy slumb'ring soul lies hid,
That, o'er the floor and down the wall,

Like ghosts the shadows rise and fall!
Oh, lady dear, hast thou no fear?
Why and what art thou dreaming here?
Sure thou art come o'er far-off seas,
A wonder to these garden trees!
Strange is thy pallor! strange thy dress!
Strange, above all, thy length of tress,
And this all solemn silentness!

The lady sleeps! Oh, may her sleep,
Which is enduring, so be deep!
Heaven have her in its sacred keep!
This chamber changed for one more holy,
This bed for one more melancholy,
I pray to God that she may lie
Forever with unopened eye,
While the pale sheeted ghosts go by!

My love, she sleeps! Oh, may her sleep,
As it is lasting, so be deep!
Soft may the worms about her creep!
Far in the forest, dim and old,
For her may some tall vault unfold—
Some vault that oft hath flung its black
And wingéd pannels fluttering back,
Triumphant, o'er the crested palls
Of her grand family funerals—
Some sepulchre, remote, alone,
Against whose portal she hath thrown,
In childhood, many an idle stone—
Some tomb from out whose sounding door
She ne'er shall force an echo more,
Thrilling to think, poor child of sin!
It was the dead who groaned within.

TO ONE IN PARADISE

Thou wast that all to me, love,
  For which my soul did pine—
A green isle in the sea, love,
  A fountain and a shrine,
All wreathed with fairy fruits and flowers,
  And all the flowers were mine.

Ah, dream too bright to last!
  Ah, starry Hope! that didst arise
But to be overcast!
  A voice from out the Future cries,
'On! on!'—but o'er the Past
  (Dim gulf!) my spirit hovering lies
Mute, motionless, aghast!

For, alas! alas! with me
  The light of Life is o'er!
No more—no more—no more—
  (Such language holds the solemn sea
To the sands upon the shore)
  Shall bloom the thunder-blasted tree,
Or the stricken eagle soar!

And all my days are trances,
  And all my nightly dreams
Are where thy grey eye glances,
  And where thy footstep gleams—
In what ethereal dances,
  By what eternal streams.

THE HAUNTED PALACE

In the greenest of our valleys
    By good angels tenanted,
Once a fair and stately palace—
    Radiant palace—reared its head.
In the monarch Thought's dominion,
    It stood there!
Never seraph spread a pinion
    Over fabric half so fair!

Banners yellow, glorious, golden,
    On its roof did float and flow
(This—all this—was in the olden
    Time long ago),
And every gentle air that dallied,
    In that sweet day,
Along the ramparts plumed and pallid,
    A wingéd odor went away.

Wanderers in that happy valley,
    Through two luminous windows, saw
Spirits moving musically,
    To a lute's well-tunéd law,
Round about a throne where, sitting,
    Porphyrogene!
In state his glory well befitting,
    The ruler of the realm was seen.

And all with pearl and ruby glowing
    Was the fair palace door,
Through which came flowing, flowing, flowing,
    And sparkling evermore,
A troop of Echoes, whose sweet duty
    Was but to sing,
In voices of surpassing beauty,
    The wit and wisdom of their king.

But evil things, in robes of sorrow,
    Assailed the monarch's high estate.
(Ah, let us mourn!—for never morrow
    Shall dawn upon him, desolate!)
And round about his home the glory
    That blushed and bloomed,
Is but a dim-remembered story
    Of the old time entombed.

And travellers, now, within that valley,
    Through the red-litten windows see
Vast forms that move fantastically
    To a discordant melody,
While, like a ghastly rapid river,
    Through the pale door
A hideous throng rush out forever,
    And laugh—but smile no more.

THE RAVEN

Once upon a midnight dreary, while I pondered, weak and
    weary,
Over many a quaint and curious volume of forgotten lore—
While I nodded, nearly napping, suddenly there came a
    tapping,
As of some one gently rapping, rapping at my chamber door.
' 'T is some visitor,' I muttered, 'tapping at my chamber door—
    Only this and nothing more.'

Ah, distinctly I remember it was in the bleak December;
And each separate dying ember wrought its ghost upon the
    floor.
Eagerly I wished the morrow;—vainly I had sought to borrow
From my books surcease of sorrow—sorrow for the lost
    Lenore—
For the rare and radiant maiden whom the angels name
    Lenore—
    Nameless *here* for evermore.

And the silken, sad, uncertain rustling of each purple curtain
Thrilled me—filled me with fantastic terrors never felt before;
So that now, to still the beating of my heart, I stood repeating,
' 'T is some visitor entreating entrance at my chamber door—
Some late visitor entreating entrance at my chamber door;—
    This it is and nothing more.'

Presently my soul grew stronger; hesitating then no longer,
'Sir,' said I, 'or Madam, truly your forgiveness I implore;
But the fact is I was napping, and so gently you came rapping,
And so faintly you came tapping, tapping at my chamber door,
That I scarce was sure I heard you'—here I opened wide the
    door;—
    Darkness there and nothing more.

Deep into that darkness peering, long I stood there wondering,
    fearing,
Doubting, dreaming dreams no mortal ever dared to dream
    before;
But the silence was unbroken, and the stillness gave no token,
And the only word there spoken was the whispered word,
    'Lenore?'
This I whispered, and an echo murmured back the word,
    'Lenore!'
    Merely this and nothing more.

Back into the chamber turning, all my soul within me burning,
Soon again I heard a tapping somewhat louder than before.
'Surely,' said I, 'surely that is something at my window lattice;
Let me see, then, what thereat is, and this mystery explore—
Let my heart be still a moment and this mystery explore;—
    'T is the wind and nothing more!'

Open here I flung the shutter, when, with many a flirt and
    flutter,
In there stepped a stately Raven of the saintly days of yore;
Not the least obeisance made he; not a minute stopped or
    stayed he;

But, with mien of lord or lady, perched above my chamber
door—
Perched upon a bust of Pallas just above my chamber door—
Perched, and sat, and nothing more.

Then this ebony bird beguiling my sad fancy into smiling,
By the grave and stern decorum of the countenance it wore,
'Though thy crest be shorn and shaven, thou,' I said, 'art sure
no craven,
Ghastly grim and ancient Raven wandering from the Nightly
shore—
Tell me what thy lordly name is on the Night's Plutonian
shore!'
Quoth the Raven, 'Nevermore.'

Much I marvelled this ungainly fowl to hear discourse so
plainly,
Though its answer little meaning—little relevancy bore;
For we cannot help agreeing that no living human being
Ever yet was blessed with seeing bird above his chamber
door—
Bird or beast upon the sculptured bust above his chamber
door,
With such name as 'Nevermore.'

But the Raven, sitting lonely on the placid bust, spoke only
That one word, as if his soul in that one word he did outpour.
Nothing farther then he uttered—not a feather then he
fluttered—
Till I scarcely more than muttered, 'Other friends have flown
before—
On the morrow *he* will leave me, as my Hopes have flown
before.'
Then the bird said, 'Nevermore.'

Startled at the stillness broken by reply so aptly spoken,
'Doubtless,' said I, 'what it utters is its only stock and store

Caught from some unhappy master whom unmerciful Disaster
Followed fast and followed faster till his songs one burden
   bore—
Till the dirges of his Hope that melancholy burden bore
    Of "Never—nevermore." '

But the Raven still beguiling my sad fancy into smiling,
Straight I wheeled a cushioned seat in front of bird and bust
   and door;
Then, upon the velvet sinking, I betook myself to linking
Fancy unto fancy, thinking what this ominous bird of yore—
What this grim, ungainly, ghastly, gaunt, and ominous bird of
   yore
    Meant in croaking 'Nevermore.'

This I sat engaged in guessing, but no syllable expressing
To the fowl whose fiery eyes now burned into my bosom's
   core;
This and more I sat divining, with my head at ease reclining
On the cushion's velvet lining that the lamp-light gloated o'er,
But whose velvet-violet lining with the lamp-light gloating
   o'er,
    She shall press, ah, nevermore!

Then, methought, the air grew denser, perfumed from an
   unseen censer
Swung by seraphim whose foot-falls tinkled on the tufted
   floor.
'Wretch,' I cried, 'thy God hath lent thee—by these angels he
   hath sent thee
Respite—respite and nepenthe from thy memories of Lenore;
Quaff, oh, quaff this kind nepenthe and forget this lost
   Lenore!'
    Quoth the Raven, 'Nevermore.'

'Prophet!' said I, 'thing of evil!—prophet still, if bird or devil!—
Whether Tempter sent, or whether tempest tossed thee here
   ashore,

Desolate yet all undaunted, on this desert land enchanted—
On this home by Horror haunted—tell me truly, I implore—
Is there—*is* there balm in Gilead?—tell me—tell me, I implore!'
    Quoth the Raven, 'Nevermore.'

'Prophet!' said I, 'thing of evil!—prophet still, if bird or devil!
By that Heaven that bends above us—by that God we both
    adore—
Tell this soul with sorrow laden if, within the distant Aidenn,
It shall clasp a sainted maiden whom the angels name Lenore—
Clasp a rare and radiant maiden whom the angels name
    Lenore.'
    Quoth the Raven, 'Nevermore.'

'Be that word our sign of parting, bird or fiend!' I shrieked,
    upstarting—
'Get thee back into the tempest and the Night's Plutonian
    shore!
Leave no black plume as a token of that lie thy soul hath
    spoken!
Leave my loneliness unbroken!—quit the bust above my door!
Take thy beak from out my heart, and take thy form from off
    my door!'
    Quoth the Raven, 'Nevermore.'

And the Raven, never flitting, still is sitting, *still* is sitting
On the pallid bust of Pallas just above my chamber door;
And his eyes have all the seeming of a demon's that is
    dreaming,
And the lamp-light o'er him streaming throws his shadow on
    the floor;
And my soul from out that shadow that lies floating on the
    floor
    Shall be lifted—nevermore!

THE BELLS

I

Hear the sledges with the bells—
 Silver bells!
What a world of merriment their melody foretells!
 How they tinkle, tinkle, tinkle,
  In the icy air of night!
 While the stars that oversprinkle
 All the heavens, seem to twinkle
  With a crystalline delight;
  Keeping time, time, time,
  In a sort of Runic rhyme,
To the tintinnabulation that so musically wells
 From the bells, bells, bells, bells,
  Bells, bells, bells—
From the jingling and the tinkling of the bells.

II

Hear the mellow wedding bells—
 Golden bells!
What a world of happiness their harmony foretells!
 Through the balmy air of night
 How they ring out their delight!—
  From the molten-golden notes,
   And all in tune,
  What a liquid ditty floats
To the turtle-dove that listens, while she gloats
  On the moon!
 Oh, from out the sounding cells,
What a gush of euphony voluminously wells!
  How it swells!
  How it dwells
  On the Future!—how it tells
  Of the rapture that impels
 To the swinging and the ringing
  Of the bells, bells, bells—

Of the bells, bells, bells, bells,
  Bells, bells, bells—
To the rhyming and the chiming of the bells!

III

Hear the loud alarum bells—
  Brazen bells!
What a tale of terror, now, their turbulency tells!
 In the startled ear of night
 How they scream out their affright!
  Too much horrified to speak,
  They can only shriek, shriek,
   Out of tune,
In a clamorous appealing to the mercy of the fire,
In a mad expostulation with the deaf and frantic fire,
  Leaping higher, higher, higher,
   With a desperate desire,
  And a resolute endeavor
  Now—now to sit, or never,
By the side of the pale-faced moon.
  Oh, the bells, bells, bells!
  What a tale their terror tells
   Of Despair!
How they clang, and clash, and roar!
What a horror they outpour
On the bosom of the palpitating air!
 Yet the ear, it fully knows,
  By the twanging
  And the clanging,
 How the danger ebbs and flows;
 Yet the ear distinctly tells,
  In the jangling
  And wrangling,
 How the danger sinks and swells,
By the sinking or the swelling in the anger of the bells—
  Of the bells,—
Of the bells, bells, bells, bells,
  Bells, bells, bells—
In the clamor and the clangor of the bells!

IV

Hear the tolling of the bells—
Iron bells!
What a world of solemn thought their monody
compels!
In the silence of the night,
How we shiver with affright
At the melancholy menace of their tone!
For every sound that floats
From the rust within their throats
Is a groan.
And the people—ah, the people—
They that dwell up in the steeple,
All alone,
And who tolling, tolling, tolling,
In that muffled monotone,
Feel a glory in so rolling
On the human heart a stone—
They are neither man nor woman—
They are neither brute nor human—
They are Ghouls:—
And their king it is who tolls:—
And he rolls, rolls, rolls,
Rolls
A pæan from the bells!
And his merry bosom swells
With the pæan of the bells!
And he dances, and he yells;
Keeping time, time, time,
In a sort of Runic rhyme,
To the pæan of the bells—
Of the bells:—
Keeping time, time, time,
In a sort of Runic rhyme,
To the throbbing of the bells—
Of the bells, bells, bells—
To the sobbing of the bells;

Keeping time, time, time,
　　As he knells, knells, knells,
In a happy Runic rhyme,
　　To the rolling of the bells—
　　Of the bells, bells, bells:—
　　To the tolling of the bells—
Of the bells, bells, bells, bells,
　　　Bells, bells, bells—
To the moaning and the groaning of the bells.

Ezra Pound

A PACT

I make a pact with you, Walt Whitman—
I have detested you long enough.
I come to you as a grown child
Who has had a pig-headed father;
I am old enough now to make friends.
It was you that broke the new wood,
Now is a time for carving.
We have one sap and one root—
Let there be commerce between us.

AN IMMORALITY

Sing we for love and idleness,
Naught else is worth the having.

Though I have been in many a land,
There is naught else in living.

And I would rather have my sweet,
Though rose-leaves die of grieving,

Than do high deeds in Hungary
To pass all men's believing.

A VIRGINAL

No, no! Go from me. I have left her lately.
I will not spoil my sheath with lesser brightness,
For my surrounding air hath a new lightness;
Slight are her arms, yet they have bound me straitly
And left me cloaked as with a gauze of æther;
As with sweet leaves; as with subtle clearness.
Oh, I have picked up magic in her nearness
To sheathe me half in half the things that sheathe her.
No, no! Go from me. I have still the flavour,
Soft as spring wind that's come from birchen bowers.
Green come the shoots, aye April in the branches,
As winter's wound with her sleight hand she staunches,
Hath of the trees a likeness of the savour:
As white their bark, so white this lady's hours.

THE RETURN

See, they return, one, and by one,
            Movements, and the slow feet,
            The trouble in the pace and the uncertain
Wavering!

See, they return, one, and by one,
With fear, as half-awakened;
As if the snow should hesitate
And murmur in the wind,
            and half turn back;
These were the 'Wing'd-with-Awe,'
            Inviolable.

Gods of the wingèd shoe!
With them the silver hounds,
            sniffing the trace of air!

Haie! Haie!
>   These were the swift to harry;
These the keen-scented;
These were the souls of blood.

Slow on the leash,
>   pallid the leash-men!

BALLAD OF THE GOODLY FERE

Simon Zelotes speaketh it somewhile after the Crucifixion

Ha' we lost the goodliest fere o' all
For the priests and the gallows tree?
Aye lover he was of brawny men,
O' ships and the open sea.

When they came wi' a host to take Our Man
His smile was good to see,
"First let these go!" quo' our Goodly Fere,
"Or I'll see ye damned," says he.

Aye he sent us out through the crossed high spears
And the scorn of his laugh rang free,
"Why took ye not me when I walked about
Alone in the town?" says he.

Oh we drunk his "Hale" in the good red wine
When we last made company,
No capon priest was the Goodly Fere
But a man o' men was he.

I ha' seen him drive a hundred men
Wi' a bundle o' cords swung free,
That they took the high and holy house
For their pawn and treasury.

They'll no' get him a' in a book I think
Though they write it cunningly;
No mouse of the scrolls was the Goodly Fere
But aye loved the open sea.

If they think they ha' snared our Goodly Fere
They are fools to the last degree.
"I'll go to the feast," quo' our Goodly Fere,
"Though I go to the gallows tree."

"Ye ha' seen me heal the lame and blind,
And wake the dead," says he,
"Ye shall see one thing to master all:
'Tis how a brave man dies on the tree."

A son of God was the Goodly Fere
That bade us his brothers be.
I ha' seen him cow a thousand men.
I have seen him upon the tree.

He cried no cry when they drave the nails
And the blood gushed hot and free,
The hounds of the crimson sky gave tongue
But never a cry cried he.

I ha' seen him cow a thousand men
On the hills o' Galilee,
They whined as he walked out calm between,
Wi' his eyes like the grey o' the sea,

Like the sea that brooks no voyaging
With the winds unleashed and free,
Like the sea that he cowed at Genseret
Wi' twey words spoke' suddently.

A master of men was the Goodly Fere,
A mate of the wind and sea,

If they think they ha' slain our Goodly Fere
They are fools eternally.

I ha' seen him eat o' the honey-comb
Sin' they nailed him to the tree.

E.P. ODE POUR L'ÉLECTION DE SON SÉPULCHRE

I

For three years, out of key with his time,
He strove to resuscitate the dead art
Of poetry; to maintain 'the sublime'
In the old sense. Wrong from the start—

No hardly, but, seeing he had been born
In a half savage country, out of date;
Bent resolutely on wringing lilies from the acorn;
Capaneus; trout for factitious bait;

Ἴδμεν γάρ τοι πάνθ', ὅσ' ἐνὶ Τροίῃ
Caught in the unstopped ear;
Giving the rocks small lee-way
The chopped seas held him, therefore, that year.

His true Penelope was Flaubert,
He fished by obstinate isles;
Observed the elegance of Circe's hair
Rather than the mottoes on sun-dials.

Unaffected by 'the march of events,'
He passed from men's memory in *l'an trentiesme
De son eage;* the case presents
No adjunct to the Muses' diadem.

II

The age demanded an image
Of its accelerated grimace,
Something for the modern stage,
Not, at any rate, an Attic grace;

Not, not certainly, the obscure reveries
Of the inward gaze;
Better mendacities
Than the classics in paraphrase!

The 'age demanded' chiefly a mould in plaster,
Made with no loss of time,
A prose kinema, not, not assuredly, alabaster
Or the 'sculpture' of rhyme.

III

The tea-rose tea-gown, etc.
Supplants the mousseline of
    Cos,
The pianola 'replaces'
Sappho's barbitos.

Christ follows Dionysus,
Phallic and ambrosial
Made way for macerations;
Caliban casts out Ariel.

All things are a flowing,
Sage Heracleitus says;
But a tawdry cheapness
Shall outlast our days.

Even the Christian beauty
Defects—after Samothrace;

We see τὸ καλὸν
Decreed in the market place.

Faun's flesh is not to us,
Nor the saint's vision.
We have the press for wafer;
Franchise for circumcision.

All men, in law, are equals,
Free of Pisistratus,
We choose a knave or an
    eunuch
To rule over us.

O bright Apollo,
τίν᾽ ἄνδρα, τίν᾽ ἥρωα, τίνα θεὸν,
What god, man, or hero,
Shall I place a tin wreath
    upon!

IV

These fought in any case,
     and some believing,
                    pro domo, in any case . . .

Some quick to arm,
some for adventure,
some from fear of weakness,
some from fear of censure,
some for love of slaughter, in imagination,
learning later . . .
some in fear, learning love of slaughter;

Died some, pro patria,
                    non 'dulce' non 'et decor' . . .
walked eye-deep in hell
believing in old men's lies, then unbelieving
came home, home to a lie,
home to many deceits,
home to old lies and new infamy;
usury age-old and age-thick
and liars in public places.

Daring as never before, wastage as never before.
Young blood and high blood,
fair cheeks, and fine bodies;

fortitude as never before

frankness as never before,
disillusions as never told in the old days,
hysterias, trench confessions,
laughter out of dead bellies.

V

There died a myriad,
And of the best, among them,
For an old bitch gone in the teeth,

For a botched civilization,
Charm, smiling at the good mouth,
Quick eyes gone under earth's lid,

For two gross of broken statues,
For a few thousand battered books.

From *Hugh Selwyn Mauberley*

ENVOI

Go, dumb-born book,
Tell her that sang me once that song of Lawes;
Hadst thou but song
As thou hast subjects known,
Then were there cause in thee that should condone
Even my faults that heavy upon me lie
And build her glories their longevity.

Tell her that sheds
Such treasure in the air,
Recking naught else but that her graces give
Life to the moment,
I would bid them live
As roses might, in magic amber laid,
Red overwrought with orange and all made
One substance and one colour
Braving time.

Tell her that goes
With song upon her lips
But sings not out the song, nor knows
The maker of it, some other mouth,
May be as fair as hers,
Might, in new ages, gain her worshippers,
When our two dusts with Waller's shall be laid,
Siftings on siftings in oblivion,
Till change hath broken down
All things save Beauty alone.

CANTO II

Hang it all, Robert Browning,
   there can be but the one 'Sordello.'
But Sordello, and my Sordello?
Lo Sordels si fo di Mantovana.
So-shu churned in the sea.
Seal sports in the spray-whited circles of cliff-wash,
Sleek head, daughter of Lir,
   eyes of Picasso
Under black fur-hood, lithe daughter of Ocean;
And the wave runs in the beach-groove:
'Eleanor, ἐλέναυς and ἐλέπτολις!'
   And poor old Homer blind, blind, as a bat,
Ear, ear for the sea-surge, murmur of old men's voices:
'Let her go back to the ships,
Back among Grecian faces, lest evil come on our own,
Evil and further evil, and a curse cursed on our children,
Moves, yes she moves like a goddess
And has the face of a god
   and the voice of Schoeney's daughters,
And doom goes with her in walking,
Let her go back to the ships,
   back among the Grecian voices.'
And by the beach-run, Tyro,
   Twisted arms of the sea-god,
Lithe sinews of water, gripping her, cross-hold,
And the blue-gray glass of the wave tents them,
Glare azure of water, cold-welter, close cover.
Quiet sun-tawny sand-stretch,
The gulls broad out their wings,
   nipping between the splay feathers;
Snipe come for their bath,
   bend out their wing-joints,
Spread wet wings to the sun-film,
And by Scios,
   to left of the Naxos passage,
Naviform rock overgrown,

           algæ cling to its edge,
There is a wine-red glow in the shallows,
           a tin flash in the sun-dazzle.

The ship landed in Scios,
           men wanting spring-water,
And by the rock-pool a young boy loggy with vine-must,
           'To Naxos? Yes, we'll take you to Naxos,
Cum' along, lad.' 'Not that way!'
'Aye, that way is Naxos.'
           And I said: 'It's a straight ship.'
And an ex-convict out of Italy
           knocked me into the fore-stays,
(He was wanted for manslaughter in Tuscany)
           And the whole twenty against me,
Mad for a little slave money.
           And they took her out of Scios
And off her course . . .
           And the boy came to, again, with the racket,
And looked out over the bows,
           and to eastward, and to the Naxos passage.
God-sleight then, god-sleight:
           Ship stock fast in sea-swirl,
Ivy upon the oars, King Pentheus,
           grapes with no seed but sea-foam,
Ivy in scupper-hole.
Aye, I, Acœtes, stood there,
           and the god stood by me,
Water cutting under the keel,
Sea-break from stern forrards,
           wake running off from the bow,
And where was gunwale, there now was vine-trunk,
And tenthril where cordage had been,
           grape-leaves on the rowlocks,
Heavy vine on the oarshafts,
And, out of nothing, a breathing,
           hot breath on my ankles,
Beasts like shadows in glass,

a furred tail upon nothingness.
Lynx-purr, and heathery smell of beasts,
              where tar smell had been,
Sniff and pad-foot of beasts,
              eye-glitter out of black air.
The sky overshot, dry, with no tempest,
Sniff and pad-foot of beasts,
              fur brushing my knee-skin,
Rustle of airy sheaths,
              dry forms in the *æther*.
And the ship like a keel in ship-yard,
              slung like an ox in smith's sling,
Ribs stuck fast in the ways,
              grape-cluster over pin-rack,
              void air taking pelt.
Lifeless air become sinewed,
              feline leisure of panthers,
Leopards sniffing the grape shoots by scupper-hole,
Crouched panthers by fore-hatch,
And the sea blue-deep about us,
              green-ruddy in shadows,
And Lyæus: 'From now, Acœtes, my altars,
Fearing no bondage,
              fearing no cat of the wood,
Safe with my lynxes,
              feeding grapes to my leopards,
Olibanum is my incense,
              the vines grow in my homage.'

The back-swell now smooth in the rudder-chains,
Black snout of a porpoise
              where Lycabs had been,
Fish-scales on the oarsmen.
              And I worship.
I have seen what I have seen.
              When they brought the boy I said:
'He has a god in him,
              though I do not know which god.'

And they kicked me into the fore-stays.
I have seen what I have seen:
   Medon's face like the face of a dory,
Arms shrunk into fins. And you, Pentheus,
Had as well listen to Tiresias, and to Cadmus,
   or your luck will go out of you.
Fish-scales over groin muscles,
   lynx-purr amid sea . . .
And of a later year,
   pale in the wine-red algæ,
If you will lean over the rock,
   the coral face under wave-tinge,
Rose-paleness under water-shift,
   Ileuthyeria, fair Dafne of sea-bords,
The swimmer's arms turned to branches,
Who will say in what year,
   fleeing what band of tritons,
The smooth brows, seen, and half seen,
   now ivory stillness.

And So-shu churned in the sea, So-shu also,
   using the long moon for a churn-stick . . .
Lithe turning of water,
   sinews of Poseidon,
Black azure and hyaline,
   glass wave over Tyro,
Close cover, unstillness,
   bright welter of wave-cords,
Then quiet water,
   quiet in the buff sands,
Sea-fowl stretching wing-joints,
   splashing in rock-hollows and sand-hollows
In the wave-runs by the half-dune;
Glass-glint of wave in the tide-rips against sunlight,
   pallor of Hesperus,
Grey peak of the wave,
   wave, colour of grape's pulp,

Olive grey in the near,
      far, smoke grey of the rock-slide,
Salmon-pink wings of the fish-hawk
      cast grey shadows in water,
The tower like a one-eyed great goose
      cranes up out of the olive-grove,
And we have heard the fauns chiding Proteus
      in the smell of hay under the olive-trees,
And the frogs singing against the fauns
      in the half-light.
And . . .

From CANTO LXXXI

What thou lovest well remains,
             the rest is dross
What thou lov'st well shall not be reft from thee
What thou lov'st well is thy true heritage
Whose world, or mine or theirs
            or is it of none?
First came the seem, then thus the palpable
    Elysium, though it were in the halls of hell,
What thou lovest well is thy true heritage

The ant's a centaur in his dragon world.
Pull down thy vanity, it is not man
Made courage, or made order, or made grace,
    Pull down thy vanity, I say pull down.
Learn of the green world what can be thy place
In scaled invention or true artistry,
Pull down thy vanity,
            Paquin pull down!
The green casque has outdone your elegance.

'Master thyself, then others shall thee beare'
    Pull down thy vanity

Thou art a beaten dog beneath the hail,
A swollen magpie in a fitful sun,
Half black half white
Nor knowst'ou wing from tail
Pull down thy vanity
        How mean thy hates
Fostered in falsity,
        Pull down thy vanity,
Rathe to destroy, niggard in charity,
Pull down thy vanity,
        I say pull down.

But to have done instead of not doing
        this is not vanity
To have, with decency, knocked
That a Blunt should open
        To have gathered from the air a live tradition
or from a fine old eye the unconquered flame
This is not vanity.
        Here error is all in the not done,
all in the diffidence that faltered

                                  From *Canto* LXXXI

ANCIENT MUSIC

Winter is icummen in,
Lhude sing Goddamm,
Raineth drop and staineth slop,
And how the wind doth ramm!
        Sing: Goddamm.
Skiddeth bus and sloppeth us,
An ague hath my ham.
Freezeth river, turneth liver,
        Damn you, sing: Goddamm.
Goddamm, Goddamm, 'tis why I am, Goddamm,
        So 'gainst the winter's balm.
Sing goddamm, damm, sing Goddamm,
Sing goddamm, sing goddamm, DAMM.

BALLAD FOR GLOOM

For God, our God is a gallant foe
That playeth behind the veil.

I have loved my God as a child at heart
That seeketh deep bosoms for rest,
I have loved my God as a maid to man—
But lo, this thing is best:

To love your God as a gallant foe that plays behind the veil;
To meet your God as the night winds meet beyond Arcturus'
    pale.

I have played with God for a woman,
I have staked with my God for truth,
I have lost to my God as a man, clear-eyed—
    His dice be not of ruth.

For I am made as a naked blade,
    But hear ye this thing in sooth:

Who loseth to God as man to man
    Shall win at the turn of the game.
I have drawn my blade where the lightnings meet
    But the ending is the same:
Who loseth to God as the sword blades lose
    Shall win at the end of the game.

For God, our God is a gallant foe that playeth behind the
    veil.
Whom God deigns not to overthrow hath need of triple mail.

CANTO XLV

With *Usura*
With usura hath no man a house of good stone
each block cut smooth and well fitting
that design might cover their face,
with usura
hath no man a painted paradise on his church wall
harpes et luthes
or where virgin receiveth message
and halo projects from incision,
with usura
seeth no man Gonzaga his heirs and his concubines
no picture is made to endure nor to live with
but it is made to sell and sell quickly
with usura, sin against nature,
is thy bread ever more of stale rags
is thy bread dry as paper,
with no mountain wheat, no strong flour
with usura the line grows thick
with usura is no clear demarcation
and no man can find site for his dwelling.
Stone cutter is kept from his stone
weaver is kept from his loom
WITH USURA
wool comes not to market
sheep bringeth no gain with usura
Usura is a murrain, usura
blunteth the needle in the maid's hand
and stoppeth the spinner's cunning. Pietro Lombardo
came not by usura
Duccio came not by usura
nor Pier della Francesca; Zuan Bellin' not by usura
nor was 'La Calunnia' painted.
Came not by usura Angelico; came not Ambrogio Praedis,
Came no church of cut stone signed: *Adamo me fecit*.
Not by usura St. Trophime

Not by usura Saint Hilaire,
Usura rusteth the chisel
It rusteth the craft and the craftsman
It gnaweth the thread in the loom
None learneth to weave gold in her pattern;
Azure hath a canker by usura; cramoisi is unbroidered
Emerald findeth no Memling
Usura slayeth the child in the womb
It stayeth the young man's courting
It hath brought palsey to bed, lyeth
between the young bride and her bridegroom
CONTRA NATURAM
They have brought whores for Eleusis
Corpses are set to banquet
at behest of usura.

ORTUS

How have I laboured?
How have I not laboured
To bring her soul to birth,
To give these elements a name and a centre!
She is beautiful as the sunlight, and as fluid.
She has no name, and no place.
How have I laboured to bring her soul into separation;
To give her a name and her being!

Surely you are bound and entwined,
You are mingled with the elements unborn;
I have loved a stream and a shadow.

I beseech you enter your life.
I beseech you learn to say "I,"
When I question you;
For you are no part, but a whole,
No portion, but a being.

THE ALCHEMIST

Chant for the Transmutation of Metals

Saîl of Claustra, Aelis, Azalais,
As you move among the bright trees;
As your voices, under the larches of Paradise
Make a clear sound,
Saîl of Claustra, Aelis, Azalais,
Raimona, Tibors, Berangèrë,
'Neath the dark gleam of the sky;
Under night, the peacock-throated,
Bring the saffron-coloured shell,
Bring the red gold of the maple,
Bring the light of the birch tree in autumn
Mirals, Cembelins, Audiarda,
                Remember this fire.

Elain, Tireis, Alcmena
'Mid the silver rustling of wheat,
Agradiva, Anhes, Ardenca,
From the plum-coloured lake, in stillness,
From the molten dyes of the water
Bring the burnished nature of fire;
Briseis, Lianor, Loica,
From the wide earth and the olive,
From the poplars weeping their amber,
By the bright flame of the fishing torch
                Remember this fire.

Midonz, with the gold of the sun, the leaf of the poplar, by
    the light of the amber,
Midonz, daughter of the sun, shaft of the tree, silver of the
    leaf, light of the yellow of the amber,
Midonz, gift of the God, gift of the light, gift of the amber
    of the sun,
                Give light to the metal.

Anhes of Rocacoart, Ardenca, Aemelis,
From the power of grass,
From the white, alive in the seed,
From the heat of the bud,

From the copper of the leaf in autumn,
From the bronze of the maple, from the sap in the bough;
Lianor, Ioanna, Loica,
By the stir of the fin,
By the trout asleep in the gray-green of water;
Vanna, Mandetta, Viera, Alodetta, Picarda, Manuela
From the red gleam of copper,
Ysaut, Ydone, slight rustling of leaves,
Vierna, Jocelynn, daring of spirits,
By the mirror of burnished copper,
                 O Queen of Cypress,
Out of Erebus, the flat-lying breadth,
Breath that is stretched out beneath the world:
Out of Erebus, out of the flat waste of air, lying beneath
    the world;
Out of the brown leaf-brown colourless
               Bring the imperceptible cool.

Elain, Tireis, Alcmena,
               Quiet this metal!
Let the manes put off their terror, let them put off their
    aqueous bodies with fire.
Let them assume the milk-white bodies of agate.
Let them draw together the bones of the metal.

Selvaggia, Guiscarda, Mandetta,
               Rain flakes of gold on the water
Azure and flaking silver of water,
Alcyon, Phætona, Alcmena,
Pallor of silver, pale lustre of Latona,
By these, from the malevolence of the dew
               Guard this alembic.
Elain, Tireis, Allodetta
               Quiet this metal.

Frederic Prokosch

THE CONSPIRATORS

And if the dead, and the dead
Of spirit now join, and in their horrifying ritual
Proceed till at last with oriental grace
End their concluding dance with the candles guttering,
The cymbals sobbing, the wind harassing the curtains,
The chill from the flood embracing the golden stairway
The scent devoured and the bowls blown clean of incense:

Ah then, farewell, sweet northern music;
No longer the flight of the mind across the continents,
The dazzling flight of our words across the tempestuous
Black, or the firelit recital of a distant battle.

No. All that we loved is lost, if the intricate
Languor of recollected centuries
Descends in its terrible sweetness on our limbs.
No shot will echo; no fire; no agonizing
Cry will resound in the city's thickets: only,
The ivy falling gently across the bridges,
The larches piercing the roofs, the reclining steeples,
The cellars rich with the agony of the reptiles,
The contemplative worms, the victorious rodents,
And at last, the climax entrancingly serene,
The inconclusive note drowned on the ascendant:
Our lovely shapes in marble still shine through the greenery,
Our exquisite silver bones still glide with the glaciers
That split our familiar hills, still fall with the avalanche
And weaving their vast wing's thunder over the Indies
The birds, the birds, sob for the time of man.

John Crowe Ransom

BELLS FOR JOHN WHITESIDE'S DAUGHTER

There was such speed in her little body,
And such lightness in her footfall,
It is no wonder her brown study
Astonishes us all.

Her wars were bruited in our high window.
We looked among orchard trees and beyond,
Where she took arms against her shadow,
Or harried unto the pond

The lazy geese, like a snow cloud
Dripping their snow on the green grass,
Tricking and stopping, sleepy and proud,
Who cried in goose, Alas,

For the tireless heart within the little
Lady with rod that made them rise
From their noon apple-dreams and scuttle
Goose-fashion under the skies!

But now go the bells, and we are ready,
In one house we are sternly stopped
To say we are vexed at her brown study,
Lying so primly propped.

CAPTAIN CARPENTER

Captain Carpenter rose up in his prime
Put on his pistols and went riding out
But he got well nigh nowhere at that time
Till he fell in with ladies in a rout.

It was a pretty lady and all her train
That played with him so sweetly but before
An hour she'd taken a sword with all her main
And twined him of his nose for evermore.

Captain Carpenter mounted up one day
And rode straightway into a stranger rogue
That looked unchristian but be that as it may
The captain did not wait upon prologue.

But drew upon him out of his great heart
The other swung against him with a club
And cracked his two legs at the shinny part
And let him roll and stick like any tub.

Captain Carpenter rode many a time
From male and female took he sundry harms
He met the wife of Satan crying "I'm
The she-wolf bids you shall bear no more arms."

Their strokes and counters whistled in the wind
I wish he had delivered half his blows
But where she should have made off like a hind
The bitch bit off his arms at the elbows.

And Captain Carpenter parted with his ears
To a black devil that used him in this wise
O Jesus ere his threescore and ten years
Another had plucked out his sweet blue eyes.

Captain Carpenter got up on his roan
And sallied from the gate in hell's despite
I heard him asking in the grimmest tone
If any enemy yet there was to fight?

"To any adversary it is fame
If he risk to be wounded by my tongue

Or burnt in two beneath my red heart's flame
Such are the perils he is cast among.

"But if he can he has a pretty choice
From an anatomy with little to lose
Whether he cut my tongue and take my voice
Or whether it be my round red heart he choose."

It was the neatest knave that ever was seen
Stepping in perfume from his lady's bower
Who at this word put in his merry mien
And fell on Captain Carpenter like a tower.

I would not knock old fellows in the dust
But there lay Captain Carpenter on his back
His weapons were the old heart in his bust
And a blade shook between rotten teeth alack.

The rogue in scarlet and gray soon knew his mind
He wished to get his trophy and depart;
With gentle apology and touch refined
He pierced him and produced the Captain's heart.

God's mercy rest on Captain Carpenter now
I thought him Sirs an honest gentleman
Citizen husband soldier and scholar enow
Let jangling kites eat of him if they can.

But God's deep curses follow after those
That shore him of his goodly nose and ears
His legs and strong arms at the two elbows
And eyes that had not watered seventy years.

The curse of hell upon the sleek upstart
Who got the Captain finally on his back
And took the red red vitals of his heart
And made the kites to whet their beaks clack clack.

HER EYES

To a woman that I knew
Were eyes of an extravagant hue:
Viz., china blue.

Those I wear upon my head
Are sometimes green and sometimes red,
I said.

My mother's eyes are wet and blear,
My little sister's are not clear,
Poor silly dear.

It must be given to but few,
A pair of eyes so utter blue
And new;

Where does she keep them from this glare
Of the monstrous sun and the wind's flare
Without any wear;

And were they never in the night
Poisoned by artificial light
Much too bright;

And had the splendid beast no heart
That boiled with tears and baked with smart
The ocular part?

I'll have no business with those eyes,
They are not kind, they are not wise,
They are lies.

A woman shooting such blue flame
I apprehend will get some blame
On her good name.

TWO IN AUGUST

Two that could not have lived their single lives
As can some husbands and wives
Did something strange; they tensed their vocal cords
And attacked each other with silences and words
Like catapulted stones and arrowed knives.

Dawn was not yet; night is for loving or sleeping,
Sweet dreams or safekeeping;
Yet he of the wide brows that were used to laurel
And she, the famed for gentleness, must quarrel,
Furious both of them, and scared, and weeping.

How sleepers groan, twitch, wake to such a mood
Is not well understood,
Nor why two entities grown almost one
Should rend and murder trying to get undone,
With individual tigers in their blood.

She in terror fled from the marriage chamber
Circuiting the dark rooms like a string of amber
Round and round and back,
And would not light one lamp against the black,
And heard the clock that clanged: Remember, Remember.

And he must tread barefooted the dim lawn,
Soon he was up and gone;
High in the trees the night-mastered birds were crying
With fear upon their tongues, no singing or flying
Which are their lovely attitudes by dawn.

Whether those bird-cries were of heaven or hell
There is no way to tell;
In the long ditch of darkness the man walked
Under the hackberry trees where the birds talked
With words too sad and strange to syllable.

PRELUDE TO AN EVENING

Do not enforce the tired wolf
Dragging his infected wound homeward
To sit tonight with the warm children
Naming the pretty kings of France.

The images of the invaded mind
Being as monsters in the dreams
Of your most brief enchanted headful,
Suppose a miracle of confusion:

That dreamed and undreamt become each other
And mix the night and day of your mind;
And it does not matter your twice crying
From mouth unbeautied against the pillow

To avert the gun of the swarthy soldier,
For cry, cock-crow, or the iron bell
Can crack the sleep-sense of outrage,
Annihilate phantoms who were nothing.

But now, by our perverse supposal,
There is a drift of fog on your mornings;
You in your peignoir, dainty at your orange-cup,
Feel poising round the sunny room

Invisible evil, deprived and bold.
All day the clock will metronome
Your gallant fear; the needles clicking,
The heels detonating the stair's cavern.

Freshening the water in the blue bowls
For the buckberries with not all your love,
You shall be listening for the low wind,
The warning sibilance of pines.

You like a waning moon, and I accusing
Our too banded Eumenides,
You shall make Noes but wanderingly,
Smoothing the heads of the hungry children.

JUDITH OF BETHULIA

Beautiful as the flying legend of some leopard
She had not yet chosen her great captain or prince
Depositary to her flesh, and our defense;
And a wandering beauty is a blade out of its scabbard.
You know how dangerous, gentlemen of threescore?
May you know it yet ten more.

Nor by process of veiling she grew the less fabulous.
Grey or blue veils, we were desperate to study
The invincible emanations of her white body,
And the winds at her ordered raiment were ominous.
Might she walk in the market, sit in the council of soldiers?
Only of the extreme elders.

But a rare chance was the girl's then, when the Invader
Trumpeted from the south, and rumbled from the north,
Beleaguered the city from four quarters of the earth,
Our soldiery too craven and sick to aid her—
Where were the arms could countervail this horde?
Her beauty was the sword.

She sat with the elders, and proved on their blear visage
How bright was the weapon unrusted in her keeping,
While he lay surfeiting on their harvest heaping,
Wasting the husbandry of their rarest vintage—
And dreaming of the broad-breasted dames for concubine?
These floated on his wine.

He was lapped with bay-leaves, and grass and fumiter weed,
And from under the wine-film encountered his mortal vision,
For even within his tent she accomplished his derision;
She loosed one veil and another, standing unafraid;
And he perished. Nor brushed her with even so much as a
    daisy?
She found his destruction easy.

The heathen are all perished. The victory was furnished,
We smote them hiding in our vineyards, barns, annexes,
And now their white bones clutter the holes of foxes,
And the chieftain's head, with grinning sockets, and var-
    nished—
Is it hung on the sky with a hideous epitaph?
No, the woman keeps the trophy.

May God send unto our virtuous lady her prince.
It is stated she went reluctant to that orgy,
Yet a madness fevers our young men, and not the clergy
Nor the elders have turned them unto modesty since.
Inflamed by the thought of her naked beauty with desire?
Yes, and chilled with fear and despair.

THE EQUILIBRISTS

Full of her long white arms and milky skin
He had a thousand times remembered sin.
Alone in the press of people traveled he,
Minding her jacinth, and myrrh, and ivory.

Mouth he remembered: the quaint orifice
From which came heat that flamed upon the kiss,
Till cold words came down spiral from the head,
Grey doves from the officious tower illsped.

Body: it was a white field ready for love,
On her body's field, with the gaunt tower above,

The lilies grew, beseeching him to take,
If he would pluck and wear them, bruise and break.

Eyes talking: Never mind the cruel words,
Embrace my flowers, but not embrace the swords.
But what they said, the doves came straightway flying
And unsaid: Honor, Honor, they came crying.

Importunate her doves. Too pure, too wise,
Clambering on his shoulder, saying, Arise,
Leave me now, and never let us meet,
Eternal distance now command thy feet.

Predicament indeed, which thus discovers
Honor among thieves, Honor between lovers.
O such a little word is Honor, they feel!
But the grey word is between them cold as steel.

At length I saw these lovers fully were come
Into their torture of equilibrium;
Dreadfully had forsworn each other, and yet
They were bound each to each, and they did not forget.

And rigid as two painful stars, and twirled
About the clustered night their prison world,
They burned with fierce love always to come near,
But Honor beat them back and kept them clear.

Ah, the strict lovers, they are ruined now!
I cried in anger. But with puddled brow
Devising for those gibbeted and brave
Came I descanting: Man, what would you have?

For spin your period out, and draw your breath,
A kinder saeculum begins with Death.
Would you ascend to Heaven and bodiless dwell?
Or take your bodies honorless to Hell?

In Heaven you have heard no marriage is,
No white flesh tinder to your lecheries,
Your male and female tissue sweetly shaped
Sublimed away, and furious blood escaped.

Great lovers lie in Hell, the stubborn ones
Infatuate of the flesh upon the bones;
Stuprate, they rend each other when they kiss,
The pieces kiss again, no end to this.

But still I watched them spinning, orbited nice.
Their flames were not more radiant than their ice.
I dug in the quiet earth and wrought the tomb
And made these lines to memorize their doom:—

Epitaph

Equilibrists lie here; stranger, tread light;
Close, but untouching in each other's sight;
Mouldered the lips and ashy the tall skull,
Let them lie perilous and beautiful.

ADDRESS TO THE SCHOLARS OF NEW ENGLAND

(*Harvard Phi Beta Kappa poem, June 23, 1939*)

When Sarah Pierrepont let her spirit rage
Her love and scorn refused the bauble earth
(Which took bloom even here, under the Bear)
And groped for the Essence sitting in himself,
Subtle, I think, for a girl's unseasoned rage.

The late and sudden extravagance of soul
By which they all were swollen exalted her
At seventeen years to Edwards' canopy,
A match pleasing to any Heaven, had not
The twelve mortal labors harassed her soul.

Thrifty and too proud were the sea-borne fathers
Who fetched the Pure Idea in a bound box
And fastened him in a steeple, to have his court
Shabby with an unkingly establishment
And Sabbath levees for the minion fathers.

The majesty of Heaven has a great house,
And even if the Indian kingdom or the fox
Ran barking mad in a wide forest place,
They had his threshold, and you had the dream
Of property in him by a steepled house.

If once the entail shall come on raffish sons,
Knife-wit scholar and merchant sharp in thumb,
With positive steel they'll pry into the steeple,
And blinking through the cracked ribs at the void
A judgment laughter rakes the cynic sons.

But like prevailing wind New England's honor
Carried, and teased small Southern boys in school,
Whose heads the temperate birds fleeing your winter
Construed for, but the stiff heroes abashed
With their frozen fingers and unearthly honor.

Scared by the holy megrims of those Pilgrims,
I thought the unhumbled and outcast and cold
Were the rich Heirs traveling incognito,
Bred too fine for the country's sweet produce
And but affecting that dog's life of pilgrims.

There used to be debate of soul and body,
The soul storming incontinent with shrew's tongue
Against what natural brilliance body had loved,
Even the green phases though deciduous
Of earth's zodiac homage to the body.

Plato, before Plotinus gentled him,
Spoke the soul's part, and though its vice is known

We're in his shadow still, and it appears
Your founders most of all the nations held
By his scandal-mongering, and established him.

Perfect was the witch foundering in water,
The blasphemer that spraddled in the stocks,
The woman branded with her sin, the whales
Of ocean taken with a psalmer's sword,
The British tea infusing the bay's water.

But they reared heads into the always clouds
And stooped to the event of war or bread,
The secular perforces and short speech
Being labors surlily done with the left hand,
The chief strength giddying with transcendent clouds.

The tangent Heavens mocked the fathers' strength,
And how the young sons know it, and study now
To take fresh conquest of the conquered earth,
But they're too strong for that, you've seen them whip
The laggard will to deeds of lunatic strength.

To incline the powerful living unto peace
With Heaven is easier now, with Earth is hard,
Yet a rare metaphysic makes them one,
A gentle Majesty, whose myrtle and rain
Enforce the fathers' gravestones unto peace.

I saw the youngling bachelors of Harvard
Lit like torches, and scrambling to disperse
Like aimless firebrands pitiful to slake,
And if there's passion enough for half their flame,
Your wisdom has done this, sages of Harvard.

Edwin Arlington Robinson

THE CHILDREN OF THE NIGHT

For those that never know the light,
　The darkness is a sullen thing;
And they, the Children of the Night,
　Seem lost in Fortune's winnowing.

But some are strong and some are weak,—
　And there's the story. House and home
Are shut from countless hearts that seek
　World-refuge that will never come.

And if there be no other life,
　And if there be no other chance
To weigh their sorrow and their strife
　Than in the scales of circumstance,

'Twere better, ere the sun go down
　Upon the first day we embark,
In life's imbittered sea to drown,
　Than sail forever in the dark.

But if there be a soul on earth
　So blinded with its own misuse
Of man's revealed, incessant worth,
　Or worn with anguish, that it views

No light but for a mortal eye,
　No rest but of a mortal sleep,
No God but in a prophet's lie,
　No faith for 'honest doubt' to keep;

If there be nothing, good or bad,
　But chaos for a soul to trust,—
God counts it for a soul gone mad,
　And if God be God, He is just.

And if God be God, He is Love;
 And though the Dawn be still so dim,
It shows us we have played enough
 With creeds that make a fiend of Him.

There is one creed, and only one,
 That glorifies God's excellence;
So cherish, that His will be done,
 The common creed of common sense.

It is the crimson, not the gray,
 That charms the twilight of all time;
It is the promise of the day
 That makes the starry sky sublime;

It is the faith within the fear
 That holds us to the life we curse;—
So let us in ourselves revere
 The Self which is the Universe!

Let us, the Children of the Night,
 Put off the cloak that hides the scar!
Let us be Children of the Light,
 And tell the ages what we are!

OH FOR A POET—FOR A BEACON BRIGHT

Oh for a poet—for a beacon bright
To rift this changeless glimmer of dead gray;
To spirit back the Muses, long astray,
And flush Parnassus with a newer light;
To put these little sonnet-men to flight
Who fashion, in a shrewd mechanic way,
Songs without souls, that flicker for a day,
To vanish in irrevocable night.
What does it mean, this barren age of ours?
Here are the men, the women, and the flowers,
The seasons, and the sunset, as before.
What does it mean? Shall there not one arise
To wrench one banner from the western skies,
And mark it with his name forevermore?

WALT WHITMAN

The master-songs are ended, and the man
That sang them is a name. And so is God
A name; and so is love, and life, and death,
And everything. But we, who are too blind
To read what we have written, or what faith
Has written for us, do not understand:
We only blink, and wonder.

Last night it was the song that was the man,
But now it is the man that is the song.
We do not hear him very much to-day:
His piercing and eternal cadence rings
Too pure for us—too powerfully pure,
Too lovingly triumphant, and too large;
But there are some that hear him, and they know
That he shall sing to-morrow for all men,
And that all time shall listen.

The master-songs are ended? Rather say
No songs are ended that are ever sung,
And that no names are dead names. When we write
Men's letters on proud marble or on sand,
We write them there forever.

ZOLA

Because he puts the compromising chart
Of hell before your eyes, you are afraid;
Because he counts the price that you have paid
For innocence, and counts it from the start,
You loathe him. But he sees the human heart
Of God meanwhile, and in His hand was weighed
Your squeamish and emasculate crusade
Against the grim dominion of his art.
Never until we conquer the uncouth
Connivings of our shamed indifference
(We call it Christian faith) are we to scan
The racked and shrieking hideousness of Truth
To find, in hate's polluted self-defence
Throbbing, the pulse, the divine heart of man.

JOHN EVERELDOWN

'Where are you going to-night, to-night,—
    Where are you going, John Evereldown?
There's never the sign of a star in sight,
    Nor a lamp that's nearer than Tilbury Town.
Why do you stare as a dead man might?
Where are you pointing away from the light?
And where are you going to-night, to-night,—
    Where are you going, John Evereldown?'

'Right through the forest, where none can see,
    There's where I'm going, to Tilbury Town.
The men are asleep,—or awake, may be,—
    But the women are calling John Evereldown.
Ever and ever they call for me,
And while they call can a man be free?
So right through the forest, where none can see,
    There's where I'm going, to Tilbury Town.'

'But why are you going so late, so late,—
    Why are you going, John Evereldown?
Though the road be smooth and the way be straight,
    There are two long leagues to Tilbury Town.
Come in by the fire, old man, and wait!
Why do you chatter out there by the gate?
And why are you going so late, so late,—
    Why are you going, John Evereldown?'

'I follow the women wherever they call,—
    That's why I'm going to Tilbury Town.
God knows if I pray to be done with it all,
    But God is no friend to John Evereldown.
So the clouds may come and the rain may fall,
The shadows may creep and the dead men crawl,—
But I follow the women wherever they call,
    And that's why I'm going to Tilbury Town.'

LUKE HAVERGAL

Go to the western gate, Luke Havergal,
There where the vines cling crimson on the wall,
And in the twilight wait for what will come.
The leaves will whisper there of her, and some,
Like flying words, will strike you as they fall;
But go, and if you listen, she will call.
Go to the western gate, Luke Havergal—
Luke Havergal.

No, there is not a dawn in eastern skies
To rift the fiery night that's in your eyes;
But there, where western glooms are gathering,
The dark will end the dark, if anything:
God slays himself with every leaf that flies,
And hell is more than half of paradise.
No, there is not a dawn in eastern skies—
In eastern skies.

Out of a grave I come to tell you this,
Out of a grave I come to quench the kiss
That flames upon your forehead with a glow
That blinds you to the way that you must go.
Yes, there is yet one way to where she is,
Bitter, but one that faith may never miss.
Out of a grave I come to tell you this—
To tell you this.

There is the western gate, Luke Havergal,
There are the crimson leaves upon the wall.
Go, for the winds are tearing them away,—
Nor think to riddle the dead words they say,
Nor any more to feel them as they fall;
But go, and if you trust her she will call.
There is the western gate, Luke Havergal—
Luke Havergal.

CHARLES CARVILLE'S EYES

A melancholy face Charles Carville had,
But not so melancholy as it seemed,
When once you knew him, for his mouth redeemed
His insufficient eyes, forever sad:
In them there was no life-glimpse, good or bad,
Nor joy nor passion in them ever gleamed;
His mouth was all of him that ever beamed,
His eyes were sorry, but his mouth was glad.

He never was a fellow that said much,
And half of what he did say was not heard
By many of us: we were out of touch
With all his whims and all his theories
Till he was dead, so those blank eyes of his
Might speak them. Then we heard them, every word.

REUBEN BRIGHT

Because he was a butcher and thereby
Did earn an honest living (and did right),
I would not have you think that Reuben Bright
Was any more a brute than you or I;
For when they told him that his wife must die,
He stared at them, and shook with grief and fright,
And cried like a great baby half that night,
And made the women cry to see him cry.

And after she was dead, and he had paid
The singers and the sexton and the rest,
He packed a lot of things that she had made
Most mournfully away in an old chest
Of hers, and put some chopped-up cedar boughs
In with them, and tore down the slaughter-house.

THE TORRENT

I found a torrent falling in a glen
Where the sun's light shone silvered and leaf-split;
The boom, the foam, and the mad flash of it
All made a magic symphony; but when
I thought upon the coming of hard men
To cut those patriarchal trees away,
And turn to gold the silver of that spray,
I shuddered. Yet a gladness now and then

Did wake me to myself till I was glad
In earnest, and was welcoming the time
For screaming saws to sound above the chime
Of idle waters, and for me to know
The jealous visionings that I had had
Were steps to the great place where trees and torrents go.

GEORGE CRABBE

Give him the darkest inch your shelf allows,
Hide him in lonely garrets, if you will,—
But his hard, human pulse is throbbing still
With the sure strength that fearless truth endows.
In spite of all fine science disavows,
Of his plain excellence and stubborn skill
There yet remains what fashion cannot kill,
Though years have thinned the laurel from his brows.

Whether or not we read him, we can feel
From time to time the vigor of his name
Against us like a finger for the shame
And emptiness of what our souls reveal
In books that are as altars where we kneel
To consecrate the flicker, not the flame.

CREDO

I cannot find my way: there is no star
In all the shrouded heavens anywhere;
And there is not a whisper in the air
Of any living voice but one so far
That I can hear it only as a bar
Of lost, imperial music, played when fair
And angel fingers wove, and unaware,
Dead leaves to garlands where no roses are.
No, there is not a glimmer, nor a call,
For one that welcomes, welcomes when he fears,
The black and awful chaos of the night;
For through it all—above, beyond it all—
I know the far-sent message of the years,
I feel the coming glory of the Light.

RICHARD CORY

Whenever Richard Cory went down town,
    We people on the pavement looked at him:
He was a gentleman from sole to crown,
    Clean favored, and imperially slim.

And he was always quietly arrayed,
    And he was always human when he talked;
But still he fluttered pulses when he said,
    "Good-morning," and he glittered when he walked.

And he was rich—yes, richer than a king,
    And admirably schooled in every grace:
In fine, we thought that he was everything
    To make us wish that we were in his place.

So on we worked, and waited for the light,
    And went without the meat, and cursed the bread;
And Richard Cory, one calm summer night,
    Went home and put a bullet through his head.

UNCLE ANANIAS

His words were magic and his heart was true,
  And everywhere he wandered he was blessed.
Out of all ancient men my childhood knew
  I choose him and I mark him for the best.
Of all authoritative liars, too,
  I crown him loveliest.

How fondly I remember the delight
  That always glorified him in the spring;
The joyous courage and the benedight
  Profusion of his faith in everything!
He was a good old man, and it was right
  That he should have his fling.

And often, underneath the apple-trees,
  When we surprised him in the summer time,
With what superb magnificence and ease
  He sinned enough to make the day sublime!
And if he liked us there about his knees,
  Truly it was no crime.

All summer long we loved him for the same
  Perennial inspiration of his lies;
And when the russet wealth of autumn came,
  There flew but fairer visions to our eyes—
Multiple, tropical, winged with a feathery flame
  Like birds of paradise.

So to the sheltered end of many a year
  He charmed the seasons out with pageantry
Wearing upon his forehead, with no fear,
  The laurel of approved iniquity.
And every child who knew him, far or near,
  Did love him faithfully.

THE DARK HILLS

Dark hills at evening in the west,
Where sunset hovers like a sound
Of golden horns that sang to rest
Old bones of warriors under ground,
Far now from all the bannered ways
Where flash the legions of the sun,
You fade—as if the last of days
Were fading, and all wars were done.

LEONORA

They have made for Leonora this low dwelling in the ground,
And with cedar they have woven the four walls round.
Like a little dryad hiding she'll be wrapped all in green,
Better kept and longer valued than by ways that would have
    been.

They will come with many roses in the early afternoon,
They will come with pinks and lilies and with Leonora soon;
And as long as beauty's garments over beauty's limbs are
    thrown,
There'll be lilies that are liars, and the rose will have its own.

There will be a wondrous quiet in the house that they have
    made,
And to-night will be a darkness in the place where she'll be
    laid;
But the builders, looking forward into time, could only see
Darker nights for Leonora than to-night shall ever be.

MINIVER CHEEVY

Miniver Cheevy, child of scorn,
　Grew lean while he assailed the seasons;
He wept that he was ever born,
　And he had reasons.

Miniver loved the days of old
　When swords were bright and steeds were prancing;
The vision of a warrior bold
　Would set him dancing.

Miniver sighed for what was not,
　And dreamed, and rested from his labors;
He dreamed of Thebes and Camelot,
　And Priam's neighbors.

Miniver mourned the ripe renown
　That made so many a name so fragrant;
He mourned Romance, now on the town,
　And Art, a vagrant.

Miniver loved the Medici,
　Albeit he had never seen one;
He would have sinned incessantly
　Could he have been one.

Miniver cursed the commonplace
　And eyed a khaki suit with loathing;
He missed the mediæval grace
　Of iron clothing.

Miniver scorned the gold he sought,
　But sore annoyed was he without it;
Miniver thought, and thought, and thought,
　And thought about it.

Miniver Cheevy, born too late,
　Scratched his head and kept on thinking;
Miniver coughed, and called it fate,
　And kept on drinking.

CASSANDRA

I heard one who said: 'Verily,
    What word have I for children here?
Your Dollar is your only Word,
    The wrath of it your only fear.

'You built it altars tall enough
    To make you see, but you are blind;
You cannot leave it long enough
    To look before you or behind.

'When Reason beckons you to pause,
    You laugh and say that you know best;
But what it is you know, you keep
    As dark as ingots in a chest.

'You laugh and answer, "We are young;
    O leave us now, and let us grow."—
Not asking how much more of this
    Will Time endure or Fate bestow.

'Because a few complacent years
    Have made your peril of your pride,
Think you that you are to go on
    Forever pampered and untried?

'What lost eclipse of history,
    What bivouac of the marching stars,
Has given the sign for you to see
    Millenniums and last great wars?

'What unrecorded overthrow
    Of all the world has ever known,
Or ever been, has made itself
    So plain to you, and you alone?

'Your Dollar, Dove and Eagle make
    A Trinity that even you

Rate higher than you rate yourselves;
  It pays, it flatters, and it's new.

'And though your very flesh and blood
  Be what your Eagle eats and drinks,
You'll praise him for the best of birds,
  Not knowing what the Eagle thinks.

'The power is yours, but not the sight;
  You see not upon what you tread;
You have the ages for your guide,
  But not the wisdom to be led.

'Think you to tread forever down
  The merciless old verities?
And are you never to have eyes
  To see the world for what it is?

'Are you to pay for what you have
  With all you are?'—No other word
We caught, but with a laughing crowd
  Moved on. None heeded, and few heard.

VAIN GRATUITIES

Never was there a man much uglier
In eyes of other women, or more grim:
"The Lord has filled her chalice to the brim,
So let us pray she's a philosopher,"
They said; and there was more they said of her—
Deeming it, after twenty years with him,
No wonder that she kept her figure slim
And always made you think of lavender.
But she, demure as ever, and as fair,
Almost, as they remembered her before
She found him, would have laughed had she been there;
And all they said would have been heard no more
Than foam that washes on an island shore
Where there are none to listen or to care.

THE MILL

The miller's wife had waited long,
    The tea was cold, the fire was dead;
And there might yet be nothing wrong
    In how he went and what he said:
"There are no millers any more,"
    Was all that she had heard him say;
And he had lingered at the door
    So long that it seemed yesterday.

Sick with a fear that had no form
    She knew that she was there at last;
And in the mill there was a warm
    And mealy fragrance of the past.
What else there was would only seem
    To say again what he had meant;
And what was hanging from a beam
    Would not have heeded where she went.

And if she thought it followed her,
    She may have reasoned in the dark
That one way of the few there were
    Would hide her and would leave no mark:
Black water, smooth above the weir
    Like starry velvet in the night,
Though ruffled once, would soon appear
    The same as ever to the sight.

MR. FLOOD'S PARTY

Old Eben Flood, climbing alone one night
Over the hill between the town below
And the forsaken upland hermitage
That held as much as he should ever know
On earth again of home, paused warily.
The road was his with not a native near;
And Eben, having leisure, said aloud,
For no man else in Tilbury Town to hear:

"Well, Mr. Flood, we have the harvest moon
Again, and we may not have many more;
The bird is on the wing, the poet says,
And you and I have said it here before.
Drink to the bird." He raised up to the light
The jug that he had gone so far to fill,
And answered huskily: "Well, Mr. Flood,
Since you propose it, I believe I will."

Alone, as if enduring to the end
A valiant armor of scarred hopes outworn,
He stood there in the middle of the road
Like Roland's ghost winding a silent horn.
Below him, in the town among the trees,
Where friends of other days had honored him,
A phantom salutation of the dead
Rang thinly till old Eben's eyes were dim.

Then, as a mother lays her sleeping child
Down tenderly, fearing it may awake,
He set the jug down slowly at his feet
With trembling care, knowing that most things break;
And only when assured that on firm earth
It stood, as the uncertain lives of men
Assuredly did not, he paced away,
And with his hand extended paused again:

"Well, Mr. Flood, we have not met like this
In a long time; and many a change has come
To both of us, I fear, since last it was
We had a drop together. Welcome home!"
Convivially returning with himself,
Again he raised the jug up to the light;
And with an acquiescent quaver said:
"Well, Mr. Flood, if you insist, I might.

"Only a very little, Mr. Flood—
For auld lang syne. No more, sir; that will do."

So, for the time, apparently it did,
And Eben evidently thought so too;
For soon amid the silver loneliness
Of night he lifted up his voice and sang,
Secure, with only two moons listening,
Until the whole harmonious landscape rang—

"For auld lang syne." The weary throat gave out,
The last word wavered, and the song was done.
He raised again the jug regretfully
And shook his head, and was again alone.
There was not much that was ahead of him,
And there was nothing in the town below—
Where strangers would have shut the many doors
That many friends had opened long ago.

THE SHEAVES

Where long the shadows of the wind had rolled,
Green wheat was yielding to the change assigned;
And as by some vast magic undivined
The world was turning slowly into gold.
Like nothing that was ever bought or sold
It waited there, the body and the mind;
And with a mighty meaning of a kind
That tells the more the more it is not told.

So in a land where all days are not fair,
Fair days went on till on another day
A thousand golden sheaves were lying there,
Shining and still, but not for long to stay—
As if a thousand girls with golden hair
Might rise from where they slept and go away.

AS IT LOOKED THEN

In a sick shade of spruce, moss-webbed, rock-fed,
Where, long unfollowed by sagacious man,
A scrub that once had been a pathway ran
Blindly from nowhere and to nowhere led,
One might as well have been among the dead
As half way there alive; so I began
Like a malingering pioneer to plan
A vain return—with one last look ahead.

And it was then that like a spoken word
Where there was none to speak, insensibly
A flash of blue that might have been a bird
Grew soon to the calm wonder of the sea—
Calm as a quiet sky that looked to be
Arching a world where nothing had occurred.

EROS TURANNOS

She fears him, and will always ask
    What fated her to choose him;
She meets in his engaging mask
    All reasons to refuse him;
But what she meets and what she fears
Are less than are the downward years,
Drawn slowly to the foamless weirs
    Of age, were she to lose him.

Between a blurred sagacity
    That once had power to sound him,
And Love, that will not let him be
    The Judas that she found him,
Her pride assuages her almost,
As if it were alone the cost.
He sees that he will not be lost,
    And waits and looks around him.

A sense of ocean and old trees
  Envelops and allures him;
Tradition, touching all he sees,
  Beguiles and reassures him;
And all her doubts of what he says
Are dimmed with what she knows of days—
Till even prejudice delays
  And fades, and she secures him.

The falling leaf inaugurates
  The reign of her confusion;
The pounding wave reverberates
  The dirge of her illusion;
And home, where passion lived and died,
Becomes a place where she can hide,
While all the town and harbor-side
  Vibrate with her seclusion.

We tell you, tapping on our brows,
  The story as it should be,
As if the story of a house
  Were told, or ever could be;
We'll have no kindly veil between
Her visions and those we have seen,—
As if we guessed what hers have been,
  Or what they are or would be.

Meanwhile we do no harm; for they
  That with a god have striven,
Not hearing much of what we say,
  Take what the god has given;
Though like waves breaking it may be,
Or like a changed familiar tree,
Or like a stairway to the sea
  Where down the blind are driven.

Theodore Roethke

PIPLING

Behold a critic, pitched like the *castrati*,
Imperious youngling, though approaching forty:
He heaps few honours on a living head,
He loves himself, and the illustrious dead;
He pipes, he squeaks, he quivers through his nose,—
Some cannot praise him: *I* am one of those.

THE SLOTH

In moving-slow he has no Peer.
You ask him something in his ear;
He thinks about it for a Year;

And then, before he says a Word
There, upside down (unlike a Bird)
He will assume that you have Heard—

A most Ex-as-per-at-ing Lug.
But should you call his manner Smug,
He'll sigh and give his Branch a Hug;

Then off again to Sleep he goes,
Still swaying gently by his Toes,
And you just know he knows he knows.

THE LOST SON

I   THE FLIGHT

At Woodlawn I heard the dead cry:
I was lulled by the slamming of iron,
A slow drip over stones,
Toads brooding in wells.
All the leaves stuck out their tongues;
I shook the softening chalk of my bones,
Saying,
Snail, snail, glister me forward,
Bird, soft-sigh me home,
Worm, be with me.
This is my hard time.

Fished in an old wound,
The soft pond of repose;
Nothing nibbled my line,
Not even the minnows came.

Sat in an empty house
Watching shadows crawl,
Scratching.
There was one fly.

Voice, come out of the silence.
Say something.
Appear in the form of a spider
Or a moth beating the curtain.

Tell me:
Which is the way I take;
Out of what door do I go,
Where and to whom?

Dark hollows said, lee to the wind,
The moon said, back of an eel,

The salt said, look by the sea,
Your tears are not enough praise,
You will find no comfort here,
In the kingdom of bang and blab.

Running lightly over spongy ground,
Past the pasture of flat stones,
The three elms,
The sheep strewn on a field,
Over a rickety bridge
Toward the quick-water, wrinkling and rippling.

Hunting along the rivers,
Down among the rubbish, the bug-riddled foliage,
By the muddy pond-edge, by the bog-holes,
By the shrunken lake, hunting, in the heat of summer.

The shape of a rat?
It's bigger than that.
It's less than a leg
And more than a nose,
Just under the water
It usually goes.

Is it soft like a mouse?
Can it wrinkle its nose?
Could it come in the house
On the tips of its toes?

Take the skin of a cat
And the back of an eel,
Then roll them in grease,—
That's the way it would feel.

It's sleek as an otter
With wide webby toes
Just under the water
It usually goes.

II   THE PIT

Where do the roots go?
  Look down under the leaves.
Who put the moss there?
  These stones have been here too long.
Who stunned the dirt into noise?
  Ask the mole, he knows.
I feel the slime of a wet nest.
  Beware Mother Mildew.
Nibble again, fish nerves.

III   THE GIBBER

At the wind's mouth,
By the cave's door,
I listened to something
I had heard before.

Dogs of the groin
Barked and howled
The sun was against me
The moon would not have me.

The weeds whined,
The snakes cried,
The cows and briars
Said to me: Die.

What a small song. What slow clouds. What dark water.
Hath the raine a father? All the caves are ice. Only the snow's
  here.
I'm cold. I'm cold all over. Rub me in father and mother.
Fear was my father, Father Fear.
His look drained the stones.

  What gliding shape
  Beckoning through halls,
  Stood poised on the stair,
  Fell dreamily down?

From the mouths of jugs
Perched on many shelves,
I saw substance flowing
That cold morning.

Like a slither of eels
That watery cheek
As my own tongue kissed
My lips awake.

Is this the storm's heart? The ground is unstilling itself.
My veins are running nowhere. Do the bones cast out their
    fire?
Is the seed leaving the old bed? These buds are live as birds.
Where, where are the tears of the world?
Let the kisses resound, flat like a butcher's palm;
Let the gestures freeze; our doom is already decided.
All the windows are burning! What's left of my life?
I want the old rage, the lash of primordial milk!
Goodbye, goodbye, old stones, the time-order is going.
I have married my hands to perpetual agitation,
I run, I run to the whistle of money.

Money money money
Water water water

How cool the grass is.
Has the bird left?
The stalk still sways.
Has the worm a shadow?
What do the clouds say?

These sweeps of light undo me.
Look, look, the ditch is running white!
I've more veins than a tree!
Kiss me, ashes, I'm falling through a dark swirl.

IV   THE RETURN

The way to the boiler was dark,
Dark all the way,
Over slippery cinders
Through the long greenhouse.

The roses kept breathing in the dark.
They had many mouths to breathe with.
My knees made little winds underneath
Where the weeds slept.

There was always a single light
Swinging by the fire-pit,
Where the fireman pulled out roses,
The big roses, the big bloody clinkers.

Once I stayed all night.
The light in the morning came slowly over the white
Snow.
There were many kinds of cool
Air.
Then came steam.

Pipe-knock.

Scurry of warm over small plants.
Ordnung! Ordnung!
Papa is coming!

A fine haze moved off the leaves;
Frost melted on far panes;
The rose, the chrysanthemum turned toward the light.
Even the hushed forms, the bent yellowy weeds
Moved in a slow up-sway.

V

It was beginning winter,
An in-between time,
The landscape still partly brown:
The bones of weeds kept swinging in the wind,
Above the blue snow.

It was beginning winter
The light moved slowly over the frozen field,
Over the dry seed-crowns,
The beautiful surviving bones
Swinging in the wind.

Light traveled over the wide field;
Stayed.
The weeds stopped swinging.
The mind moved, not alone,
Through the clear air, in the silence.

Was it light?
Was it light within?
Was it light within light?
Stillness becoming alive,
Yet still?

A lively understandable spirit
Once entertained you.
It will come again.
Be still.
Wait.

I KNEW A WOMAN, LOVELY IN HER BONES

I knew a woman, lovely in her bones,
When small birds sighed, she would sigh back at them;
Ah, when she moved, she moved more ways than one:
The shapes a bright container can contain!

Of her choice virtues only gods should speak,
Or English poets who grew up on Greek
(I'd have them sing in chorus, cheek to cheek.)

How well her wishes went! She stroked my chin,
She taught me Turn, and Counter-turn, and Stand;
She taught me Touch, that undulant white skin:
I nibbled meekly from her proffered hand;
She was the sickle; I, poor I, the rake,
Coming behind her for her pretty sake
(But what prodigious mowing we did make.)

Love likes a gander, and adores a goose:
Her full lips pursed, the errant note to seize;
She played it quick, she played it light and loose;
My eyes, they dazzled at her flowing knees;
Her several parts could keep a pure repose,
Or one hip quiver with a mobile nose
(She moved in circles, and those circles moved.)

Let seed be grass, and grass turn into hay:
I'm martyr to a motion not my own;
What's freedom for? To know eternity.
I swear she cast a shadow white as stone.
But who would count eternity in days?
These old bones live to learn her wanton ways:
(I measure time by how a body sways.)

ELEGY FOR JANE

(My student, thrown by a horse)

I remember the neckcurls, limp and damp as tendrils;
And her quick look, a sidelong pickerel smile;
And how, once startled into talk, the light syllables leaped for
    her,
And she balanced in the delight of her thought,
A wren, happy, tail into the wind,

Her song trembling the twigs and small branches.
The shade sang with her;
The leaves, their whispers turned to kissing,
And the mould sang in the bleached valleys under the rose.

Oh, when she was sad, she cast herself down into such a pure
   depth,
Even a father could not find her:
Scraping her cheek against straw,
Stirring the clearest water.

My sparrow, you are not here,
Waiting like a fern, making a spiney shadow.
The sides of wet stones cannot console me,
Nor the moss, wound with the last light.

If only I could nudge you from this sleep,
My maimed darling, my skittery pigeon.
Over this damp grave I speak the words of my love:
I, with no rights in this matter,
Neither father nor lover.

THE PARTNER

Between such animal and human heat
I find myself perplexed. What is desire?—
The impulse to make someone else complete?
That woman would set sodden straw on fire.
Was I the servant of a sovereign wish,
Or ladle rattling in an empty dish?

We played a measure with commingled feet:
The lively dead had taught us to be fond.
Who can embrace the body of his fate?
Light altered light along the living ground.
She kissed me close, and then did something else.
My marrow beat as wildly as my pulse.

I'd say it to my horse: we live beyond
Our outer skin. Who's whistling up my sleeve?
I see a heron prancing in his pond;
I know a dance the elephants believe.
The living all assemble! What's the cue?—
Do what the clumsy partner wants to do!

Things loll and loiter. Who condones the lost?
This joy outleaps the dog. Who cares? Who cares?
I gave her kisses back, and woke a ghost.
O what lewd music crept into our ears!
The body and the soul know how to play
In that dark world where gods have lost their way.

Edwin Rolfe

A POEM TO DELIGHT MY FRIENDS WHO LAUGH AT SCIENCE-FICTION

That was the year
the small birds in their frail and delicate battalions
committed suicide against the Empire State,
having, in some never-explained manner,
lost their aerial radar, or ignored it.

That was the year
men and women everywhere stopped dying natural deaths.
The aged, facing sleep, took poison;
the infant, facing life, died with the mother in childbirth;
and the whole wild remainder of the population,
despairing but deliberate, crashed in auto accidents
on roads as clear and uncluttered as ponds.

That was the year every ship on every ocean,
every lake, harbor, river, vanished without trace;
and even ships docked at quays
turned over like wounded animals, harpooned whales, or
    Normandies.

Yes, and the civilian transcontinental planes
found, like the war-planes, the sky-lanes crowded
and, praising Icarus, plunged to earth in flames.

Many, mild stay-at-homes, slipped in bathtubs,
others, congenital indoors-men, descending stairs,
and some, irrepressible roisterers, playing musical chairs.
Tots fell from scooter cars and tricycles
and casual passersby were stabbed by falling icicles.

Ah, what carnage! It was reported
that even bicarb and aspirin turned fatal,
and seconal too, to those with mild headaches,
Whose stomachs were slightly acid, or who found they could
   not sleep.
All lovers died in bed, as all seafarers on the deep.

Till finally the only people left alive
were the soldiers sullenly spread on battlefields
among the shell-pocked hills and the charred trees.
Thus, even the indispensable wars died of ennui.

But not the expendable conscripts: they remained as always.
However, since no transport was available anywhere,
and home, in any case, was dead, and bare,
the soldiers wandered eternally
in their dazed, early-Chirico landscapes,
like drunken stars in their shrinking orbits
round and round and round and round

and (since I too died in the world-wide suicide)
they may still, for all I know, be there.
Like forsaken chessmen abandoned by paralyzed players,
they may still be there,
may still be there.

Muriel Rukeyser

EYES OF NIGHT-TIME

On the roads at night I saw the glitter of eyes:
my dark around me let shine one ray; that black
allowed their eyes: spangles in the cat's, air in the moth's eye
    shine,
mosaic of the fly, ruby-eyed beetle, the eyes that never weep,
the horned toad sitting and its tear of blood,
fighters and prisoners in the forest, people
aware in this almost total dark, with the difference,
the one broad fact of light.

Eyes on the road at night, sides of a road like rhyme;
the floor of the illumined shadow sea
and shallows with their assembling flash and show
of sight, root, holdfast, eyes of the brittle stars.
And your eyes in the shadowy red room,
scent of the forest entering, various time
calling and the light of wood along the ceiling
and over us birds calling and their circuit eyes.
And in our bodies the eyes of the dead and the living
giving us gifts at hand, the glitter of all their eyes.

EASTER EVE

Wary of time O it seizes the soul tonight
I wait for the great morning of the west
confessing with every breath mortality.
Moon of this wild sky struggles to stay whole
and on the water silvers the ships of war.
I go alone in the black-yellow light
all night waiting for day, while everywhere the sure
death of light, the leaf's sure return to the root
is repeated in million, death of all man to share.

Whatever world I know shines ritual death,
wide under this moon they stand gathering fire,
fighting with flame, stand fighting in their graves.
All shining with life as the leaf, as the wing shines,
the stone deep in the mountain, the drop in the green wave.
Lit by their energies, secretly, all things shine.
Nothing can black that glow of life; although
      each part go crumbling down
      itself shall rise up whole.

Now I say there are new meanings; now I name
death our black honor and feast of possibility
to celebrate casting of life on life. This earth-long day
between blood and resurrection where we wait
remembering sun, seed, fire; remembering
that fierce Judaean Innocent who risked
every immortal meaning on one life.
Given to our year as sun and spirit are,
as seed we are blessed only in needing freedom.
Now I say that the peace the spirit needs is peace,
not lack of war, but fierce continual flame.
For all men: effort is freedom, effort's peace,
it fights. And along these truths the soul goes home,
      flies in its blazing to a place
      more safe and round than Paradise.

Night of the soul, our dreams in the arms of dreams
dissolving into eyes that look upon us.
Dreams the sources of action, the meeting and the end,
a resting-place among the flight of things.
And love which contains all human spirit, all wish,
the eyes and hands, sex, mouth, hair, the whole woman—
fierce peace I say at last, and the sense of the world.
In the time of conviction of mortality
whatever survive, I remember what I am.—
The nets of this night are on fire with sun and moon
pouring both lights into the open tomb.

Whatever arise, it comes in the shape of peace,
fierce peace which is love, in which moves all the stars,
and the breathing of universes, filling, falling away,
and death on earth cast into the human dream.
What fire survive forever
myself is for my time.

READING TIME: 1 MINUTE 26 SECONDS

The fear of poetry is the
fear: mystery and fury of a midnight street
of windows whose low voluptuous voice
issues, and after that there is no peace.

That round waiting moment in the
theatre: curtain rises, dies into the ceiling
and here is played the scene with the mother
bandaging a revealed son's head. The bandage is torn off.
Curtain goes down. And here is the moment of proof.

That climax when the brain acknowledges the world,
all values extended into the blood awake.
Moment of proof. And as they say Brancusi did,
building his bird to extend through soaring air,
as Kafka planned stories that draw to eternity
through time extended. And the climax strikes.

Love touches so, that months after the look of
blue stare of love, the footbeat on the heart
is translated into the pure cry of birds
following air-cries, or poems, the new scene.
Moment of proof. That strikes long after act.

They fear it. They turn away, hand up palm out
fending off moment of proof, the straight look, poem.
The prolonged wound-consciousness after the bullet's shot.
The prolonged love after the look is dead,
the yellow joy after the song of the sun.

ROTTEN LAKE ELEGY

As I went down to Rotten Lake I remembered
the wrecked season, haunted by plans of salvage,
snow, the closed door, footsteps and resurrections,
    machinery of sorrow.

The warm grass gave to the feet and the stilltide water
was floor of evening and magnetic light and
reflection of wish, the black-haired beast with my eyes
    walking beside me.

The green and yellow lights, the street of water standing
point to the image of that house whose destruction
I weep when I weep you. My door (no), poems, rest,
    (don't say it!) untamable need.

❁

When you have left the river you are a little way
nearer the lake; but I leave many times.
Parents parried my past; the present was poverty,
the future depended on my unfinished spirit.
There were no misgivings because there was no choice,
only regret for waste, and the wild knowledge:
growth and sorrow and discovery.

When you have left the river you proceed alone;
all love is likely to be illicit; and few
friends to command the soul; they are too feeble.
Rejecting the subtle and contemplative minds
as being too thin in the bone; and the gross thighs
and unevocative hands fail also. But the poet
and his wife, those who say Survive, remain;
and those two who were with me on the ship
leading me to the sum of the years, in Spain.

When you have left the river you will hear the war.
In the mountains, with tourists, in the insanest groves

the sound of kill, the precious face of peace.
And the sad frightened child, continual minor,
returns, nearer whole circle, O and nearer
all that was loved, the lake, the naked river,
what must be crossed and cut out of your heart,
what must be stood beside and straightly seen.

*

As I went down to Rotten Lake I remembered
how the one crime is need. The man lifting the loaf
with hunger as motive can offer no alibi, is always condemned.

These are the lines at the employment bureau
and the tense students at their examinations;
needing makes clumsy and robs them of their wish,
      in one fast gesture

plants on them failure of the imagination;
and lovers who lower their bodies into the chair
gently and sternly as if the flesh had been wounded,
      never can conquer.

Their need is too great, their vulnerable bodies
rigidly joined will snap, turn love away,
fear parts them, they lose their hands and voices,
      never get used to the world.

Walking at night, they are asked Are you your best friend's
best friend? and must say No, not yet, they are
love's vulnerable, and they go down to Rotten Lake
      hoping for wonders.

Dare it arrive, the day when weakness ends?
When the insistence is strong, the wish converted?
I prophesy the meeting by the water
      of these desires.

I know what this, I have known the waking
when every night ended in one cliff-dream

of faces drowned beneath the porous rock
   brushed by the sea;

suffered the change: deprived erotic dreams
to images of that small house where peace
walked room to room and always with one face
   telling her stories,

and needed that, past loss, past fever, and the
attractive enemy who in my bed
touches all night the body of my sleep,
   improves my summer

with madness, impossible loss, and the dead music
of altered promise, a room torn up by the roots,
the desert that crosses from the door to the wall,
   continual bleeding,

and all the time that will which cancels enmity,
seeks its own Easter, arrives at the water-barrier;
must face it now, biting the lakeside ground;
   looks for its double,

the twin that must be met again, changeling need,
blazing in color somewhere, flying yellow
into the forest with its lucid edict:
   take to the world,

this is the honor of your flesh, the offering
of strangers, the faces of cities, honor of all your wish.
Immortal undoing! I say in my own voice. These prophecies
   may all come true,

out of the beaten season. I look in Rotten Lake
wait for the flame reflection, seeing only
the free beast flickering black along my side
   animal of my need,

and cry I want! I want! rising among the world
to gain my converted wish, the amazing desire
that keeps me alive, though the face be still, be still,
the slow dilated heart know nothing but lack,
now I begin again the private rising,
the ride to survival of that consuming bird
beating, up from dead lakes, ascents of fire.

Carl Sandburg

THE PEOPLE WILL LIVE ON

The people will live on.
The learning and blundering people will live on.
They will be tricked and sold and again sold
And go back to the nourishing earth for rootholds,
The people so peculiar in renewal and comeback,
You can't laugh off their capacity to take it.
The mammoth rests between his cyclonic dramas.
The people so often sleepy, weary, enigmatic,
is a vast huddle with many units saying:
"I earn my living
I make enough to get by
and it takes all my time.
If I had more time
I could do more for myself
and maybe for others.
I could read and study
and talk things over
and find out about things.
It takes time.
I wish I had the time."

The people is a tragic and comic two-face:
hero and hoodlum: phantom and gorilla twisting to moan with a gargoyle mouth: "They
buy me and sell me . . . it's a game . . .
sometime I'll break loose . . ."

> Once having marched
> Over the margins of animal necessity,
> Over the grim line of sheer subsistence
> Then man came
> To the deeper rituals of his bones,
> To the lights lighter than any bones,
> To the time for thinking things over,
> To the dance, the song, the story,
> Or the hours given over to dreaming,
> Once having so marched.

Between the finite limitations of the five senses
and the endless yearnings of man for the beyond
the people hold to the humdrum bidding of work and food
while reaching out when it comes their way
for lights beyond the prison of the five senses,
for keepsakes lasting beyond any hunger or death.
> This reaching is alive.
The panderers and liars have violated and smutted it.
> Yet this reaching is alive yet
> for lights and keepsakes.

> The people know the salt of the sea
> and the strength of the winds
> lashing the corners of the earth.
> The people take the earth
> as a tomb of rest and a cradle of hope.
> Who else speaks for the Family of Man?
> They are in tune and step
> with constellations of universal law.

The people is a polychrome,
a spectrum and a prism

held in a moving monolith,
a console organ of changing themes,
a clavilux of color poems
wherein the sea offers fog
and the fog moves off in rain
and the Labrador sunset shortens
to a nocturne of clear stars
serene over the shot spray
of northern lights.

The steel mill sky is alive.
The fire breaks white and zigzag
shot on a gun-metal gloaming.
Man is a long time coming.
Man will yet win.
Brother may yet line up with brother:

This old anvil laughs at many broken hammers.
There are men who can't be bought.
The fireborn are at home in fire.
The stars make no noise.
You can't hinder the wind from blowing.
Time is a great teacher.
Who can live without hope?

In the darkness with a great bundle of grief
the people march.
In the night, and overhead a shovel of stars for
keeps, the people march:
"Where to? What next?"

CHICAGO

Hog Butcher for the World,
Tool Maker, Stacker of Wheat,
Player with Railroads and the Nation's Freight
Handler;

Stormy, husky, brawling,
    City of the Big Shoulders:
They tell me you are wicked and I believe them, for I have
    seen your painted women under the gas lamps luring the
    farm boys.
And they tell me you are crooked and I answer: Yes, it is
    true I have seen the gunman kill and go free to kill again.
And they tell me you are brutal and my reply is: On the faces
    of women and children I have seen the marks of wanton
    hunger.
And having answered so I turn once more to those who sneer
    at this my city, and I give them back the sneer and say to
    them:
Come and show me another city with lifted head singing so
    proud to be alive and coarse and strong and cunning.
Flinging magnetic curses amid the toil of piling job on job,
    here is a tall bold slugger set vivid against the little soft
    cities;
Fierce as a dog with tongue lapping for action, cunning as a
    savage pitted against the wilderness,
        Bareheaded,
        Shoveling,
        Wrecking,
        Planning,
        Building, breaking, rebuilding.
Under the smoke, dust all over his mouth, laughing with
    white teeth,
Under the terrible burden of destiny laughing as a young man
    laughs,
Laughing even as an ignorant fighter laughs who has never
    lost a battle,
Bragging and laughing that under his wrist is the pulse, and
    under his ribs the heart of the people,
                Laughing!
Laughing the stormy, husky, brawling laughter of Youth,
    half-naked, sweating, proud to be Hog Butcher, Tool
    Maker, Stacker of Wheat, Player with Railroads and
    Freight Handler to the Nation.

FOUR PRELUDES ON PLAYTHINGS OF THE WIND

I

The woman named Tomorrow
sits with a hairpin in her teeth
and takes her time
and does her hair the way she wants it
and fastens at last the last braid and coil
and puts the hairpin where it belongs
and turns and drawls: Well, what of it?
My grandmother, Yesterday, is gone.
What of it? Let the dead be dead.

II

The doors were cedar
and the panel strips of gold
and the girls were golden girls
and the panels read and the girls chanted:
> We are the greatest city,
> and the greatest nation:
> nothing like us ever was.

The doors are twisted on broken hinges.
Sheets of rain swish through on the wind
> where the golden girls ran and the panels
> read:
> We are the greatest city,
> the greatest nation,
> nothing like us ever was.

III

It has happened before.
Strong men put up a city and got
a nation together,
And paid singers to sing and women
to warble: We are the greatest city,
the greatest nation,
nothing like us ever was.

And while the singers sang
and the strong men listened
and paid the singers well,
> there were rats and lizards who listened
> . . . and the only listeners left now
> . . . are . . . the rats . . . and the lizards.
And there are black crows
crying, "Caw, caw,"
bringing mud and sticks
building a nest
over the words carved
on the doors where the panels were cedar
and the strips on the panels were gold
and the golden girls came singing:
> We are the greatest city,
> the greatest nation:
> nothing like us ever was.

The only singers now are crows crying, "Caw, caw,"
And the sheets of rain whine in the wind and doorways.
And the only listeners now are . . . the rats . . . and the lizards.

IV

The feet of the rats
scribble on the doorsills;
the hieroglyphs of the rat footprints
chatter the pedigrees of the rats
and babble of the blood
and gabble of the breed
of the grandfathers and the great-grandfathers
of the rats.
And the wind shifts
and the dust on a doorsill shifts
and even the writing of the rat footprints
tells us nothing, nothing at all
about the greatest city, the greatest nation
where the strong men listened
and the women warbled: Nothing like us ever was.

George Santayana

A MINUET ON REACHING THE AGE OF 50

Old Age, on tiptoe, lays her jewelled hand
Lightly in mine.—Come, tread a stately measure,
Most gracious partner, nobly posed and bland.
   Ours be no boisterous pleasure,
But smiling conversation, with quick glance
And memories dancing lightlier than we dance,
   Friends who a thousand joys
Divide and double, save one joy supreme
   Which many a pang alloys.
   Let wanton girls and boys
Cry over lovers' woes and broken toys.
Our waking life is sweeter than their dream.

Dame Nature, with unwitting hand,
Has sparsely strewn the black abyss with lights
Minute, remote, and numberless. We stand
   Measuring far depths and heights,
   Arched over by a laughing heaven,
Intangible and never to be scaled.
If we confess our sins, they are forgiven.
   We triumph, if we know we failed.

   Tears that in youth you shed,
Congealed to pearls, now deck your silvery hair;
   Sighs breathed for loves long dead
Frosted the glittering atoms of the air
     Into the veils you wear
Round your soft bosom and most queenly head;
    The shimmer of your gown
Catches all tints of autumn, and the dew
Of gardens where the damask roses blew;

The myriad tapers from these arches hung
      Play on your diamonded crown;
And stars, whose light angelical caressed
      Your virgin days,
Give back in your calm eyes their holier rays.
    The deep past living in your breast
    Heaves these half-merry sighs;
    And the soft accents of your tongue
    Breathe unrecorded charities.

      Hasten not; the feast will wait.
This is a master-night without a morrow.
No chill and haggard dawn, with after-sorrow,
      Will snuff the spluttering candle out,
Or blanch the revellers homeward straggling late.
      Before the rout
Wearies or wanes, will come a calmer trance.
Lulled by the poppied fragrance of this bower,
      We'll cheat the lapsing hour,
And close our eyes, still smiling, on the dance.

AS IN THE MIDST OF BATTLE THERE IS ROOM

As in the midst of battle there is room
For thoughts of love, and in foul sin for mirth;
As gossips whisper of a trinket's worth
Spied by the death-bed's flickering candle-gloom;
As in the crevices of Caesar's tomb
The sweet herbs flourish on a little earth:
So in this great disaster of our birth
We can be happy, and forget our doom.
For morning, with a ray of tenderest joy
Gilding the iron heaven, hides the truth,
And evening gently woos us to employ
Our grief in idle catches. Such is youth;
Till from that summer's trance we wake, to find
Despair before us, vanity behind.

Delmore Schwartz

THE STARLIGHT'S INTUITIONS PIERCED THE TWELVE

The starlight's intuitions pierced the twelve,
The brittle night sky sparkled like a tune
Tinkled and tapped out on the xylophone.
Empty and vain, a glittering dune, the moon
Arose too big, and, in the mood which ruled,
Seemed like a useless beauty in a pit;
And then one said, after he carefully spat:
'No matter what we do, he looks at it!

'I cannot see a child or find a girl
Beyond his smile which glows like that spring moon.'
'—Nothing no more the same,' the second said,
'Though all may be forgiven, never quite healed
The wound I bear as witness, standing by;
No ceremony surely appropriate,
Nor secret love, escape or sleep because
No matter what I do, he looks at it—'

'Now,' said the third, 'no thing will be the same:
I am as one who never shuts his eyes,
The sea and sky no more are marvellous,
I know no more true freshness or surprise!'
'Now,' said the fourth, 'nothing will be enough,
—I heard his voice accomplishing all wit:
No word can be unsaid, no deed withdrawn,
—No matter what is said, he measures it!'

'Vision, imagination, hope or dream
Believed, denied, the scene we wished to see?
It does not matter in the least: for what
Is altered if it is not true? That we
Saw goodness, as it is—*this* is the awe
And the abyss which we will not forget,

His story now the skull which holds all thought:
No matter what I think, I think of it!'

'And I will never be what once I was,'
Said one for long as single as a knife,
'And we will never be as once we were;
We have died once, this is a second life.'
'My mind is spilled in moral chaos,' one
Righteous as Job exclaimed, 'now infinite
Suspicion of my heart stems what I will,
—No matter what I choose, he stares at it!'

'I am as one native in summer places,
—Ten weeks' excitement paid for by the rich;
Debauched by that, and then all winter bored,'
The sixth declared, 'his peak left us a ditch.'
'He came to make this life more difficult,'
The seventh said, 'No one will ever fit
His measures' heights, all is inadequate:
No matter what we have, what good is it?'

'He gave forgiveness to us: what a gift!'
The eighth chimed in. 'But now we know *how much*
Must be forgiven. But if forgiven, what?
The crime which was will be; and the least touch
Revives the memory: what is forgiveness worth?'
The ninth spoke thus: 'Who now will ever sit
At ease in Zion at the Easter feast?
No matter what the place, he touches it!'

'And I will always stammer, since he spoke,'
One, who had been most eloquent, said, stammering,
'I looked too long at the sun; like too much light,
Too much of goodness is a boomerang,'
Laughed the eleventh of the troop, 'I must
Try what he tried: I saw the infinite
Who walked the lake and raised the hopeless dead:
No matter what the feat, he first accomplished it!'

So spoke the twelfth; and then the twelve in chorus:
'Unspeakable unnatural goodness is
Risen and shines, and never will ignore us;
He glows forever in all consciousness;
Forgiveness, love, and hope possess the pit,
And bring our endless guilt, like shadow's bars:
No matter what we do, he stares at it!
What pity can each deny? what debt defer?
We know he looks at us like all the stars,
And we shall never be as once we were,
This life will never be what once it was!'

THE HEAVY BEAR WHO GOES WITH ME

"the witness of the body"—WHITEHEAD

The heavy bear who goes with me,
A manifold honey to smear his face,
Clumsy and lumbering here and there,
The central ton of every place,
The hungry beating brutish one
In love with candy, anger, and sleep,
Crazy factotum, dishevelling all,
Climbs the building, kicks the football,
Boxes his brother in the hate-ridden city.

Breathing at my side, that heavy animal,
That heavy bear who sleeps with me,
Howls in his sleep for a world of sugar,
A sweetness intimate as the water's clasp,
Howls in his sleep because the tight-rope
Trembles and shows the darkness beneath.
—The strutting show-off is terrified,
Dressed in his dress-suit, bulging his pants,
Trembles to think that his quivering meat
Must finally wince to nothing at all.

That inescapable animal walks with me,
Has followed me since the black womb held,
Moves where I move, distorting my gesture,
A caricature, a swollen shadow,
A stupid clown of the spirit's motive,
Perplexes and affronts with his own darkness,
The secret life of belly and bone,
Opaque, too near, my private, yet unknown,
Stretches to embrace the very dear
With whom I would walk without him near,
Touches her grossly, although a word
Would bare my heart and make me clear,
Stumbles, flounders, and strives to be fed
Dragging me with him in his mouthing care,
Amid the hundred million of his kind,
The scrimmage of appetite everywhere.

IN THE NAKED BED, IN PLATO'S CAVE

In the naked bed, in Plato's cave,
Reflected headlights slowly slid the wall,
Carpenters hammered under the shaded window,
Wind troubled the window curtains all night long.
A fleet of trucks strained uphill, grinding,
Their freights covered, as usual.
The ceiling lightened again, the slanting diagram
Slid slowly forth.
                    Hearing the milkman's chop,
His striving up the stair, the bottle's chink,
I rose from bed, lit a cigarette,
And walked to the window. The stony street
Displayed the stillness in which buildings stand,
The street-lamp's vigil and the horse's patience.
The winter sky's pure capital
Turned me back to bed with exhausted eyes.

Strangeness grew in the motionless air. The loose
Film grayed. Shaking wagons, hooves' waterfalls,
Sounded far off, increasing, louder and nearer.
A car coughed, starting. Morning, softly
Melting the air, lifted the half-covered chair
From underseas, kindled the looking-glass,
Distinguished the dresser and the white wall.
The bird called tentatively, whistled, called,
Bubbled and whistled, so! Perplexed, still wet
With sleep, affectionate, hungry and cold. So, so,
O son of man, the ignorant night, the travail
Of early morning, the mystery of beginning
Again and again,
                         while History is unforgiven.

TIRED AND UNHAPPY, YOU THINK OF HOUSES

Tired and unhappy, you think of houses
Soft-carpeted and warm in the December evening,
While snow's white pieces fall past the window,
And the orange firelight leaps.
                         A young girl sings
That song of Gluck where Orpheus pleads with Death;
Her elders watch, nodding their happiness
To see time fresh again in her self-conscious eyes:
The servants bring the coffee, the children retire,
Elder and younger yawn and go to bed,
The coals fade and glow, rose and ashen,
It is time to shake yourself! and break this
Banal dream, and turn your head
Where the underground is charged, where the weight
Of the lean buildings is seen,
Where close in the subway rush, anonymous
In the audience, well-dressed or mean,
So many surround you, ringing your fate,
Caught in an anger exact as a machine!

FOR THE ONE WHO WOULD TAKE MAN'S LIFE IN HIS HANDS

Tiger Christ unsheathed his sword,
Threw it down, became a lamb.
Swift spat upon the species, but
Took two women to his heart.
Samson who was strong as death
Paid his strength to kiss a slut.
Othello that stiff warrior
Was broken by a woman's heart.
Troy burned for a sea-tax, also for
Possession of a charming whore.
What do all examples show?
What must the finished murderer know?

You cannot sit on bayonets,
Nor can you eat among the dead.
When all are killed, you are alone,
A vacuum comes where hate has fed.
Murder's fruit is silent stone,
The gun increases poverty.
With what do these examples shine?
The soldier turned to girls and wine.
Love is the tact of every good,
The only warmth, the only peace.

'What have I said?' asked Socrates,
'Affirmed extremes, cried yes and no,
Taken all parts, denied myself,
Praised the caress, extolled the blow,
Soldier and lover quite deranged
Until their motions are exchanged.
—What do all examples show?
What can any actor know?
The contradiction in every act,
The infinite task of the human heart.'

Karl Shapiro

AUTO WRECK

Its quick soft silver bell beating, beating,
And down the dark one ruby flare
Pulsing out red light like an artery,
The ambulance at top speed floating down
Past beacons and illuminated clocks
Wings in a heavy curve, dips down,
And brakes speed, entering the crowd.
The doors leap open, emptying light;
Stretchers are laid out, the mangled lifted
And stowed into the little hospital.
Then the bell, breaking the hush, tolls once,
And the ambulance with its terrible cargo
Rocking, slightly rocking, moves away,
As the doors, an afterthought, are closed.

We are deranged, walking among the cops
Who sweep glass and are large and composed.
One is still making notes under the light.
One with a bucket douches ponds of blood
Into the street and gutter.
One hangs lanterns on the wrecks that cling,
Empty husks of locusts, to iron poles.

Our throats were tight as tourniquets,
Our feet were bound with splints, but now
Like convalescents intimate and gauche,
We speak through sickly smiles and warn
With the stubborn saw of common sense,
The grim joke and the banal resolution.
The traffic moves around with care,
But we remain, touching a wound
That opens to our richest horror.

Already old, the question Who shall die?
Becomes unspoken Who is innocent?

For death in war is done by hands;
Suicide has cause and stillbirth, logic.
But this invites the occult mind,
Cancels our physics with a sneer,
And spatters all we knew of dénouement
Across the expedient and wicked stones.

A DOME OF SUNDAY

With focus sharp as Flemish-painted face
In film of varnish brightly fixed
And through a polished hand-lens deeply seen,
Sunday at noon through hyaline thin air
Sees down the street,
And in the camera of my eye depicts
Row-houses and row-lives:
Glass after glass, door after door the same,
Face after face the same, the same,
The brutal visibility the same;

As if one life emerging from one house
Would pause, a single image caught between   •
Two facing mirrors where vision multiplies
Beyond perspective,
A silent clatter in the high-speed eye
Spinning out photo-circulars of sight.

I see slip to the curb the long machines
Out of whose warm and windowed rooms pirouette
Shellacked with silk and light
The hard legs of our women.
Our women are one woman, dressed in black.
The carmine printed mouth
And cheeks as soft as muslin-glass belong
Outright to one dark dressy man
Merely a swagger at her curvy side.

This is their visit to themselves:
All day from porch to porch they weave

A nonsense pattern through the even glare,
Stealing in surfaces
Cold vulgar glances at themselves.

And high up in the heated room all day
I wait behind the plate glass pane for one,
Hot as a voyeur for a glimpse of one,
The vision to blot out this woman's sheen;
All day my sight records expensively
Row-houses and row-lives.

But nothing happens; no diagonal
With melting shadow falls across the curb:
Neither the blinded negress lurching through fatigue,
Nor exiles bleeding from their pores,
Nor that bright bomb slipped lightly from its rack
To splinter every silvered glass and crystal prism,
Witch-bowl and perfume bottle
And billion candle-power dressing-bulb,
No direct hit to smash the shatter-proof
And lodge at last the quivering needle
Clean in the eye of one who stands transfixed
In fascination of her brightness.

SCYROS

snuffle and sniff and handkerchief

The doctor punched my vein
The captain called me Cain
Upon my belly sat the sow of fear
With coins on either eye
The President came by
And whispered to the braid what none could hear

High over where the storm
Stood steadfast cruciform
The golden eagle sank in wounded wheels

White negroes laughing still
Crept fiercely on Brazil
Turning the navies upward on their keels

Now one by one the trees
Stripped to their naked knees
To dance upon the heaps of shrunken dead
The roof of England fell
Great Paris tolled her bell
And China staunched her milk and wept for bread

No island singly lay
But lost its name that day
The Ainu dived across the plunging sands
From dawn to dawn to dawn
King George's birds came on
Strafing the tulips from his children's hands

Thus in the classic sea
Southeast from Thessaly
The dynamited mermen washed ashore
And tritons dressed in steel
Trolled heads with rod and reel
And dredged potatoes from the Aegean floor

Hot is the sky and green
Where Germans have been seen
The moon leaks metal on the Atlantic fields
Pink boys in birthday shrouds
Loop lightly through the clouds
Or coast the peaks of Finland on their shields

That prophet year by year
Lay still but could not hear
Where scholars tapped to find his new remains
Gog and Magog ate pork
In vertical New York
And war began next Monday on the Danes.

NOSTALGIA

My soul stands at the window of my room,
　　And I ten thousand miles away;
My days are filled with Ocean's sound of doom,
　　Salt and cloud and the bitter spray.
Let the wind blow, for many a man shall die.

My selfish youth, my books with gilded edge,
　　Knowledge and all gaze down the street;
The potted plants upon the window ledge
　　Gaze down with selfish lives and sweet.
Let the wind blow, for many a man shall die.

My night is now her day, my day her night,
　　So I lie down, and so I rise;
The sun burns close, the star is losing height,
　　The clock is hunted down the skies.
Let the wind blow, for many a man shall die.

Truly a pin can make the memory bleed,
　　A world explode the inward mind
And turn the skulls and flowers never freed
　　Into the air, no longer blind.
Let the wind blow, for many a man shall die.

Laughter and grief join hands. Always the heart
　　Clumps in the breast with heavy stride;
The face grows lined and wrinkled like a chart,
　　The eyes bloodshot with tears and tide.
Let the wind blow, for many a man shall die.

THE FLY

O hideous little bat, the size of snot,
With polyhedral eye and shabby clothes,
To populate the stinking cat you walk
The promontory of the dead man's nose,

Climb with the fine leg of a Duncan Phyfe
    The smoking mountains of my food
        And in a comic mood
    In mid-air take to bed a wife.

Riding and riding with your filth of hair
On gluey foot or wing, forever coy,
Hot from the compost and green sweet decay
Sounding your buzzer like an urchin toy;
You dot all whiteness with diminutive stool;
    In the tight belly of the dead
        Burrow with hungry head
    And inlay maggots like a jewel.

At your approach the great horse stomps and paws
Bringing the hurricane of his heavy tail;
Shod in disease you dare to kiss my hand
Which sweeps against you like an angry flail;
Still you return, return, trusting your wing
    To draw you from the hunter's reach
        That learns to kill to teach
    Disorder to the tinier thing.

My peace is your disaster. For your death
Children like spiders cup their pretty hands
And wives resort to chemistry of war.
In fens of sticky paper and quicksands
You glue yourself to death. Where you are stuck
    You struggle hideously and beg;
        You amputate your leg
    Imbedded in the amber muck.

But I, a man, must swat you with my hate,
Slap you across the air and crush your flight,
Must mangle with my shoe and smear your blood,
Expose your little guts pasty and white,
Knock your head sidewise like a drunkard's hat,
    Pin your wings under like a crow's,

Tear off your flimsy clothes
And beat you as one beats a rat.

Then like Gargantua I stride among
The corpses strewn like raisins in the dust,
The broken bodies of the narrow dead
That catch the throat with fingers of disgust.
I sweep. One gyrates like a top and falls
And stunned, stone blind, and deaf
Buzzes its frightful F
And dies between three cannibals.

Hy Sobiloff

PAINTING OF A LOBSTER BY PICASSO

This claw remains alive,
Stands aside and swings on fantasy;
It hangs from a drapery rod
Against the wall of a room
And near the window.
This claw seizes the sunlight,
Lies in a crib of muscle
Tied to a string.
The claw surrounds the egg
As in the room the whole lobster sleeps
On a cracked plate,
Lobster eaten by a butterfly
On a checkered table cloth, blue and white.

PITTSBURGH

Near the road brim
Man's devil burned on the ground
His mouth pouring forth anger
In shades of white and gray,
A tongue cracked and discolored,

As earth stirred her iron ire.
A thousand pots boiled raw hills
A spectacle of sparkling soup,
Boiling bubbles popping,
Bones and scars of stone breeding new giants.

Man's devil dug in an open hearth
Melting mountains and losing ground.
Witches writhed in gorged voices
Spreading phantom scars
Heaping screaming flames to the four corners.
A smoldering canyon of melting steel
Patched their leaky skin, disguised their zinc faces.
Only when the wind blew
Did the fiery cinders light up their secret eyes.

Doomsday blasted with dynamite sticks dressed as Sabbath
    candles
Casting the rolling pilgrims into bronze statues,
Targets for dumb boulders rolling down the mountains.
Crust or ashes or late white smoke covered the clouds
While man's cranial fright plowed the old ground,
And raked the quarry to stoke his volcanic heart.

MY MOTHER'S TABLE

My mother's table was round like her face
Round and covered with fingerstains
And crumbs that stuck to my fingertips.
At that table each child wanted everything:
My father gave everything, emptied himself
Into the pockets round my mother's table.
We ate hard crust and made a hatbrim of hard crust,
Ate each other around my mother's table.
Ashamed to age alone,
My sister cried for too many dresses,
Grabbed for my dessert,

But I hid my chocolate under my pillow,
Stalked about the bedpost
Disappeared among the beams in our attic.
I counted my fingers and toes like a miser
Shouted to myself in my own language.
I grew by making promises to myself;
In lonely baths the fear of love became my religion.
Then one year they erected new fences for me to climb,
Prepared sticks and stones to destroy me
And I flew off at a tangent from my mother's round table.
The hobby horses were playing
And my childhood carrousel
Was still a familiar wonderland,
But when I crossed out chimneys and attics
The world became a strange neighborhood
Where I climbed a ladder of birthdays,
Reading my father's face.

AIRSHIP

I slept in a sleepy field
Floated on cloud pastures
The shepherd led my chariot

I rolled in the skies' creases
The roadbed near a dream
Yet the sky has a flat face

I scratched my eye out to look out
On the white breasts of vapor
And I heard the trumpets blowing earthly sounds

Theodore Spencer

THE INFLATABLE GLOBE

When the allegorical man came calling,
He told us all he would show us a trick,
And he showed us a flat but inflatable ball.
'Look at this ball,' he told us all;
'Look at the lines marked out on this ball.'
We looked at the ball and the lines on the ball:
England was red, and France was blue;
Germany orange and Russia brown:
'Look at this ball,' he told us all,
'With a blow of my breath I inflate this ball.'
He blew, and it bounced, and bouncing, falling,
He bounced it against the wall with a kick.
'But without my breath it will flatten and fall,'
Said the allegorical man; and down
Flat came his hand and squashed the ball,
And it fell on the floor with no life at all
Once his breath had gone out of the ball . . .
It seemed to us all a stupid trick.

EDEN: OR ONE VIEW OF IT

We come by a terrible gate;
We go out by a terrible gate;
The thunder blares and the lightning blares,
At the trembling gates there is lightning and thunder.
In between is there green? Lilacs?
Oranges in between the roses?
Are there flowers there at all, or a garden?

O lost flowers, abandoned garden,
Oranges lost between the roses,
Is the green lost between the lilacs,

Between the gates of trembling thunder?
Where thunder blares and lightning blares
As we enter the terrible gate;
And go out by the terrible gate.

William Stafford

ONE HOME

Mine was a Midwest home—you can keep your world.
Plain black hats rode the thoughts that made our code.
We sang hymns in the house; the roof was near God.

The light bulb that hung in the pantry made a wan light,
but we could read by it the names of preserves—
outside, the buffalo grass, and the wind in the night.

A wildcat sprang at Grandpa on the Fourth of July
when he was cutting plum bushes for fuel,
before Indians pulled the West over the edge of the sky.

To anyone who looked at us we said, 'My friend';
liking the cut of a thought, we could say 'Hello'.
(But plain black hats rode the thoughts that made our code.)

The sun was over our town; it was like a blade.
Kicking cottonwood leaves we ran toward storms.
Wherever we looked the land would hold us up.

A RITUAL TO READ TO EACH OTHER

If you don't know the kind of person I am
and I don't know the kind of person you are
a pattern that others made may prevail in the world
and following the wrong god home we may miss our star.

For there is many a small betrayal in the mind,
a shrug that lets the fragile sequence break
sending with shouts the horrible errors of childhood
storming out to play through the broken dyke.

And as elephants parade holding each elephant's tail,
but if one wanders the circus won't find the park,
I call it cruel and maybe the root of all cruelty
to know what occurs but not recognize the fact.

And so I appeal to a voice, to something shadowy,
a remote important region in all who talk:
though we could fool each other, we should consider—
lest the parade of our mutual life get lost in the dark.

For it is important that awake people be awake,
or a breaking line may discourage them back to sleep;
the signals we give—yes or no, or maybe—
should be clear: the darkness around us is deep.

Gertrude Stein

I AM ROSE

I am Rose my eyes are blue
I am Rose and who are you
I am Rose and when I sing
I am Rose like anything

Wallace Stevens

OF MODERN POETRY

The poem of the mind in the act of finding
What will suffice. It has not always had
To find: the scene was set; it repeated what
Was in the script.
                              Then the theatre was changed
To something else. Its past was a souvenir.

It has to be living, to learn the speech of the place.
It has to face the men of the time and to meet
The women of the time. It has to think about war
And it has to find what will suffice. It has
To construct a new stage. It has to be on that stage
And, like an insatiable actor, slowly and
With meditation speak words that in the ear,
In the delicatest ear of the mind, repeat,
Exactly, that which it wants to hear, at the sound
Of which, an invisible audience listens,
Not to the play, but to itself, expressed
In an emotion as of two people, as of two
Emotions becoming one. The actor is
A metaphysician in the dark, twanging
An instrument, twanging a wiry string that gives
Sounds passing through sudden rightnesses, wholly
Containing the mind, below which it cannot descend,
Beyond which it has no will to rise.
                                                      It must
Be the finding of a satisfaction, and may
Be of a man skating, a woman dancing, a woman
Combing. The poem of the act of the mind.

MARTIAL CADENZA

Only this evening I saw again low in the sky
The evening star, at the beginning of winter, the star
That in spring will crown every western horizon,
Again . . . as if it came back, as if life came back,
Not in a later son, a different daughter, another place,
But as if evening found us young, still young,
Still walking in a present of our own.

It was like sudden time in a world without time,
This world, this place, the street in which I was,
Without time: as that which is not has no time,
Is not, or is of what there was, is full
Of the silence before the armies, armies without
Either trumpets or drums, the commanders mute, the arms
On the ground, fixed fast in a profound defeat.

What had this star to do with the world it lit,
With the blank skies over England, over France
And above the German camps? It looked apart.
Yet it is this that shall maintain—Itself
Is time, apart from any past, apart
From any future, the ever-living and being,
The ever-breathing and moving, the constant fire,

The present close, the present realized,
Not the symbol but that for which the symbol stands,
The vivid thing in the air that never changes,
Though the air change. Only this evening I saw it again,
At the beginning of winter, and I walked and talked
Again, and lived and was again, and breathed again
And moved again and flashed again, time flashed again.

DANCE OF THE MACABRE MICE

In the land of turkeys in turkey weather
At the base of the statue, we go round and round.
What a beautiful history, beautiful surprise!
Monsieur is on horseback. The horse is covered with mice.

This dance has no name. It is a hungry dance.
We dance it out to the tip of Monsieur's sword,
Reading the lordly language of the inscription,
Which is like zithers and tambourines combined:

The Founder of the State. Whoever founded
A state that was free, in the dead of winter, from mice?
What a beautiful tableau tinted and towering,
The arm of bronze outstretched against all evil!

THE EMPEROR OF ICE-CREAM

Call the roller of big cigars,
The muscular one, and bid him whip
In kitchen cups concupiscent curds.
Let the wenches dawdle in such dress
As they are used to wear, and let the boys
Bring flowers in last month's newspapers.
Let be be finale of seem.
The only emperor is the emperor of ice-cream.

Take from the dresser of deal,
Lacking the three glass knobs, that sheet
On which she embroidered fantails once
And spread it so as to cover her face.
If her horny feet protrude, they come
To show how cold she is, and dumb.
Let the lamp affix its beam.
The only emperor is the emperor of ice-cream.

ANECDOTE OF THE JAR

I placed a jar in Tennessee,
And round it was, upon a hill.
It made the slovenly wilderness
Surround that hill.

The wilderness rose up to it,
And sprawled around, no longer wild.
The jar was round upon the ground
And tall and of a port in air.

It took dominion everywhere.
The jar was gray and bare.
It did not give of bird or bush,
Like nothing else in Tennessee.

SUNDAY MORNING

Complacencies of the peignoir, and late
Coffee and oranges in a sunny chair,
And the green freedom of a cockatoo
Upon a rug mingle to dissipate
The holy hush of ancient sacrifice.
She dreams a little, and she feels the dark
Encroachment of that old catastrophe,
As a calm darkens among water-lights.
The pungent oranges and bright, green wings
Seem things in some procession of the dead,
Winding across wide water, without sound.
The day is like wide water, without sound,
Stilled for the passing of her dreaming feet
Over the seas, to silent Palestine,
Dominion of the blood and sepulchre.

Why should she give her bounty to the dead?
What is divinity if it can come
Only in silent shadows and in dreams?

Shall she not find in comforts of the sun,
In pungent fruit and bright, green wings, or else
In any balm or beauty of the earth,
Things to be cherished like the thought of heaven?
Divinity must live within herself:
Passions of rain, or moods in falling snow;
Grievings in loneliness, or unsubdued
Elations when the forest blooms; gusty
Emotions on wet roads on autumn nights;
All pleasures and all pains, remembering
The bough of summer and the winter branch.
These are the measures destined for her soul.

Jove in the clouds had his inhuman birth.
No mother suckled him, no sweet land gave
Large-mannered motions to his mythy mind.
He moved among us, as a muttering king,
Magnificent, would move among his hinds,
Until our blood, commingling, virginal,
With heaven, brought such requital to desire
The very hinds discerned it, in a star.
Shall our blood fail? Or shall it come to be
The blood of paradise? And shall the earth
Seem all of paradise that we shall know?
The sky will be much friendlier then than now,
A part of labor and a part of pain,
And next in glory to enduring love,
Not this dividing and indifferent blue.

She says, "I am content when wakened birds,
Before they fly, test the reality
Of misty fields, by their sweet questionings;
But when the birds are gone, and their warm fields
Return no more, where, then, is paradise?"
There is not any haunt of prophecy,
Nor any old chimera of the grave,
Neither the golden underground, nor isle
Melodious, where spirits gat them home,

Nor visionary south, nor cloudy palm
Remote on heaven's hill, that has endured
As April's green endures; or will endure
Like her remembrance of awakened birds,
Or her desire for June and evening, tipped
By the consummation of the swallow's wings.

She says, "But in contentment I still feel
The need of some imperishable bliss."
Death is the mother of beauty; hence from her,
Alone, shall come fulfilment to our dreams
And our desires. Although she strews the leaves
Of sure obliteration on our paths,
The path sick sorrow took, the many paths
Where triumph rang its brassy phrase, or love
Whispered a little out of tenderness,
She makes the willow shiver in the sun
For maidens who were wont to sit and gaze
Upon the grass, relinquished to their feet.
She causes boys to pile new plums and pears
On disregarded plate. The maidens taste
And stray impassioned in the littering leaves.

Is there no change of death in paradise?
Does ripe fruit never fall? Or do the boughs
Hang always heavy in that perfect sky,
Unchanging, yet so like our perishing earth,
With rivers like our own that seek for seas
They never find, the same receding shores
That never touch with inarticulate pang?
Why set the pear upon those river-banks
Or spice the shores with odors of the plum?
Alas, that they should wear our colors there,
The silken weavings of our afternoons,
And pick the strings of our insipid lutes!
Death is the mother of beauty, mystical,
Within whose burning bosom we devise
Our earthly mothers waiting, sleeplessly.

Supple and turbulent, a ring of men
Shall chant in orgy on a summer morn
Their boisterous devotion to the sun,
Not as a god, but as a god might be,
Naked among them, like a savage source.
Their chant shall be a chant of paradise,
Out of their blood, returning to the sky;
And in their chant shall enter, voice by voice,
The windy lake wherein their lord delights,
The trees, like serafim, and echoing hills,
That choir among themselves long afterward.
They shall know well the heavenly fellowship
Of men that perish and of summer morn.
And whence they came and whither they shall go
The dew upon their feet shall manifest.

She hears, upon that water without sound,
A voice that cries, "The tomb in Palestine
Is not the porch of spirits lingering.
It is the grave of Jesus, where He lay."
We live in an old chaos of the sun,
Or old dependency of day and night,
Or island solitude, unsponsored, free,
Of that wide water, inescapable.
Deer walk upon our mountains, and the quail
Whistle about us their spontaneous cries;
Sweet berries ripen in the wilderness;
And, in the isolation of the sky,
At evening, casual flocks of pigeons make
Ambiguous undulations as they sink,
Downward to darkness, on extended wings.

CONVERSATION WITH THREE WOMEN OF NEW ENGLAND

The mode of the person becomes the mode of the world,
For that person, and, sometimes, for the world itself.
The contents of the mind become solid show
Or almost solid seem show—the way a fly bird

Fixes itself in its inevitable bush . . .
It follows that to change modes is to change the world.

Now, you, for instance, are of this mode: You say
That in that ever-dark central, wherever it is,
In the central of earth or sky or thought,
There is a drop that is life's element,
Sole, single source and minimum patriarch,
The one thing common to all life, the human
And inhuman same, the likeness of things unlike.

And you, you say that the capital things of the mind
Should be as natural as natural objects,
So that a carved king found in a jungle, huge
And weathered, should be part of a human landscape,
That a figure reclining among columns toppled down,
Stiff in eternal lethargy, should be,
Not the beginning but the end of artifice,
A nature of marble in a marble world.

And then, finally, it is you that say
That only in man's definitions of himself,
Only encompassed in humanity, is he
Himself. The author of man's canons is man,
Not some outer patron and imaginer.

In which one of these three worlds are the four of us
The most at home? Or is it enough to have seen
And felt and known the difference we have seen
And felt and known in the colors in which we live,
In the excellences of the air we breathe,
The bouquet of being—enough to realize
That the sense of being changes as we talk,
That talk shifts the cycle of the scenes of kings?

THE COMEDIAN AS THE LETTER C

I

The World without Imagination

Nota: man is the intelligence of his soil,
The sovereign ghost. As such, the Socrates
Of snails, musician of pears, principium
And lex. Sed quæritur: is this same wig
Of things, this nincompated pedagogue,
Preceptor to the sea? Crispin at sea
Created, in his day, a touch of doubt.
An eye most apt in gelatines and jupes,
Berries of villages, a barber's eye,
An eye of land, of simple salad-beds,
Of honest quilts, the eye of Crispin, hung
On porpoises, instead of apricots,
And on silentious porpoises, whose snouts
Dibbled in waves that were mustachios,
Inscrutable hair in an inscrutable world.
One eats one paté, even of salt, quotha.
It was not so much the lost terrestrial,
The snug hibernal from that sea and salt,
That century of wind in a single puff.
What counted was mythology of self,
Blotched out beyond unblotching. Crispin,
The lutanist of fleas, the knave, the thane,
The ribboned stick, the bellowing breeches, cloak
Of China, cap of Spain, imperative haw
Of hum, inquisitorial botanist,
And general lexicographer of mute
And maidenly greenhorns, now beheld himself,
A skinny sailor peering in the sea-glass.
What word split up in clickering syllables
And storming under multitudinous tones
Was name for this short-shanks in all that brunt?
Crispin was washed away by magnitude.
The whole of life that still remained in him

Dwindled to one sound strumming in his ear,
Ubiquitous concussion, slap and sigh,
Polyphony beyond his baton's thrust.

Could Crispin stem verboseness in the sea,
The old age of a watery realist,
Triton, dissolved in shifting diaphanes
Of blue and green? A wordy, watery age
That whispered to the sun's compassion, made
A convocation, nightly, of the sea-stars,
And on the clopping foot-ways of the moon
Lay grovelling. Triton incomplicate with that
Which made him Triton, nothing left of him,
Except in faint, memorial gesturings,
That were like arms and shoulders in the waves,
Here, something in the rise and fall of wind
That seemed hallucinating horn, and here,
A sunken voice, both of remembering
And of forgetfulness, in alternate strain.
Just so an ancient Crispin was dissolved.
The valet in the tempest was annulled.
Bordeaux to Yucatan, Havana next,
And then to Carolina. Simple jaunt.
Crispin, merest minuscule in the gales,
Dejected his manner to the turbulence.
The salt hung on his spirit like a frost,
The dead brine melted in him like a dew
Of winter, until nothing of himself
Remained, except some starker, barer self
In a starker, barer world, in which the sun
Was not the sun because it never shone
With bland complaisance on pale parasols,
Beetled, in chapels, on the chaste bouquets.
Against his pipping sounds a trumpet cried
Celestial sneering boisterously. Crispin
Became an introspective voyager.

Here was the veritable ding an sich, at last,
Crispin confronting it, a vocable thing,

But with a speech belched out of hoary darks
Noway resembling his, a visible thing,
And excepting negligible Triton, free
From the unavoidable shadow of himself
That lay elsewhere around him. Severance
Was clear. The last distortion of romance
Forsook the insatiable egotist. The sea
Severs not only lands but also selves.
Here was no help before reality.
Crispin beheld and Crispin was made new.
The imagination, here, could not evade,
In poems of plums, the strict austerity
Of one vast, subjugating, final tone.
The drenching of stale lives no more fell down.
What was this gaudy, gusty panoply?
Out of what swift destruction did it spring?
It was caparison of wind and cloud
And something given to make whole among
The ruses that were shattered by the large.

II

Concerning the Thunderstorms of Yucatan

In Yucatan, the Maya sonneteers
Of the Caribbean amphitheatre,
In spite of hawk and falcon, green toucan
And jay, still to the night-bird made their plea,
As if raspberry tanagers in palms,
High up in orange air, were barbarous.
But Crispin was too destitute to find
In any commonplace the sought-for aid.
He was a man made vivid by the sea,
A man come out of luminous traversing,
Much trumpeted, made desperately clear,
Fresh from discoveries of tidal skies,
To whom oracular rockings gave no rest.
Into a savage color he went on.

How greatly had he grown in his demesne,
This auditor of insects! He that saw
The stride of vanishing autumn in a park
By way of decorous melancholy; he
That wrote his couplet yearly to the spring,
As dissertation of profound delight,
Stopping, on voyage, in a land of snakes,
Found his vicissitudes had much enlarged
His apprehension, made him intricate
In moody rucks, and difficult and strange
In all desires, his destitution's mark.
He was in this as other freemen are,
Sonorous nutshells rattling inwardly.
His violence was for aggrandizement
And not for stupor, such as music makes
For sleepers halfway waking. He perceived
That coolness for his heat came suddenly,
And only, in the fables that he scrawled
With his own quill, in its indigenous dew,
Of an æsthetic tough, diverse, untamed,
Incredible to prudes, the mint of dirt,
Green barbarism turning paradigm.
Crispin foresaw a curious promenade
Or, nobler, sensed an elemental fate,
And elemental potencies and pangs,
And beautiful barenesses as yet unseen,
Making the most of savagery of palms,
Of moonlight on the thick, cadaverous bloom
That yuccas breed, and of the panther's tread.
The fabulous and its intrinsic verse
Came like two spirits parleying, adorned
In radiance from the Atlantic coign,
For Crispin and his quill to catechize.
But they came parleying of such an earth,
So thick with sides and jagged lops of green,
So intertwined with serpent-kin encoiled
Among the purple tufts, the scarlet crowns,
Scenting the jungle in their refuges,

So streaked with yellow, blue and green and red
In beak and bud and fruity gobbet-skins,
That earth was like a jostling festival
Of seeds grown fat, too juicily opulent,
Expanding in the gold's maternal warmth.

So much for that. The affectionate emigrant found
A new reality in parrot-squawks.
Yet let that trifle pass. Now, as this odd
Discoverer walked through the harbor streets
Inspecting the cabildo, the façade
Of the cathedral, making notes, he heard
A rumbling, west of Mexico, it seemed,
Approaching like a gasconade of drums.
The white cabildo darkened, the façade,
As sullen as the sky, was swallowed up
In swift, successive shadows, dolefully.
The rumbling broadened as it fell. The wind,
Tempestuous clarion, with heavy cry,
Came bluntly thundering, more terrible
Than the revenge of music on bassoons.
Gesticulating lightning, mystical,
Made pallid flitter. Crispin, here, took flight.
An annotator has his scruples, too.
He knelt in the cathedral with the rest,
This connoisseur of elemental fate,
Aware of exquisite thought. The storm was one
Of many proclamations of the kind,
Proclaiming something harsher than he learned
From hearing signboards whimper in cold nights
Or seeing the midsummer artifice
Of heat upon his pane. This was the span
Of force, the quintessential fact, the note
Of Vulcan, that a valet seeks to own,
The thing that makes him envious in phrase.

And while the torrent on the roof still droned
He felt the Andean breath. His mind was free

And more than free, elate, intent, profound
And studious of a self possessing him,
That was not in him in the crusty town
From which he sailed. Beyond him, westward, lay
The mountainous ridges, purple balustrades,
In which the thunder, lapsing in its clap,
Let down gigantic quavers of its voice,
For Crispin to vociferate again.

III

Approaching Carolina

The book of moonlight is not written yet
Nor half begun, but, when it is, leave room
For Crispin, fagot in the lunar fire,
Who, in the hubbub of his pilgrimage
Through sweating changes, never could forget
That wakefulness or meditating sleep,
In which the sulky strophes willingly
Bore up, in time, the somnolent, deep songs.
Leave room, therefore, in that unwritten book
For the legendary moonlight that once burned
In Crispin's mind above a continent.
America was always north to him,
A northern west or western north, but north,
And thereby polar, polar-purple, chilled
And lank, rising and slumping from a sea
Of hardy foam, receding flatly, spread
In endless ledges, glittering, submerged
And cold in a boreal mistiness of the moon.
The spring came there in clinking pannicles
Of half-dissolving frost, the summer came,
If ever, whisked and wet, not ripening,
Before the winter's vacancy returned.
The myrtle, if the myrtle ever bloomed,
Was like a glacial pink upon the air.
The green palmettoes in crepuscular ice
Clipped frigidly blue-black meridians,
Morose chiaroscuro, gauntly drawn.

How many poems he denied himself
In his observant progress, lesser things
Than the relentless contact he desired;
How many sea-masks he ignored; what sounds
He shut out from his tempering ear; what thoughts,
Like jades affecting the sequestered bride;
And what descants, he sent to banishment!
Perhaps the Arctic moonlight really gave
The liaison, the blissful liaison,
Between himself and his environment,
Which was, and is, chief motive, first delight,
For him, and not for him alone. It seemed
Illusive, faint, more mist than moon, perverse,
Wrong as a divagation to Peking,
To him that postulated as his theme
The vulgar, as his theme and hymn and flight,
A passionately niggling nightingale.
Moonlight was an evasion, or, if not,
A minor meeting, facile, delicate.
Thus he conceived his voyaging to be
An up and down between two elements,
A fluctuating between sun and moon,
A sally into gold and crimson forms,
As on this voyage, out of goblinry,
And then retirement like a turning back
And sinking down to the indulgences
That in the moonlight have their habitude.
But let these backward lapses, if they would.
Grind their seductions on him, Crispin knew
It was a flourishing tropic he required
For his refreshment, an abundant zone,
Prickly and obdurate, dense, harmonious,
Yet with a harmony not rarefied
Nor fined for the inhibited instruments
Of over-civil stops. And thus he tossed
Between a Carolina of old time,
A little juvenile, an ancient whim,
And the visible, circumspect presentment drawn

From what he saw across his vessel's prow.

He came. The poetic hero without palms
Or jugglery, without regalia.
And as he came he saw that it was spring,
A time abhorrent to the nihilist
Or searcher for the fecund minimum.
The moonlight fiction disappeared. The spring,
Although contending featly in its veils,
Irised in dew and early fragrancies,
Was gemmy marionette to him that sought
A sinewy nakedness. A river bore
The vessel inward. Tilting up his nose,
He inhaled the rancid rosin, burly smells
Of dampened lumber, emanations blown
From warehouse doors, the gustiness of ropes,
Decays of sacks, and all the arrant stinks
That helped him round his rude æsthetic out.
He savored rankness like a sensualist.
He marked the marshy ground around the dock,
The crawling railroad spur, the rotten fence,
Curriculum for the marvelous sophomore.
It purified. It made him see how much
Of what he saw he never saw at all.
He gripped more closely the essential prose
As being, in a world so falsified,
The one integrity for him, the one
Discovery still possible to make,
To which all poems were incident, unless
That prose should wear a poem's guise at last.

IV

The Idea of a Colony

Nota: his soil is man's intelligence.
That's better. That's worth crossing seas to find.
Crispin in one laconic phrase laid bare
His cloudy drift and planned a colony.

Exit the mental moonlight, exit lex,
Rex and principium, exit the whole
Shebang. Exeunt omnes. Here was prose
More exquisite than any tumbling verse:
A still new continent in which to dwell.
What was the purpose of his pilgrimage,
Whatever shape it took in Crispin's mind,
If not, when all is said, to drive away
The shadow of his fellows from the skies,
And, from their stale intelligence released,
To make a new intelligence prevail?
Hence the reverberations in the words
Of his first central hymns, the celebrants
Of rankest trivia, tests of the strength
Of his æsthetic, his philosophy,
The more invidious, the more desired.
The florist asking aid from cabbages,
The rich man going bare, the paladin
Afraid, the blind man as astronomer,
The appointed power unwielded from disdain.
His western voyage ended and began.
The torment of fastidious thought grew slack,
Another, still more bellicose, came on.
He, therefore, wrote his prolegomena,
And, being full of the caprice, inscribed
Commingled souvenirs and prophecies.
He made a singular collation. Thus:
The natives of the rain are rainy men.
Although they paint effulgent, azure lakes,
And April hillsides wooded white and pink,
Their azure has a cloudy edge, their white
And pink, the water bright that dogwood bears.
And in their music showering sounds intone.
On what strange froth does the gross Indian dote,
What Eden sapling gum, what honeyed gore,
What pulpy dram distilled of innocence,
That streaking gold should speak in him
Or bask within his images and words?

If these rude instances impeach themselves
By force of rudeness, let the principle
Be plain. For application Crispin strove,
Abhorring Turk as Esquimau, the lute
As the marimba, the magnolia as rose.

Upon these premises propounding, he
Projected a colony that should extend
To the dusk of a whistling south below the south,
A comprehensive island hemisphere.
The man in Georgia waking among pines
Should be pine-spokesman. The responsive man,
Planting his pristine cores in Florida,
Should prick thereof, not on the psaltery,
But on the banjo's categorical gut,
Tuck, tuck, while the flamingoes flapped his bays.
Sepulchral señors, bibbling pale mescal,
Oblivious to the Aztec almanacs,
Should make the intricate Sierra scan.
And dark Brazilians in their cafés,
Musing immaculate, pampean dits,
Should scrawl a vigilant anthology,
To be their latest, lucent paramour.
These are the broadest instances. Crispin,
Progenitor of such extensive scope,
Was not indifferent to smart detail.
The melon should have apposite ritual,
Performed in verd apparel, and the peach,
When its black branches came to bud, belle day,
Should have an incantation. And again,
When piled on salvers its aroma steeped
The summer, it should have a sacrament
And celebration. Shrewd novitiates
Should be the clerks of our experience.
These bland excursions into time to come,
Related in romance to backward flights,
However prodigal, however proud,
Contained in their afflatus the reproach

That first drove Crispin to his wandering.
He could not be content with counterfeit,
With masquerade of thought, with hapless words
That must belie the racking masquerade,
With fictive flourishes that preordained
His passion's permit, hang of coat, degree
Of buttons, measure of his salt. Such trash
Might help the blind, not him, serenely sly.
It irked beyond his patience. Hence it was,
Preferring text to gloss, he humbly served
Grotesque apprenticeship to chance event,
A clown, perhaps, but an aspiring clown.
There is a monotonous babbling in our dreams
That makes them our dependent heirs, the heirs
Of dreamers buried in our sleep, and not
The oncoming fantasies of better birth.
The apprentice knew these dreamers. If he dreamed
Their dreams, he did it in a gingerly way.
All dreams are vexing. Let them be expunged.
But let the rabbit run, the cock declaim.

Trinket pasticcio, flaunting skyey sheets,
With Crispin as the tiptoe cozener?
No, no: veracious page on page, exact.

V

A Nice Shady Home

Crispin as hermit, pure and capable,
Dwelt in the land. Perhaps if discontent
Had kept him still the pricking realist,
Choosing his element from droll confect
Of was and is and shall or ought to be,
Beyond Bordeaux, beyond Havana, far
Beyond carked Yucatan, he might have come
To colonize his polar planterdom
And jig his chits upon a cloudy knee.
But his emprize to that idea soon sped.

Crispin dwelt in the land and dwelling there
Slid from his continent by slow recess
To things within his actual eye, alert
To the difficulty of rebellious thought
When the sky is blue. The blue infected will.
It may be that the yarrow in his fields
Sealed pensive purple under its concern.
But day by day, now this thing and now that
Confined him, while it cosseted, condoned,
Little by little, as if the suzerain soil
Abashed him by carouse to humble yet
Attach. It seemed haphazard denouement.
He first, as realist, admitted that
Whoever hunts a matinal continent
May, after all, stop short before a plum
And be content and still be realist.
The words of things entangle and confuse.
The plum survives its poems. It may hang
In the sunshine placidly, colored by ground
Obliquities of those who pass beneath,
Harlequined and mazily dewed and mauved
In bloom. Yet it survives in its own form,
Beyond these changes, good, fat, guzzly fruit.
So Crispin hasped on the surviving form,
For him, of shall or ought to be in is.
Was he to bray this in profoundest brass
Arointing his dreams with fugal requiems?
Was he to company vastest things defunct
With a blubber of tom-toms harrowing the sky?
Scrawl a tragedian's testament? Prolong
His active force in an inactive dirge,
Which, let the tall musicians call and call,
Should merely call him dead? Pronounce amen
Through choirs infolded to the outmost clouds?
Because he built a cabin who once planned
Loquacious columns by the ructive sea?
Because he turned to salad-beds again?
Jovial Crispin, in calamitous crape?

Should he lay by the personal and make
Of his own fate an instance of all fate?
What is one man among so many men?
What are so many men in such a world?
Can one man think one thing and think it long?
Can one man be one thing and be it long?
The very man despising honest quilts
Lies quilted to his poll in his despite.
For realists, what is is what should be.

And so it came, his cabin shuffled up,
His trees were planted, his duenna brought
Her prismy blonde and clapped her in his hands,
The curtains flittered and the door was closed.
Crispin, magister of a single room,
Latched up the night. So deep a sound fell down
It was as if the solitude concealed
And covered him and his congenial sleep.
So deep a sound fell down it grew to be
A long soothsaying silence down and down.
The crickets beat their tambours in the wind,
Marching a motionless march, custodians.

In the presto of the morning, Crispin trod,
Each day, still curious, but in a round
Less prickly and much more condign than that
He once thought necessary. Like Candide,
Yeoman and grub, but with a fig in sight,
And cream for the fig and silver for the cream,
A blonde to tip the silver and to taste
The rapey gouts. Good star, how that to be
Annealed them in their cabin ribaldries!
Yet the quotidian saps philosophers
And men like Crispin like them in intent,
If not in will, to track the knaves of thought.
But the quotidian composed as his,
Of breakfast ribands, fruits laid in their leaves,
The tomtit and the cassia and the rose,

Although the rose was not the noble thorn
Of crinoline spread, but of a pining sweet,
Composed of evenings like cracked shutters flung
Upon the rumpling bottomness, and nights
In which those frail custodians watched,
Indifferent to the tepid summer cold,
While he poured out upon the lips of her
That lay beside him, the quotidian
Like this, saps like the sun, true fortuner.
For all it takes it gives a humped return
Exchequering from piebald fiscs unkeyed.

VI

And Daughters with Curls

Portentous enunciation, syllable
To blessed syllable affined, and sound
Bubbling felicity in cantilene,
Prolific and tormenting tenderness
Of music, as it comes to unison,
Forgather and bell boldly Crispin's last
Deduction. Thrum with a proud douceur
His grand pronunciamento and devise.
The chits came for his jigging, bluet-eyed,
Hands without touch yet touching poignantly,
Leaving no room upon his cloudy knee,
Prophetic joint, for its diviner young.
The return to social nature, once begun,
Anabasis or slump, ascent or chute,
Involved him in midwifery so dense
His cabin counted as phylactery,
Then place of vexing palankeens, then haunt
Of children nibbling at the sugared void,
Infants yet eminently old, then dome
And halidom for the unbraided femes,
Green crammers of the green fruits of the world,
Bidders and biders for its ecstasies,

True daughters both of Crispin and his clay.
All this with many multings of the man,
Effective colonizer sharply stopped
In the door-yard by his own capacious bloom.
But that this bloom grown riper, showing nibs
Of its eventual roundness, puerile tints
Of spiced and weathery rouges, should complex
The stopper to indulgent fatalist
Was unforeseen. First Crispin smiled upon
His goldenest demoiselle, inhabitant,
She seemed, of a country of the capuchins,
So delicately blushed, so humbly eyed,
Attentive to a coronal of things
Secret and singular. Second, upon
A second similar counterpart, a maid
Most sisterly to the first, not yet awake
Excepting to the motherly footstep, but
Marvelling sometimes at the shaken sleep.
Then third, a thing still flaxen in the light,
A creeper under jaunty leaves. And fourth,
Mere blusteriness that gewgaws jollified,
All din and gobble, blasphemously pink.
A few years more and the vermeil capuchin
Gave to the cabin, lordlier than it was,
The dulcet omen fit for such a house.
The second sister dallying was shy
To fetch the one full-pinioned one himself
Out of her botches, hot embosomer.
The third one gaping at the orioles
Lettered herself demurely as became
A pearly poetess, peaked for rhapsody.
The fourth, pent now, a digit curious.
Four daughters in a world too intricate
In the beginning, four blithe instruments
Of differing struts, four voices several
In couch, four more personæ, intimate
As buffo, yet divers, four mirrors blue
That should be silver, four accustomed seeds

Hinting incredible hues, four selfsame lights
That spread chromatics in hilarious dark,
Four questioners and four sure answerers.

Crispin concocted doctrine from the rout.
The world, a turnip once so readily plucked,
Sacked up and carried overseas, daubed out
Of its ancient purple, pruned to the fertile main.
And sown again by the stiffest realist,
Came reproduced in purple, family font,
The same insoluble lump. The fatalist
Stepped in and dropped the chuckling down his craw,
Without grace or grumble. Score this anecdote
Invented for its pith, not doctrinal
In form though in design, as Crispin willed,
Disguised pronunciamento, summary,
Autumn's compendium, strident in itself
But muted, mused, and perfectly revolved
In those portentous accents, syllables,
And sounds of music coming to accord
Upon his law, like their inherent sphere,
Seraphic proclamations of the pure
Delivered with a deluging onwardness.
Or if the music sticks, if the anecdote
Is false, if Crispin is a profitless
Philosopher, beginning with green brag,
Concluding fadedly, if as a man
Prone to distemper he abates in taste,
Fickle and fumbling, variable, obscure,
Glozing his life with after-shining flicks,
Illuminating, from a fancy gorged
By apparition, plain and common things,
Sequestering the fluster from the year,
Making gulped potions from obstreperous drops,
And so distorting, proving what he proves
Is nothing, what can all this matter since
The relation comes, benignly, to its end?

So may the relation of each man be clipped.

CRUDE FOYER

Thought is false happiness: the idea
That merely by thinking one can,
Or may, penetrate, not may,
But can, that one is sure to be able—

That there lies at the end of thought
A foyer of the spirit in a landscape
Of the mind, in which we sit
And wear humanity's bleak crown;

In which we read the critique of paradise
And say it is the work
Of a comedian, this critique;
In which we sit and breathe

An innocence of an absolute,
False happiness, since we know that we use
Only the eye as faculty, that the mind
Is the eye, and that this landscape of the mind

Is a landscape only of the eye; and that
We are ignorant men incapable
Of the least, minor, vital metaphor, content,
At last, there, when it turns out to be here.

IT IS THE CELESTIAL ENNUI OF APARTMENTS

It is the celestial ennui of apartments
That sends us back to the first idea, the quick
Of this invention; and yet so poisonous

Are the ravishments of truth, so fatal to
The truth itself, the first idea becomes
The hermit in a poet's metaphors,

Who comes and goes and comes and goes all day.
May there be an ennui of the first idea?
What else, prodigious scholar, should there be?

The monastic man is an artist. The philosopher
Appoints man's place in music, say, today.
But the priest desires. The philosopher desires.

And not to have is the beginning of desire.
To have what is not is its ancient cycle.
It is desire at the end of winter, when

It observes the effortless weather turning blue
And sees the myosotis on its bush.
Being virile, it hears the calendar hymn.

It knows that what it has is what is not
And throws it away like a thing of another time,
As morning throws off stale moonlight and shabby sleep.

THE LION ROARS AT THE ENRAGING DESERT

The lion roars at the enraging desert,
Reddens the sand with his red-colored noise,
Defies red emptiness to evolve his match,

Master by foot and jaws and by the mane,
Most supple challenger. The elephant
Breaches the darkness of Ceylon with blares,

The glitter-goes on surfaces of tanks,
Shattering velvetest far-away. The bear,
The ponderous cinnamon, snarls in his mountain

At summer thunder and sleeps through winter snow.
But you, ephebe, look from your attic window,
Your mansard with a rented piano. You lie

In silence upon your bed. You clutch the corner
Of the pillow in your hand. You writhe and press
A bitter utterance from your writhing, dumb,

Yet voluble of dumb violence. You look
Across the roofs as sigil and as ward
And in your centre mark them and are cowed . . .

These are the heroic children whom time breeds
Against the first idea—to lash the lion,
Caparison elephants, teach bears to juggle.

IT FEELS GOOD AS IT IS WITHOUT THE GIANT

It feels good as it is without the giant,
A thinker of the first idea. Perhaps
The truth depends on a walk around a lake,

A composing as the body tires, a stop
To see hepatica, a stop to watch
A definition growing certain and

A wait within that certainty, a rest
In the swags of pine-trees bordering the lake.
Perhaps there are times of inherent excellence,

As when the cock crows on the left and all
Is well, incalculable balances,
At which a kind of Swiss perfection comes

And a familiar music of the machine
Sets up its Schwärmerei, not balances
That we achieve but balances that happen,

As a man and woman meet and love forthwith.
Perhaps there are moments of awakening,
Extreme, fortuitous, personal, in which

We more than awaken, sit on the edge of sleep,
As on an elevation, and behold
The academies like structures in a mist.

BETHOU ME, SAID SPARROW

Bethou me, said sparrow, to the crackled blade,
And you, and you, bethou me as you blow,
When in my coppice you behold me be.

Ah, ké! the bloody wren, the felon jay,
Ké-ké, the jug-throated robin pouring out,
Bethou, bethou, bethou me in my glade.

There was such idiot minstrelsy in rain,
So many clappers going without bells,
That these bethous compose a heavenly gong.

One voice repeating, one tireless chorister,
The phrases of a single phrase, ké-ké,
A single text, granite monotony,

One sole face, like a photograph of fate,
Glass-blower's destiny, bloodless episcopus,
Eye without lid, mind without any dream—

These are of minstrels lacking minstrelsy,
Of an earth in which the first leaf is the tale
Of leaves, in which the sparrow is a bird

Of stone, that never changes. Bethou him, you
And you, bethou him and bethou. It is
A sound like any other. It will end.

SOLDIER, THERE IS A WAR BETWEEN THE MIND

Soldier, there is a war between the mind
And sky, between thought and day and night. It is
For that the poet is always in the sun,

Patches the moon together in his room
To his Virgilian cadences, up down,
Up down. It is a war that never ends.

Yet it depends on yours. The two are one.
They are a plural, a right and left, a pair,
Two parallels that meet if only in

The meeting of their shadows or that meet
In a book in a barrack, a letter from Malay.
But your war ends. And after it you return

With six meats and twelve wines or else without
To walk another room . . . Monsieur and comrade,
The soldier is poor without the poet's lines,

His petty syllabi, the sounds that stick,
Inevitably modulating, in the blood.
And war for war, each has its gallant kind.

How simply the fictive hero becomes the real;
How gladly with proper words the soldier dies,
If he must, or lives on the bread of faithful speech.

From *Notes Toward a Supreme Fiction*

MRS. ALFRED URUGUAY

So what said the others and the sun went down
And, in the brown blues of evening, the lady said,
In the donkey's ear, "I fear that elegance

Must struggle like the rest." She climbed until
The moonlight in her lap, mewing her velvet,
And her dress were one and she said, "I have said no
To everything, in order to get at myself.
I have wiped away moonlight like mud. Your innocent ear
And I, if I rode naked, are what remain."

The moonlight crumbled to degenerate forms,
While she approached the real, upon her mountain,
With lofty darkness. The donkey was there to ride,
To hold by the ear, even though it wished for a bell,
Wished faithfully for a falsifying bell.
Neither the moonlight could change it. And for her,
To be, regardless of velvet, could never be more
Than to be, she could never differently be,
Her no and no made yes impossible.

Who was it passed her there on a horse all will,
What figure of capable imagination?
Whose horse clattered on the road on which she rose,
As it descended, blind to her velvet and
The moonlight? Was it a rider intent on the sun,
A youth, a lover with phosphorescent hair,
Dressed poorly, arrogant of his streaming forces,
Lost in an integration of the martyrs' bones,
Rushing from what was real; and capable?

The villages slept as the capable man went down,
Time swished on the village clocks and dreams were alive,
The enormous gongs gave edges to their sounds,
As the rider, no chevalere and poorly dressed,
Impatient of the bells and midnight forms,
Rode over the picket rocks, rode down the road,
And, capable, created in his mind,
Eventual victor, out of the martyrs' bones,
The ultimate elegance: the imagined land.

PRESENCE OF AN EXTERNAL MASTER OF KNOWLEDGE

Under the shape of his sail, Ulysses,
Symbol of the seeker, crossing by night
The giant sea, read his own mind.
He said, "As I know, I am and have
The right to be." He guided his boat
Beneath the middle stars and said:

"Here I feel the human loneliness
And that, in space and solitude,
Which knowledge is: the world and fate,
The right within me and about me,
Joined in a triumphant vigor,
Like a direction on which I depend . . .

A longer, deeper breath sustains
This eloquence of right, since knowing
And being are one—the right to know
Is equal to the right to be.
The great Omnium descends on me,
Like an absolute out of this eloquence."

The sharp sail of Ulysses seemed,
In the breathings of that soliloquy,
Alive with an enigma's flittering,
And bodying, and being there,
As he moved, straightly, on and on,
Through clumped stars dangling all the way.

CONTINUAL CONVERSATION WITH A SILENT MAN

The old brown hen and the old blue sky,
Between the two we live and die—
The broken cartwheel on the hill.

As if, in the presence of the sea,
We dried our nets and mended sail
And talked of never-ending things,

Of the never-ending storm of will,
One will and many wills, and the wind,
Of many meanings in the leaves,

Brought down to one below the eaves,
Link, of that tempest, to the farm,
The chain of the turquoise hen and sky

And the wheel that broke as the cart went by.
It is not a voice that is under the eaves.
It is not speech, the sound we hear

In this conversation, but the sound
Of things and their motion: the other man,
A turquoise monster moving round.

HOLIDAY IN REALITY

I

It was something to see that their white was different,
Sharp as white paint in the January sun;

Something to feel that they needed another yellow,
Less Aix than Stockholm, hardly a yellow at all,

A vibrancy not to be taken for granted, from
A sun in an almost colorless, cold heaven.

They had known that there was not even a common speech,
Palabra of a common man who did not exist.

Why should they not know they had everything of their own
As each had a particular woman and her touch?

After all, they knew that to be real each had
To find for himself his earth, his sky, his sea.

And the words for them and the colors that they possessed.
It was impossible to breathe at Durand-Ruel's.

II

The flowering Judas grows from the belly or not at all.
The breast is covered with violets. It is a green leaf.

Spring is umbilical or else it is not spring.
Spring is the truth of spring or nothing, a waste, a fake.

These trees and their argentines, their dark-spiced branches,
Grow out of the spirit or they are fantastic dust.

The bud of the apple is desire, the down-falling gold,
The catbird's gobble in the morning half-awake—

These are real only if I make them so. Whistle
For me, grow green for me and, as you whistle and grow
    green,

Intangible arrows quiver and stick in the skin
And I taste at the root of the tongue the unreal of what is real.

Trumbull Stickney

MT. LYKAION

Alone on Lykaion since man hath been
Stand on the height two columns, where at rest
Two eagles hewn of gold sit looking East
Forever; and the sun goes up between.
Far down around the mountain's oval green
An order keeps the falling stones abreast.
Below within the chaos last and least
A river like a curl of light is seen.
Beyond the river lies the even sea,
Beyond the sea another ghost of sky,—
O God, support the sickness of my eye
Lest the far space and long antiquity
Suck out my heart, and on this awful ground
The great wind kill my little shell with sound.

THE SOUL OF TIME

                   Time's a circumference
Whereof the segment of our station seems
A long straight line from nothing into naught.
Therefore we say "progress," "infinity"—
Dull words whose object
Hangs in the air of error and delights
Our boyish minds ahunt for butterflies.
For aspiration studies not the sky
But looks for stars; the victories of faith
Are soldiered none the less with certainties,
And all the multitudinous armies decked
With banners blown ahead and flute before
March not to the desert or th' Elysian fields,
But in the track of some discovery,
The grip and cognizance of something true,
Which won resolves a better distribution
Between the dreaming mind and real truth.

I cannot understand you.
                        'Tis because
You lean over my meaning's edge and feel
A dizziness of the things I have not said.

BE STILL. THE HANGING GARDENS WERE A DREAM

Be still. The Hanging Gardens were a dream
That over Persian roses flew to kiss
The curlèd lashes of Semiramis.
Troy never was, nor green Skamander stream.
Provence and Troubadour are merest lies,
The glorious hair of Venice was a beam
Made within Titian's eye. The sunsets seem,
The world is very old and nothing is.
Be still. Thou foolish thing, thou canst not wake,
Nor thy tears wedge thy soldered lids apart,

But patter in the darkness of thy heart.
Thy brain is plagued. Thou art a frighted owl
Blind with the light of life thou'ldst not forsake,
And error loves and nourishes thy soul.

LIVE BLINDLY

Live blindly and upon the hour. The Lord,
Who was the Future, died full long ago.
Knowledge which is the Past is folly. Go,
Poor child, and be not to thyself abhorred.
Around thine earth sun-wingèd winds do blow
And planets roll; a meteor draws his sword;
The rainbow breaks his seven-coloured chord
And the long strips of river-silver flow:
Awake! Give thyself to the lovely hours.
Drinking their lips, catch thou the dream in flight
About their fragile hairs' aërial gold.
Thou art divine, thou livest,—as of old
Apollo springing naked to the light,
And all his island shivered into flowers.

ON SOME SHELLS FOUND INLAND

These are my murmur-laden shells that keep
A fresh voice tho' the years lie very gray.
The wave that washed their lips and tuned their lay
Is gone, gone with the faded ocean sweep,
The royal tide, gray ebb and sunken neap
And purple midday,—gone! To this hot clay
Must sing my shells, where yet the primal day,
Its roar and rhythm and splendour will not sleep.
What hand shall join them to their proper sea
If all be gone? Shall they forever feel
Glories undone and worlds that cannot be?—
'T were mercy to stamp out this agèd wrong,
Dash them to earth and crunch them with the heel
And make a dust of their seraphic song.

Ruth Stone

THE MAGNET

I loved my lord, my black-haired lord, my young love
Thin faced, pointed like a fox,
And he, singing and sighing, with the bawdy went crying
Up the hounds, through thicket he leaped, through bramble,
And crossed the river on rocks.
And there alongside the sheep and among the ewes and lambs,
With terrible sleep he cunningly laid his hoax.

Ah fey, and ill-gotten, and wicked his tender heart,
Even as they with their bahs and their niggles, rumped up the
    thistle and bit
With their delicate teeth the flowers and the seeds and the leaf,
He leaped with a cry as coarse as the herders, "Come, I will
    start,
Come now my pretties, and dance, to the hunting horn and
    the slit
Of your throbbing throats, and make me a coat out of grief."
And they danced, he was fey, they did dance, and the coat
    they made
Turned all of an innocent mind, and a single love, into beasts
    afraid.

Was it I called him back? was it hunger? was it the world?
Not my tears, not those cries of the murdered, but 'twas the fox
Hid in the wood who called, and the smell of the fox, burned
    in his mind,
The fox in his den, smiling, around his red body his fine plume
    curled,
Out of the valley and across the river, leaving his sheep's hair,
    he left the maligned flocks,
I heard him coming through brambles, through narrow forests,
    I bid my nights unwind,
I bid my days turn back, I broke my windows, I unsealed my
    locks.

Allen Tate

THE MEDITERRANEAN

Quem das finem, rex magne, dolorum?

Where we went in the boat was a long bay
A slingshot wide, walled in by towering stone—
Peaked margin of antiquity's delay,
And we went there out of time's monotone:

Where we went in the black hull no light moved
But a gull white-winged along the feckless wave,
The breeze, unseen but fierce as a body loved,
That boat drove onward like a willing slave:

Where we went in the small ship the seaweed
Parted and gave to us the murmuring shore
And we made feast and in our secret need
Devoured the very plates Aeneas bore:

Where derelict you see through the low twilight
The green coast that you, thunder-tossed, would win,
Drop sail, and hastening to drink all night
Eat dish and bowl to take that sweet land in!

Where we feasted and caroused on the sandless
Pebbles, affecting our day of piracy,
What prophecy of eaten plates could landless
Wanderers fulfil by the ancient sea?

We for that time might taste the famous age
Eternal here yet hidden from our eyes
When lust of power undid its stuffless rage;
They, in a wineskin, bore earth's paradise.

Let us lie down once more by the breathing side
Of Ocean, where our live forefathers sleep
As if the Known Sea still were a month wide—
Atlantis howls but is no longer steep!

What country shall we conquer, what fair land
Unman our conquest and locate our blood?
We've cracked the hemispheres with careless hand!
Now, from the Gates of Hercules we flood

Westward, westward till the barbarous brine
Whelms us to the tired land where tasseling corn,
Fat beans, grapes sweeter than muscadine
Rot on the vine: in that land were we born.

SONNETS AT CHRISTMAS

I

This is the day His hour of life draws near,
Let me get ready from head to foot for it
Most handily with eyes to pick the year
For small feed to reward a feathered wit.
Some men would see it an epiphany
At ease, at food and drink, others at chase
Yet I, stung lassitude, with ecstasy
Unspent argue the season's difficult case
So: Man, dull critter of enormous head,
What would he look at in the coiling sky?
But I must kneel again unto the Dead
While Christmas bells of paper white and red,
Figured with boys and girls spilt from a sled,
Ring out the silence I am nourished by.

II

Ah, Christ, I love you rings to the wild sky
And I must think a little of the past:
When I was ten I told a stinking lie
That got a black boy whipped; but now at last
The going years, caught in an accurate glow,
Reverse like balls englished upon green baize—
Let them return, let the round trumpets blow
The ancient crackle of the Christ's deep gaze.
Deafened and blind, with senses yet unfound,

Am I, untutored to the after-wit
Of knowledge, knowing a nightmare has no sound;
Therefore with idle hands and head I sit
In late December before the fire's daze
Punished by crimes of which I would be quit.

AENEAS AT WASHINGTON

I myself saw furious with blood
Neoptolemus, at his side the black Atridae,
Hecuba and the hundred daughters, Priam
Cut down, his filth drenching the holy fires.
In that extremity I bore me well,
A true gentleman, valorous in arms,
Disinterested and honourable. Then fled:
That was a time when civilization
Run by the few fell to the many, and
Crashed to the shout of men, the clang of arms:
Cold victualing I seized, I hoisted up
The old man my father upon my back,
In the smoke made by sea for a new world
Saving little—a mind imperishable
If time is, a love of past things tenuous
As the hesitation of receding love.

(To the reduction of uncitied littorals
We brought chiefly the vigor of prophecy,
Our hunger breeding calculation
And fixed triumphs)

I saw the thirsty dove
In the glowing fields of Troy, hemp ripening
And tawny corn, the thickening Blue Grass
All lying rich forever in the green sun.
I see all things apart, the towers that men
Contrive I too contrived long, long ago.
Now I demand little. The singular passion
Abides its object and consumes desire
In the circling shadow of its appetite.
There was a time when the young eyes were slow,

Their flame steady beyond the firstling fire,
I stood in the rain, far from home at nightfall
By the Potomac, the great Dome lit the water,
The city my blood had built I knew no more
While the screech-owl whistled his new delight
Consecutively dark.

                                        Stuck in the wet mire
Four thousand leagues from the ninth buried city
I thought of Troy, what we had built her for.

WINTER MASK

To the memory of W. B. Yeats

Towards nightfall when the wind
Tries the eaves and casements
(A winter wind of the mind
Long gathering its will)
I lay the mind's contents
Bare, as upon a table,
And ask, in a time of war,
Whether there is still
To a mind frivolously dull
Anything worth living for.

If I am meek and dull
And a poor sacrifice
Of perverse will to cull
The act from the attempt,
Just look into damned eyes
And give the returning glare;
For the damned like it, the more
Damnation is exempt
From what would save its heir
With a thing worth living for.

The poisoned rat in the wall
Cuts through the wall like a knife,
Then blind, drying, and small
And driven to cold water,
Dies of the water of life:
Both damned in eternal ice,
The traitor become the boor
Who had led his friend to slaughter,
Now bites his head—not nice,
The food that he lives for.

I supposed two scenes of hell,
Two human bestiaries,
Might uncommonly well
Convey the doom I thought;
But lest the horror freeze
The gentler estimation
I go to the sylvan door
Where nature has been bought
In rational proration
As a thing worth living for.

Should the buyer have been
    beware?
It is an uneven trade
For man has wet his hair
Under the winter weather
With only fog for shade:
His mouth a bracketed hole
Picked by the crows that bore
Nature to their hanged
    brother,
Who rattles against the bole
The thing that he lived for.

I asked the master Yeats
Whose great style could not
    tell
Why it is man hates
His own salvatiòn,
Prefers the way to hell,
And finds his last safety
In the self-made curse that
    bore
Him towards damnatiòn:
The drowned undrowned by
    the sea,
The sea worth living for.

SEASONS OF THE SOUL

To the memory of John Peale Bishop, 1892–1944

*Allor porsi la mano un poco avante,
e colsi un ramicel da un gran pruno;
e il tronco suo gridò: Perchè mi schiante?*

I. SUMMER

Summer, this is our flesh,
The body you let mature;
If now while the body is
    fresh
You take it, shall we give
The heart, lest heart endure
The mind's tattering
Blow of greedy claws?
Shall mind itself still live
If like a hunting king
It falls to the lion's jaws?

Under the summer's blast
The soul cannot endure

Unless by sleight or fast
It seize or deny its day
To make the eye secure.
Brothers-in-arms, remember
The hot wind dries and
    draws
With circular delay
The flesh, ash from the
    ember,
Into the summer's jaws.

It was a gentle sun
When, at the June solstice

Green France was overrun
With caterpillar feet.
No head knows where its rest
    is
Or may lie down with reason
When war's usurping claws
Shall take the heart escheat—
Green field in burning season
To stain the weevil's jaws.

The southern summer dies
Evenly in the fall:
We raise our tired eyes
Into a sky of glass,
Blue, empty, and tall
Without tail or head
Where burn the equal laws
For Balaam and his ass
Above the invalid dead,
Who cannot lift their jaws.

When was it that the
    summer
(Daylong a liquid light)

And a child, the new-comer,
Bathed in the same green
    spray,
Could neither guess the
    night?
The summer had no reason;
Then, like a primal cause
It had its timeless day
Before it kept the season
Of time's engaging jaws.

Two men of our summer
    world
Descended winding hell
And when their shadows
    curled
They fearfully confounded
The vast concluding shell:
Stopping, they saw in the
    narrow
Light a centaur pause
And gaze, then his astounded
Beard, with a notched arrow,
Part back upon his jaws.

II. AUTUMN

It had an autumn smell
And that was how I knew
That I was down a well:
I was no longer young;
My lips were numb and blue,
The air was like fine sand
In a butcher's stall
Or pumice to the tongue:

And when I raised my hand
I stood in the empty hall.

The round ceiling was high
And the gray light like shale
Thin, crumbling and dry:
No rug on the bare floor
Nor any carved detail

To which the eye could glide;
I counted along the wall
Door after closed door
Through which a shade
    might slide
To the cold and empty hall.

I will leave this house, I
    said,
There is the autumn
    weather—
Here, nor living nor dead;
The lights burn in the town
Where men fear together.
Then on the bare floor,
But tiptoe lest I fall,
I walked years down
Towards the front door
At the end of the empty hall.

The door was false—no key
Or lock, and I was caught
In the house; yet I could see
I had been born to it
For miles of running brought
Me back where I began.
I saw now in the wall

A door open a slit
And a fat grizzled man
Come out into the hall:

As in a moonlit street
Men meeting are too shy
To check their hurried feet
But raise their eyes and
    squint
As through a needle's eye
Into the faceless gloom,—
My father in a gray shawl
Gave me an unseeing glint
And entered another room!
I stood in the empty hall

And watched them come and
    go
From one room to another,
Old men, old women—slow,
Familiar; girls, boys;
I saw my downcast mother
Clad in her street-clothes,
Her blue eyes long and small,
Who had no look or voice
For him whose vision froze
Him in the empty hall.

III. WINTER

Goddess sea-born and bright,
Return into the sea
Where eddying twilight
Gathers upon your people—
Cold goddess, hear our plea!

Leave the burnt earth, Venus,
For the drying God above,
Hanged in his windy steeple,
No longer bears for us
The living wound of love.

All the sea-gods are dead.
You, Venus, come home
To your salt maidenhead,
The tossed anonymous sea
Under shuddering foam—
Shade for lovers, where
A shark swift as your dove
Shall pace our company
All night to nudge and tear
The livid wound of love.

And now the winter sea:
Within her hollow rind
What sleek facility
Of sea-conceited scop
To plumb the nether mind!
Eternal winters blow
Shivering flakes, and shove
Bodies that wheel and drop—
Cold soot upon the snow
Their livid wound of love.

Beyond the undertow
The gray sea-foliage
Transpires a phosphor glow
Into the circular miles:
In the centre of his cage
The pacing animal

Surveys the jungle cove
And slicks his slithering wiles
To turn the venereal awl
In the livid wound of love.

Beyond the undertow
The rigid madrepore
Resists the winter's flow—
Headless, unageing oak
That gives the leaf no more.
Wilfully as I stood
Within the thickest grove
I seized a branch, which
    broke;
I heard the speaking blood
(From the livid wound of
    love)

Drip down upon my toe:
'We are the men who died
Of self-inflicted woe,
Lovers whose stratagem
Led to their suicide.'
I touched my sanguine hair
And felt it drip above
Their brother who, like them,
Was maimed and did not
    bear
The living wound of love.

IV. SPRING

Irritable spring, infuse
Into the burning breast
Your combustible juice
That as a liquid soul
Shall be the body's guest

Who lights, but cannot stay
To comfort this unease
Which, like a dying coal,
Hastens the cooler day
Of the mother of silences.

Back in my native prime
I saw the orient corn
All space but no time,
Reaching for the sun
Of the land where I was
    born:
It was a pleasant land
Where even death could
    please
Us with an ancient pun—
All dying for the hand
Of the mother of silences.

In time of bloody war
Who will know the time?
Is it a new spring star
Within the timing chill,
Talking, or just a mime,
That rises in the blood—
Thin Jack-and-Jilling seas
Without the human will?
Its light is at the flood,
Mother of silences!

It burns us each alone
Whose burning arrogance
Burns up the rolling stone,
This earth—Platonic cave
Of vertiginous chance!
Come, tired Sisyphus,

Cover the cave's egress
Where light reveals the slave,
Who rests when sleeps with
    us
The mother of silences.

Come, old woman, save
Your sons who have gone
    down
Into the burning cave:
Come, mother, and lean
At the window with your son
And gaze through its light
    frame
These fifteen centuries
Upon the shirking scene
Where men, blind, go lame:
Then, mother of silences,

Speak, that we may hear;
Listen, while we confess
That we conceal our fear;
Regard us, while the eye
Discerns by sight or guess
Whether, as sheep foregather
Upon their crooked knees,
We have begun to die;
Whether your kindness,
    mother,
Is mother of silences.

MORE SONNETS AT CHRISTMAS

Ten Years Later

I

Again the native hour lets down the locks
Uncombed and black, but gray the bobbing beard;
Ten years ago His eyes, fierce shuttlecocks,
Pierced the close net of what I failed: I feared
The belly-cold, the grave-clout, that betrayed
Me dithering in the drift of cordial seas;
Ten years are time enough to be dismayed
By mummy Christ, head crammed between his knees.

Suppose I take an arrogant bomber, stroke
By stroke, up to the frazzled sun to hear
Sun-ghostlings whisper: Yes, the capital yoke—
Remove it and there's not a ghost to fear
This crucial day, whose decapitate joke
Languidly winds into the inner ear.

II

The day's at end and there's nowhere to go,
Draw to the fire, even this fire is dying;
Get up and once again politely lying
Invite the ladies toward the mistletoe
With greedy eyes that stare like an old crow.
How pleasantly the holly wreaths did hang
And how stuffed Santa did his reindeer clang
Above the golden oaken mantel, years ago!

Then hang this picture for a calendar,
As sheep for goat, and pray most fixedly
For the cold martial progress of your star,
With thoughts of commerce and society,
Well-milked Chinese, Negroes who cannot sing,
The Huns gelded and feeding in a ring.

III

Give me this day a faith not personal
As follows: The American people fully armed
With assurance policies, righteous and harmed,
Battle the world of which they're not at all.
That lying boy of ten who stood in the hall,
His hat in hand (thus by his father charmed:
"You may be President"), was not alarmed
Nor even left uneasy by his fall.

Nobody said that he could be a plumber,
Carpenter, clerk, bus-driver, bombardier;
Let little boys go into violent slumber,
Aegean squall and squalor where their fear
Is of an enemy in remote oceans
Unstalked by Christ: these are the better notions.

IV

Gay citizen, myself, and thoughtful friend,
Your ghosts are Plato's Christians in the cave.
Unfix your necks, turn to the door; the nave
Gives back the cheated and light dividend
So long sequestered; now, new-rich, you'll spend
Flesh for reality inside a stone
Whose light obstruction, like a gossamer bone,
Dead or still living, will not break or bend.

Thus light, your flesh made pale and sinister
And put off like a dog that's had his day,
You will be Plato's kept philosopher,
Albino man bleached from the mortal clay,
Mild-mannered, gifted in your master's ease
While the sun squats upon the waveless seas.

Edward Taylor

UPON A SPIDER CATCHING A FLY

Thou sorrow, venom Elf:
  Is this thy play,
To spin a web out of thyself
  To Catch a Fly?
    For why?

I saw a pettish wasp
  Fall foul therein:
Whom yet thy whorl pins did
    not hasp
  Lest he should fling
    His sting.

But as afraid, remote
  Didst stand hereat,
And with thy little fingers
    stroke
  And gently tap
    His back.

Thus gently him didst treat
  Lest he should pet,
And in a froppish, aspish
    heat
  Should greatly fret
    Thy net.

Whereas the silly Fly,
  Caught by its leg,
Thou by the throat took'st
    hastily,
  And 'hind the head
    Bite Dead.

This goes to pot, that not
  Nature doth call.
Strive not above what
    strength hath got,
  Lest in the brawl
    Thou fall.

This Fray seems thus to us:
  Hell's Spider gets
His intrails spun to whip
    Cords thus,
  And wove to nets,
    And sets.

To tangle Adam's race
  In's stratagems
To their Destructions,
    Spoil'd, made base
  By venom things,
    Damn'd Sins.

But mighty, Gracious Lord,
  Communicate
Thy Grace to break the Cord;
    afford
  Us Glory's Gate
    And State.

We'll Nightingale sing like,
  When perch'd on high
In Glory's Cage, thy glory,
    bright:
  Yea, thankfully,
    For joy.

HOUSEWIFERY

Make me, O Lord, thy Spinning Wheel complete;
   Thy Holy Word my Distaff make for me.
Make mine Affections thy Swift Flyers neat,
   And make my Soul thy holy Spool to be.
   My Conversation make to be thy Reel,
   And reel the yarn thereon spun of thy Wheel.

Make me thy Loom then, knit therein this Twine:
   And make thy Holy Spirit, Lord, wind quills:
Then weave the Web thyself. The yarn is fine.
   Thine Ordinances make my Fulling Mills.
   Then die the same in Heavenly Colours Choice,
   All pink'd with Varnish'd Flowers of Paradise.

Then clothe, therewith mine Understanding, Will,
   Affections, Judgment, Conscience, Memory;
My Words and Actions, that their shine may fill
   My ways with glory and thee glorify.
   Then mine apparel shall display before ye
   That I am Cloth'd in Holy robes for glory.

THE REFLECTION

Lord, art thou at the Table Head above
   Meat, Med'cine, Sweetness, sparkling Beauties, to
Enamour Souls with Flaming Flakes of Love,
   And not my Trencher, nor my Cup o'erflow?
   Ben't I a bidden guest? Oh! sweat mine Eye:
   O'erflow with Tears: Oh! draw thy fountains dry.

Shall I not smell thy sweet, oh! Sharon's Rose?
   Shall not mine Eye salute thy Beauty? Why?
Shall thy sweet leaves their Beauteous sweets upclose?
   As half ashamed my sight should on them lie?
   Woe's me! For this my sighs shall be in grain,
   Offer'd on Sorrow's Altar for the same.

Had not my Soul's, thy Conduit, Pipes stopt been
    With mud, what Ravishment would'st thou Convey?
Let Grace's Golden Spade dig till the Spring
    Of tears arise, and clear this filth away.
    Lord, let thy Spirit raise my sighings till
    These Pipes my soul do with thy sweetness fill.

Earth once was Paradise of Heaven below,
    Till inkefac'd sin had it with poyson stockt;
And Chast this Paradise away into
    Heav'ns upmost Loft, and it in Glory Lockt.
    But thou, sweet Lord, hast with thy golden Key
    Unlockt the Door, and made a golden day.

Once at thy Feast, I saw thee Pearle-like stand
    'Tween Heaven and Earth, where Heaven's Bright glory all
In streams fell on thee, as a floodgate and
    Like Sun Beams through thee on the World to Fall.
    Oh! Sugar sweet then! My Deare sweet Lord, I see
    Saints' Heaven-lost Happiness restor'd by thee.

Shall Heaven and Earth's bright Glory all up lie,
    Like Sun Beams bundled in the sun in thee?
Dost thou sit Rose at Table Head, where I
    Do sit, and Carv'st no morsel sweet for me?
    So much before, so little now! Sprindge, Lord,
    Thy Rosy Leaves, and me their Glee afford.

Shall not thy Rose my Garden fresh perfume?
    Shall not thy Beauty my dull Heart assail?
Shall not thy golden gleams run through this gloom?
    Shall my black Velvet Mask thy fair Face Veil?
    Pass o'er my Faults: shine forth, bright sun; arise!
    Enthrone thy Rosy-self within mine Eyes.

SACRAMENTAL MEDITATION VI

Am I thy gold? Or Purse, Lord, for thy Wealth;
  Whether in mine or mint refind for thee?
I'm counted so, but count me o'er thyself,
  Lest gold washt face, and brass in Heart I be.
  I Fear my Touchstone touches when I try
  Me, and my Counted Gold too overly.

Am I new minted by thy Stamp indeed?
  Mine Eyes are dim; I cannot clearly see.
Be thou my Spectacles that I may read
  Thine Image and Inscription stampt on me.
  If thy bright Image do upon me stand,
  I am a Golden Angel in thy hand.

Lord, make my Soul thy Plate: thine Image bright
  Within the Circle of the same enfoil.
And on its brims in golden Letters write
  Thy Superscription in an Holy style.
  Then I shall be thy Money, thou my Hoard:
  Let me thy Angel be, be thou my Lord.

Dunstan Thompson

A KNIGHT OF GHOSTS AND SHADOWS

Cold. Cold. Cold winds and colder heart.
The night blows cold from East to West, and love
Grows cold as England. What fire consoles? Prove
Me these smiles, these fair ways, and here swear no hurt
To death, else cavalier lies hand in glove
With gentlemen of gravest fashion. I move
Wands, wishes. But you stand still and words apart.

Silence. And all my sailing lovers come
To grief, cry up a violent sea, wraith-tossed

Unlucky sea, the sea whose lustrous ghost
Glides through the central blue, your eyes. This time
Is tidal. Mariners of friendship, lost
Greenmen by harbor mouth, who, kissing almost
Their own land, foundered, here watch my welcome home.

Now when the fire fails and loneliness kills
And the soul longs to be gone from where it is,
I appear bemused to you, wondering—would a kiss
Make the gesture, or change of feature? How these miles
Between us freeze, sparkling through darkness. His
Hands, one thinks, might film my murder but miss
The meaning, as though that wedding bell which chills
You rang for the dead. "Remember, whom no one wills
Love to, whom no one tries to cherish." Unless
This weather for despair breaks soon, the trees
Are hung with suicides. And what of these guiles,
These gaudy manners, should your flatterer's dress
Be pockets out and no cash left? May it please
God, you shall have a good friend. This rude air stills.
And I imagine roses for a moment on the winter hills.

NOR MARS HIS SWORD

To Richard Hager

My life is legends of the yellow haired
Who coin their eyes with money from my hand
And, seeing through me their good looks endeared
To the rough boatman, go, laughing, to a far land.
Each burnished boy, his riches squandered, spends
My fortune to persuade me we are friends.

You were the first—but may not be the last
Contriver, O death-in-life long lover. Time
Which we failed at school; time when devotions past
Reason ransacked us—what moonlight for crime:
That time runs out. Now I oppose a bad age
With courage. And you in a wrecked square rage.

Tomorrow I may not give you. But today
My heart, as instance, for your faithful watch?
Why, you shall have it, if one word I say
Lights up the nightshade by a striking match.
You turned me once against myself, and for
Your welfare I can offer nothing more.

At moments such as this my failure takes
Wing like the swan, and, singing, flies through death,
Air of the sad daredevil. Tears, these snowflakes,
Mantle the ruined duchies underneath
My eyes. "God have mercy on us both," you said,
And looked in the mirror at the glassy dead.

Angel of anguish, suicidal saint,
Dear friend with a sunburst for a martyr's crown,
I am your praising enemy, a faint
Fellow, but the broken voice is still my own.
Pray, rest—the world is wide awake. In heaven,
I believe, even our deaths are forgiven.

THE LAY OF THE BATTLE OF TOMBLAND

"Whatever you want is yours,"
    Said the Man with the Lopside Head;
"Girls, diamonds, and motor cars,
    If you'll love me, love me in bed."

So he prayed, and the sirens sang
    Their wrongs, O sang to me
Lost in the blackout, "You're young
    But wait till you're old as we."

I stayed where I was, afraid
    To leave the Club Foot Man;
"Behind the mirror," he said, "we'll hide.
    The dead have a death-ray plan."

"Welcome! Welcome!" the searchlights wrote.
  "The End of the World is here."
They spelt their names and then went out,
  And the poor lay everywhere.

What could I cry but "Bombs Away,"
  When the Man who was Hunchback spoke.
"O live through this, and be my boy,"
  He laughed, and his true voice broke.

"God, be nimble," the dicers begged,
  "Christ, be quick;" but they rolled too short,
Their fears embraced, and the whirlers bragged
  "In our heartbreak arms is sport."

The Harelip Man knelt down to drink
  Blood from the sewers, swore
"You'll kiss me yet, and you'll thank
  Me later, later, after the war."

Through air of flares the statues ran
  Shrouded in silk. "Be warned,"
They wirelessed, "for marble men
  Are the friends you never mourned."

O bathed in fire my mobster stood,
  The Man with the Artificial Eyes,
"Falling in love with love," he said,
  "Is falling in love with lies."

This piteous city gave up the ghost
  In the toll of all her towers;
Parachute princes held me fast,
  "Rest," they ordered, "the rest is ours."

John Thompson, Jr.

A LOVE FOR PATSY

See the little maunderer
Stretch out on the grass!
His heart is burst asunder
The pieces cry Alas.

Upright, fat pink pieces
Of fluffy cloud float overhead.
The little facets of his eyes
Split by salty tears, so tired

Of seeing pieces of the world,
Close, and rustling grass,
Caws of an old unpleasant bird
Are sounds that say Alas;

They float like notes in the funny paper,
Round notes with sharp little tails.
Oh I'm blue, the supine moper
Says, I'm trapped in the toils

Of Patsy's black black hair.
Her hair is like the cool dry night
That waves through the window-bar
Where a moody jailbird sits apart

Shuffling his broken heart. I'm sad
As I can be. Her black
Black hair can never be compared
To dull dichotomic

Trees or prickly grass, inflated
Clouds, even a great
One draped on the sun. Over-rated
Senseless things to stare at,

One here one there they're strewn,
Impinging pieces left out of
The world. Her eyes are green!
Oh oh, he says, I die of love.

See the weeping little wretch
He rolls in a frenzy!
In all the world no two things match
But the green eyes of Patsy.

Henry David Thoreau

SIC VITA

I am a parcel of vain strivings tied
    By a chance bond together,
Dangling this way and that, their links
    Were made so loose and wide,
            Methinks,
        For milder weather.

A bunch of violets without their roots,
    And sorrel intermixed,
Encircled by a wisp of straw
    Once coiled about their shoots,
            The law
        By which I'm fixed.

A nosegay which Time clutched from out
    Those fair Elysian fields,
With weeds and broken stems, in haste,
    Doth make the rabble rout
            That waste
        The day he yields.

And here I bloom for a short hour unseen,
  Drinking my juices up,
    With no root in the land
      To keep my branches green,
        But stand
        In a bare cup.

Some tender buds were left upon my stem
  In mimicry of life,
    But ah! the children will not know,
      Till time has withered them,
        The woe
        With which they're rife.

But now I see I was not plucked for naught,
  And after in life's vase
    Of glass set while I might survive,
      But by a kind hand brought
        Alive
        To a strange place.

That stock thus thinned will soon redeem its hours,
  And by another year,
    Such as God knows, with freer air,
      More fruits and fairer flowers
        Will bear,
        While I droop here.

WINTER MEMORIES

Within the circuit of this plodding life
There enter moments of an azure hue,
Untarnished fair as is the violet
Or anemone, when the spring strews them
By some meandering rivulet, which make
The best philosophy untrue that aims
But to console man for his grievances.

I have remembered when the winter came,
High in my chamber in the frosty nights,
When in the still light of the cheerful moon,
On every twig and rail and jutting spout,
The icy spears were adding to their length
Against the arrows of the coming sun,
How in the shimmering noon of summer past
Some unrecorded beam slanted across
The upland pastures where the Johnswort grew;
Or heard, amid the verdure of my mind,
The bee's long smothered hum, on the blue flag
Loitering amidst the mead; or busy rill,
Which now through all its course stands still and dumb
Its own memorial,—purling at its play
Along the slopes, and through the meadows next,
Until its youthful sound was hushed at last
In the staid current of the lowland stream;
Or seen the furrows shine but late upturned,
And where the fieldfare followed in the rear,
When all the fields around lay bound and hoar
Beneath a thick integument of snow.
So by God's cheap economy made rich
To go upon my winter's task again.

Parker Tyler

TO A PHOTOGRAPH

To Ch. B.

It is the littleness I would keep
    Of this big frail moment, or the frail
Bigness and qualitative issue of it, for
    It is a thing of lines, this amorphous
        Being that
        I would keep.

And now is set its law: as of a
 Crystal age whose masses pierce and pierce
The white depth of the page, easily
 And automatically, as the
  Letters beat on,
  And the words.

The crystalline great sex: that
 Hiding behind all lighted planes, round
As a rose, whose leaf is the poem, whose
 Child is surfaces, such as this
  Snapshot, precise
  And yet blurred.

Neither can arms embrace the typewriter
 Nor, though instanter life should leave
Me, any air give birth except to breath
 Alone. But somewhere love corpuscular
  Imitates cor-
  Puscular love!

For that crook of leg, and thickness
 Of flesh, and fold of lax and simple
Tension, in those: look! is a music
 Caught and reduced, whose wild vast
  Will threatened death
  To kiss it all.

And did, in a way; and in more ways, when
 The light taps and the soft vents of verse
And glance's infinitesimal weight
 Of wing, stole along life's great
  Abstract curves, so
  Formless there till now.

So substanceless till now: the true sag
 And sift of monumental gaze
Theoretically having for all time's warp

Itself to gag and give, weep on and woo,
    Muffled above, and
    Below, with ink.

Organically, I move with all my
    Named and nameless fingers, where the voice
Shows as on a map, nowhere, the single
    Sigh that delivers up, and will,
        All history's weft
        To syllabled lip.

For this, deep, would I not keep it still
    Because I could not, shallow, unless I
Statued it as statues do, but would I,
    Making all lucid, keep its loose matter-
        Of-fact mystery
        Of all frames clear,

Where, dubious at night and solemn-quick,
    The heart's eye, and the twin breasts', hug
Those paths no camera took, or ever can,
    Swallowed their own motion, and dead their rhythm:
        Immutable to rhyme,
        Impossible to scan.

Mark Van Doren

THE DISTANT RUNNERS

Six great horses of Spain, set free after his death by De Soto's men, ran West and restored to America the wild race lost there some thousands of years ago.   —A legend.

    Ferdinand De Soto lies
    Soft again in river mud.
    Birds again, as on the day
    Of his descending, rise and go

Straightly West, and do not know
Of feet beneath that faintly thud.

If I were there in other time,
Between the proper sky and stream;
If I were there and saw the six
Abandoned manes, and ran along,
I could sing the fetlock song
That now is chilled within a dream.

Ferdinand De Soto, sleeping
In the river, never heard
Four-and-twenty Spanish hooves
Fling off their iron and cut the green,
Leaving circles new and clean
While overhead the wing-tips whirred.

Neither I nor any walker
By the Mississippi now
Can see the dozen nostrils open
Half in pain for death of men—
But half in gladness, neighing then
As loud as loping would allow.

On they rippled, tail and back,
A prairie day, and swallows knew
A dark, uneven current there.
But not a sound came up the wind,
And toward the night their shadow thinned
Before the black that flooded through.

If I were there to bend and look,
The sky would know them as they sped
And turn to see. But I am here,
And they are far, and time is old.
Within my dream the grass is cold;
The legs are locked; the sky is dead.

Mona Van Duyn

THE GENTLE SNORER

When summer came, we locked up our lives and fled
to the woods in Maine, and pulled up over our heads
a comforter filled with batts of piney dark,
tied with crickets' chirretings and the *bork*
of frogs; we hid in a sleep of strangeness from
the human humdrum.

A pleasant noise the unordered world makes wove
around us. Burrowed, we heard the scud of waves,
wrack of bending branch, or plop of a fish
on his heavy home; the little beasts rummaged the brush.
We dimmed to silence, slipped from the angry pull
of wishes and will.

And then we had a three-weeks cabin guest
who snored; he broke the otherness of our rest.
As all night long he sipped the succulent air,
that rhythm we shared made visible to the ear
a rich refreshment of the blood. We fed in
unison with him.

A sound we dreamed and woke to, over the snuff
of wind, not loud enough to scare off the roof
the early morning chipmunks. Under our skins
we heard, as after disease, the bright, thin
tick of our time. Sleeping, he mentioned death
and celebrated breath.

He went back home. The water flapped the shore.
A thousand bugs drilled at the darkness. Over
the lake a loon howled. Nothing spoke up for us,
Salvagers always of what we have always lost;
and we thought that what the night needed was more of man,
he left us so partisan.

Byron Vazakas

THE PAVILION ON THE PIER

A sunstruck spray sifts back breakwater waves,
while out the bay a cackling naphtha launch
slits water whitely up the back. I squint
behind sunglasses with their green ground glass,
and stomp the steel-strut pier whose fishhooks hook
the fish, our kindred; and stuffed seagulls dive
to rise like mermaids at the Hippodrome.
Horsehair horizons pencil-line my eyes
till backward, on the boardwalk, grandma rides
her wicker rolling chair, and bats the breeze.
And backward, on a fatal figure-eight,
I'm somersaulted to a child again.
Head over heels . . . still, clammy hands hold tight
that waltz with mother like a record grooved
three-quarter time in pity. But the salt
air heals the salt rubbed in by coming back
till recognition rounds a sheepish grin
at mother as a whalebone collared Madame
X, the unknown woman; and the looking back
sands down disaster to a souvenir
of polk-a-dotted parasols above the beach
where mother sits forever for her photograph.

MIDSUMMER NIGHT'S DREAM

The canvas leaves, the painted trees
    seem natural. Perspectives deepen
    with the curtain's rise; and the
    back-drop swims in a pale blue

Light. The music fades out quietly.
    The audience crinkles the programs,
    and awaits the act. All eyes turn
    toward the stage, as though a

Single face looked forth; as though a
    single wish became the characters
    beyond the footlights and the red
    plush seats. This is the forest

Of all imagining; this is the unheard
    orchestra, the music of the mind.
    Here, foliage is rich and dark
    and sensual; and silence is a

Place. As love seems understanding,
    so this forest's mystery becomes
    desire accomplished, the ripened
    promise of desire fulfilled. In

Grottoes of damp, the trickling water
    cools the mossy stones. The
    insects hum. The verdure glistens.
    The moonlight, like the audience,

Seems true, or more so, the imaginary
    raised to the imaginative.
    Beyond the haze of balconies,
    the tensing dreams attain reality,

And the actual becomes their gift.
    The stage is a mirror where
    the actors amplify the self,
    communicate the personal. Puck

And the lovers play out plots,
    investigate dilemmas soon
    dissolved. Within this wood
    the secret and delightful night

Exists forever. Oberon sparkles
    like madness. And like a child,
    Titania strokes the ass's head
    beneath his dark and lucid gaze.

Jones Very

THE HAND AND FOOT

The hand and foot that stir not, they shall find
Sooner than all the rightful place to go:
Now in their motion free as roving wind,
Though first no snail so limited and slow;
I mark them full of labor all the day,
Each active motion made in perfect rest;
They cannot from their path mistaken stray,
Though 't is not theirs, yet in it they are blest;
The bird has not their hidden track found out,
The cunning fox though full of art he be;
It is the way unseen, the certain route,
Where ever bound, yet thou art ever free;
The path of Him, whose perfect law of love
Bids spheres and atoms in just order move.

YOURSELF

'Tis to yourself I speak; you cannot know
Him whom I call in speaking such a one,
For you beneath the earth lie buried low,
Which he alone as living walks upon:
You may at times have heard him speak to you,
And often wished perchance that you were he;
And I must ever wish that it were true,
For then you could hold fellowship with me:
But now you hear us talk as strangers, met
Above the room wherein you lie abed;
A word perhaps loud spoken you may get,
Or hear our feet when heavily they tread;
But he who speaks, or him who's spoken to,
Must both remain as strangers still to you.

Robert Penn Warren

REVELATION

Because he had spoken harshly to his mother,
The day became astonishingly bright,
The enormity of distance crept to him like a dog now,
And earth's own luminescence seemed to repel the night.

Loud the roof was rent like paper torn to admit
Sun-sulphurous splendor where had been before
But the submarine glimmer by kindly countenances lit,
As slow, phosphorescent dignities light the ocean floor.

By walls, by walks, chrysanthemum and aster,
All hairy, fat-petalled species, lean, confer,
And his ears, and heart, should burn at that insidious whisper
Which concerns him so, he knows; but he cannot make out
  the words.

The peacock screamed, and his feathered fury made
Legend shake, all day, while the sky ran pale as milk;
That night, all night, the buck rabbit stamped in the moonlit
  glade,
And the owl's brain glowed like a coal in the grove's com-
  bustible, dark.

When Sulla smote and Rome was rent, Augustine
Recalled how Nature, shuddering, tore her gown,
And kind changed kind, and the blunt herbivorous tooth
  dripped blood;
At Duncan's death, at Dunsinane, chimneys blew down.

But, oh! his mother was kinder than ever Rome,
Dearer than Duncan—no wonder, then, Nature's frame
Thrilled in voluptuous hemispheres far off from his home;
But not in terror: only as the bride, as the bride.

In separateness only does love learn definition,
Though Brahma smiles beneath the dappled shade,

Though tears, that night, wet the pillow where the boy's head
    was laid
Dreamless of splendid antipodal agitation;

And though across what tide and tooth Time is,
He was to lean back toward that recalcitrant face,
He would think, than Sulla more fortunate, how once he had
    learned
Something important above love, and about love's grace.

PURSUIT

The hunchback on the corner, with gum and shoelaces,
Has his own wisdom and pleasures, and may not be lured
To divulge them to you, for he has merely endured
Your appeal for his sympathy and your kind purchases;

And wears infirmity but as the general who turns
Apart, in his famous old greatcoat there on the hill
At dusk when the rapture and cannonade are still,
To muse withdrawn from the dead, from his gorgeous
    subalterns;

Or stares from the thicket of his familiar pain, like a fawn
That meets you a moment, wheels, in imperious innocence is
    gone.

Go to the clinic. Wait in the outer room
Where like an old possum the snag-nailed hand will hump
On its knee in murderous patience, and the pomp
Of pain swells like the Indies, or a plum.

And there you will stand, as on the Roman hill,
Stunned by each withdrawn gaze and severe shape,
The first barbarian victor stood to gape
At the sacrificial fathers, white-robed, still;

And even the feverish old Jew stares stern with authority
Till you feel like one who has come too late, or improperly
    clothed, to a party.

The doctor will take you now. He is burly and clean;
Listening, like lover or worshiper, bends at your heart;
But cannot make out just what it tries to impart;
So smiles; says you simply need a change of scene.

Of scene, of solace: therefore Florida,
Where Ponce de Leon clanked among the lilies,
Where white sails skit on blue and cavort like fillies,
And the shoulder gleams in the moonlit corridor.
A change of love: if love is a groping Godward, though blind,
No matter what crevice, creek, chink, bright in dark, the pale
    tentacle find.

In Florida consider the flamingo
Its color passion but its neck a question;
Consider even that girl the other guests shun
On beach, at bar, in bed, for she may know
The secret you are seeking, after all;
Or the child you humbly sit by, excited and curly,
That screams on the shore at the sea's sunlit hurlyburly,
Till the mother calls its name, toward nightfall.
Till you sit alone: in the dire meridians, off Ireland, in fury
Of spume-tooth and dawnless sea-heave, salt rimes the look-
    out's devout eye.

Till you sit alone—which is the beginning of error—
Behind you the music and lights of the great hotel:
Solution, perhaps, is public, despair personal,
But history held to your breath clouds like a mirror.
There are many states, and towns in them, and faces,
But meanwhile, the little old lady in black, by the wall,
Who admires all the dancers, and tells you how just last fall
Her husband died in Ohio, and damp mists her glasses;
She blinks & croaks, like a toad or a Norn, in the horrible light,
And rattles her crutch, which may put forth a small bloom,
    perhaps white.

TERROR

I Volontari Americani Presso Eserciti Stranieri Non Perdono La Cittadinanza.
Il Messaggero, Roma, Sabato, 27 Gennaio, 1940.

Not picnics or pageants or the improbable
Powers of air whose tongues exclaim dominion
And gull the great man to follow his terrible
Star, suffice; not the window-box, or the bird on

The ledge, which means so much to the invalid,
Nor the joy you leaned after, as by the tracks the grass
In the emptiness after the lighted Pullmans fled,
Suffices; nor faces, which, like distraction, pass
Under the street-lamps, teasing to faith or pleasure,
Suffice you, born to no adequate definition of terror.

For yours, like a puppy, is darling and inept,
Though his cold nose brush your hand while you laugh at his
    clowning;
Or the kitten you sleep with, though once or twice while you
    slept
It tried to suck your breath, and you dreamed of drowning,
Perjured like Clarence, sluiced from the perilous hatches;
But never of lunar wolf-waste or the arboreal
Malignancy, with the privy breath, which watches
And humps in the dark; but only a dream, after all.
At the worst, you think, with a little twinge of distress,
That contagion may nook in the comforting fur you love to
    caress.

Though some, unsatisfied and sick, have sought
That immitigable face, whose smile is ice,
And fired their hearts like pitch-pine, for they thought
Rather flame than the damp worm-tooth of compromise:
So Harry L. I knew, whose whores and gin
Had dwindled to a slick smile in the drug store
But for the absurd contraption of a plane,
Which flung on air the unformulable endeavor
While heart bled speed to lave the applauded name.
The crash was in an old cornfield; not even flame.

So some, whose passionate emptiness and tidal
Lust swayed toward the debris of Madrid,
And left New York to loll in their fierce idyll
Among the olives, where the snipers hid;
And now the North, to seek that visioned face
And polarize their iron of despair,
Who praise no beauty like the boreal grace

Which greens the dead eye under the rocket's flare.
They fight old friends, for their obsession knows
Only the immaculate itch, not human friends or foes.

They sought a secret which fat Franco's Moor,
Hieratic, white-robed, pitiless, might teach,
Who duped and dying but for pride, therefore
Hugged truth which cause or conscience scarcely reach.
As Jacob all night with the angelic foe,
They wrestled him who did not speak, but died,
And wrestle now, by frozen fen and floe,
New Courier, in fury sanctified;
And seek that face which, greasy, frost-breathed, in furs,
Bends to the bomb-sight over bitter Helsingfors.

Blood splashed on the terrorless intellect creates
Corrosive fizzle like the spattered lime,
And its enseamed stew but satiates
Itself, in that lewd and faceless pantomime.
You know, by radio, how hotly the world repeats,
When the brute crowd roars or the blunt boot-heels resound
In the Piazza or the Wilhelmplatz,
The crime of Onan, spilled upon the ground;
You know, whose dear hope Alexis Carrel kept
Alive in a test tube, where it monstrously grew, and slept.

But it is dead, and you now, guiltless, sink
To rest in lobbies, or pace gardens where
The slow god crumbles and the fountains prink,
Nor heed the criminal king, who paints the air
With discoursed madness and protruding eye,
Nor give the alarm, nor ask tonight where sleeps
That head which hooped the jewel Fidelity,
But like an old melon now, in the dank ditch, seeps;
But you crack nuts, while the conscience-stricken stare
Kisses the terror; for you see an empty chair.

Edward Weismiller

TO THE WOMAN IN BOND STREET STATION

Madam, you are right; the fight was a great pity.
Two soldiers against a third, an ally—perhaps
No worse could befall, as you feel, in this tense city.

Violence broke out so sharply: sudden fear
Fell on the watchers, who recoiled, and gasped,
And did not recall the girl who had disappeared.

Certainly the boy alone was very young.
It was brutal to smash at him so with the torch. But, madam,
Though what I mean, and would say, is not on my tongue,

It was late; all three are gone now, home to their places,
Their hatreds dimmed. And those who today are damned
Are not such furious boys with blood on their faces.

John Hall Wheelock

AFTERNOON: AMAGANSETT BEACH

                              The broad beach,
Sea-wind and the sea's irregular rhythm,
Great dunes with their pale grass, and on the beach
Driftwood, tangle of bones, an occasional shell,
Now coarse, now carven and delicate—whorls of time

Stranded in space, deaf ears listening
To lost time, old oceanic secrets.
Along the water's edge, in pattern casual
As the pattern of the stars, the pin-point air-holes
Left by the sand-flea under the receding spume
Wink and blink out again. A gull drifts over,
Wide wings crucified against the sky—
His shadow travels the shore, upon its margins
You will find his signature: one long line,
Two shorter lines curving out from it, a nearly
Perfect graph of the bird himself in flight.
His footprint is his image fallen from heaven.

Walt Whitman

I CELEBRATE MYSELF

I celebrate myself, and sing myself,
And what I assume you shall assume,
For every atom belonging to me as good belongs to you.
I loafe and invite my soul,
I lean and loafe at my ease observing a spear of summer grass.
My tongue, every atom of my blood, form'd from this soil,
    this air,
Born here of parents born here from parents the same, and
    their parents the same,
I, now thirty-seven years old in perfect health begin,
Hoping to cease not till death.
Creeds and schools in abeyance,
Retiring back a while sufficed at what they are, but never
    forgotten,
I harbor for good or bad, I permit to speak at every hazard,
Nature without check with original energy.

From Song of Myself

DAREST THOU NOW O SOUL

Darest thou now O soul,
Walk out with me toward the unknown region,
Where neither ground is for the feet nor any path to follow?

No map there, nor guide,
Nor voice sounding, nor touch of human hand,
Nor face with blooming flesh, nor lips, nor eyes, are in that
        land.

I know it not O soul,
Nor dost thou, all is a blank before us,
All waits undream'd of in that region, that inaccessible land.

Till when the ties loosen,
All but the ties eternal, Time and Space,
Nor darkness, gravitation, sense, nor any bounds bounding us.

Then we burst forth, we float,
In Time and Space O soul, prepared for them,
Equal, equipt at last, (O joy! O fruit of all!) them to fulfil
        O soul.

WHISPERS OF HEAVENLY DEATH

Whispers of heavenly death murmur'd I hear,
Labial gossip of night, sibilant chorals,
Footsteps gently ascending, mystical breezes wafted soft and
        low,
Ripples of unseen rivers, tides of a current flowing, forever
        flowing,
(Or is it the plashing of tears? the measureless waters of hu-
        man tears?)

I see, just see skyward, great cloud-masses,
Mournfully slowly they roll, silently swelling and mixing,
With at times a half-dimm'd, sadden'd far-off star,
Appearing and disappearing.

(Some parturition rather, some solemn immortal birth;
On the frontiers to eyes impenetrable,
Some soul is passing over.)

ANIMALS

I think I could turn and live with animals, they are so placid
  and self-contained;
I stand and look at them long and long,
They do not sweat and whine about their condition;
They do not lie awake in the dark and weep for their sins;
They do not make me sick discussing their duty to God;
Not one is dissatisfied—not one is demented with the mania of
  owning things;
Not one kneels to another, nor to his kind that lived thousands
  of years ago;
Not one is respectable or industrious over the whole earth.

From Song of Myself

GRASS

A child said *What is the grass?* fetching it to me with full
  hands;
How could I answer the child? I do not know what it is any
  more than he.

I guess it must be the flag of my disposition, out of hopeful
  green stuff woven.
Or I guess it is the handkerchief of the Lord,
A scented gift and remembrancer designedly dropt,
Bearing the owner's name some way in the corners, that we
  may see and remark, and say *Whose?*
Or I guess the grass is itself a child, the produced babe of the
  vegetation.
Or I guess it is a uniform hieroglyphic,
And it means, Sprouting alike in broad zones and narrow
  zones,
Growing among black folks as among white,
Kanuck, Tuckahoe, Congressman, Cuff, I give them the same,
  I receive them the same.

And now it seems to me the beautiful uncut hair of graves.
Tenderly will I use you curling grass,
It may be you transpire from the breasts of young men,
It may be if I had known them I would have loved them,
It may be you are from old people, or from offspring taken
    soon out of their mother's laps,
And here you are the mother's laps.

This grass is very dark to be from the white heads of old
    mothers,
Darker than the colorless beards of old men,
Dark to come from under the faint red roofs of mouths.

O I perceive after all so many uttering tongues,
And I perceive they do not come from the roofs of mouths for
    nothing.
I wish I could translate the hints about the dead young men
    and women,
And the hints about old men and mothers, and the offspring
    taken soon out of their laps.

What do you think has become of the young and old men?
And what do you think has become of the women and chil-
    dren?

They are alive and well somewhere,
The smallest sprout shows there is really no death,
And if ever there was it led forward life, and does not wait at
    the end to arrest it,
And ceas'd the moment life appear'd.
All goes onward and outward, nothing collapses,
And to die is different from what any one supposed, and
    luckier.

From *Song of Myself*

MY BARBARIC YAWP

The spotted hawk swoops by and accuses me, he complains
    of my gab and my loitering.
I too am not a bit tamed, I too am untranslatable,
I sound my barbaric yawp over the roofs of the world.

The last scud of day holds back for me,
It flings my likeness after the rest and true as any on the
    shadow'd wilds,
It coaxes me to the vapor and the dusk.

I depart as air, I shake my white locks at the runaway sun,
I effuse my flesh in eddies, and drift it in lacy jags.
I bequeath myself to the dirt to grow from the grass I love,
If you want me again look for me under your boot-soles.

You will hardly know what I am or what I mean,
But I shall be good health to you nevertheless,
And filter and fibre your blood.

Failing to fetch me at first keep encouraged,
Missing me one place search another,
I stop somewhere waiting for you.

From Song of Myself

O CAPTAIN! MY CAPTAIN!

O Captain! my Captain! our fearful trip is done,
The ship has weather'd every rack, the prize we sought is won,
The port is near, the bells I hear, the people all exulting,
While follow eyes the steady keel, the vessel grim and daring;
        But O heart! heart! heart!
          O the bleeding drops of red,
            Where on the deck my Captain lies,
             Fallen cold and dead.

O Captain! my Captain! rise up and hear the bells;
Rise up—for you the flag is flung—for you the bugle trills,
For you bouquets and ribbon'd wreaths—for you the shores
   a-crowding,
For you they call, the swaying mass, their eager faces turning;
       Here Captain! dear father!
         The arm beneath your head!
          It is some dream that on the deck,
           You've fallen cold and dead.

My Captain does not answer, his lips are pale and still,
My father does not feel my arm, he has no pulse nor will,
The ship is anchor'd safe and sound, its voyage closed and
   done,
From fearful trip the victor ship comes in with object won;
       Exult O shores, and ring O bells!
        But I with mournful tread,
         Walk the deck my Captain lies,
         Fallen cold and dead.

OUT OF THE CRADLE ENDLESSLY ROCKING

Out of the cradle endlessly rocking,
Out of the mocking-bird's throat, the musical shuttle,
Out of the Ninth-month midnight,
Over the sterile sands and the fields beyond, where the child
   leaving his bed wandered alone, bareheaded, barefoot,
Down from the showered halo,
Up from the mystic play of shadows twining and twisting as
   if they were alive,
Out from the patches of briers and blackberries,
From the memories of the bird that chanted to me,
From your memories, sad brother, from the fitful risings and
   fallings I heard,
From under that yellow half-moon late-risen and swollen as if
   with tears,
From those beginning notes of yearning and love there in the
   mist,

From the thousand responses of my heart never to cease,
From the myriad thence-aroused words,
From the word stronger and more delicious than any,
From such as now they start the scene revisiting,
As a flock, twittering, rising, or overhead passing,
Borne hither, ere all eludes me, hurriedly,
A man, yet by these tears a little boy again,
Throwing myself on the sand, confronting the waves,
I, chanter of pains and joys, uniter of here and hereafter,
Taking all hints to use them, but swiftly leaping beyond them,
A reminiscence sing.

Once Paumanok,
When the lilac-scent was in the air and Fifth-month grass was
    growing,
Up this seashore in some briers,
Two feathered guests from Alabama, two together,
And their nest, and four light-green eggs spotted with brown,
And every day the he-bird to and fro near at hand,
And every day the she-bird crouched on her nest, silent, with
    bright eyes,
And every day I, a curious boy, never too close, never disturb-
    ing them,
Cautiously peering, absorbing, translating.

Shine! shine! shine!
Pour down your warmth, great sun!
While we bask, we two together.
Two together!
Winds blow south, or winds blow north,
Day come white, or night come black,
Home, or rivers and mountains from home,
Singing all time, minding no time,
While we two keep together.

Till of a sudden,
Maybe killed, unknown to her mate,
One forenoon the she-bird crouched not on the nest,
Nor returned that afternoon, nor the next,

Nor ever appeared again.
And thenceforward all summer in the sound of the sea,
And at night under the full of the moon in calmer weather,
Over the hoarse surging of the sea,
Or flitting from brier to brier by day,
I saw, I heard at intervals the remaining one, the he-bird,
The solitary guest from Alabama.
Blow! blow! blow!
Blow up sea-winds along Paumanok's shore;
I wait and I wait till you blow my mate to me.
Yes, when the stars glistened,
All night long on the prong of a moss-scalloped stake,
Down almost amid the slapping waves,
Sat the lone singer wonderful causing tears.

He called on his mate,
He poured forth the meanings which I of all men know.
Yes, my brother, I know,—
The rest might not, but I have treasured every note,
For more than once dimly down to the beach gliding,
Silent, avoiding the moonbeams, blending myself with the
    shadows,
Recalling now the obscure shapes, the echoes, the sounds and
    sights after their sorts,
The white arms out in the breakers tirelessly tossing,
I, with bare feet, a child, the wind wafting my hair,
Listened long and long.
Listened to keep, to sing, now translating the notes,
Following you, my brother.

Soothe! soothe! soothe!
Close on its wave soothes the wave behind,
And again another behind embracing and lapping, every one
    close,
But my love soothes not me, not me.
Low hangs the moon, it rose late,
It is lagging—O I think it is heavy with love, with love.
O madly the sea pushes upon the land,
With love, with love.

*O night! do I not see my love fluttering out among the
    breakers?*
What is that little black thing I see there in the white?
Loud! loud! loud!
Loud I call to you, my love!
High and clear I shoot my voice over the waves,
Surely you must know who is here, is here,
You must know who I am, my love.
Low-hanging moon!
What is that dusky spot in your brown yellow?
O it is the shape, the shape of my mate!
O moon, do not keep her from me any longer.
Land! land! O land!
*Whichever way I turn, O I think you could give me my mate
    back again if you only would,*
For I am almost sure I see her dimly whichever way I look.
O rising stars!
*Perhaps the one I want so much will rise, will rise with some
    of you.*
O throat! O trembling throat!
Sound clearer through the atmosphere!
Pierce the woods, the earth,
Somewhere listening to catch you must be the one I want.
Shake out carols!
Solitary here, the night's carols!
Carols of lonesome love! death's carols!
Carols under that lagging, yellow, waning moon!
*O under that moon where she droops almost down into the
    sea!*
O reckless despairing carols!
But soft! sink low!
Soft! let me just murmur,
And do you wait a moment, you husky-noised sea,
For somewhere I believe I heard my mate responding to me,
So faint, I must be still, be still to listen,
*But not altogether still, for then she might not come imme-
    diately to me.*

Hither, my love!
Here I am! here!
With this just-sustained note I announce myself to you,
This gentle call is for you my love, for you.

Do not be decoyed elsewhere:
That is the whistle of the wind, it is not my voice,
That is the fluttering, the fluttering of the spray,
Those are the shadows of leaves.

O darkness! O in vain!
O I am very sick and sorrowful.
O brown halo in the sky near the moon, drooping upon the
* sea!*
O troubled reflection in the sea!
O throat! O throbbing heart!
And I singing uselessly, uselessly all the night.

O past! O happy life! O songs of joy!
In the air, in the woods, over fields,
Loved! loved! loved! loved! loved!
But my mate no more, no more with me!
We two together no more.

The aria sinking.
All else continuing, the stars shining,
The winds blowing, the notes of the bird continuous echoing,
With angry moans the fierce old mother incessantly moaning,
On the sands of Paumanok's shore gray and rustling,
The yellow half-moon enlarged, sagging down, drooping, the
  face of the sea almost touching,
The boy ecstatic, with his bare feet the waves, with his hair
  the atmosphere dallying,
The love in the heart long pent, now loose, now at last tumul-
  tuously bursting,
The aria's meaning, the ears, the soul, swiftly depositing,
The strange tears down the cheeks coursing,
The colloquy there, the trio, each uttering,

The undertone, the savage old mother incessantly crying,
To the boy's soul's questions sullenly timing, some drowned
secret hissing,
To the outsetting bard.

Demon or bird (said the boy's soul)
Is it indeed toward your mate you sing? or is it really to me?
For I, that was a child, my tongue's use sleeping, now I have
heard you,
Now in a moment I know what I am for, I awake,
And already a thousand singers, a thousand songs, clearer,
louder and more sorrowful than yours,
A thousand warbling echoes have started to life within me,
never to die.

O you singer solitary, singing by yourself, projecting me,
O solitary me listening, never more shall I cease perpetuating
you,
Never more shall I escape, never more the reverberations,
Never more the cries of unsatisfied love be absent from me.
Never again leave me to be the peaceful child I was before
what there in the night,
By the sea under the yellow and sagging moon,
The messenger there aroused, the fire, the sweet hell within,
The unknown want, the destiny of me.
O give me the clew! (It lurks in the night here somewhere)
O if I am to have so much, let me have more!
A word then, (for I will conquer it)
The word final, superior to all,
Subtle, sent up—what is it?—I listen;
Are you whispering it, and have been all the time, you sea-
waves?
Is that it from your liquid rims and wet sands?

Whereto answering, the sea,
Delaying not, hurrying not,
Whispered me through the night, & very plainly before day-
break,
Lisped to me the low and delicious word death,

And again death, death, death, death,
Hissing melodious, neither like the bird nor like my aroused
    child's heart,
But edging near as privately for me, rustling at my feet,
Creeping thence steadily up to my ears and laving me softly
    all over,
Death, death, death, death, death.

Which I do not forget,
But fuse the song of my dusky demon and brother,
That he sang to me in the moonlight on Paumanok's gray
    beach,
With the thousand responsive songs at random,
My own songs awaked from that hour,
And with them the key, the word up from the waves,
The word of the sweetest song and all songs,
That strong and delicious word which, creeping to my feet,
(Or like some old crone rocking the cradle, swathed in sweet
    garments, bending aside)
The sea whispered me.

A NOISELESS PATIENT SPIDER

A noiseless patient spider,
I mark'd where on a little promontory it stood isolated,
Mark'd how to explore the vacant vast surrounding,
It launch'd forth filament, filament, filament, out of itself.
Ever unreeling them, ever tirelessly speeding them.

And you O my soul where you stand,
Surrounded, detached, in measureless oceans of space,
Ceaselessly musing, venturing, throwing, seeking the spheres
    to connect them.
Till the bridge you will need be form'd, till the ductile anchor
    hold,
Till the gossamer thread you fling catch somewhere, O my
    soul.

NATIVE MOMENTS

Native moments—when you come upon me—ah you are here
    now,
Give me now libidinous joys only,
Give me the drench of my passions, give me life coarse and
    rank,
To-day I go consort with Nature's darlings, to-night too,
I am for those who believe in loose delights, I share the mid-
    night orgies of young men,
I dance with the dancers and drink with the drinkers,
The echoes ring with our indecent calls, I pick out some low
    person for my dearest friend,
He shall be lawless, rude, illiterate, he shall be one condemned
    by others for deeds done,
I will play a part no longer, why should I exile myself from
    my companions?
O you shunn'd persons, I at least do not shun you,
I come forthwith in your midst, I will be your poet,
I will be more to you than to any of the rest.

ONCE I PASS'D THROUGH A POPULOUS CITY

Once I pass'd through a populous city imprinting my brain for
    future use with its shows, architecture, customs, traditions,
Yet now of all that city I remember only a woman I casually
    met there who detain'd me for love of me,
Day by day and night by night we were together—all else has
    long been forgotten by me,
I remember I saw only that woman who passionately clung to
    me,
Again we wander, we love, we separate again,
Again she holds me by the hand, I must not go,
I see her close beside me with silent lips sad and tremulous.

I HEARD YOU, SOLEMN-SWEET PIPES OF THE ORGAN

I heard you, solemn-sweet pipes of the organ, as last Sunday
    morn I pass'd the church,
Winds of autumn, as I walk'd the woods at dusk I heard your
    long-stretch'd sighs up above so mournful,
I heard the perfect Italian tenor singing at the opera, I heard
    the soprano in the midst of the quartet singing;
Heart of my love! you too I heard murmuring low through one
    of the wrists around my head,
Heard the pulse of you when all was still ringing little bells
    last night under my ear.

IN PATHS UNTRODDEN

In paths untrodden,
In the growths by margins of pond-waters,
Escaped from the life that exhibits itself,
From all the standards hitherto publish'd, from the pleasures,
    profits, conformities,
Which too long I was offering to feed my soul,
Clear to me now standards not yet publish'd, clear to me that
    my soul,
That the soul of the man I speak for rejoices in comrades,
Here by myself away from the clank of the world,
Tallying and talk'd to here by tongues aromatic,
No longer abash'd, (for in this secluded spot I can respond as
    I would not dare elsewhere,)
Strong upon me the life that does not exhibit itself, yet con-
    tains all the rest,
Resolv'd to sing no songs to-day but those of manly attach-
    ment,
Projecting them along that substantial life,
Bequeathing hence types of athletic love,
Afternoon this delicious Ninth-month in my forty-first year,
I proceed for all who are or have been young men,
To tell the secret of my nights and days,
To celebrate the need of comrades.

WHEN I HEARD AT THE CLOSE OF THE DAY

When I heard at the close of the day how my name had been
    receiv'd with plaudits in the capitol, still it was not a happy
    night for me that follow'd,
And else when I carous'd, or when my plans were accom-
    plish'd, still I was not happy,
But the day when I rose at dawn from the bed of perfect
    health, refresh'd, singing, inhaling the ripe breath of
    autumn,
When I saw the full moon in the west grow pale and disappear
    in the morning light,
When I wander'd alone over the beach, and undressing
    bathed, laughing with the cool waters, and saw the sun rise.
And when I thought how my dear friend my lover was on his
    way coming, O then I was happy,
O then each breath tasted sweeter, and all that day my food
    nourish'd me more, and the beautiful day pass'd well,
And the next came with equal joy, and with the next at eve-
    ning came my friend,
And that night while all was still I heard the waters roll slowly
    continually up the shores,
I heard the hissing rustle of the liquid and sands as directed
    to me whispering to congratulate me,
For the one I love most lay sleeping by me under the same
    cover in the cool night,
In the stillness in the autumn moonbeams his face was in-
    clined toward me,
And his arm lay lightly around my breast—and that night I
    was happy.

I SAW IN LOUISIANA A LIVE-OAK GROWING

I saw in Louisiana a live-oak growing,
All alone stood it and the moss hung down from the branches,
Without any companion it grew there uttering joyous leaves
    of dark green,
And its look, rude, unbending, lusty, made me think of myself,
But I wonder'd how it could utter joyous leaves standing alone

there without its friend near, for I knew I could not,

And I broke off a twig with a certain number of leaves upon it, and twined around it a little moss,

And brought it away, and I have placed it in sight, in my room,

It is not needed to remind me as of my own dear friends,

(For I believe lately I think of little else than of them,)

Yet it remains to me a curious token, it makes me think of manly love;

For all that, and though the live-oak glistens there in Louisiana solitary in a wide flat space,

Uttering joyous leaves all its life without a friend a lover near,

I know very well I could not.

A GLIMPSE

A glimpse through an interstice caught,

Of a crowd of workmen and drivers in a bar-room around the stove late of a winter night, and I unremark'd seated in a corner,

Of a youth who loves me and whom I love, silently approaching and seating himself near, that he may hold me by the hand,

A long while amid the noises of coming and going, of drinking and oath and smutty jest,

There we two, content, happy in being together, speaking little, perhaps not a word.

EARTH, MY LIKENESS

Earth, my likeness,

Though you look so impassive, ample and spheric there,

I now suspect that is not all;

I now suspect there is something fierce in you eligible to burst forth,

For an athlete is enamour'd of me, and I of him,

But toward him there is something fierce and terrible in me eligible to burst forth,

I dare not tell it in words, not even in these songs.

NOT HEAVING FROM MY RIBB'D BREAST ONLY

Not heaving from my ribb'd breast only,
Not in sighs at night in rage dissatisfied with myself,
Not in those long-drawn, ill-supprest sighs,
Not in many an oath and promise broken,
Not in my wilful and savage soul's volition,
Not in the subtle nourishment of the air,
Not in this beating and pounding at my temples and wrists,
Not in the curious systole and diastole within which will one
    day cease,
Not in many a hungry wish told to the skies only,
Not in cries, laughter, defiances, thrown from me when alone
    far in the wilds,
Not in husky pantings through clinch'd teeth,
Not in sounded and resounded words, chattering words,
    echoes, dead words,
Not in the murmurs of my dreams while I sleep,
Nor the other murmurs of these incredible dreams of every
    day,
Nor in the limbs and senses of my body that take you and
    dismiss you continually—not there,
Not in any or all of them O adhesiveness! O pulse of my life!
Need I that you exist and show yourself any more than in these
    songs.

OF THE TERRIBLE DOUBT OF APPEARANCES

Of the terrible doubt of appearances,
Of the uncertainty after all, that we may be deluded,
That may-be reliance and hope are but speculations after all,
That may-be identity beyond the grave is a beautiful fable
    only,
May-be the things I perceive, the animals, plants, men, hills,
    shining and flowing waters,
The skies of day and night, colors, densities, forms, may-be
    these are (as doubtless they are) only apparitions, and the
    real something has yet to be known,

(How often they dart out of themselves as if to confound me and mock me!
How often I think neither I know, nor any man knows, aught of them,)
May-be seeming to me what they are (as doubtless they indeed but seem) as from my present point of view, and might prove (as of course they would) nought of what they appear, or nought anyhow, from entirely changed points of view;
To me these and the like of these are curiously answer'd by my lovers, my dear friends,
When he whom I love travels with me or sits a long while holding me by the hand,
When the subtle air, the impalpable, the sense that words and reason hold not, surround us and pervade us,
Then I am charged with untold and untellable wisdom, I am silent, I require nothing further,
I cannot answer the question of appearances or that of identity beyond the grave,
But I walk or sit indifferent, I am satisfied,
He ahold of my hand has completely satisfied me.

THE BASE OF ALL METAPHYSICS

And now gentlemen,
A word I give to remain in your memories and minds,
As base and finalè too for all metaphysics.
(So to the students the old professor,
At the close of his crowded course.)

Having studied the new and antique, the Greek and Germanic systems,
Kant having studied and stated, Fichte and Schelling and Hegel,
Stated the lore of Plato, and Socrates greater than Plato,
And greater than Socrates sought and stated, Christ divine having studied long,
I see reminiscent to-day those Greek and Germanic systems,

See the philosophies all, Christian churches and tenets see,
Yet underneath Socrates clearly see, and underneath Christ
    the divine I see,
The dear love of man for his comrade, the attraction of friend
    to friend,
Of the well-married husband and wife, of children and
    parents,
Of city for city and land for land.

RECORDERS AGES HENCE

Recorders ages hence,
Come, I will take you down underneath this impassive ex-
    terior, I will tell you what to say of me,
Publish my name and hang up my picture as that of the ten-
    derest lover,
The friend the lover's portrait, of whom his friend his lover
    was fondest,
Who was not proud of his songs, but of the measureless ocean
    of love within him, and freely pour'd it forth,
Who often walk'd lonesome walks thinking of his dear friends,
    his lovers,
Who pensive away from one he lov'd often lay sleepless and
    dissatisfied at night,
Who knew too well the sick, sick dread lest the one he lov'd
    might secretly be indifferent to him,
Whose happiest days were far away through fields, in woods,
    on hills, he and another wandering hand in hand, they twain
    apart from other men,
Who oft as he saunter'd the streets curv'd with his arm the
    shoulder of his friend, while the arm of his friend rested
    upon him also.

ARE YOU THE NEW PERSON DRAWN TOWARD ME?

Are you the new person drawn toward me?
To begin with take warning, I am surely far different from
    what you suppose;
Do you suppose you will find in me your ideal?

Do you think it is so easy to have me become your lover?
Do you think the friendship of me would be unalloy'd satisfaction?
Do you think I am trusty and faithful?
Do you see no further than this façade, this smooth and tolerant manner of me?
Do you suppose yourself advancing on real ground toward a real heroic man?
Have you no thought O dreamer that it may be all maya, illusion?

ROOTS AND LEAVES THEMSELVES ALONE

Roots and leaves themselves alone are these,
Scents brought to men and women from the wild woods and pond-side,
Breast-sorrel and pinks of love, fingers that wind around tighter than vines,
Gushes from the throats of birds hid in the foliage of trees as the sun is risen,
Breezes of land and love sent from living shores to you on the living sea, to you O sailors!
Frost-mellow'd berries and Third-month twigs offer'd fresh to young persons wandering out in the fields when the winter breaks up,
Love-buds put before you and within you whoever you are,
Buds to be unfolded on the old terms,
If you bring the warmth of the sun to them they will open and bring form, color, perfume, to you,
If you become the aliment and the wet they will become flowers, fruits, tall branches and trees.

NOT HEAT FLAMES UP AND CONSUMES

Not heat flames up and consumes,
Not sea-waves hurry in and out,
Not the air delicious and dry, the air of ripe summer, bears lightly along white down-balls of myriads of seeds,

Wafted, sailing gracefully, to drop where they may;
Not these, O none of these more than the flames of me, con-
  suming, burning for his love whom I love,
O none more than I hurrying in and out;
Does the tide hurry, seeking something, and never give up?
  O I the same,
O nor down-balls nor perfumes, nor the high rain-emitting
  clouds, are borne through the open air,
Any more than my soul is borne through the open air,
Wafted in all directions O love, for friendship, for you.

THE FIRST DANDELION

Simple and fresh and fair from winter's close emerging,
As if no artifice of fashion, business, politics, had ever been,
Forth from its sunny nook of shelter'd grass—innocent, golden,
  calm as the dawn,
The spring's first dandelion shows its trustful face.

TO-DAY AND THEE

The appointed winners in a long-stretch'd game;
The course of Time and nations—Egypt, India, Greece and
  Rome;
The past entire, with all its heroes, histories, arts, experiments,
Its store of songs, inventions, voyages, teachers, books,
Garner'd for now and thee—To think of it!
The heirdom all converged in thee!

AFTER THE DAZZLE OF DAY

After the dazzle of day is gone,
Only the dark, dark night shows to my eyes the stars;
After the clangor of organ majestic, or chorus, or perfect band,
Silent, athwart my soul, moves the symphony true.

HALCYON DAYS

Not from successful love alone,
Nor wealth, nor honor'd middle age, nor victories of politics
   or war;
But as life wanes, and all the turbulent passions calm,
As gorgeous, vapory, silent hues cover the evening sky,
As softness, fullness, rest, suffuse the frame, like fresher,
   balmier air,
As the days take on a mellower light, and the apple at last
   hangs really finish'd and indolent-ripe on the tree,
Then for the teeming quietest, happiest days of all!
The brooding and blissful halcyon days!

SONG OF THE OPEN ROAD

I

Afoot and light-hearted I take to the open road,
Healthy, free, the world before me,
The long brown path before me leading wherever I choose.
Henceforth I ask not good-fortune, I myself am good-fortune,
Henceforth I whimper no more, postpone no more, need
   nothing,
Done with indoor complaints, libraries, querulous criticisms,
Strong and content I travel the open road.
The earth, that is sufficient,
I do not want the constellations any nearer,
I know they are very well where they are,
I know they suffice for those who belong to them.

(Still here I carry my old delicious burdens,
I carry them, men and women, I carry them with me wherever
   I go,
I swear it is impossible for me to get rid of them,
I am fill'd with them; and I will fill them in return.)

II

You road I enter upon and look around, I believe you are not
   all that is here,

I believe that much unseen is also here.

Here the profound lesson of reception, nor preference nor denial,

The black with his woolly head, the felon, the diseas'd, the illiterate person, are not denied;

The birth, the hasting after the physician, the beggar's tramp, the drunkard's stagger, the laughing party of mechanics,

The escaped youth, the rich person's carriage, the fop, the eloping couple,

The early market-man, the hearse, the moving of furniture into the town, the return back from the town,

They pass, I also pass, any thing passes, none can be interdicted,

None but are accepted, none but shall be dear to me.

III

You air that serves me with breath to speak!

You objects that call from diffusion my meanings and give them shape!

You light that wraps me and all things in delicate equable showers!

You paths worn in the irregular hollows by the roadsides!

I believe you are latent with unseen existences, you are so dear to me.

You flagg'd walks of the cities! you strong curbs at the edges!

You ferries! you planks and posts of wharves! you timberlined sides! you distant ships!

You rows of houses! you window-pierc'd façades! you roofs!

You porches and entrances! you copings and iron guards!

You windows whose transparent shells might expose so much!

You doors and ascending steps! you arches!

You gray stones of interminable pavements! you trodden crossings!

From all that has touch'd you I believe you have imparted to yourselves, and now would impart the same secretly to me,

From the living and the dead you have peopled your impassive surfaces, and the spirits thereof would be evident and amicable with me.

IV

The earth expanding right hand and left hand,
The picture alive, every part in its best light,
The music falling in where it is wanted, and stopping where
    it is not wanted,
The cheerful voice of the public road, the gay fresh sentiment
    of the road.

O highway I travel, do you say to me *Do not leave me?*
Do you say *Venture not—if you leave me you are lost?*
Do you say *I am already prepared, I am well-beaten and un-
    denied, adhere to me?*

O public road, I say back I am not afraid to leave you, yet I
    love you,
You express me better than I can express myself,
You shall be more to me than my poem.

I think heroic deeds were all conceiv'd in the open air, and
    all free poems also,
I think I could stop here myself and do miracles,
I think whatever I shall meet on the road I shall like, and
    whoever beholds me shall like me,
I think whoever I see must be happy.

V

From this hour I ordain myself loos'd of limits and imaginary
    lines,
Going where I list, my own master total and absolute,
Listening to others, considering well what they say,
Pausing, searching, receiving, contemplating,
Gently, but with undeniable will, divesting myself of the holds
    that would hold me.

I inhale great draughts of space,
The east and the west are mine, and the north and the south
    are mine.

I am larger, better than I thought,
I did not know I held so much goodness.

All seems beautiful to me,
I can repeat over to men and women You have done such
    good to me I would do the same to you,

I will recruit for myself and you as I go,
I will scatter myself among men and women as I go,
I will toss a new gladness and roughness among them,
Whoever denies me it shall not trouble me,
Whoever accepts me he or she shall be blessed and shall bless
   me.

VI

Now if a thousand perfect men were to appear it would not
   amaze me,
Now if a thousand beautiful forms of women appear'd it would
   not astonish me.
Now I see the secret of the making of the best persons,
It is to grow in the open air and to eat and sleep with the
   earth.
Here a great personal deed has room,
(Such a deed seizes upon the hearts of the whole race of men,
Its effusion of strength and will overwhelms law and mocks all
   authority and all argument against it.)

Here is the test of wisdom,
Wisdom is not finally tested in schools,
Wisdom cannot be pass'd from one having it to another not
   having it,
Wisdom is of the soul, is not susceptible of proof, is its own
   proof,
Applies to all stages and objects and qualities and is content,
Is the certainty of the reality and immortality of things, and
   the excellence of things;
Something there is in the float of the sight of things that pro-
   vokes it out of the soul.

Now I re-examine philosophies and religions,
They may prove well in lecture-rooms, yet not prove at all
   under the spacious clouds and along the landscape and
   flowing currents.
Here is realization,
Here is a man tallied—he realizes here what he has in him,
The past, the future, majesty, love—if they are vacant of you,
   you are vacant of them.

Only the kernel of every object nourishes;
Where is he who tears off the husks for you and me?
Where is he that undoes stratagems and envelopes for you
and me?
Here is adhesiveness, it is not previously fashion'd, it is
apropos;
Do you know what it is as you pass to be loved by strangers?
Do you know the talk of those turning eye-balls?

VII

Here is the efflux of the soul,
The efflux of the soul comes from within through embower'd
gates, ever provoking questions,
These yearnings why are they? these thoughts in the darkness
why are they?
Why are there men and women that while they are nigh me
the sunlight expands my blood?
Why when they leave me do my pennants of joy sink flat and
lank?
Why are there trees I never walk under but large and melo-
dious thoughts descend upon me?
(I think they hang there winter and summer on those trees
and always drop fruit as I pass;)
What is it I interchange so suddenly with strangers?
What with some driver as I ride on the seat by his side?
What with some fisherman drawing his seine by the shore as
I walk by and pause?
What gives me to be free to a woman's and man's good-will?
what gives them to be free to mine?

VIII

The efflux of the soul is happiness, here is happiness,
I think it pervades the open air, waiting at all times,
Now it flows unto us, we are rightly charged.
Here rises the fluid and attaching character,
The fluid and attaching character is the freshness and sweet-
ness of man and woman,
(The herbs of the morning sprout no fresher and sweeter

every day out of the roots of themselves, than it sprouts
fresh and sweet continually out of itself.)
Toward the fluid and attaching character exudes the sweat of
the love of young and old,
From it falls distill'd the charm that mocks beauty and at-
tainments,
Toward it heaves the shuddering longing ache of contact.

IX

Allons! whoever you are come travel with me!
Traveling with me you find what never tires.
The earth never tires,
The earth is rude, silent, incomprehensible at first, Nature is
rude and incomprehensible at first,
Be not discouraged, keep on, there are divine things well
envelop'd,
I swear to you there are divine things more beautiful than
words can tell.
Allons! we must not stop here,
However sweet these laid-up stores, however convenient this
dwelling we cannot remain here,
However shelter'd this port and however calm these waters
we must not anchor here,
However welcome the hospitality that surrounds us we are
permitted to receive it but a little while.

X

Allons! the inducements shall be greater,
We will sail pathless and wild seas,
We will go where winds blow, waves dash, and the Yankee
clipper speeds by under full sail.
Allons! with power, liberty, the earth, the elements,
Health, defiance, gayety, self-esteem, curiosity;
Allons! from all formules!
From your formules, O bat-eyed and materialistic priests.
The stale cadaver blocks up the passage—the burial waits no
longer.
Allons! yet take warning!

He traveling with me needs the best blood, thews, endurance,
None may come to the trial till he or she bring courage and
health,
Come not here if you have already spent the best of yourself,
Only those may come who come in sweet and determin'd
bodies,
No diseas'd person, no rum-drinker or venereal taint is per-
mitted here.
(I and mine do not convince by arguments, similes, rhymes,
We convince by our presence.)

XI

Listen! I will be honest with you,
I do not offer the old smooth prizes, but offer rough new
prizes,
These are the days that must happen to you:
You shall not heap up what is call'd riches,
You shall scatter with lavish hand all that you earn or achieve,
You but arrive at the city to which you were destin'd, you
hardly settle yourself to satisfaction before you are call'd
by an irresistible call to depart,
You shall be treated to the ironical smiles and mockings of
those who remain behind you,
What beckonings of love you receive you shall only answer
with passionate kisses of parting,
You shall not allow the hold of those who spread their reach'd
hands toward you.

XII

Allons! after the great Companions, and to belong to them!
They too are on the road—they are the swift and majestic
men—they are the greatest women,
Enjoyers of calms of seas and storms of seas,
Sailors of many a ship, walkers of many a mile of land,
Habitués of many distant countries, habitués of far-distant
dwellings,
Trusters of men and women, observers of cities, solitary
toilers,

Pausers and contemplators of tufts, blossoms, shells of the
shore,

Dancers at wedding-dances, kissers of brides, tender helpers
of children, bearers of children,

Soldiers of revolts, standers by gaping graves, lowerers-down
of coffins,

Journeyers over consecutive seasons, over the years, the curious years each emerging from that which preceded it,

Journeyers as with companions, namely their own diverse
phases,

Forth-steppers from the latent unrealized baby-days,

Journeyers gayly with their own youth, journeyers with their
bearded and well-grain'd manhood,

Journeyers with their womanhood, ample, unsurpass'd, content,

Journeyers with their own sublime old age of manhood or
womanhood,

Old age, calm, expanded, broad with the haughty breadth of
the universe,

Old age, flowing free with the delicious near-by freedom of
death.

XIII

Allons! to that which is endless as it was beginningless,

To undergo much, tramps of days, rests of nights,

To merge all in the travel they tend to, and the days and
nights they tend to,

Again to merge them in the start of superior journeys,

To see nothing anywhere but what you may reach it and pass
it,

To conceive no time, however distant, but what you may
reach it and pass it,

To look up or down no road but it stretches and waits for you,
however long but it stretches and waits for you,

To see no being, not God's or any, but you also go thither,

To see no possession but you may possess it, enjoying all without labor or purchase, abstracting the feast yet not abstracting one particle of it,

To take the best of the farmer's farm and the rich man's elegant villa, and the chaste blessings of the well-married couple, and the fruits of orchards and flowers of gardens,

To take to your use out of the compact cities as you pass through,

To carry buildings and streets with you afterward wherever you go,

To gather the minds of men out of their brains as you encounter them, to gather the love out of their hearts,

To take your lovers on the road with you, for all that you leave them behind you,

To know the universe itself as a road, as many roads, as roads for traveling souls.

All parts away for the progress of souls,

All religion, all solid things, arts, governments—all that was or is apparent upon this globe or any globe, falls into niches and corners before the procession of souls along the grand roads of the universe.

Of the progress of the souls of men and women along the grand roads of the universe, all other progress is the needed emblem and sustenance.

Forever alive, forever forward,

Stately, solemn, sad, withdrawn, baffled, mad, turbulent, feeble, dissatisfied,

Desperate, proud, fond, sick, accepted by men, rejected by men,

They go! they go! I know that they go, but I know not where they go,

But I know that they go toward the best—toward something great.

Whoever you are, come forth! or man or woman come forth!

You must not stay sleeping and dallying there in the house, though you built it, or though it has been built for you.

Out of the dark confinement! out from behind the screen!

It is useless to protest. I know all and expose it.

Behold through you as bad as the rest,

Through the laughter, dancing, dining, supping, of people,

Inside of dresses and ornaments, inside of those wash'd and
trimm'd faces,
Behold a secret silent loathing and despair.

No husband, no wife, no friend, trusted to hear the con-
fession,
Another self, a duplicate of every one, skulking and hiding it
goes,
Formless and wordless through the streets of the cities, polite
and bland in the parlors,
In the cars of railroads, in steamboats, in the public assembly,
Home to the houses of men and women, at the table, in the
bedroom, everywhere,
Smartly attired, countenance smiling, form upright, death
under the breast-bones, hell under the skull-bones,
Under the broadcloth and gloves, under the ribbons and arti-
ficial flowers,
Keeping fair with the customs, speaking not a syllable of itself,
Speaking of any thing else but never of itself.

XIV

Allons! through struggles and wars!
The goal that was named cannot be countermanded.
Have the past struggles succeeded?
What has succeeded? yourself? your nation? Nature?
Now understand me well—it is provided in the essence of
things that from any fruition of success, no matter what,
shall come forth something to make a greater struggle
necessary.
My call is the call of battle, I nourish active rebellion,
He going with me must go well arm'd,
He going with me goes often with spare diet, poverty, angry
enemies, desertions.

XV

Allons! the road is before us!
It is safe—I have tried it—my own feet have tried it well—
be not detain'd!
Let the paper remain on the desk unwritten, and the book on
the shelf unopen'd!

Let the tools remain in the workshop! let the money remain
    unearn'd!

Let the school stand! mind not the cry of the teacher!

Let the preacher preach in his pulpit! let the lawyer plead in
    the court, and the judge expound the law.

Camerado, I give you my hand!

I give you my love more precious than money,

I give you myself before preaching or law;

Will you give me yourself? will you come travel with me?

Shall we stick by each other as long as we live?

TEARS

Tears! tears! tears!

In the night, in solitude, tears,

On the white shore dripping, dripping, suck'd in by the sand,

Tears, not a star shining, all dark and desolate,

Moist tears from the eyes of a muffled head;

O who is that ghost? that form in the dark, with tears?

What shapeless lump is that, bent, crouch'd there on the sand?

Streaming tears, sobbing tears, throes, choked with wild cries;

O storm, embodied, rising, careering with swift steps along
    the beach!

O wild and dismal night storm, with wind—O belching and
    desperate!

O shade so sedate and decorous by day, with calm counte-
    nance and regulated pace,

But away at night as you fly, none looking—O then the un-
    loosen'd ocean,

Of tears! tears! tears!

TO THE MAN-OF-WAR-BIRD

Thou who has slept all night upon the storm,

Waking renew'd on thy prodigious pinions,

(Burst the wild storm? above it thou ascended'st,

And rested on the sky, thy slave that cradled thee,)

Now a blue point, far, far in heaven floating,

As to the light emerging here on deck I watch thee,
 (Myself a speck, a point on the world's floating vast.)
Far, far at sea,
After the night's fierce drifts have strewn the shore with
    wrecks,
With re-appearing day as now so happy and serene,
The rosy and elastic dawn, the flashing sun,
The limpid spread of air cerulean,
Thou also re-appearest.

Thou born to match the gale, (thou art all wings,)
To cope with heaven and earth and sea and hurricane,
Thou ship of air that never furl'st thy sails,
Days, even weeks untired and onward, through spaces, realms
    gyrating,
At dusk that look'st on Senegal, at morn America,
That sport'st amid the lightning-flash and thunder-cloud,
In them, in thy experiences, had'st thou my soul,
What joys! what joys were thine!

ABOARD AT A SHIP'S HELM

Aboard at a ship's helm,
A young steersman steering with care.
Through fog on a sea-coast dolefully ringing,
An ocean-bell—O a warning bell, rock'd by the waves.
O you give good notice indeed, you bell by the sea-reefs ring-
    ing,
Ringing, ringing, to warn the ship from its wreck-place.
For as on the alert O steersman, you mind the loud admoni-
    tion,
The bows turn, the freighted ship tacking speeds away under
    her gray sails,
The beautiful and noble ship with all her precious wealth
    speeds away gayly and safe.

But O the ship, the immortal ship! O ship aboard the ship!
Ship of the body, ship of the soul, voyaging, voyaging, voyag-
    ing.

ON THE BEACH AT NIGHT

On the beach at night,
Stands a child with her father,
Watching the east, the autumn sky.

Up through the darkness,
While ravening clouds, the burial clouds, in black masses
     spreading,
Lower sullen and fast athwart and down the sky,
Amid a transparent clear belt of ether yet left in the east,
Ascends large and calm the lord-star Jupiter,
And nigh at hand, only a very little above,
Swim the delicate sisters the Pleiades.

From the beach the child holding the hand of her father,
Those burial clouds that lower victorious soon to devour all,
Watching, silently weeps.

Weep not, child,
Weep not, my darling,
With these kisses let me remove your tears,
The ravening clouds shall not long be victorious,
They shall not long possess the sky, they devour the stars only
     in apparition,

Jupiter shall emerge, be patient, watch again another night,
     the Pleiades shall emerge,
They are immortal, all those stars both silvery and golden
     shall shine out again,
The great stars and the little ones shall shine out again, they
     endure,
The vast immortal suns and the long-enduring pensive moons
     shall again shine.

Then dearest child mournest thou only for Jupiter?
Considerest thou alone the burial of the stars?

Something there is,
(With my lips soothing thee, adding I whisper,

I give thee the first suggestion, the problem and indirection,)
Something there is more immortal even than the stars,
(Many the burials, many the days and nights, passing away,)
Something that shall endure longer even than lustrous Jupiter,
Longer than sun or any revolving satellite,
Or the radiant sisters the Pleiades.

THE WORLD BELOW THE BRINE

The world below the brine,
Forests at the bottom of the sea, the branches and leaves,
Sea-lettuce, vast lichens, strange flowers and seeds, the thick
    tangle, openings, and pink turf,
Different colors, pale gray and green, purple, white, and gold,
    the play of light through the water,
Dumb swimmers there among the rocks, coral, gluten, grass,
    rushes, and the aliment of the swimmers,
Sluggish existences grazing there suspended, or slowly crawl-
    ing close to the bottom,
The sperm-whale at the surface blowing air and spray, or
    disporting with his flukes,
The leaden-eyed shark, the walrus, the turtle, the hairy sea-
    leopard, and the sting-ray,
Passions there, wars, pursuits, tribes, sight in those ocean-
    depths, breathing that thick-breathing air, as so many do,
The change thence to the sight here, and to the subtle air
    breathed by beings like us who walk this sphere,
The change onward from ours to that of beings who walk
    other spheres.

ON THE BEACH AT NIGHT ALONE

On the beach at night alone,
As the old mother sways her to and fro singing her husky
    song,
As I watch the bright stars shining, I think a thought of the
    clef of the universes and of the future.

A vast similitude interlocks all,

All spheres, grown, ungrown, small, large, suns, moons, planets,

All distances of place however wide,

All distances of time, all inanimate forms,

All souls, all living bodies though they be ever so different, or in different worlds,

All gaseous, watery, vegetable, mineral processes, the fishes, the brutes,

All nations, colors, barbarisms, civilizations, languages,

All indentities that have existed or may exist on this globe, or any globe

All lives and deaths, all of the past, present, future,

This vast similitude spans them, and always has spann'd,

And shall forever span them and compactly hold and enclose them.

SONG FOR ALL SEAS, ALL SHIPS

I

To-day a rude brief recitative,

Of ships sailing the seas, each with its special flag or ship-signal,

Of unnamed heroes in the ships—of waves spreading and spreading far as the eye can reach,

Of dashing spray, and the winds piping and blowing,

And out of these a chant for the sailors of all nations,

Fitful, like a surge.

Of sea-captains young or old, and the mates, and of all intrepid sailors,

Of the few, very choice, taciturn, whom fate can never surprise nor death dismay,

Pick'd sparingly without noise by thee old ocean chosen by thee,

Thou sea that pickest and cullest the race in time, and unitest nations,

Suckled by thee, old husky nurse, embodying thee,

Indomitable, untamed as thee.

(Ever the heroes on water or on land, by ones or twos appearing,
Ever the stock preserv'd and never lost, though rare, enough
for seed preserv'd.)

II

Flaunt out O sea your separate flags of nations!
Flaunt out visible as ever the various ship-signals!
But do you reserve especially for yourself and for the soul of
man one flag above all the rest,
A spiritual woven signal for all nations, emblem of man elate
above death,
Token of all brave captains and all intrepid sailors and mates,
And all that went down doing their duty,
Reminiscent of them, twined from all intrepid captains young
or old,
A pennant universal, subtly waving all time, o'er all brave
sailors,
All seas, all ships.

PATROLLING BARNEGAT

Wild, wild the storm, and the sea high running,
Steady the roar of the gale, with incessant undertone mutter-
ing,
Shouts of demoniac laughter fitfully piercing and pealing,
Waves, air, midnight, their savagest trinity lashing,
Out in the shadows there milk-white combs careering,
On beachy slush and sand spirts of snow fierce slanting,
Where through the murk the easterly death-wind breasting,
Through cutting swirl and spray watchful and firm advancing,
(That in the distance! is that a wreck? is the red signal flar-
ing?)
Slush and sand of the beach tireless till daylight wending,
Steadily, slowly, through hoarse roar never remitting,
Along the midnight edge by those milk-white combs career-
ing,
A group of dim, weird forms, struggling, the night confront-
ing,
That savage trinity warily watching.

AFTER THE SEA-SHIP

After the sea-ship, after the whistling winds,
After the white-gray sails taut to their spars and ropes,
Below, a myriad myriad waves hastening, lifting up their
        necks,
Tending in ceaseless flow toward the track of the ship,
Waves of the ocean bubbling and gurgling, blithely prying,
Waves, undulating waves, liquid, uneven, emulous waves,
Toward that whirling current, laughing and buoyant, with
        curves,
Where the great vessel sailing and tacking displaced the sur-
        face,
Larger and smaller waves in the spread of the ocean yearn-
        fully flowing,
The wake of the sea-ship after she passes, flashing and frolic-
        some under the sun,
A motley procession with many a fleck of foam and many
        fragments,
Following the stately and rapid ship, in the wake following.

THE UNEXPRESS'D

How dare one say it?
After the cycles, poems, singers, plays,
Vaunted Ionia's, India's—Homer, Shakspere—the long, long
        times, thick dotted roads, areas,
The shining clusters and the Milky Ways of stars—Nature's
        pulses reap'd,
All retrospective passions, heroes, war, love, adoration,
All ages' plummets dropt to their utmost depths,
All human lives, throats, wishes, brains—all experiences' ut-
        terance;
After the countless songs, or long or short, all tongues, all
        lands,
Still something not yet told in poesy's voice or print—some-
        thing lacking,
(Who knows? the best yet unexpress'd and lacking.)

John Greenleaf Whittier

THE SADDEST WORDS

. . . . Of all sad words of tongue or pen,
The saddest are these: "It might have been!"

From Maud Muller

PROEM

I love the old melodious lays
Which softly melt the ages through,
    The songs of Spenser's golden days,
    Arcadian Sidney's silvery phrase,
Sprinkling our noon of time with freshest morning dew.

    Yet, vainly in my quiet hours
To breathe their marvellous notes I try;
    I feel them, as the leaves and flowers
    In silence feel the dewy showers,
And drink with glad, still lips the blessing of the sky.

    The rigor of a frozen clime,
The harshness of an untaught ear,
    The jarring words of one whose rhyme
    Beat often Labor's hurried time,
Or Duty's rugged march through storm and strife, are here.

    Of mystic beauty, dreamy grace,
No rounded art the lack supplies;
    Unskilled the subtle lines to trace,
    Or softer shades of Nature's face,
I view her common forms with unanointed eyes.

    Nor mine the seer-like power to show
The secrets of the heart and mind;
    To drop the plummet-line below
    Our common world of joy and woe,
A more intense despair or brighter hope to find.

Yet here at least an earnest sense
Of human right and weal is shown;
A hate of tyranny intense,
And hearty in its vehemence,
As if my brother's pain and sorrow were my own.

O Freedom! if to me belong
Nor mighty Milton's gift divine,
Nor Marvell's wit and graceful song,
Still with a love as deep and strong
As theirs, I lay, like them, my best gifts on thy shrine.

Richard Wilbur

TYWATER

Death of Sir Nihil, book the *nth*,
Upon the charred and clotted sward,
Lacking the lily of our Lord,
Alases of the hyacinth.

Could flicker from behind his ear
A whistling silver throwing knife,
And with a holler punch the life
Out of a swallow in the air.

Behind the lariat's butterfly
Shuttled his white and gritted grin,
And cuts of sky would roll within
The noose-hole, when he spun it high.

The violent, neat and practiced skill
Was all he loved and all he learned;
When he was hit, his body turned
To clumsy dirt before it fell.

And what to say of him, God knows.
Such violence. And such repose.

JUGGLER

A ball will bounce, but less and less. It's not
A light-hearted thing, resents its own resilience.
Falling is what it loves, and the earth falls
So in our hearts from brilliance,
Settles and is forgot.
It takes a skyblue juggler with five red balls

To shake our gravity up. Whee, in the air
The balls roll round, wheel on his wheeling hands,
Learning the ways of lightness, alter to spheres
Grazing his finger ends,
Cling to their courses there,
Swinging a small heaven about his ears.

But a heaven is easier made of nothing at all
Than the earth regained, and still and sole within
The spin of worlds, with a gesture sure and noble
He reels that heaven in,
Landing it ball by ball,
And trades it all for a broom, a plate, a table.

Oh, on his toe the table is turning, the broom's
Balancing up on his nose, and the plate whirls
On the tip of the broom! Damn, what a show, we cry:
The boys stamp, and the girls
Shriek, and the drum booms
And all comes down, and he bows and says goodbye.

If the juggler is tired now, if the broom stands
In the dust again, if the table starts to drop
Through the daily dark again, and though the plate
Lies flat on the table top,
For him we batter our hands
Who has won for once over the world's weight.

STILL, CITIZEN SPARROW

Still, citizen sparrow, this vulture which you call
Unnatural, let him but lumber again to air
Over the rotten office, let him bear
The carrion ballast up, and at the tall

Tip of the sky lie cruising. Then you'll see
That no more beautiful bird is in heaven's height,
No wider more placid wings, no watchfuller flight;
He shoulders nature there, the frightfully free,

The naked-headed one. Pardon him, you
Who dart in the orchard aisles, for it is he
Devours death, mocks mutability,
Has heart to make an end, keeps nature new.

Thinking of Noah, childheart, try to forget
How for so many bedlam hours his saw
Soured the song of birds with its wheezy gnaw,
And the slam of his hammer all the day beset

The people's ears. Forget that he could bear
To see the towns like coral under the keel,
And the fields so dismal deep. Try rather to feel
How high and weary it was, on the waters where

He rocked his only world, and everyone's.
Forgive the hero, you who would have died
Gladly with all you knew; he rode that tide
To Ararat; all men are Noah's sons.

MUSEUM PIECE

The good grey guardians of art
Patrol the halls on spongy shoes,
Impartially protective, though
Perhaps suspicious of Toulouse.

Here dozes one against the wall,
Disposed upon a funeral chair.
A Degas dancer pirouettes
Upon the parting of his hair.

See how she spins! The grace is there,
But strain as well is plain to see.
Degas loved the two together:
Beauty joined to energy.

Edgar Degas purchased once
A fine El Greco, which he kept
Against the wall beside his bed
To hang his pants on while he slept.

AT YEAR'S-END

Now winter downs the dying of the year,
And night is all a settlement of snow;
From the soft street the rooms of houses show
A gathered light, a shapen atmosphere,
Like frozen-over lakes whose ice is thin
And still allows some stirring down within.

I've known the wind by water banks to shake
The late leaves down, which frozen where they fell
And held in ice as dancers in a spell
Fluttered all winter long into a lake;
Graved on the dark in gestures of descent,
They seemed their own most perfect monument.

There was perfection in the death of ferns
Which laid their fragile cheeks against the stone
A million years. Great mammoths overthrown
Composedly have made their long sojourns,
Like palaces of patience, in the gray
And changeless lands of ice. And at Pompeii

The little dog lay curled and did not rise
But slept the deeper as the ashes rose
And found the people incomplete, and froze
The random hands, the loose unready eyes
Of men expecting yet another sun
To do the shapely thing they had not done.

These sudden ends of time must give us pause.
We fray into the future, rarely wrought
Save in the tapestries of afterthought.
More time, more time. Barrages of applause
Come muffled from a buried radio.
The Newyear bells are wrangling with the snow.

MIND

Mind in its purest play is like some bat
That beats about in caverns all alone,
Contriving by a kind of senseless wit
Not to conclude against a wall of stone.

It has no need to falter or explore;
Darkly it knows what obstacles are there,
And so may weave and flitter, dip and soar
In perfect courses through the blackest air.

And has this simile a like perfection?
The mind is like a bat. Precisely. Save
That in the very happiest intellection
A graceful error may correct the cave.

LOVE CALLS US TO THE THINGS OF THIS WORLD

The eyes open to a cry of pulleys,
And spirited from sleep, the astounded soul

Hangs for a moment bodiless and simple
As false dawn.
                    Outside the open window
The morning air is all awash with angels.

Some are in bed-sheets, some are in blouses,
Some are in smocks: but truly there they are.
Now they are rising together in calm swells
Of halcyon feeling, filling whatever they wear
With the deep joy of their impersonal breathing;

Now they are flying in place, conveying
The terrible speed of their omnipresence, moving
And staying like white water; and now of a sudden
They swoon down into so rapt a quiet
That nobody seems to be there.
                                        The soul shrinks

From all that it is about to remember,
From the punctual rape of every blessèd day,
And cries,
              'Oh, let there be nothing on earth but laundry,
Nothing but rosy hands in the rising steam
And clear dances done in the sight of heaven.'

Yet, as the sun acknowledges
With a warm look the world's hunks and colors,
The soul descends once more in bitter love
To accept the waking body, saying now
In a changed voice as the man yawns and rises,

'Bring them down from their ruddy gallows;
Let there be clean linen for the backs of thieves;
Let lovers go sweet and fresh to be undone,
And the heaviest nuns walk in a pure floating
Of dark habits,
                    keeping their difficult balance.'

Oscar Williams

THE LAST SUPPER

I

Apostles of the hidden sun
Are come unto the room of breath
Hung with the banging blinds of death,
The body twelve, the spirit one,
Far as the eye, in earth arrayed,
The night shining, the supper laid.

II

The wine shone on the table that evening of history
Like an enormous ruby in the bauble and mystery.

In the glowing walls of the flickering decanter
There moved His face as at the world's center.

The hands of Judas showed up red and hurried
And the light hit them so, like a cross carried.

The faces of the others were there and moving
In the crystal of the dome, swiftly hovering.

The saints, under a lens, shrunken to pigmies,
Gesticulated in birds or in colored enigmas.

Outside there was a storm, the sound of temblors,
The blood bubbled and sprang into the tumblers.

When the morning came like a white wall of stone,
The day lay in the glass and the blood was gone.

I SING AN OLD SONG

I sing an old song, bird on a charcoal bough,
Silver voice on the black black bough, singing,
Rolling heirloom eyes, burning holes in time,
Drenching the flank of nearness with drip-music:
The disturbed owner who hides everywhere
Lumbers through the miles of thick indignation:
The subconscious parts the nap-gold of afternoon.

I sing an old song, bird scything the silence,
Bundling sabres at the cornerstone of sense:
Bird, pulley on a hillheap of elves' eyelashes,
Silver piston sunk to a bud on the bough,
Sing, bird, sing, from the black black bough,
Shake the enormous atmosphere from your small fist
Of body, tear the colossal ear of the all around
Hanging loosely, like forest outside a window:
Open all the fluteholes of days until the world
Weeps music, and sweats light from every facet,
And tumbles to the smoking knees of its orbit.

I sing an old song, bead in the hair of the park,
Bird-knot in the weave of leaves, nugget in sieve
Straining gravel of Utopia to shining beginnings,
Deed, navel of matter, fleck of the future,
Knuckle knock on finality, sing, bird, sing:
Ride the groundswell of heartbreak, tap thick wrist
Of branch, lump of utterance in the cup of sunlight
Melt into the sweetness of reality, O:
Sprinkle effigies on the gauze of stillness,
Aim your gold beak from the nest, from the crook
Of the leafy black arm, toward the poised sun
Swing girders from your beak through tin pretense
Into the underground room of man, the pallid palace.

I sing an old song, bird, toe-hold of song on bough,
Bundle in the bush of radiance: birth-cry of poem!

THE MIRAGE

I lived a life without love, and saw the being
I loved on every branch; then that bare tree
Stood up with all its branches up, a great harp
Growing straight out of the ground, and there I saw
A squadron of bright birds clothing the bare limbs;
The music notes sat on the harp; it was all love.

This was the heart inside the starved body;
Love grew images like cactus, and planted roses
On the walls of the mirage, and the garden grew
Shining with perfume and the senses dwindled to dew,
The century was rolled into one formation aloft,
A cloud, like St. Veronica's handkerchief of love.

There I saw the face of the one without whom
I lived, two soft jewels implanted in her face,
Her hair pouring around her face without sound,
And her love for me sprang on her skin like dew,
Pearl-grey as the flower of the brain she lay
Quivering on the soft cushion of the great day.

I heard a roar of buildings at my conscience,
I looked up and saw a wall of windows glowing,
And there my love leaned out of each window,
There she leaned out multiplied like heaven
In that vast wall of lights, every light her face,
Suns of a thousand mornings ranging on one day.

And all the machines were running, and yes, great
Was the sound of their running downward and down
Into the blind chutes of their rooted feet,
And all of the windows quivered with my many loves,
Like apples they fell off, at one windfall, all,
And I awoke on the starved pavements of no love.

ON MEETING A STRANGER IN A BOOKSHOP

We stand talking in the cave whose walls are
The colors—like rock under a veil of nettles—
Of the books' backs embedded as if forever;
The writing on the wall is overweening with titles.

I talk to you, the bare light burns above
Like the apple of Eden pulsating its sparks,
And in this small space we sail as in a closed
Balloon through the vast astronomical works.   ·

I tell you the most intimate thing I am,
My name, and yours floats out to me, creeps
Into ears' trumpets, folds itself around my brain:
Holding hands thus we sail off into the deeps.

We sail off and are the angels again and again
Affirming the sensational power of a thought;
We leap down a star to the land of shouldn't,
Or stand looking wanly into the window of ought.

The world (it's a world!) leans heavily outside
Its breathing against the walls of the cave;
Strangely, we are flying both inside and outside,
We blow to cool off a Venus rising on a wave.

Our wings are bright doubts hoisting at our backs
With an elaborateness that embarrasses the dragon
Of gravitation who looks up with large sweet orbs
Of chagrin and churns up conventions in his wagon.

We have stepped out with the buoyant daring step
Of a rainbow on its seven-league spread of color;
Chips of philosophy and verse, platitudes' powder,
Star-pollen, too, softly cling to our shoulders.

We come to the ten black birds facing each other
Like fingers of the hands under a tree's bent back
And busily lacing the twigs of the long boot—
Good-bye, we say, to the problem there in its track.

Finally like children we have run out of ourselves.
I put on my coat and you pretend to be hurried.
We let go our clinging eyes and the cave caves in:
The books tumble on our heads and we are buried.

BY FIAT OF ADORATION

This is what we really want
Who drink the kingdom of the heart
A toast to the imagination

She is flowering in a doorway
Eyes cheeks haze of hair
Stepping out of time into here

This is what we really have
Who see the one we adore becoming
The two that she is in the light

Ah God bounces all the waters
From hand to jubilant hand
He cannot contain Himself

But comes over into being
With benediction of painted cloud
The being whom to look at is to become

By fiat of adoration do we reach
The very muscle of miracle
The ease with which beauty is beauty

THE PRAYING MANTIS VISITS A PENTHOUSE

The praying Mantis with its length of straw
Out of the nowhere's forehead born full armed
Engages the century at my terrace door.
Focused at inches the dinosaur insect sends
Broadsides of epic stillness at my eye,
Above the deafening projects of the age.
My wife, who fears the thunder of its poise,
Has seen it and cries out. The clouds like curls
Fall in my faith as I seize a stick to stop
This Martian raid distilled to a straw with legs,
To wisps of prowess. Bristling with motionlessness
The Mantis prays to the Stick twice armed with Man.

I strike, the stick whistles, shearing off two legs
Which run off by themselves beneath some boards.
The Mantis spreads out tints of batlike wing,
The many colored pennants of its blood,
And hugs my weapon; the frantic greens come out,
The reds and yellows blurt out from the straw,
All sinews doubtless screaming insect death.
Against the railing's edge I knock the stick
Sending that gay mad body into the gulf.
Such noisy trappings in defeat wake doubts.
I search my mind for possible wounds and feel
The victim's body heavy on the victor's heart.

THE LEG IN THE SUBWAY

When I saw the woman's leg on the floor of the subway train,
Protrude beyond the panel (while her body overflowed my
    mind's eye),
When I saw the pink stocking, black shoe, curve bulging with
    warmth,
The delicate etching of the hair behind the flesh-colored
    gauze,
When I saw the ankle of Mrs. Nobody going nowhere for a
    nickel,

When I saw this foot motionless on the moving motionless
    floor,
My mind caught on a nail of a distant star, I was wrenched
    out
Of the reality of the subway ride, I hung in a socket of dis-
    tance: and this is what I saw:

The long tongue of the earth's speed was licking the leg,
Upward and under and around went the long tongue of
    speed:
It was made of a flesh invisible, it dripped the saliva of miles:
It drank moment, lit shivers of insecurity in niches between
    bones:
It was full of eyes, it stopped licking to look at the passengers:
It was as alive as a worm, and busier than anybody in the
    train:
It spoke saying: To whom does this leg belong? Is it a bonus
    leg
For the rush hour? Is it a forgotten leg? Among the many
Myriads of legs did an extra leg fall in from the Out There?

O Woman, sliced off bodily by the line of the panel, shall I
    roll
Your leg into the abdominal nothing, among digestive teeth?
Or shall I fit it in with the pillars that hold up the headlines?
But nobody spoke, though all the faces were talking silently,
As the train zoomed, a zipper closing up swiftly the seam of
    time.

Alas, said the long tongue of the speed of the earth quite
    faintly,
What is one to do with an incorrigible leg that will not melt—
But everybody stopped to listen to the train vomiting
    cauldrons
Of silence, while somebody's jolted-out afterthought trickled
    down
The blazing shirt-front solid with light bulbs, and just then

The planetary approach of the next station exploded atoms of
   light,
And when the train stopped, the leg had grown a surprising
   mate,
And the long tongue had slipped hurriedly out through a
   window:

I perceived through the hole left by the nail of the star in my
   mind
How civilization was as dark as a wood and dimensional with
   things
And how birds dipped in chromium sang in the crevices of
   our deeds.

THE MAN COMING TOWARD YOU

I

The man coming toward you is falling forward on all fronts:
He has just come in from the summer hot box of circumstance,
His obedient arm pulls a ticket from the ticket machine,
A bell announces to the long tables his presence on the scene;
The room is crowded with Last Suppers and the air is angry;
The halleluiahs lift listless heads; the man is hungry.

He looks at the people, the rings of lights, the aisles, the
   chairs,
They mass and attack his eyes and they take him unawares,
But in a moment it is over and the immense hippopotamus
   cries
And swims away to safety in the vast past of his eyes;
The weeks recoil before the days, the years before the months;
The man is hungry and keeps moving forward on all fronts.

His hair is loosening, his teeth are at bay, he breathes fear,
His nails send futile tendrils into the belly of the atmosphere;
Every drop of his blood is hanging loose in the universe,
His children's faces everywhere bring down the college doors;
He is growing old on all fronts; his foes and his friends
Are bleeding behind invisible walls bedecked with dividends;

His wife is aging, and his skin puts on its anonymous gloves;
The man is helpless, surrounded by two billion hates and
loves;
Look at him squirm inside his clothes, the harpies around his
ears,
In just one minute his brothers will have aged four thousand
years.
Who records his stupendous step on the delicate eardrum
of Chance?
The man coming toward you is marching forward on all fronts.

II

Incoming train chattering opposite one's consciousness
With wheels moving restlessly inside the face of distance—
So the breath of the everyday expands through the station
Churning up a cloud of coffins above the advancing pistons.

Now the feet of the station are off the ground of Christian
love,
The station is skipping rope with an elegant swish of arches:
A massive airiness, skirts blowing with a mass music of mind,
While the herd of backs, the trek from the subconscious,
lurches.

Landing field of the strange strangers from the Mars of mo-
ment,
This is the land where the cat heads of the comets are buried:
The great clock of the nation peers under the sheet of history,
Like an eye staring amazed in the middle of the hostile fore-
head.

The ticket sellers are buried seated in the incandescent walls
But manage to meet the human race all gloved in travel
dither:
Somewhere the long legs of highways stretch in torture under
The cavernous breach of landscape at the other end of the
tether.

A canyonful of bells shivers to bits in a fit of innocence:
The railway station bends its head around the napes of
silence:

Everywhere the shadows are budding on the tree of substance
Flowering into large leopards grounded swiftly on the pylons.

The train pulls in, tugging luminously at the leash of rails:
All the books are emptying their characters into the station:
The people who are quaintly decorating the mouthful of light
Reach for their hats and pasts and the luggage of frustration.

And the amazing direction called home branches everywhere,
Dizzying the dutiful compass and the compliant elements:
The attenuated female cry of struck iron bites at the wind,
And a powerful charge of flesh overloads the filaments.

This ant hill overrunning with nerves, with maggots of myth,
This tuft of winter lightning blooming in the cheek of travel,
This immense bulb wired in the bosom of a sullen universe,
This gathering of huddled veins—who shall unravel, unravel?

Who shall unravel this knot of light, the tangled sinews of
    man,
This kink composed of heroes and harpies, aims and omens?
For all the knots are Gordian knots until the mind is won,
The tyrant mind of the present unturned by the many
    poems. . . .

SHOPPING FOR MEAT IN WINTER

What lewd, naked and revolting shape is this?
A frozen oxtail in the butcher's shop
Long and lifeless upon the huge block of wood
On which the ogre's axe begins *chop chop.*

The sun like incense fumes on the smoky glass,
The street frets with people, the winter wind
Throws knives, prices dangle from shoppers' mouths
While the grim vegetables, on parade, bring to mind

The great countryside bathed in golden sleep,
The trees, the bees, the soft peace everywhere—
I think of the cow's tail, how all summer long
It beat the shapes of harps into the air.

DWARF OF DISINTEGRATION

I

Who is it runs through the many-storied mansion of myth
With the exaggerated child's-head among pillars and palings,
Holding in his grip the balloons of innumerable windows
And chased by the flowing malevolent army of the ceilings?

It is the dwarf, the yellow dwarf, with the minted cheeks,
With the roots of the fingers, with the wafer-thin cry,
In a maze of walls, lost in the nurseries of definition—
Shadows dance on shins of trumpets in a waning sky.

Voices are wired in the walls, rats are gnawing rumors,
The throat of music is bursting with the leadpipes of lust,
And the giant's face on the dwarf's shoulders is frightened
As the battle sounds strike the panes from the near-by past.·

The pillars in the palace are reclining about like pistons:
The horses of parenthesis have run away into the woods:
The king is caught on the vast flypaper of the people:
There are holes as big as hovels in the wall of platitude.

The queen is ill from planting the garden with progeny
And her eyes are crossed off by vicious marks from her face:
She telephones the dwarf who puts his head in the instrument
To find his features come out in glacial coal-bins of space.

The orgasms of distant guns attack at the lustful curtains
And soldiers are standing about in historical knots of lies
Warming frozen tag-ends of lives around the spontaneous
Combustion of bosses who are stoking hollows of hired eyes.

The swine bulge in the snake bellies of the telegraph wires
And bellow under flat clouds of ceilings in the interior;
Communication swallows the quicksilver swords of distance;
Headlines perform, in squadrons of plumes, on the warriors.

But the draughty palace of fable is full of feeble splendor:
The yellow dwarf now in possession of knowing documents
Runs after the newspapers cackling on the edge of freedom—
The golden cupboards tremble for the aging sentiments.

The music of battlefields exhilarates the hidden overhead
And injects into the air a breakdown sense of release,
And the numerals wriggle off the lock boxes of the world
Unloosing a swarm of the venomous vultures of the peace.

But the dwarf, the yellow dwarf, with sunspots for eyes
Is hunting in the archives in the moth holes in the palace,
And he tightens the torture boot around the spinal column,
The steel twilight gleaming with the sweat of his malice.

II

Now that the battle is on, keep off the palace grounds,
You can hear the dwarf rummaging in the elephant inside:
It's better to draw a curtain of birds around your eyes—
Fall into the picture book under the thumb of a landslide—

Than to come upon spiders eating the iris of the eyeball,
Glimpse the yellow dwarf digesting the members of princes,
Or see famous paintings loll, like tongues, from their frames
Into a roomful of heroes pretending to harass pretenses.

The sagging structure propped between thought and thinker,
The gilded lawns flow on under the smokescreen of the laws:
The allover attack of a decaying body infiltrates to the atom,
Even the beast in the violin hangs out with lopped-off paws.

Run! run into the first thicket of verbs, the nest of deeds!
Place a skyline between yourself and the grandiose emblem!
For the inquisition wears the hypocritical jowls of a palace,
There's nothing here to salvage, and yours is another problem.

VARIATIONS ON A THEME

I

ON THE DEATH OF AN ACQUAINTANCE

Friend, when I think of your delicate feminine face
And of your little hopes common as hearing or seeing,
How singlehanded you moved the massive stone of space
To find a cranny for the flower from the soil of your being,

And how now you manage to keep open in the universe
Under all-time strain that lighted crack in the reckoning
I am haunted by your grimace O steadily getting worse
Awaiting the vast glad look that reduces everything.

For long I thought you another human being in doubt,
One of the millions ordinary as daylight is everywhere,
One of those usual people that one meets with all about—
Now I see you were capable of decision and despair.

Forgive me if my heart cringes with those who die,
Forgive me, friend, when even in thought I cannot be brave
Who think of your clear face agonized under tons of sky
Hourly growing more haggard from the weight of the grave.

II

THE SPRITELY DEAD

There was a man within our tenement
who died upon a worn down step of day:
the wreath they hung upon the doorway meant
that there was nothing else for him to do.

But he was obstinate, he would not rest:
he dragged the flesh of silence everywhere
on crippled wings, and we would hear him whir
while on our memory's sill his eyes would roost.

We saw him wring his thoughts in deep despair
and stamp the color from our backyard scene:
careless, without his body, he would peer
to find out if we noticed his new sin.

He was afraid, afraid: he climbed our vines
and hid, on hands and knees, along our veins.

III

THE BORROWER OF SALT

The man who saw the light hanging on the tall end
Of the road thought it was a lantern on the distant wall
Of the mysterious neighbor, so he said, friend, friend,
I am coming out to borrow some of the savor of your salt.

Wherewith he started running toward the light that hung
In the neighbor's window, and as he kept going the light
Danced, saying with a mocking step, isn't it wrong
That I dance in my glory while you walk in the night?

Yes, said the man, it is wrong, and what is worse
The wind is getting bad, the mud thicker, the road
Harder to follow and I move as slowly as a hearse,
In fact I feel my body itself turning into the load.

The gleam tittered like a light on the end of a spar
But the man was up to his knees in road as if roots
Sprouted from his feet; alas, said the man, it is too hard,
Those who would walk in great men's tracks wear boots.

He turned around and the wind opened spigots of swift air
On his head, up his thighs he felt the earth's lips creep,
And lo, the light gleamed spiritedly from his own fair
Housetop, but he couldn't move, the track was so deep.

William Carlos Williams

THE YACHTS

contend in a sea which the land partly encloses
shielding them from the too heavy blows
of an ungoverned ocean which when it chooses

tortures the biggest hulls, the best man knows
to pit against its beatings, and sinks them pitilessly.
Mothlike in mists, scintillant in the minute

brilliance of cloudless days, with broad bellying sails
they glide to the wind tossing green water
from their sharp prows while over them the crew crawls

ant like, solicitously grooming them, releasing,
making fast as they turn, lean far over and having
caught the wind again, side by side, head for the mark.

In a well guarded arena of open water surrounded by
lesser and greater craft which, sycophant, lumbering
and flittering follow them, they appear youthful, rare

as the light of a happy eye, live with the grace
of all that in the mind is feckless, free and
naturally to be desired. Now the sea which holds them

is moody, lapping their glossy sides, as if feeling
for some slightest flaw but fails completely.
Today no race. Then the wind comes again. The yachts

move, jockeying for a start, the signal is set and they
are off. Now the waves strike at them but they are too
well made, they slip through, though they take in canvas.

Arms with hands grasping seek to clutch at the prows.
Bodies thrown recklessly in the way are cut aside.
It is a sea of faces about them in agony, in despair

until the horror of the race dawns staggering the mind,
the whole sea become an entanglement of watery bodies
lost to the world bearing what they cannot hold. Broken,

beaten, desolate, reaching from the dead to be taken up
they cry out, failing, failing! their cries rising
in waves still as the skillful yachts pass over.

THE FORGOTTEN CITY

When I was coming down from the country
with my mother, the day of the storm,
trees were across the road and small branches
kept rattling on the roof of the car.
There was ten feet or more of water
making the parkways impassable with the wind
bringing more rain in sheets. Brown torrents
gushed up through new sluiceways in the
valley floor so that I had to take any road
I could find bearing to the south and west,
to get back to the city. I passed through
extraordinary places, as vivid as any
I ever saw where the storm had broken
the barrier and let through
a strange commonplace: Long, deserted avenues
with unrecognized names at the corners and
drunken looking people with completely
foreign manners. Monuments, institutions
and in one place a large body of water
startled me with an acre or more of hot
jets spouting up symmetrically over it. Parks.
I had no idea where I was and promised
myself I would some day go back to study

this curious and industrious people who lived
in these apartments, at these sharp
corners and turns of intersecting avenues
with so little apparent communication
with an outside world. How did they get
cut off this way from representation in our
newspapers and other means of publicity
when so near the metropolis, so closely
surrounded by the familiar and the famous.

BURNING THE CHRISTMAS GREENS

Their time past, pulled down
cracked and flung to the fire
—go up in a roar

All recognition lost, burnt
   clean
clean in the flame, the green
dispersed, a living red,
flame red, red as blood wakes
on the ash—

and ebbs to a steady burning
the rekindled bed become
a landscape of flame

At the winter's midnight
we went to the trees, the
   coarse
holly, the balsam and
the hemlock for their green

At the thick of the dark
the moment of the cold's
deepest plunge we brought
   branches
cut from the green trees

to fill our need, and over
doorways, about paper
Christmas
bells covered with tinfoil
and fastened by red ribbons

we stuck the green prongs
in the windows hung
woven wreaths and above
   pictures
the living green. On the

mantel we built a green
   forest
and among those hemlock
sprays put a herd of small
white deer as if they

were walking there. All this!

and it seemed gentle and
    good
to us. Their time past,
relief! The room bare. We

stuffed the dead grate
with them upon the half
    burntout
log's smouldering eye, open-
    ing
red and closing under them

and we stood there looking
    down.
Green is a solace
a promise of peace, a fort
against the cold (though we

did not say so) a challenge
above the snow's
hard shell. Green (we might
have said) that, where

small birds hide and dodge
and lift their plaintiff
rallying cries, blocks for them
and knocks down

the unseeing bullets of
the storm. Green spruce
    boughs

pulled down by a weight of
snow—Transformed!

Violence leaped and
    appeared.
Recreant! roared to life
as the flame rose through and
our eyes recoiled from it.

In the jagged flames green
to red, instant and alive.
    Green!
those sure abutments. Gone!
lost to mind

and quick in the contracting
tunnel of the grate
appeared a world! Black
mountains, black and red—as

yet uncolored—and ash white,
an infant landscape shim-
    mering
ash and flame and we, in
that instant, lost,

breathless to be witnesses,
as if we stood
ourselves refreshed among
the shining fauna of that fire.

TRACT

I will teach you my townspeople
how to perform a funeral—
for you have it over a troupe
of artists—
unless one should scour the world—
you have the ground sense necessary.

See! the hearse leads.
I begin with a design for a hearse.
For Christ's sake not black—
nor white either—and not polished!
Let it be weathered—like a farm wagon—
with gilt wheels (this could be
applied fresh at small expense)
or no wheels at all:
a rough dray to drag over the ground.

Knock the glass out!
My God—glass, my townspeople!
For what purpose? Is it for the dead
to look out or for us to see
how well he is housed or to see
the flowers or the lack of them—
or what?
To keep the rain and snow from him?
He will have a heavier rain soon:
pebbles and dirt and what not.
Let there be no glass—
and no upholstery! phew!
and no little brass rollers
and small easy wheels on the bottom—
my townspeople what are you thinking of!
A rough plain hearse then
with gilt wheels and no top at all.
On this the coffin lies
by its own weight.

No wreaths please—
especially no hot-house flowers.
Some common memento is better,
something he prized and is known by:
his old clothes—a few books perhaps—
God knows what! You realize
how we are about these things,
my townspeople—
something will be found—anything—
even flowers if he had come to that.
So much for the hearse.

For heaven's sake though see to the driver!
Take off the silk hat! In fact
that's no place at all for him
up there unceremoniously
dragging our friend out to his own dignity!
Bring him down—bring him down!
Low and inconspicuous! I'd not have him ride
on the wagon at all—damn him—
the undertaker's understrapper!
Let him hold the reins
and walk at the side
and inconspicuously too!

Then briefly as to yourselves:
Walk behind—as they do in France,
seventh class, or if you ride
Hell take curtains! Go with some show
of inconvenience; sit openly—
to the weather as to grief.
Or do you think you can shut grief in?
What—from us? We who have perhaps
nothing to lose? Share with us
share with us—it will be money
in your pockets.
                           Go now
I think you are ready.

Elinor Wylie

HYMN TO EARTH

Farewell, incomparable element,
Whence man arose, where he shall not return;
And hail, imperfect urn
Of his last ashes, and his firstborn fruit;
Farewell, the long pursuit,
And all the adventures of his discontent;
The voyages which sent
His heart averse from home:
Metal of clay, permit him that he come
To thy slow-burning fire as to a hearth;
Accept him as a particle of earth.

Fire, being divided from the other three,
It lives removed, or secret at the core;
Most subtle of the four,
When air flies not, nor water flows,
It disembodied goes,
Being light, elixir of the first degree,
More volatile than he;
With strength and power to pass
Through space, where never his least atom was:
He has no part in it, save as his eyes
Have drawn its emanation from the skies.

A wingless creature heavier than air,
He is rejected of its quintessence;
Coming and going hence,
In the twin minutes of his birth and death,
He may inhale as breath,
As breath relinquish heaven's atmosphere,
Yet in it have no share,
Nor can survive therein

Where its outer edge is filtered pure and thin:
It doth but lend its crystal to his lungs
For his early crying, and his final songs.

The element of water has denied
Its child; it is no more his element;
It never will relent;
Its silver harvests are more sparsely given
Than the rewards of heaven,
And he shall drink cold comfort at its side:
The water is too wide:
The seamew and the gull
Feather a nest made soft and pitiful
Upon its foam; he has not any part
In the long swell of sorrow at its heart.

Hail and farewell, beloved element,
Whence he departed, and his parent once;
See where thy spirit runs
Which for so long hath had the moon to wife;
Shall this support his life
Until the arches of the waves be bent
And grow shallow and spent?
Wisely it cast him forth
With his dead weight of burdens nothing worth,
Leaving him, for the universal years,
A little seawater to make his tears.

Hail, element of earth, receive thy own,
And cherish, at thy charitable breast,
This man, this mongrel beast:
He ploughs the sand, and, at his hardest need,
He sows himself for seed;
He ploughs the furrow, and in this lies down
Before the corn is grown;
Between the apple bloom
And the ripe apple is sufficient room
In time, and matter, to consume his love
And make him parcel of a cypress grove.

Receive him as thy lover for an hour
Who will not weary, by a longer stay,
The kind embrace of clay;
Even within thine arms he is dispersed
To nothing, as at first;
The air flings downward from its four-quartered tower
Him whom the flames devour;
At the full tide, at the flood,
The sea is mingled with his salty blood:
The traveller dust, although the dust be vile,
Sleeps as thy lover for a little while.

O VIRTUOUS LIGHT

A private madness has prevailed
Over the pure and valiant mind;
The instrument of reason failed
And the star-gazing eyes struck blind.

Sudden excess of light has wrought
Confusion in the secret place
Where the slow miracles of thought
Take shape through patience into grace.

Mysterious as steel and flint
The birth of this destructive spark
Whose inward growth has power to print
Strange suns upon the natural dark.

O break the walls of sense in half
And make the spirit fugitive!
This light begotten of itself
Is not a light by which to live!

The fire of farthing tallow dips
Dispels the menace of the skies
So it illuminate the lips
And enter the discerning eyes.

O virtuous light, if thou be man's
Or matter of the meteor stone,
Prevail against this radiance
Which is engendered of its own!

WINTER SLEEP

When against earth a wooden heel
Clicks as loud as stone and steel,
When snow turns flour instead of flakes,
And frost bakes clay as fire bakes,
When the hard-bitten fields at last
Crack like iron flawed in the cast,
When the world is wicked and cross and old,
I long to be quit of the cruel cold.

Little birds like bubbles of glass
Fly to other Americas,
Birds as bright as sparkles of wine
Fly in the night to the Argentine,
Birds of azure and flame-birds go
To the tropical Gulf of Mexico:
They chase the sun, they follow the heat,
It is sweet in their bones, O sweet, sweet, sweet!
It's not with them that I'd love to be,
But under the roots of the balsam tree.

Just as the spiniest chestnut-burr
Is lined within with the finest fur,
So the stony-walled, snow-roofed house
Of every squirrel and mole and mouse
Is lined with thistledown, sea-gull's feather,
Velvet mullein-leaf, heaped together
With balsam and juniper, dry and curled,
Sweeter than anything else in the world.
O what a warm and darksome nest
Where the wildest things are hidden to rest!
It's there that I'd love to lie and sleep,
Soft, soft, soft, and deep, deep, deep!

LET NO CHARITABLE HOPE

Now let no charitable hope
Confuse my mind with images
Of eagle and of antelope:
I am in nature none of these.

I was, being human, born alone;
I am, being woman, hard beset;
I live by squeezing from a stone
The little nourishment I get.

In masks outrageous and austere
The years go by in single file;
But none has merited my fear,
And none has quite escaped my smile.

I HEREBY SWEAR THAT TO UPHOLD YOUR HOUSE

I hereby swear that to uphold your house
I would lay my bones in quick destroying lime
Or turn my flesh to timber for all time;
Cut down my womanhood; lop off the boughs
Of that perpetual ecstasy that grows
From the heart's core; condemn it as a crime
If it be broader than a beam, or climb
Above the stature that your roof allows.
I am not the hearthstone nor the cornerstone
Within this noble fabric you have builded;
Not by my beauty was its cornice gilded;
Not on my courage were its arches thrown:
My lord, adjudge my strength, and set me where
I bear a little more than I can bear.

Index of Authors and Titles

Index of Authors and Titles

ABOUT THE EDITOR

Oscar Williams, editor of *The New Pocket Anthology of American Verse,* is himself a distinguished poet. He is the author of four books of poetry, of which the most recent is *Selected Poems* published by Charles Scribner's Sons. Dylan Thomas has written: "Oscar Williams is without a doubt a very real and important American poet. . . . His powerful imagery and unique personal idiom will add a permanent page to American poetry, I feel sure." Mr. Williams is originator and general editor of *The Little Treasury Series* published by Scribner's. His *A Little Treasury of Modern Poetry, Immortal Poems of the English Language* and *The Pocket Book of Modern Verse* are accepted as the present-day classics in their fields and are in wide use in colleges and universities. Robert Lowell has written in *The Sewanee Review:* "Oscar Williams is probably the best anthologist in America."

In addition, Mr. Williams has lectured and read poetry at leading universities in California, Missouri, Iowa, and other states, and at Harvard. He has also been a leader in Poetry at writers' conferences held at the universities of Utah and Connecticut, and New York University.

Oliver Wendell Holmes

Herman Melville

Sidney Lanier

Stephen Crane

Edgar Lee Masters

Elinor Wylie

William Carlos Williams

Conrad Aiken

Ogden Nash

Karl Shapiro

Richard Wilbur

Robert Lowell